GETTING STARTED

WELCOME

Congratulations, you have just gained access to the highest quality practice tests for the AWS Cloud Practitioner Certification Exam. These practice tests will prepare you thoroughly for the real exam so that you get to pass with flying colors.

There are **6 practice exams with 65 questions** each and each set of practice exams includes questions from all domains of the latest **CLF-C01** exam. All **390 practice questions** were designed to reflect the difficulty of the real AWS exam. With these Practice Tests, you'll know when you are ready to pass your AWS Certified Cloud Practitioner exam the first time! We recommend re-taking these practice tests until you consistently score 80% or higher - that's when you're ready to sit the exam and achieve a great score!

If you want easy to pass questions, then these Practice Tests are <u>not</u> for you! Our students love these high-quality practice tests because they **match the level of difficulty and exam pattern** of the actual certification exam and help them understand the AWS concepts. Students who have recently passed the CLF-C01 exam confirm that these AWS practice questions are the most similar to the real exam.

I hope you get great value from this resource that has been well received by our pool of over 500,000 students. Through diligent study of these questions, you will be in the perfect position to ace your AWS Cloud Practitioner exam first time.

Wishing you the best for every step in your cloud journey!

Neal Davis

Neal Davis

Founder of Digital Cloud Training

WHAT DO OTHER STUDENTS SAY?

Check out the excellent reviews from our many students who passed their AWS exam with an average passing score of over 850:

* * * * *

These practice exams are very helpful when preparing for the AWS Certified Cloud Practitioner exam. The questions are similar to those on the exam and follow the format of the questions on the exam, and are of the appropriate difficulty level as the exam. Highly recommended.

* * * * *

What I liked the most is the fact that the wrong answers are explained as to why they are wrong. In understanding the correct answer, you also learn the additional information. I like the option to answer the questions with or without the correct answer being shown.

* * * * *

This book is a great resource to prepare for the AWS Certified Cloud Practitioner exam. In particular, I appreciate that the answers for each question explain why that particular answer is correct/incorrect, thus reinforcing learning.

HOW TO BEST USE THIS RESOURCE

We have organized the 390 practice questions into 6 sets and each set is repeated once <u>without</u> answers and explanations and once <u>with</u> answers and explanations. This allows you to choose from two methods of preparation.

1. Exam simulation

To simulate the exam experience, use the "PRACTICE QUESTIONS ONLY" sets. Grab a pen and paper to record your answers for all 65 questions. After completing each set, check your answers using the "PRACTICE QUESTIONS, ANSWERS & EXPLANATIONS" section.

To calculate your total score, sum up the number of correct answers and multiply them by 1.54 (weighting out of 100%) to get your percentage score out of 100%. For example, if you got 50 questions right, the calculation would be 50 x 1.54 = 77%. The pass mark of the official AWS exam is 70%.

2. Training mode

To use the practice questions as a learning tool, use the "PRACTICE QUESTIONS, ANSWERS & EXPLANATIONS" sets to view the answers and read the in-depth explanations as you move through the questions.

KEY TRAINING ADVICE

AIM FOR A MINIMUM SCORE OF 80%: Although the actual AWS exam has a pass mark of 70%, we recommend that you repeatedly retake our AWS practice exams until you consistently score 80% or higher. We encourage you to put in the work and study the explanations in detail. Once you achieve the recommended score in the practice tests - you are ready to sit the exam and achieve a great score!

FAMILIARIZE YOURSELF WITH THE QUESTION STYLE: Using our AWS practice exams helps you gain experience with the test question format and exam approach for the latest CLF-C01 exam. You'll become intimately familiar with how the questions in the real AWS exam are structured and will be adequately prepared for the real AWS exam experience.

DEEPEN YOUR KNOWLEDGE: Please note that though we match the AWS exam pattern, our AWS practice exams are NOT brain dumps. Don't expect to pass the real AWS certification exam by simply memorizing answers. Instead, we encourage you to use these practice tests to deepen your knowledge. This is your best chance to successfully pass your exam - no matter what questions you are presented with.

YOUR PATHWAY TO SUCCESS

✓ Enroll in Instructor-led Video Course
  Familiarize yourself with the AWS platform

✓ Take our AWS Practice Exams
  Identify your strengths and weaknesses and assess your exam readiness

✓ Study Training Notes
  Focus your study on the knowledge areas where you need to most

✓ Get AWS Certified
  This pathway will let you pass your AWS exam first time with confidence

Instructor-led Video Course

If you're new to AWS, we'd suggest first enrolling in the online instructor-led AWS Certified Cloud Practitioner Video Course from Digital Cloud Training to familiarize yourself with the AWS platform before assessing your exam readiness with these practice exams.

To learn more, visit https://digitalcloud.training/aws-certified-cloud-practitioner/

Apply coupon code **AMZ20** at checkout for a 20% discount.

Online practice exam simulator

If you are looking for practice questions online, enroll in the practice exam course from Digital Cloud Training. Our online Practice Exams are delivered in 4 different variations:

- **Exam Mode**

In exam simulation mode, you complete one full-length practice exam and answer all 65 questions within the allotted time. You are then presented with a pass / fail score report showing your overall score and performance in each knowledge area to identify your strengths and weaknesses.

- **Training Mode**

When taking the practice exam in training mode, you will be shown the answers and explanations for every question after clicking "check". Upon completion of the exam, the score report will show your overall score and performance in each knowledge area.

- **Knowledge Reviews**

Now that you have identified your strengths and weaknesses, you get to dive deep into specific areas with our knowledge reviews. You are presented with a series of questions focused on a specific topic. There is no time limit and you can view the answer to each question as you go through them.

- **Final Exam Simulator**

The exam simulator randomly selects 65 questions from our pool of over 500 unique questions – mimicking the real AWS exam environment. The practice exam has the same format, style, time limit and passing score as the real AWS exam

To learn more, visit https://digitalcloud.training/aws-certified-cloud-practitioner/

Apply coupon code **AMZ20** at checkout for a 20% discount.

Training Notes

Use the Training Notes for the AWS Certified Cloud Practitioner from Digital Cloud to get a more detailed understanding of the AWS services and focus your study on the knowledge areas where you need to most. Deep dive into the CLF-C01 exam objectives with 200 pages of detailed facts, tables and diagrams to shortcut your time to success.

To learn more, visit https://digitalcloud.training/aws-certified-cloud-practitioner/

Apply coupon code **AMZ20** at checkout for a 20% discount.

LIMITED TIME BONUS OFFER

As a special bonus, we are now offering **FREE Access to the Final Exam Simulator** on the Digital Cloud Training website. The practice exam has the same format, style, time limit and passing score as the real AWS exam. With over 500 practice questions, you get to evaluate your progress and identify your strengths and weaknesses. Simply the best way to assess your exam readiness.

Navigate to the BONUS OFFER section at end of this book for instructions on how to claim your bonus.

EXTENDED PDF VERSION

Based on the feedback we've received from our Amazon clients, we understand that studying complex diagrams in black and white or accessing reference links from a kindle may NOT offer the best learning experience.

That's why we've decided to provide you with a PDF of this book at no additional charge. This extended version includes additional diagrams, images and reference links that will enable you to access additional information. To access your free PDF version, simply navigate to the Conclusion of this book for download instructions.

CONTACT, FEEDBACK & SHARING

We want you to get great value from these training resources. If for any reason you are not 100% satisfied, please contact us at support@digitalcloud.training. We promise to address all questions and concerns, typically within 24hrs. We really want you to have a 5-star learning experience!

The AWS platform is evolving quickly, and the exam tracks these changes with a typical lag of around 6 months. We are therefore reliant on student feedback to keep track of what is appearing in the exam. If there are any topics in your exam that weren't covered in our training resources, please provide us with feedback using this form https://digitalcloud.training/student-feedback/. We appreciate any feedback that will help us further improve our AWS training resources.

REVIEWS REALLY MATTER

If you enjoy reading reviews, please consider paying it forward. Reviews guide students and help us continuously improve our courses. We celebrate every honest review and truly appreciate it. We'd be thrilled if you could leave a rating at amazon.com/ryp or your local amazon store (e.g. amazon.co.uk/ryp).

JOIN THE AWS COMMUNITY

Our private Facebook group is a great place to ask questions and share knowledge and exam tips with the AWS community. Join the AWS Certification QA group on Facebook and share your exam feedback with the AWS community: https://www.facebook.com/groups/awscertificationqa

To join the discussion about all things related to Amazon Web Services on Slack, visit: http://digitalcloud.training/slack for instructions.

CONNECT WITH NEAL ON SOCIAL MEDIA

To learn more about the different ways of connecting with Neal, visit: https://digitalcloud.training/neal-davis

 digitalcloud.training/neal-davis

 youtube.com/c/digitalcloudtraining

 facebook.com/digitalcloudtraining

 Twitter @nealkdavis

 linkedin.com/in/nealkdavis

 Instagram @digitalcloudtraining

TABLE OF CONTENTS

SET 1: PRACTICE QUESTIONS ONLY

For training purposes, go directly to Set 1: Practice Questions, Answers & Explanations

QUESTION 1

What advantages does a database administrator obtain by using the Amazon Relational Database Service (RDS)?

1. RDS provides 99.99999999999% reliability and durability.
2. RDS databases automatically scale based on load.
3. RDS enables users to dynamically adjust CPU and RAM resources.
4. RDS simplifies relational database administration tasks.

QUESTION 2

A Cloud Practitioner requires point-in-time recovery (PITR) for an Amazon DynamoDB table. Who is responsible for configuring and performing backups?

1. AWS is responsible for both tasks.
2. The customer is responsible for configuring and AWS is responsible for performing backups.
3. The customer is responsible for both tasks.
4. AWS is responsible for configuring and the user is responsible for performing backups.

QUESTION 3

A large company is interested in avoiding long-term contracts and moving from fixed costs to variable costs.

What is the value proposition of AWS for this company?

1. Economies of scale
2. Pay-as-you-go pricing
3. Volume pricing discounts
4. Automated cost optimization

QUESTION 4

A customer needs to determine Total Cost of Ownership (TCO) for a workload that requires physical isolation. Which hosting model should be accounted for?

1. Dedicated Hosts
2. Reserved Instances
3. On-Demand Instances
4. Spot Instances

QUESTION 5

Which tasks can a user complete using the AWS Cost Management tools? (Select TWO.)

1. Automatically terminate AWS resources if budget thresholds are exceeded.
2. Break down AWS costs by day, service, and linked AWS account.
3. Create budgets and receive notifications if current or forecasted usage exceeds the budgets.
4. Launch either EC2 Spot instances or On-Demand instances based on the current pricing.
5. Move data stored in Amazon S3 Standard to an archiving storage class to reduce cost.

QUESTION 6

Which of the following AWS services are compute services? (Select TWO.)

1. AWS Batch

2. AWS CloudTrail
3. AWS Elastic Beanstalk
4. Amazon EFS
5. Amazon Inspector

QUESTION 7

Which design principles are enabled by the AWS Cloud to improve the operation of workloads? (Select TWO.)

1. Minimize platform design
2. Loose coupling
3. Customized hardware
4. Remove single points of failure
5. Minimum viable product

QUESTION 8

A user is planning to launch three EC2 instances behind a single Elastic Load Balancer. The deployment should be highly available.

1. Launch the instances across multiple Availability Zones in a single AWS Region.
2. Launch the instances as EC2 Spot Instances in the same AWS Region and the same Availability Zone.
3. Launch the instances in multiple AWS Regions, and use Elastic IP addresses.
4. Launch the instances as EC2 Reserved Instances in the same AWS Region, but in different Availability Zones.

QUESTION 9

Which resource should a new user on AWS use to get help with deploying popular technologies based on AWS best practices, including architecture and deployment instructions?

1. AWS CloudFormation
2. AWS Artifact
3. AWS Config
4. AWS Quick Starts

QUESTION 10

A company needs to publish messages to a thousands of subscribers simultaneously using a push mechanism.

Which AWS service should the company use?

1. AWS Step Functions
2. Amazon Simple Workflow Service (SWF)
3. Amazon Simple Notification Service (Amazon SNS)
4. Amazon Simple Queue Service (Amazon SQS)

QUESTION 11

A company uses Amazon EC2 instances to run applications that are dedicated to different departments. The company needs to break out the costs of these applications and allocate them to the relevant department. The EC2 instances run in a single VPC.

How can the company achieve these requirements?

1. Enable billing access for IAM users and view the costs in Cost Explorer.
2. Enable billing alerts through Amazon CloudWatch and Amazon SNS.
3. Create tags by department on the instances and then run a cost allocation report.
4. Add additional Amazon VPCs and launch each application in a separate VPC.

QUESTION 12

An application uses a PostgreSQL database running on a single Amazon EC2 instance. A Cloud Practitioner has been asked to increase the availability of the database so there is automatic recovery in the case of a failure.

Which tasks can the Cloud Practitioner take to meet this requirement?

1. Migrate the database to Amazon RDS and enable the Multi-AZ feature.
2. Configure an Elastic Load Balancer in front of the EC2 instance.
3. Configure EC2 Auto Recovery to move the instance to another Region.
4. Set the DeleteOnTermination value to false for the EBS root volume.

QUESTION 13

A company is launching a new website which is expected to have highly variable levels of traffic. The website will run on Amazon EC2 and must be highly available.

What is the MOST cost-effective approach?

1. Use the AWS CLI to launch and terminate Amazon EC2 instances to match demand.
2. Create an Amazon EC2 Auto Scaling group and configure an Elastic Load Balancer.
3. Determine the highest expected traffic and use an appropriate instance type.
4. Launch the website using an Amazon EC2 instance running on a dedicated host.

QUESTION 14

Which of the following statements best describes the concept of agility in relation to cloud computing on AWS? (Select TWO.)

1. The speed at which AWS rolls out new features.
2. The ability to experiment quickly.
3. The elimination of wasted capacity.
4. The ability to automatically scale capacity.
5. The speed at which AWS resources can be created.

QUESTION 15

A company runs a batch job on an Amazon EC2 instance and it takes 6 hours to complete. The workload is expected to double in volume each month with a proportional increase in processing time.

What is the most efficient cloud architecture to address the growing workload?

1. Run the batch job on a larger Amazon EC2 instance type with more CPU.
2. Change the Amazon EC2 volume type to a Provisioned IOPS SSD volume.
3. Run the application on a bare metal Amazon EC2 instance.
4. Run the batch workload in parallel across multiple Amazon EC2 instances.

QUESTION 16

An individual IAM user must be granted access to an Amazon S3 bucket using a bucket policy. Which element in the S3 bucket policy should be updated to define the user account for which access will be granted?

1. Action
2. Principal
3. Resource
4. Condition

QUESTION 17

A Cloud Practitioner needs a tool that can assist with viewing and managing AWS costs and usage over time. Which tool should the Cloud Practitioner use?

1. AWS Budgets

2. Amazon Inspector
3. AWS Organizations
4. AWS Cost Explorer

QUESTION 18

A company plans to deploy a relational database on AWS. The IT department will perform database administration. Which service should the company use?

1. Amazon EC2
2. Amazon RedShift
3. Amazon ElastiCache
4. Amazon DynamoDB

QUESTION 19

A company is planning to move a number of legacy applications to the AWS Cloud. The solution must be cost-effective. Which approach should the company take?

1. Migrate the applications to dedicated hosts on Amazon EC2.
2. Rehost the applications on Amazon EC2 instances that are right-sized.
3. Use AWS Lambda to host the legacy applications in the cloud.
4. Use an Amazon S3 static website to host the legacy application code.

QUESTION 20

A company must provide access to AWS resources for their employees. Which security practices should they follow? (Select TWO.)

1. Enable multi-factor authentication for users.
2. Create IAM policies based on least privilege principles.
3. Disable password policies and management console access.
4. Create IAM users in different AWS Regions.
5. Create IAM Roles and apply them to IAM groups.

QUESTION 21

An Amazon Virtual Private Cloud (VPC) can include multiple:

1. AWS Regions.
2. Edge locations.
3. Internet gateways.
4. Availability Zones.

QUESTION 22

A Cloud Practitioner anticipates an increase in application traffic at a future date and time when a sales event will take place. How can the Cloud Practitioner configure Amazon EC2 Auto Scaling to ensure the right number of Amazon EC2 instances are available ahead of the event?

1. Configure predictive scaling.
2. Configure a target tracking scaling policy.
3. Configure a scheduled scaling policy.
4. Configure a step scaling policy.

QUESTION 23

A company is deploying an application on Amazon EC2 that requires low-latency access to application components in an on-premises data center. Which AWS service or resource can the company use to extend their existing VPC to the on-premises data center?

1. Amazon Connect
2. AWS Outposts
3. AWS Direct Connect
4. Amazon Workspaces

QUESTION 24

Which type of credential should a Cloud Practitioner use for programmatic access to AWS resources from the AWS CLI/API?

1. SSL/TLS certificate
2. SSH public keys
3. Access keys
4. User name and password

QUESTION 25

A company is designing a new a service that must align with the operational excellence pillar of the AWS Well-Architected Framework.

Which design principles should the company follow? (Select TWO.)

1. Anticipate failure.
2. Make large-scale changes.
3. Perform operations as code.
4. Perform manual operations.
5. Create static operational procedures.

QUESTION 26

A website has a global customer base and users have reported poor performance when connecting to the site.

Which AWS service will improve the customer experience by reducing latency?

1. AWS Direct Connect
2. Amazon EC2 Auto Scaling
3. Amazon CloudFront
4. Amazon ElastiCache

QUESTION 27

What is one method of protecting against distributed denial of service (DDoS) attacks in the AWS Cloud?

1. Use Amazon CloudWatch monitoring.
2. Configure a firewall in front of resources.
3. Monitor the Service Health Dashboard.
4. Enable AWS CloudTrail logging.

QUESTION 28

How much data can a company store in the Amazon S3 service?

1. 1 PB
2. 100 TB
3. 100 PB
4. Virtually unlimited

QUESTION 29

A company is deploying a new workload and software licensing requirements dictate that the workload must be run on a specific, physical server.

Which Amazon EC2 instance deployment option should be used?

1. Dedicated Instances
2. Spot Instances
3. Reserved Instances
4. Dedicated Hosts

QUESTION 30

Which of the following are valid benefits of using the AWS Cloud? (Select TWO.)

1. Outsource all operational risk.
2. Total control over data center infrastructure.
3. Fast provisioning of IT resources.
4. Ability to go global quickly.
5. Outsource all application development to AWS.

QUESTION 31

Which tasks require the use of the AWS account root user? (Select TWO.)

1. Enabling encryption for S3.
2. Viewing AWS CloudTrail logs.
3. Changing the account name.
4. Changing AWS Support plans.
5. Changing payment currency.

QUESTION 32

Which AWS service can a company use to discover and protect sensitive data that is stored in Amazon S3 buckets.

1. Amazon GuardDuty
2. AWS Policy Generator
3. Amazon Detective
4. Amazon Macie

QUESTION 33

Which benefits can a company gain by deploying a relational database on Amazon RDS instead of Amazon EC2? (Select TWO.)

1. Automated backups
2. Schema management
3. Indexing of tables
4. Software patching
5. Root access to OS

QUESTION 34

A company is planning to deploy an application with a relational database on AWS. The application layer requires access to the database instance's operating system in order to run scripts.

The company prefer to keep management overhead to a minimum. Which deployment should be used for the database?

1. Amazon RDS
2. Amazon DynamoDB
3. Amazon EC2
4. Amazon S3

QUESTION 35

Customers using AWS services must patch operating systems on which of the following services?

1. AWS Lambda
2. Amazon EC2
3. AWS Fargate
4. Amazon DynamoDB

QUESTION 36

Which AWS feature can be used to launch a pre-configured Amazon Elastic Compute Cloud (EC2) instance?

1. Amazon Elastic Block Store (EBS)
2. Amazon EC2 Systems Manager
3. Amazon Machine Image (AMI)
4. Amazon AppStream 2.0

QUESTION 37

Which of the following AWS features or services can be used to provide root storage volumes for Amazon EC2 instances?

1. Amazon Elastic Block Store (EBS)
2. Amazon Machine Image
3. Amazon Elastic File System (EFS)
4. Amazon Simple Storage Service (S3)

QUESTION 38

Which AWS service or feature can assist with protecting a website that is hosted outside of AWS?

1. Amazon VPC route tables
2. Amazon EC2 security groups
3. Amazon VPC network ACLs
4. AWS Web Application Firewall (WAF)

QUESTION 39

Which AWS service can a team use to deploy infrastructure on AWS using familiar programming languages?

1. AWS Cloud Development Kit (AWS CDK)
2. Amazon CodeGuru
3. AWS Config
4. AWS CodeCommit

QUESTION 40

When running applications in the AWS Cloud, which common tasks can AWS manage on behalf of their customers? (Select TWO.)

1. Patching database software
2. Application source code auditing
3. Creating a database schema
4. Taking a backup of a database
5. Application security testing

QUESTION 41

Which of the following will help a user determine if they need to request an Amazon EC2 service limit increase?

1. AWS Personal Health Dashboard
2. AWS Cost Explorer
3. AWS Trusted Advisor
4. AWS Service Health Dashboard

QUESTION 42

How does the AWS cloud increase the speed and agility of execution for customers? (Select TWO.)

1. Fast provisioning of resources
2. Private connections to data centers
3. Secured data centers
4. Lower cost of deployment
5. Scalable compute capacity

QUESTION 43

A company has multiple AWS accounts and is using AWS Organizations with consolidated billing. Which advantages will they benefit from? (Select TWO.)

1. They will receive one bill for the accounts in the Organization.
2. The default service limits in all accounts will be increased.
3. They will receive a fixed discount for all usage across accounts.
4. They may benefit from lower unit pricing for aggregated usage.
5. They will be automatically enrolled in a business support plan.

QUESTION 44

Which of the following represents a value proposition for using the AWS Cloud?

1. AWS is responsible for securing your applications.
2. It is not necessary to enter into long term contracts.
3. Customers can request specialized hardware.
4. AWS provides full access to their data centers.

QUESTION 45

A company has many underutilized compute resources on-premises. Which AWS Cloud feature will help resolve this issue?

1. High availability
2. Elasticity
3. Global deployment
4. Fault tolerance

QUESTION 46

What can a Cloud Practitioner use to categorize and track AWS costs by project?

1. Cost Allocation Tags
2. AWS Trusted Advisor
3. Consolidated billing
4. Multiple accounts

QUESTION 47

A company is deploying a MySQL database on AWS. The database must easily scale and have automatic backup enabled.

Which AWS service should the company?

1. Amazon Athena

2. Amazon DynamoDB
3. Amazon Aurora
4. Amazon DocumentDB

QUESTION 48

A company plans to use reserved instances to get discounted pricing for Amazon EC2 instances. The company may need to change the EC2 instance type during the one year period.

Which instance purchasing option is the MOST cost-effective for this use case?

1. Standard Reserved Instances
2. Convertible Reserved Instances
3. Zonal Reserved Instances
4. Regional Reserved Instances

QUESTION 49

Which of the following is a sole responsibility of AWS?

1. Application deployment
2. Patch management
3. Availability Zone management
4. Customer data access controls

QUESTION 50

Which AWS service provides a managed software version control system?

1. Amazon CodeDeploy
2. AWS CodePipeline
3. AWS DataSync
4. AWS CodeCommit

QUESTION 51

Which of the following deployments involves the reliability pillar of the AWS Well-Architected Framework?

1. Amazon RDS Multi-AZ deployment
2. Amazon EBS provisioned IOPS volume
3. Attach a WebACL to a CloudFront distribution
4. Use CloudFormation to deploy infrastructure

QUESTION 52

A Cloud Practitioner needs to monitor a new Amazon EC2 instances CPU and network utilization. Which AWS service should be used?

1. Amazon Inspector
2. AWS CloudTrail
3. AWS Systems Manager
4. Amazon CloudWatch

QUESTION 53

AWS are able to continually reduce their pricing due to:

1. Economies of scale.
2. Pay-as-you go pricing.
3. Elastic compute services.

4. Compute savings plans.

QUESTION 54

Which AWS services can a company use to gather information about activity in their AWS account? (Select TWO.)

1. Amazon CloudFront
2. AWS CloudTrail
3. AWS Trusted Advisor
4. Amazon Connect
5. Amazon CloudWatch

QUESTION 55

A company is deploying an application in the AWS Cloud. How can they secure the application? (Select TWO.)

1. Enable encryption for the application data at rest.
2. Configure public access for the AWS services used by the application.
3. Enable monitoring by turning off encryption for data in transit.
4. Limit access privileges according to the principal of least privilege.
5. Provide full admin access to developer and operations staff.

QUESTION 56

A Cloud Practitioner is developing a new application and wishes to integrate features of AWS services directly into the application.

Which of the following is the BEST tool for this purpose?

1. AWS Software Development Kit
2. AWS CodeDeploy
3. AWS Command Line Interface (CLI)
4. AWS CodePipeline

QUESTION 57

A user needs to identify underutilized Amazon EC2 instances to reduce costs.

Which AWS service or feature will meet this requirement?

1. AWS CodeBuild
2. AWS Trusted Advisor
3. AWS Cost Explorer
4. AWS Personal Health Dashboard

QUESTION 58

Which of the following can an AWS customer use to launch a new ElastiCache cluster? (Select TWO.)

1. AWS CloudFormation
2. AWS Concierge
3. AWS Systems Manager
4. AWS Management Console
5. AWS Data Pipeline

QUESTION 59

A company is deploying a new web application in a single AWS Region that will be used by users globally.

Which AWS services will assist with lowering latency and improving transfer speeds for the global users? (Select TWO.)

1. AWS Direct Connect

2. AWS Global Accelerator
3. Amazon CloudFront
4. AWS Transfer Gateway
5. AWS Snowcone

QUESTION 60

For what purpose would a Cloud Practitioner access AWS Artifact?

1. Download configuration details for all AWS resources.
2. Access training materials for AWS services.
3. Create a security assessment report for AWS services.
4. Gain access to AWS security and compliance documents.

QUESTION 61

Which AWS Cloud service provides recommendations on how to optimize performance for AWS services?

1. Amazon Inspector
2. AWS Trusted Advisor
3. Amazon CloudWatch
4. AWS CloudTrail

QUESTION 62

A company is migrating a monolithic application that does not scale well into the cloud and refactoring it into a microservices architecture.

Which best practice of the AWS Well-Architected Framework does this plan relate to?

1. Stop spending money on undifferentiated heavy lifting.
2. Implement loosely coupled services.
3. Manage change in automation.
4. Use multiple solutions to improve performance.

QUESTION 63

What are AWS Identity and Access Management (IAM) access keys used for?

1. Logging in to the AWS Management Console.
2. Ensuring the integrity of log files.
3. Making programmatic calls to AWS from AWS APIs.
4. Enabling encryption in transit for web servers.

QUESTION 64

What is the best practice for managing AWS IAM access keys?

1. There is no need to manage access keys.
2. Customers should rotate access keys regularly.
3. AWS rotate access keys on a schedule.
4. Never use access keys, always use IAM roles.

QUESTION 65

According to the AWS shared responsibility model, which of the following is a responsibility of AWS?

1. Configuring network ACLs to block malicious attacks.
2. Patching software running on Amazon EC2 instances.
3. Updating the firmware on the underlying EC2 hosts.

4. Updating security group rules to enable connectivity.

SET 1: PRACTICE QUESTIONS AND ANSWERS

QUESTION 1

What advantages does a database administrator obtain by using the Amazon Relational Database Service (RDS)?

1. RDS provides 99.99999999999% reliability and durability.
2. RDS databases automatically scale based on load.
3. RDS enables users to dynamically adjust CPU and RAM resources.
4. RDS simplifies relational database administration tasks.

Answer: 4

Explanation:

Amazon RDS is a managed relational database service on which you can run several types of database software. The service is managed so this reduces the database administration tasks an administrator would normally undertake. The managed service includes hardware provisioning, database setup, patching and backups.

CORRECT: "RDS simplifies relational database administration tasks" is the correct answer.

INCORRECT: "RDS databases automatically scale based on load" is incorrect. This is not true, storage auto scaling is possible but for compute it scales by changing instance type (manual).

INCORRECT: "RDS provides 99.99999999999% reliability and durability" is incorrect. This is not true of Amazon RDS.

INCORRECT: "RDS enables users to dynamically adjust CPU and RAM resources" is incorrect. You cannot adjust CPU and RAM dynamically, you must change the instance type and reboot the database instance.

References:

https://aws.amazon.com/rds/

Save time with our exam-specific cheat sheets:

https://digitalcloud.training/certification-training/aws-certified-cloud-practitioner/aws-databases/

QUESTION 2

A Cloud Practitioner requires point-in-time recovery (PITR) for an Amazon DynamoDB table. Who is responsible for configuring and performing backups?

1. AWS is responsible for both tasks.
2. The customer is responsible for configuring and AWS is responsible for performing backups.
3. The customer is responsible for both tasks.
4. AWS is responsible for configuring and the user is responsible for performing backups.

Answer: 2

Explanation:

Point-in-time recovery (PITR) provides continuous backups of your DynamoDB table data. When enabled, DynamoDB maintains incremental backups of your table for the last 35 days until you explicitly turn it off. It is a customer responsibility to enable PITR on and AWS is responsible for actually performing the backups.

CORRECT: "The customer is responsible for configuring and AWS is responsible for performing backups" is the correct answer.

INCORRECT: "AWS is responsible for configuring and the user is responsible for performing backups" is incorrect. This is backwards, users are responsible for configuring and AWS is responsible for performing backups.

INCORRECT: "AWS is responsible for both tasks" is incorrect. This is not true as users must configure PITR.

INCORRECT: "The customer is responsible for both tasks" is incorrect. This is not true, AWS perform the backups.

References:

https://aws.amazon.com/blogs/aws/new-amazon-dynamodb-continuous-backups-and-point-in-time-recovery-pitr/

Save time with our exam-specific cheat sheets:

https://digitalcloud.training/certification-training/aws-certified-cloud-practitioner/aws-databases/

QUESTION 3

A large company is interested in avoiding long-term contracts and moving from fixed costs to variable costs.

What is the value proposition of AWS for this company?

1. Economies of scale
2. Pay-as-you-go pricing
3. Volume pricing discounts
4. Automated cost optimization

Answer: 2

Explanation:

Pay-as-you-go pricing helps companies move away from fixed costs to variable costs in a model in which they only pay for what they actually use. There are no fixed term contracts with AWS so that requirement is also met.

CORRECT: "Pay-as-you-go pricing" is the correct answer.

INCORRECT: "Economies of scale" is incorrect. You do get good pricing because of the economies of scale leveraged by AWS. However, the value proposition for companies wishing to avoid fixed costs is pay-as-you-go pricing. This flexibility can be more important in some cases than the actual cost per unit.

INCORRECT: "Volume pricing discounts" is incorrect. This is not the value proposition for this company as they are seeking to avoid long-term contracts and fixed costs, not to achieve a discount.

INCORRECT: "Automated cost optimization" is incorrect. This is a not a feature that relates to the value proposition for this customer.

References:

https://aws.amazon.com/pricing/

Save time with our exam-specific cheat sheets:

https://digitalcloud.training/certification-training/aws-certified-cloud-practitioner/aws-billing-and-pricing/

QUESTION 4

A customer needs to determine Total Cost of Ownership (TCO) for a workload that requires physical isolation. Which hosting model should be accounted for?

1. Dedicated Hosts
2. Reserved Instances
3. On-Demand Instances
4. Spot Instances

Answer: 1

Explanation:

An Amazon EC2 Dedicated Host is a physical server with EC2 instance capacity fully dedicated to your use. Dedicated Hosts allow you to use your existing per-socket, per-core, or per-VM software licenses, including Windows Server, Microsoft SQL Server, SUSE, and Linux Enterprise Server.

Note that dedicated hosts can be considered "hosting model" as it determines that actual underlying infrastructure that is used for running your workload. All of the other answers are simply pricing plans for shared hosting models.

CORRECT: "Dedicated Hosts" is the correct answer.

INCORRECT: "Reserved Instances" is incorrect as this pricing model does not support physical isolation.

INCORRECT: "On-Demand Instances" is incorrect as this pricing model does not support physical isolation.

INCORRECT: "Spot Instances" is incorrect as this hosting pricing does not support physical isolation.

References:

https://docs.aws.amazon.com/AWSEC2/latest/UserGuide/dedicated-hosts-overview.html

Save time with our exam-specific cheat sheets:

https://digitalcloud.training/certification-training/aws-certified-cloud-practitioner/aws-compute/

QUESTION 5

Which tasks can a user complete using the AWS Cost Management tools? (Select TWO.)

1. Automatically terminate AWS resources if budget thresholds are exceeded.
2. Break down AWS costs by day, service, and linked AWS account.
3. Create budgets and receive notifications if current or forecasted usage exceeds the budgets.
4. Launch either EC2 Spot instances or On-Demand instances based on the current pricing.
5. Move data stored in Amazon S3 Standard to an archiving storage class to reduce cost.

Answer: 2,3

Explanation:

The AWS Cost Management tools includes services, tools, and resources to organize and track cost and usage data, enhance control through consolidated billing and access permissions, enable better planning through budgeting and forecasts, and further lower costs with resources and pricing optimizations.

CORRECT: "Break down AWS costs by day, service, and linked AWS account" is a correct answer.

CORRECT: "Create budgets and receive notifications if current or forecasted usage exceeds the budgets" is also a correct answer.

INCORRECT: "Automatically terminate AWS resources if budget thresholds are exceeded" is incorrect. The cost management tools will not do this for you but they could generate an alert which could be processed by another service to terminate resources.

INCORRECT: "Launch either EC2 Spot instances or On-Demand instances based on the current pricing" is incorrect. The cost management tools do not integrate with the tools used to launch EC2 instances and cannot choose the best pricing plan.

INCORRECT: "Move data stored in Amazon S3 Standard to an archiving storage class to reduce cost" is incorrect. This is performed using lifecycle management in Amazon S3, it is not a task performed by cost management tools.

References:

https://aws.amazon.com/aws-cost-management/

Save time with our exam-specific cheat sheets:

https://digitalcloud.training/certification-training/aws-certified-cloud-practitioner/aws-billing-and-pricing/

QUESTION 6

Which of the following AWS services are compute services? (Select TWO.)

1. AWS Batch
2. AWS CloudTrail
3. AWS Elastic Beanstalk
4. Amazon EFS
5. Amazon Inspector

Answer: 1,3

Explanation:

AWS Batch enables developers, scientists, and engineers to easily and efficiently run hundreds of thousands of batch computing jobs on AWS.

AWS Elastic Beanstalk is an easy-to-use service for deploying and scaling web applications and services developed with Java, .NET, PHP, Node.js, Python, Ruby, Go, and Docker on familiar servers such as Apache, Nginx, Passenger, and IIS.

CORRECT: "AWS Batch" is a correct answer.

CORRECT: "AWS Elastic Beanstalk" is also a correct answer.

INCORRECT: "AWS CloudTrail" is incorrect. CloudTrail is used for auditing.

INCORRECT: "Amazon EFS" is incorrect. The Elastic File System (EFS) is used for storing data and is mounted by EC2 instances.

INCORRECT: "Amazon Inspector" is incorrect. Amazon Inspector is an automated security assessment service that helps improve the security and compliance of applications deployed on AWS.

References:

https://aws.amazon.com/batch/

https://aws.amazon.com/elasticbeanstalk/

QUESTION 7

Which design principles are enabled by the AWS Cloud to improve the operation of workloads? (Select TWO.)

1. Minimize platform design
2. Loose coupling
3. Customized hardware
4. Remove single points of failure
5. Minimum viable product

Answer: 2,4

Explanation:

Loose coupling is when you break systems down into smaller components that are loosely coupled together. This reduces interdependencies between systems components. This is achieved in the cloud using messages buses, notification and messaging services.

Removing single points of failure ensures fault tolerance and high availability. This is easily achieved in the cloud as the architecture and features of the cloud support the implementation of highly available and fault tolerant systems.

CORRECT: "Loose coupling" is a correct answer.

CORRECT: "Remove single points of failure" is also a correct answer.

INCORRECT: "Customized hardware" is incorrect. You cannot customize hardware in the cloud.

INCORRECT: "Minimize platform design" is incorrect. This is not an operational advantage for workloads in the cloud.

INCORRECT: "Minimum viable product" is incorrect. This is not an operational advantage for workloads in the cloud.

References:

https://d1.awsstatic.com/whitepapers/AWS_Cloud_Best_Practices.pdf

Save time with our exam-specific cheat sheets:

https://digitalcloud.training/certification-training/aws-certified-cloud-practitioner/architecting-for-the-cloud/

QUESTION 8

A user is planning to launch three EC2 instances behind a single Elastic Load Balancer. The deployment should be highly available.

1. Launch the instances across multiple Availability Zones in a single AWS Region.
2. Launch the instances as EC2 Spot Instances in the same AWS Region and the same Availability Zone.
3. Launch the instances in multiple AWS Regions, and use Elastic IP addresses.
4. Launch the instances as EC2 Reserved Instances in the same AWS Region, but in different Availability Zones.

Answer: 1

Explanation:

To make the deployment highly available the user should launch the instances across multiple Availability Zones in a single AWS Region. Elastic Load Balancers can only serve targets in a single Region so it is not possible to deploy across Regions.

CORRECT: "Launch the instances across multiple Availability Zones in a single AWS Region" is the correct answer.

INCORRECT: "Launch the instances as EC2 Spot Instances in the same AWS Region and the same Availability Zone" is incorrect. The pricing model is not relevant to high availability and deploying in a single AZ does not result in a highly available deployment.

INCORRECT: "Launch the instances in multiple AWS Regions, and use Elastic IP addresses" is incorrect. You cannot use an ELB with instances in multiple Regions and using an EIP does not help.

INCORRECT: "Launch the instances as EC2 Reserved Instances in the same AWS Region, but in different Availability Zones" is incorrect. Using reserved instances may not be appropriate as we do not know whether this is going to be a long-term workload or not.

References:

https://aws.amazon.com/about-aws/global-infrastructure/regions_az/

Save time with our exam-specific cheat sheets:

https://digitalcloud.training/certification-training/aws-certified-cloud-practitioner/aws-global-infrastructure/

QUESTION 9

Which resource should a new user on AWS use to get help with deploying popular technologies based on AWS best practices, including architecture and deployment instructions?

1. AWS CloudFormation
2. AWS Artifact
3. AWS Config
4. AWS Quick Starts

Answer: 4

Explanation:

Quick Starts are built by Amazon Web Services (AWS) solutions architects and partners to help you deploy popular technologies on AWS, based on AWS best practices for security and high availability. These accelerators reduce hundreds of manual procedures into just a few steps, so you can build your production environment quickly and start using it immediately.

Each Quick Start includes AWS CloudFormation templates that automate the deployment and a guide that discusses the architecture and provides step-by-step deployment instructions.

CORRECT: "AWS Quick Starts" is the correct answer.

INCORRECT: "AWS CloudFormation" is incorrect. CloudFormation is used to deploy infrastructure from templates, the Quick Starts use CloudFormation.

INCORRECT: "AWS Artifact" is incorrect. Artifact provides on-demand access to AWS security and compliance reports.

INCORRECT: "AWS Config" is incorrect. Config is a service used for compliance relating the configuration of AWS resources.

References:

https://aws.amazon.com/quickstart/

QUESTION 10

A company needs to publish messages to a thousands of subscribers simultaneously using a push mechanism.

Which AWS service should the company use?

1. AWS Step Functions
2. Amazon Simple Workflow Service (SWF)
3. Amazon Simple Notification Service (Amazon SNS)
4. Amazon Simple Queue Service (Amazon SQS)

Answer: 3

Explanation:

Amazon SNS is a publisher/subscriber notification service that uses a push mechanism to publish messages to multiple subscribers. Amazon SNS enables you to send messages or notifications directly to users with SMS text messages to over 200 countries, mobile push on Apple, Android, and other platforms or email (SMTP).

CORRECT: "Amazon Simple Notification Service (Amazon SNS)" is the correct answer.

INCORRECT: "Amazon Simple Queue Service (Amazon SQS)" is incorrect. SQS is a message queue service used for decoupling applications.

INCORRECT: "Amazon Simple Workflow Service (SWF)" is incorrect. SWF is a workflow orchestration service, not a messaging service.

INCORRECT: "AWS Step Functions" is incorrect. AWS Step Functions is a serverless workflow orchestration service for modern applications.

References:

Save time with our exam-specific cheat sheets:

QUESTION 11

A company uses Amazon EC2 instances to run applications that are dedicated to different departments. The company needs to break out the costs of these applications and allocate them to the relevant department. The EC2 instances run in a single VPC.

How can the company achieve these requirements?

1. Enable billing access for IAM users and view the costs in Cost Explorer.
2. Enable billing alerts through Amazon CloudWatch and Amazon SNS.
3. Create tags by department on the instances and then run a cost allocation report.
4. Add additional Amazon VPCs and launch each application in a separate VPC.

Answer: 3

Explanation:

The company should create cost allocation tags that specify the department and assign them to resources. These tags must be activated so they are visible in the cost allocation report. Once this is done and a monthly cost allocation report has been configured it will be easy to monitor the costs for each department.

CORRECT: "Create tags by department on the instances and then run a cost allocation report" is the correct answer.

INCORRECT: "Enable billing access for IAM users and view the costs in Cost Explorer" is incorrect. Cost explorer will not show a breakdown of the costs by department.

INCORRECT: "Enable billing alerts through Amazon CloudWatch and Amazon SNS" is incorrect. A billing alert simply lets you know you have reached a cost threshold.

INCORRECT: "Add additional Amazon VPCs and launch each application in a separate VPC" is incorrect. This will not help as billing is not broken out by VPC so they will not be able to determine the costs per department using this method.

References:

https://docs.aws.amazon.com/awsaccountbilling/latest/aboutv2/configurecostallocreport.html

Save time with our exam-specific cheat sheets:

https://digitalcloud.training/certification-training/aws-certified-cloud-practitioner/aws-billing-and-pricing/

QUESTION 12

An application uses a PostgreSQL database running on a single Amazon EC2 instance. A Cloud Practitioner has been asked to increase the availability of the database so there is automatic recovery in the case of a failure.

Which tasks can the Cloud Practitioner take to meet this requirement?

1. Migrate the database to Amazon RDS and enable the Multi-AZ feature.
2. Configure an Elastic Load Balancer in front of the EC2 instance.
3. Configure EC2 Auto Recovery to move the instance to another Region.
4. Set the DeleteOnTermination value to false for the EBS root volume.

Answer: 1

Explanation:

Moving the database to Amazon RDS means that the database can take advantage of the built-in Multi-AZ feature. This feature creates a standby instance in another Availability Zone and synchronously replicates to it. In the event of a failure that affects the primary database an automatic failover can occur and the database will become functional on the standby instance.

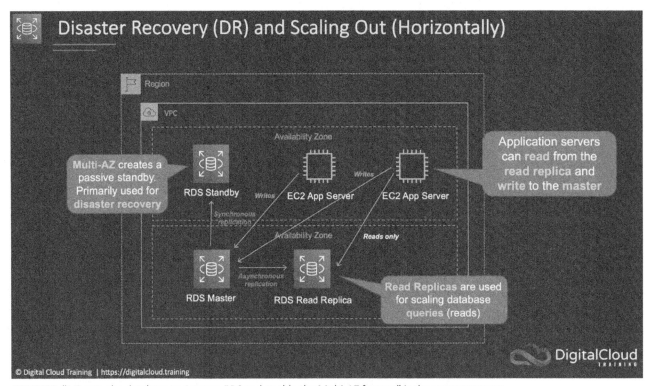

CORRECT: "Migrate the database to Amazon RDS and enable the Multi-AZ feature" is the correct answer.

INCORRECT: "Configure an Elastic Load Balancer in front of the EC2 instance" is incorrect. You cannot use an ELB to distribute traffic to a database and with a single instance there's no benefit here at all.

INCORRECT: "Configure EC2 Auto Recovery to move the instance to another Region" is incorrect. The auto recovery feature of EC2 automatically moves the instance to another host, not to another Region.

INCORRECT: "Set the DeleteOnTermination value to false for the EBS root volume" is incorrect. This will simply preserve the root volume; it will not perform automatic recovery

References:

https://aws.amazon.com/rds/features/multi-az/

Save time with our exam-specific cheat sheets:

https://digitalcloud.training/certification-training/aws-certified-cloud-practitioner/aws-databases/

QUESTION 13

A company is launching a new website which is expected to have highly variable levels of traffic. The website will run on Amazon EC2 and must be highly available.

What is the MOST cost-effective approach?

1. Use the AWS CLI to launch and terminate Amazon EC2 instances to match demand.
2. Create an Amazon EC2 Auto Scaling group and configure an Elastic Load Balancer.
3. Determine the highest expected traffic and use an appropriate instance type.
4. Launch the website using an Amazon EC2 instance running on a dedicated host.

Answer: 2

Explanation:

The most cost-effective approach for ensuring the website is highly available on Amazon EC2 instances is to use an Auto Scaling group. This will ensure that the appropriate number of instances is always available to service the demand. An Elastic Load Balancer can be placed in front of the instances to distribute incoming connections.

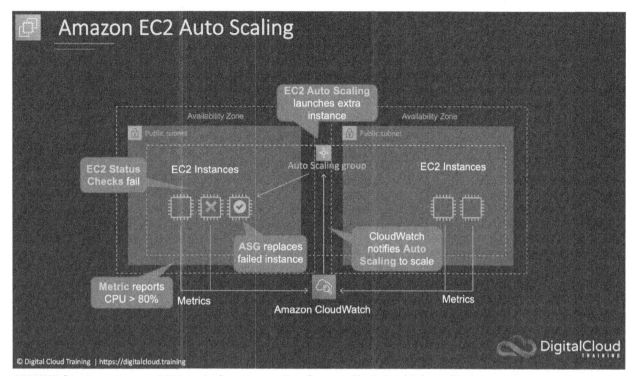

Amazon EC2 Auto Scaling

EC2 Auto Scaling launches extra instance

Availability Zone

Public subnet

EC2 Status Checks fail

EC2 Instances

Auto Scaling group

Availability Zone

Public subnet

EC2 Instances

ASG replaces failed instance

CloudWatch notifies Auto Scaling to scale

Metric reports CPU > 80%

Metrics

Amazon CloudWatch

Metrics

© Digital Cloud Training | https://digitalcloud.training

DigitalCloud
TRAINING

CORRECT: "Create an Amazon EC2 Auto Scaling group and configure an Elastic Load Balancer" is the correct answer.

INCORRECT: "Use the AWS CLI to launch and terminate Amazon EC2 instances to match demand" is incorrect. This is a manual approach and would not be recommended.

INCORRECT: "Determine the highest expected traffic and use an appropriate instance type" is incorrect. This approach will result in the company overpaying when the demand is low.

INCORRECT: "Launch the website using an Amazon EC2 instance running on a dedicated host" is incorrect. This is an expensive solution as dedicated hosts are very costly and should only be used when physical isolation of resources or host visibility is required.

References:

https://aws.amazon.com/ec2/autoscaling/

Save time with our exam-specific cheat sheets:

https://digitalcloud.training/certification-training/aws-certified-cloud-practitioner/elastic-load-balancing-and-auto-scaling/

QUESTION 14

Which of the following statements best describes the concept of agility in relation to cloud computing on AWS? (Select TWO.)

1. The speed at which AWS rolls out new features.
2. The ability to experiment quickly.
3. The elimination of wasted capacity.
4. The ability to automatically scale capacity.
5. The speed at which AWS resources can be created.

Answer: 2,5

Explanation:

In a cloud computing environment, new IT resources are only a click away, which means that you reduce the time to make those resources available to your developers from weeks to just minutes. This results in a dramatic increase in agility for the organization, since the cost and time it takes to experiment and develop is significantly lower.

CORRECT: "The ability to experiment quickly" is a correct answer.

CORRECT: "The speed at which AWS resources can be created" is also a correct answer.

INCORRECT: "The speed at which AWS rolls out new features" is incorrect. This is not a statement that describes agility.

INCORRECT: "The elimination of wasted capacity" is incorrect. This is also known as right-sizing and it is a cost benefit of running in the cloud. It is not a statement that describes agility.

INCORRECT: "The ability to automatically scale capacity" is incorrect. Auto scaling ensures you have the right amount of capacity available.

References:

https://docs.aws.amazon.com/whitepapers/latest/aws-overview/six-advantages-of-cloud-computing.html

Save time with our exam-specific cheat sheets:

https://digitalcloud.training/certification-training/aws-certified-cloud-practitioner/cloud-computing-concepts/

QUESTION 15

A company runs a batch job on an Amazon EC2 instance and it takes 6 hours to complete. The workload is expected to double in volume each month with a proportional increase in processing time.

What is the most efficient cloud architecture to address the growing workload?

1. Run the batch job on a larger Amazon EC2 instance type with more CPU.
2. Change the Amazon EC2 volume type to a Provisioned IOPS SSD volume.
3. Run the application on a bare metal Amazon EC2 instance.
4. Run the batch workload in parallel across multiple Amazon EC2 instances.

Answer: 4

Explanation:

The most efficient option is to use multiple EC2 instances and distribute the workload across them. This is an example of horizontal scaling and will allow the workload to keep growing in size without any issue and without increasing the overall processing timeframe.

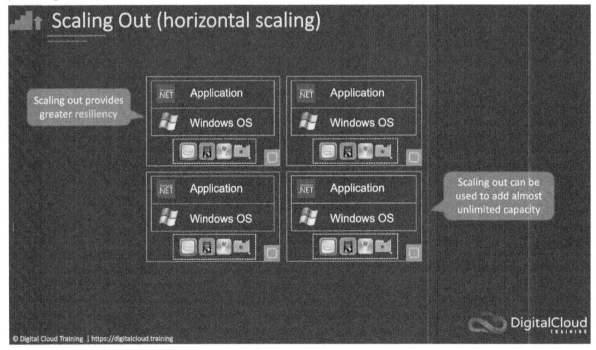

CORRECT: "Run the batch workload in parallel across multiple Amazon EC2 instances" is the correct answer.

INCORRECT: "Run the batch job on a larger Amazon EC2 instance type with more CPU" is incorrect. This may help initially but over time this will not scale well and the workload will take many days to complete.

INCORRECT: "Change the Amazon EC2 volume type to a Provisioned IOPS SSD volume" is incorrect. This will improve the underlying performance of the EBS volume but does not assist with processing (more CPU is needed, i.e. by spreading across instances).

INCORRECT: "Run the application on a bare metal Amazon EC2 instance" is incorrect. Bare metal instances are used for workloads that require access to the hardware feature set (such as Intel VT-x), for applications that need to run in non-virtualized environments for licensing or support requirements, or for customers who wish to use their own hypervisor.

References:

https://wa.aws.amazon.com/wellarchitected/2020-07-02T19-33-23/wat.concept.horizontal-scaling.en.html

Save time with our exam-specific cheat sheets:

https://digitalcloud.training/certification-training/aws-certified-cloud-practitioner/architecting-for-the-cloud/

QUESTION 16

An individual IAM user must be granted access to an Amazon S3 bucket using a bucket policy. Which element in the S3 bucket policy should be updated to define the user account for which access will be granted?

1. Action
2. Principal
3. Resource
4. Condition

Answer: 2

Explanation:

The Principal element specifies the user, account, service, or other entity that is allowed or denied access to a resource. The bucket policy below has a Principal element set to * which is a wildcard meaning any user. To grant access to a specific IAM user the following format can be used:

"Principal":{"AWS":"arn:aws:iam::AWSACCOUNTNUMBER:user/username"}

```
{
    "Version":"2012-10-17",
    "Statement":[
      {
        "Sid":"PublicRead",
        "Effect":"Allow",
        "Principal": "*",
        "Action":["s3:GetObject","s3:GetObjectVersion"],
        "Resource":["arn:aws:s3:::DOC-EXAMPLE-BUCKET/*"]
      }
    ]
}
```

CORRECT: "Principal" is the correct answer.

INCORRECT: "Action" is incorrect. Actions are the permissions that you can specify in a policy.

INCORRECT: "Resource" is incorrect. Resources are the ARNs of resources you wish to specify permissions for.

INCORRECT: "Condition" is incorrect. Conditions define certain conditions to apply when granting permissions such as the source IP address of the caller.

References:

https://docs.aws.amazon.com/AmazonS3/latest/userguide/s3-bucket-user-policy-specifying-principal-intro.html

Save time with our exam-specific cheat sheets:

https://digitalcloud.training/certification-training/aws-certified-cloud-practitioner/aws-storage/

QUESTION 17

A Cloud Practitioner needs a tool that can assist with viewing and managing AWS costs and usage over time. Which tool should the Cloud Practitioner use?

1. AWS Budgets
2. Amazon Inspector
3. AWS Organizations
4. AWS Cost Explorer

Answer: 4

Explanation:

AWS Cost Explorer has an easy-to-use interface that lets you visualize, understand, and manage your AWS costs and usage over time. AWS Cost Explorer provides you with a set of default reports that you can use as the starting place for your analysis. From there, use the filtering and grouping capabilities to dive deeper into your cost and usage data and generate custom insights.

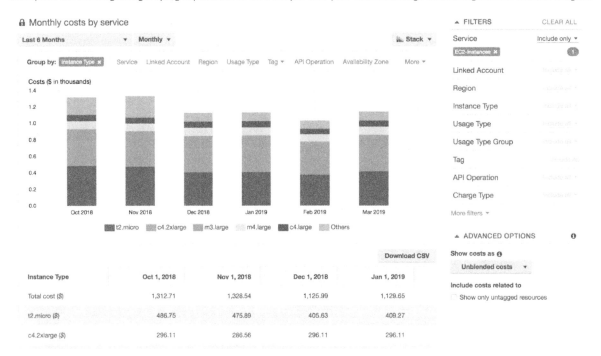

CORRECT: "AWS Cost Explorer" is the correct answer.

INCORRECT: "AWS Budgets" is incorrect. AWS Budgets allows you to set custom budgets to track your cost and usage from the simplest to the most complex use cases.

INCORRECT: "Amazon Inspector" is incorrect. Amazon Inspector is an automated security assessment service that helps improve the security and compliance of applications deployed on AWS

INCORRECT: "AWS Organizations" is incorrect. AWS Organizations allows you to organize accounts, create accounts programmatically, and leverage consolidated billing.

References:

https://aws.amazon.com/aws-cost-management/aws-cost-explorer/

Save time with our exam-specific cheat sheets:

https://digitalcloud.training/certification-training/aws-certified-cloud-practitioner/aws-billing-and-pricing/

QUESTION 18

A company plans to deploy a relational database on AWS. The IT department will perform database administration. Which service should the company use?

1. Amazon EC2
2. Amazon RedShift
3. Amazon ElastiCache
4. Amazon DynamoDB

Answer: 1

Explanation:

A self-managed relational database can be installed on Amazon EC2. When using this deployment you can choose the operating system and instance type that suits your needs and then install and manage any database software you require.

The table below helps you to understand when to use different types of database deployment:

Data Store	Use Case
Database on EC2	• Need full control over instance and database
	• Third-party database engine (not available in RDS)
Amazon RDS	• Need traditional relational database
	• e.g. Oracle, PostgreSQL, Microsoft SQL, MariaDB, MySQL
	• Data is well-formed and structured
Amazon DynamoDB	• NoSQL database
	• In-memory performance
	• High I/O needs
	• Dynamic scaling
Amazon RedShift	• Data warehouse for large volumes of aggregated data
Amazon ElastiCache	• Fast temporary storage for small amounts of data
	• In-memory database
Amazon EMR	• Analytics workloads using the Hadoop framework

CORRECT: "Amazon EC2" is the correct answer.

INCORRECT: "Amazon RedShift" is incorrect. RedShift is managed data warehouse solution and is better suited to use cases where analytics of data is required.

INCORRECT: "Amazon ElastiCache" is incorrect. ElastiCache is a managed service for in-memory, high-performance caching of database content.

INCORRECT: "Amazon DynamoDB" is incorrect. DynamoDB is a non-relational (NoSQL) type of database.

Save time with our exam-specific cheat sheets:

https://digitalcloud.training/certification-training/aws-certified-cloud-practitioner/aws-databases/

QUESTION 19

A company is planning to move a number of legacy applications to the AWS Cloud. The solution must be cost-effective. Which approach should the company take?

1. Migrate the applications to dedicated hosts on Amazon EC2.
2. Rehost the applications on Amazon EC2 instances that are right-sized.
3. Use AWS Lambda to host the legacy applications in the cloud.
4. Use an Amazon S3 static website to host the legacy application code.

Answer: 2

Explanation:

The most cost-effective solution that works is to use Amazon EC2 instances that are right-sized with the most optimum instance types. Right-sizing is the process of ensuring that the instance type selected for each application provides the right amount of resources for the application.

CORRECT: "Rehost the applications on Amazon EC2 instances that are right-sized" is the correct answer.

INCORRECT: "Migrate the applications to dedicated hosts on Amazon EC2" is incorrect. Dedicated hosts are expensive and there is no need to use them with this solution.

INCORRECT: "Use AWS Lambda to host the legacy applications in the cloud" is incorrect. It is unlikely that you can simply host legacy applications using AWS Lambda.

INCORRECT: "Use an Amazon S3 static website to host the legacy application code" is incorrect. You cannot host legacy application code in an S3 static website, only static content is possible.

References:

https://d1.awsstatic.com/whitepapers/cost-optimization-right-sizing.pdf

Save time with our exam-specific cheat sheets:

https://digitalcloud.training/certification-training/aws-certified-cloud-practitioner/aws-compute/

QUESTION 20

A company must provide access to AWS resources for their employees. Which security practices should they follow? (Select TWO.)

1. Enable multi-factor authentication for users.
2. Create IAM policies based on least privilege principles.
3. Disable password policies and management console access.
4. Create IAM users in different AWS Regions.
5. Create IAM Roles and apply them to IAM groups.

Answer: 1, 2

Explanation:

There are a several security best practices for AWS IAM that are listed in the document shared below. Enabling multi-factor authentication is a best practice to require a second factor of authentication when logging in. Another best practice is to grant least privilege access when configuring users and password policies.

CORRECT: "Enable multi-factor authentication for users" is a correct answer.

CORRECT: "Create IAM policies based on least privilege principles" is also a correct answer.

INCORRECT: "Disable password policies and management console access" is incorrect. This is not a security best practice. There is no need to disable management console access and password policies should be used.

INCORRECT: "Create IAM users in different AWS Regions" is incorrect. You cannot create IAM users in different Regions as the IAM service is a global service.

INCORRECT: "Create IAM Roles and apply them to IAM groups" is incorrect. You cannot apply roles to groups, you apply policies to groups.

References:

https://docs.aws.amazon.com/IAM/latest/UserGuide/best-practices.html

Save time with our exam-specific cheat sheets:

https://digitalcloud.training/certification-training/aws-certified-cloud-practitioner/identity-and-access-management/

QUESTION 21

An Amazon Virtual Private Cloud (VPC) can include multiple:

1. AWS Regions.
2. Edge locations.
3. Internet gateways.
4. Availability Zones.

Answer: 4

Explanation:

An Amazon VPC includes multiple Availability Zones. Within a VPC you can create subnets in each AZ that is available in the Region and distribute your resources across these subnets for high availability.

CORRECT: "Availability Zones" is the correct answer.

INCORRECT: "AWS Regions" is incorrect. A VPC cannot include multiple Regions.

INCORRECT: "Edge locations" is incorrect. A VPC cannot include multiple Edge locations as these are independent of the Regions in which a VPC is created.

INCORRECT: "Internet gateways" is incorrect. You can only attach one Internet gateway to each VPC.

References:

https://aws.amazon.com/vpc

Save time with our exam-specific cheat sheets:

https://digitalcloud.training/certification-training/aws-certified-cloud-practitioner/aws-networking/

QUESTION 22

A Cloud Practitioner anticipates an increase in application traffic at a future date and time when a sales event will take place. How can the Cloud Practitioner configure Amazon EC2 Auto Scaling to ensure the right number of Amazon EC2 instances are available ahead of the event?

1. Configure predictive scaling.
2. Configure a target tracking scaling policy.
3. Configure a scheduled scaling policy.
4. Configure a step scaling policy.

Answer: 3

Explanation:

Scheduled scaling helps you to set up your own scaling schedule according to predictable load changes. For example, let's say that every week the traffic to your web application starts to increase on Wednesday, remains high on Thursday, and starts to decrease on Friday. You can configure a schedule for Amazon EC2 Auto Scaling to increase capacity on Wednesday and decrease capacity on Friday.

CORRECT: "Configure a scheduled scaling policy" is the correct answer.

INCORRECT: "Configure predictive scaling" is incorrect. Predictive scaling uses daily and weekly trends to determine when to scale. In this case the Cloud Practitioner knows about the event that will require more resources.

INCORRECT: "Configure a target tracking scaling policy" is incorrect. This policy will cause the ASG to attempt to keep resource utilization at the target value.

INCORRECT: "Configure a step scaling policy" is incorrect. Step scaling will launch resources in response to demand, this will not ensure the resource are ready at the right time as there will be a delay.

References:

https://docs.aws.amazon.com/autoscaling/ec2/userguide/schedule_time.html

Save time with our exam-specific cheat sheets:

https://digitalcloud.training/certification-training/aws-certified-cloud-practitioner/elastic-load-balancing-and-auto-scaling/

QUESTION 23

A company is deploying an application on Amazon EC2 that requires low-latency access to application components in an on-premises data center. Which AWS service or resource can the company use to extend their existing VPC to the on-premises data center?

1. Amazon Connect
2. AWS Outposts
3. AWS Direct Connect
4. Amazon Workspaces

Answer: 2

Explanation:

AWS Outposts is a fully managed service that offers the same AWS infrastructure, AWS services, APIs, and tools to virtually any datacenter, co-location space, or on-premises facility for a truly consistent hybrid experience. With AWS Outposts you can extend your VPC into the on-premises data center as in the following diagram:

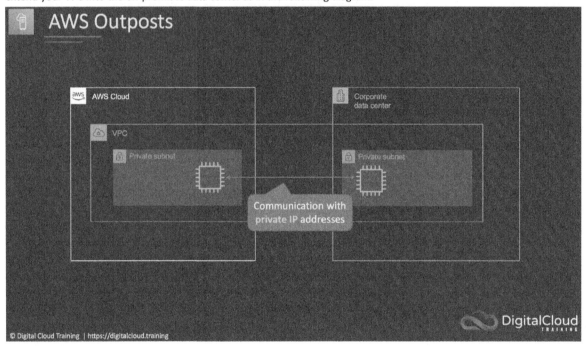

CORRECT: "AWS Outposts" is the correct answer.

INCORRECT: "Amazon Connect" is incorrect. Amazon Connect provides a seamless omnichannel experience through a single unified contact center for voice, chat, and task management.

INCORRECT: "AWS Direct Connect" is incorrect. Direct Connect is used for creating a low-latency private connection to an on-premises data center but it cannot be used to extend the VPC.

INCORRECT: "Amazon Workspaces" is incorrect. Amazon WorkSpaces is a managed, secure Desktop-as-a-Service (DaaS) solution.

References:

https://aws.amazon.com/outposts/

Save time with our exam-specific cheat sheets:

https://digitalcloud.training/certification-training/aws-certified-cloud-practitioner/aws-networking/

QUESTION 24

Which type of credential should a Cloud Practitioner use for programmatic access to AWS resources from the AWS CLI/API?

1. SSL/TLS certificate
2. SSH public keys
3. Access keys
4. User name and password

Answer: 3

Explanation:

Access keys are long-term credentials for an IAM user or the AWS account root user. You can use access keys to sign programmatic requests to the AWS CLI or AWS API (directly or using the AWS SDK).

Access keys consist of two parts: an access key ID (for example, AKIAIOSFODNN7EXAMPLE) and a secret access key (for example, wJalrXUtnFEMI/K7MDENG/bPxRfiCYEXAMPLEKEY).

Like a user name and password, you must use both the access key ID and secret access key together to authenticate your requests. Manage your access keys as securely as you do your user name and password.

CORRECT: "Access keys" is the correct answer.

INCORRECT: "SSL/TLS certificate" is incorrect. Certificates are not used by users for authenticating to AWS services.

INCORRECT: "SSH public keys" is incorrect. These are used for connections using the SSH protocol.

INCORRECT: "User name and password" is incorrect. An IAM user name and password can be used for console access but cannot be used with the CLI or API.

References:

https://docs.aws.amazon.com/IAM/latest/UserGuide/id_credentials_access-keys.html

Save time with our exam-specific cheat sheets:

https://digitalcloud.training/certification-training/aws-certified-cloud-practitioner/aws-compute/

QUESTION 25

A company is designing a new a service that must align with the operational excellence pillar of the AWS Well-Architected Framework.

Which design principles should the company follow? (Select TWO.)

1. Anticipate failure.
2. Make large-scale changes.
3. Perform operations as code.
4. Perform manual operations.
5. Create static operational procedures.

Answer: 1,3

Explanation:

AWS Well-Architected helps cloud architects build secure, high-performing, resilient, and efficient infrastructure for their applications and workloads. There are 5 pillars and under the operational excellence pillar the following best practices are recommended:

- Perform operations as code
- Make frequent, small, reversible changes
- Refine operations procedures frequently
- Anticipate failure
- Learn from all operational failures

CORRECT: "Anticipate failure" is a correct answer.

CORRECT: "Perform operations as code" is also a correct answer.

INCORRECT: "Make large-scale changes" is incorrect. This is not an operational best practice.

INCORRECT: "Perform manual operations" is incorrect. This is not an operational best practice.

INCORRECT: "Create static operational procedures" is incorrect. This is not an operational best practice.

References:

https://aws.amazon.com/architecture/well-architected/

Save time with our exam-specific cheat sheets:

https://digitalcloud.training/certification-training/aws-certified-cloud-practitioner/architecting-for-the-cloud/

QUESTION 26

A website has a global customer base and users have reported poor performance when connecting to the site.

Which AWS service will improve the customer experience by reducing latency?

1. AWS Direct Connect
2. Amazon EC2 Auto Scaling
3. Amazon CloudFront
4. Amazon ElastiCache

Answer: 3

Explanation:

Amazon CloudFront is a fast content delivery network (CDN) service that securely delivers data, videos, applications, and APIs to customers globally with low latency, high transfer speeds, all within a developer-friendly environment.

CORRECT: "Amazon CloudFront" is the correct answer.

INCORRECT: "AWS Direct Connect" is incorrect. Direct Connect is a private network connection between an on-premises data center and AWS.

INCORRECT: "Amazon EC2 Auto Scaling" is incorrect. Auto Scaling launches and terminates instances, this does not reduce latency for global users.

INCORRECT: "Amazon ElastiCache" is incorrect. ElastiCache is a database caching service, it is not used to cache websites.

References:

https://aws.amazon.com/cloudfront/

Save time with our exam-specific cheat sheets:

https://digitalcloud.training/certification-training/aws-certified-cloud-practitioner/content-delivery-and-dns-services/

QUESTION 27

What is one method of protecting against distributed denial of service (DDoS) attacks in the AWS Cloud?

1. Use Amazon CloudWatch monitoring.
2. Configure a firewall in front of resources.
3. Monitor the Service Health Dashboard.
4. Enable AWS CloudTrail logging.

Answer: 2

Explanation:

Some forms of DDoS mitigation are included automatically with AWS services. You can further improve your DDoS resilience by using an AWS architecture with specific services and by implementing additional best practices. Using a firewall with AWS resources is recommended to reduce the attack surface of your services which can mitigate some DDoS attacks.

CORRECT: "Configure a firewall in front of resources" is the correct answer.

INCORRECT: "Use Amazon CloudWatch monitoring" is incorrect. Performance monitoring will not protect against DDoS.

INCORRECT: "Enable AWS CloudTrail logging" is incorrect. Logging API calls will not protect against DDoS.

INCORRECT: "Monitor the Service Health Dashboard" is incorrect. The service health dashboard is not personalized to your resources so is not useful for monitoring and will not protect against DDoS.

QUESTION 28

How much data can a company store in the Amazon S3 service?

1. 1 PB
2. 100 TB
3. 100 PB
4. Virtually unlimited

Answer: 4

Explanation:

The Amazon Simple Storage Service (S3) offers virtually unlimited storage. The total volume of data and number of objects you can store are unlimited. Individual Amazon S3 objects can range in size from a minimum of 0 bytes to a maximum of 5 terabytes. The largest object that can be uploaded in a single PUT is 5 gigabytes.

CORRECT: "Virtually unlimited" is the correct answer.

INCORRECT: "1 PB" is incorrect. There is no such limit.

INCORRECT: "100 TB" is incorrect. There is no such limit.

INCORRECT: "100 PB" is incorrect. There is no such limit.

References:

https://aws.amazon.com/s3/faqs/

Save time with our exam-specific cheat sheets:

https://digitalcloud.training/certification-training/aws-certified-cloud-practitioner/aws-storage/

QUESTION 29

A company is deploying a new workload and software licensing requirements dictate that the workload must be run on a specific, physical server.

Which Amazon EC2 instance deployment option should be used?

1. Dedicated Instances
2. Spot Instances
3. Reserved Instances
4. Dedicated Hosts

Answer: 4

Explanation:

An Amazon EC2 Dedicated Host is a physical server fully dedicated for your use, so you can help address corporate compliance requirements. Amazon EC2 Dedicated Hosts allow you to use your eligible software licenses from vendors such as Microsoft and Oracle on Amazon EC2, so that you get the flexibility and cost effectiveness of using your own licenses, but with the resiliency, simplicity and elasticity of AWS

CORRECT: "Dedicated Hosts" is the correct answer.

INCORRECT: "Dedicated Instances" is incorrect. With dedicated instances you are not given a specific physical server to run your instances on.

INCORRECT: "Spot Instances" is incorrect. This deployment option does not provide a specific physical server.

INCORRECT: "Reserved Instances" is incorrect. This deployment option does not provide a specific physical server.

References:

https://aws.amazon.com/ec2/dedicated-hosts/

QUESTION 30

Which of the following are valid benefits of using the AWS Cloud? (Select TWO.)

1.   Outsource all operational risk.
2.   Total control over data center infrastructure.
3.   Fast provisioning of IT resources.
4.   Ability to go global quickly.
5.   Outsource all application development to AWS.

Answer: 3, 4

Explanation:

The ability to provision IT resources quickly and easily and also globally are valid benefits of using the AWS cloud. These are covered in AWS' 6 advantages of cloud which include "Increase speed and agility" and "Go global in minutes".

CORRECT: "Fast provisioning of IT resources" is a correct answer.

CORRECT: "Ability to go global quickly" is also a correct answer.

INCORRECT: "Outsource all operational risk" is incorrect. You do not outsource all operational risk; you still have to manage risk for the applications you run on AWS.

INCORRECT: "Total control over data center infrastructure" is incorrect. You don't have any control over data center infrastructure in the AWS Cloud.

INCORRECT: "Outsource all application development to AWS" is incorrect. You must still develop your own applications on the AWS Cloud.

References:

https://docs.aws.amazon.com/whitepapers/latest/aws-overview/six-advantages-of-cloud-computing.html

QUESTION 31

Which tasks require the use of the AWS account root user? (Select TWO.)

1.   Enabling encryption for S3.
2.   Viewing AWS CloudTrail logs.
3.   Changing the account name.
4.   Changing AWS Support plans.
5.   Changing payment currency.

Answer: 3,4

Explanation:

Some tasks can only be performed by the root user of an AWS account. This includes changing the account name and changing AWS support plans. For more information view the AWS article referenced below.

CORRECT: "Changing the account name" is a correct answer.

CORRECT: "Changing AWS Support plans" is also a correct answer.

INCORRECT: "Enabling encryption for S3" is incorrect. This does not require root.

INCORRECT: "Viewing AWS CloudTrail logs" is incorrect. This does not require root.

INCORRECT: "Changing payment currency" is incorrect. This does not require root.

References:

https://docs.aws.amazon.com/general/latest/gr/root-vs-iam.html

https://digitalcloud.training/certification-training/aws-certified-cloud-practitioner/identity-and-access-management/

QUESTION 32

Which AWS service can a company use to discover and protect sensitive data that is stored in Amazon S3 buckets.

1. Amazon GuardDuty
2. AWS Policy Generator
3. Amazon Detective
4. Amazon Macie

Answer: 4

Explanation:

Amazon Macie is a fully managed data security and data privacy service that uses machine learning and pattern matching to discover and protect your sensitive data in AWS. Amazon Macie automates the discovery of sensitive data at scale and lowers the cost of protecting your data.

Macie automatically provides an inventory of Amazon S3 buckets including a list of unencrypted buckets, publicly accessible buckets, and buckets shared with AWS accounts outside those you have defined in AWS Organizations.

Then, Macie applies machine learning and pattern matching techniques to the buckets you select to identify and alert you to sensitive data, such as personally identifiable information (PII).

CORRECT: "Amazon Macie" is the correct answer.

INCORRECT: "Amazon GuardDuty" is incorrect. Amazon GuardDuty is a threat detection service that continuously monitors for malicious activity and unauthorized behavior to protect your AWS accounts, workloads, and data stored in Amazon S3.

INCORRECT: "AWS Policy Generator" is incorrect. The AWS Policy Generator is a tool that enables you to create policies that control access to Amazon Web Services (AWS) products and resources.

INCORRECT: "Amazon Detective" is incorrect. Amazon Detective automatically processes terabytes of event data records about IP traffic, AWS management operations, and malicious or unauthorized activity.

References:

https://aws.amazon.com/macie/

Save time with our exam-specific cheat sheets:

https://digitalcloud.training/certification-training/aws-certified-cloud-practitioner/cloud-security/

QUESTION 33

Which benefits can a company gain by deploying a relational database on Amazon RDS instead of Amazon EC2? (Select TWO.)

1. Automated backups
2. Schema management
3. Indexing of tables
4. Software patching
5. Root access to OS

Answer: 1, 4

Explanation:

Two of the benefits of using a managed Amazon RDS service instead of a self-managed database on EC2 are that you get automated backups and automatic software patching.

CORRECT: "Automated backups" is a correct answer.

CORRECT: "Software patching" is also a correct answer.

INCORRECT: "Schema management" is incorrect. This is not a feature of the managed service.

INCORRECT: "Indexing of tables" is incorrect. This is not a feature of the managed service.

INCORRECT: "Root access to OS" is incorrect. You do not get root access to an RDS instance's operating system.

References:

Save time with our exam-specific cheat sheets:

https://digitalcloud.training/certification-training/aws-certified-cloud-practitioner/aws-databases/

QUESTION 34

A company is planning to deploy an application with a relational database on AWS. The application layer requires access to the database instance's operating system in order to run scripts.

The company prefer to keep management overhead to a minimum. Which deployment should be used for the database?

1. Amazon RDS
2. Amazon DynamoDB
3. Amazon EC2
4. Amazon S3

Answer: 3

Explanation:

The company would like to keep management overhead to a minimum so RDS would be good to meet that requirement. However, with RDS you cannot access the operating system so the requirement for running scripts on the OS rules RDS out. Therefore, the next best solution is to deploy on an Amazon EC2 instances as the other options presented are unsuitable for a relational database.

CORRECT: "Amazon EC2" is the correct answer.

INCORRECT: "Amazon RDS" is incorrect as the application would not be able to access the OS of the RDS instance to run scripts.

INCORRECT: "Amazon DynamoDB" is incorrect. This is a non-relational database.

INCORRECT: "Amazon S3" is incorrect. This is an object-storage system and is not suitable for running a relational database.

References:

https://aws.amazon.com/rds/

Save time with our exam-specific cheat sheets:

https://digitalcloud.training/certification-training/aws-certified-cloud-practitioner/aws-databases/

QUESTION 35

Customers using AWS services must patch operating systems on which of the following services?

1. AWS Lambda
2. Amazon EC2
3. AWS Fargate
4. Amazon DynamoDB

Answer: 2

Explanation:

Amazon EC2 is an infrastructure as a service (IaaS) solution. This means the underlying hardware and software layer for running a virtual server are managed for you. As a customer you must then manage the operating system and any software you install. This includes installing patches on the operating system as part of regular maintenance activities.

CORRECT: "Amazon EC2" is the correct answer.

INCORRECT: "AWS Lambda" is incorrect. This is a serverless service and you do not need to manage patches.

INCORRECT: "AWS Fargate" is incorrect. This is a serverless service and you do not need to manage patches.

INCORRECT: "Amazon DynamoDB" is incorrect. This is a serverless service and you do not need to manage patches.

References:

https://aws.amazon.com/ec2/

Save time with our exam-specific cheat sheets:

https://digitalcloud.training/certification-training/aws-certified-cloud-practitioner/aws-compute/

QUESTION 36

Which AWS feature can be used to launch a pre-configured Amazon Elastic Compute Cloud (EC2) instance?

1. Amazon Elastic Block Store (EBS)
2. Amazon EC2 Systems Manager
3. Amazon Machine Image (AMI)
4. Amazon AppStream 2.0

Answer: 3

Explanation:

An Amazon Machine Image (AMI) provides the information required to launch an instance. You must specify an AMI when you launch an instance. You can launch multiple instances from a single AMI when you need multiple instances with the same configuration. You can use different AMIs to launch instances when you need instances with different configurations.

CORRECT: "Amazon Machine Image (AMI)" is the correct answer.

INCORRECT: "Amazon Elastic Block Store (EBS)" is incorrect. EBS is block-based storage for EC2.

INCORRECT: "Amazon EC2 Systems Manager" is incorrect . AWS Systems Manager gives you visibility and control of your infrastructure on AWS.

INCORRECT: "Amazon AppStream 2.0" is incorrect. Amazon AppStream 2.0 is a fully managed non-persistent application and desktop streaming service.

References:

https://docs.aws.amazon.com/AWSEC2/latest/UserGuide/AMIs.html

Save time with our exam-specific cheat sheets:

https://digitalcloud.training/certification-training/aws-certified-cloud-practitioner/aws-compute/

QUESTION 37

Which of the following AWS features or services can be used to provide root storage volumes for Amazon EC2 instances?

1. Amazon Elastic Block Store (EBS)
2. Amazon Machine Image
3. Amazon Elastic File System (EFS)
4. Amazon Simple Storage Service (S3)

Answer: 1

Explanation:

The Amazon Elastic Block Store (EBS) provides block-based storage volumes for Amazon EC2 instances. Root volumes are where the operating system is installed and can be either EBS volumes or instance store volumes.

CORRECT: "Amazon Elastic Block Store (EBS)" is the correct answer.

INCORRECT: "Amazon Machine Image" is incorrect. An AMI provides the information required to launch an instance including the mapping of EBS volumes.

INCORRECT: "Amazon Elastic File System (EFS)" is incorrect. EFS volumes cannot be used for the root storage volume but can be mounted to store data.

INCORRECT: "Amazon Simple Storage Service (S3)" is incorrect. Amazon S3 buckets cannot be attached to EC2 instances in any way, it is a service that is accessed via a REST API.

References:

https://docs.aws.amazon.com/opsworks/latest/userguide/best-practices-storage.html

Save time with our exam-specific cheat sheets:

https://digitalcloud.training/certification-training/aws-certified-cloud-practitioner/aws-compute/

QUESTION 38

Which AWS service or feature can assist with protecting a website that is hosted outside of AWS?

1. Amazon VPC route tables
2. Amazon EC2 security groups
3. Amazon VPC network ACLs
4. AWS Web Application Firewall (WAF)

Answer: 4

Explanation:

AWS WAF can be used to protect on-premises resources if they are deployed behind an Application Load Balancer (ALB). In this scenario the on-premises website servers are added to a target group by IP address. The ALB has a WAF WebACL attached to it and distributes connections to the on-premises website.

CORRECT: "AWS Web Application Firewall (WAF)" is the correct answer.

INCORRECT: "Amazon VPC route tables" is incorrect. A route table cannot be used for protecting resources running outside AWS.

INCORRECT: "Amazon EC2 security groups" is incorrect. Security groups can only be attached to EC2 instances.

INCORRECT: "Amazon VPC network ACLs" is incorrect. Network ACLs only filter traffic entering and leaving a VPC subnet.

References:

https://aws.amazon.com/waf/features/

Save time with our exam-specific cheat sheets:

https://digitalcloud.training/certification-training/aws-certified-cloud-practitioner/cloud-security/

QUESTION 39

Which AWS service can a team use to deploy infrastructure on AWS using familiar programming languages?
1. AWS Cloud Development Kit (AWS CDK)
2. Amazon CodeGuru
3. AWS Config
4. AWS CodeCommit

Answer: 1

Explanation:

The AWS Cloud Development Kit (AWS CDK) is an open source software development framework to define cloud application resources using familiar programming languages. With AWS CDK you can stick to using programming languages that are familiar to you and have infrastructure deployed using AWS CloudFormation.

CORRECT: "AWS Cloud Development Kit (AWS CDK)" is the correct answer.

INCORRECT: "Amazon CodeGuru" is incorrect. CodeGuru is used to review code and provide intelligent recommendations for improvement.

INCORRECT: "AWS Config" is incorrect. AWS Config is used for configuration compliance management.

INCORRECT: "AWS CodeCommit" is incorrect. CodeCommit is a fully-managed source control service.

References:

https://aws.amazon.com/cdk/

Save time with our exam-specific cheat sheets:

https://digitalcloud.training/certification-training/aws-certified-cloud-practitioner/additional-aws-services-tools/

QUESTION 40

When running applications in the AWS Cloud, which common tasks can AWS manage on behalf of their customers? (Select TWO.)
1. Patching database software
2. Application source code auditing
3. Creating a database schema
4. Taking a backup of a database

    5.   Application security testing

Answer: 1, 4

Explanation:

With AWS managed services you can reduce your time spent performing common IT tasks. With services such as Amazon RDS, AWS will patch the database host operating system and database software and perform patch management activities.

CORRECT: "Patching database software" is a correct answer.

CORRECT: "Taking a backup of a database" is also a correct answer.

INCORRECT: "Application source code auditing" is incorrect. AWS does not audit your source code. You can use Amazon CodeGuru for recommendations for improvement though.

INCORRECT: "Creating a database schema" is incorrect. AWS does not create your schema; this is something that's in the customer's control.

INCORRECT: "Application security testing" is incorrect. AWS does not perform any security testing of your applications.

References:

https://aws.amazon.com/rds/

Save time with our exam-specific cheat sheets:

https://digitalcloud.training/certification-training/aws-certified-cloud-practitioner/aws-databases/

QUESTION 41

Which of the following will help a user determine if they need to request an Amazon EC2 service limit increase?
1.   AWS Personal Health Dashboard
2.   AWS Cost Explorer
3.   AWS Trusted Advisor
4.   AWS Service Health Dashboard

Answer: 3

Explanation:

AWS Trusted Advisor is an online tool that provides you real time guidance to help you provision your resources following AWS best practices. Trusted Advisor checks help optimize your AWS infrastructure, improve security and performance, reduce your overall costs, and monitor service limits.

CORRECT: "AWS Trusted Advisor" is the correct answer.

INCORRECT: "AWS Personal Health Dashboard" is incorrect. The personal health dashboard shows issues or upcoming events that may impact your resources. It does not notify of service limit breaches.

INCORRECT: "AWS Service Health Dashboard" is incorrect. This dashboard simply shows the current service health and any issues across Regions.

INCORRECT: "AWS Cost Explorer" is incorrect. Cost Explorer is used for viewing costs and will not assist with service limits.

References:

https://aws.amazon.com/premiumsupport/technology/trusted-advisor/

Save time with our exam-specific cheat sheets:

https://digitalcloud.training/certification-training/aws-certified-cloud-practitioner/aws-cloud-management/

QUESTION 42

How does the AWS cloud increase the speed and agility of execution for customers? (Select TWO.)

1. Fast provisioning of resources
2. Private connections to data centers
3. Secured data centers
4. Lower cost of deployment
5. Scalable compute capacity

Answer: 1, 5

Explanation:

The ability to quickly provision resources on AWS is a good example of speed and agility. On AWS the resources are readily available and can be deployed extremely quickly. Scalable compute capacity is another example as it gives you the agility to easily reconfigure your resources with more or less capacity as is required.

CORRECT: "Fast provisioning of resources" is a correct answer.

CORRECT: "Scalable compute capacity" is also a correct answer.

INCORRECT: "Private connections to data centers" is incorrect. A private connection to a data center is not an example of speed and agility.

INCORRECT: "Secured data centers" is incorrect. Secured data centers are not an example of speed and agility.

INCORRECT: "Lower cost of deployment" is incorrect. This is not an example of speed and agility.

References:

https://docs.aws.amazon.com/whitepapers/latest/aws-overview/six-advantages-of-cloud-computing.html

Save time with our exam-specific cheat sheets:

https://digitalcloud.training/certification-training/aws-certified-cloud-practitioner/cloud-computing-concepts/

QUESTION 43

A company has multiple AWS accounts and is using AWS Organizations with consolidated billing. Which advantages will they benefit from? (Select TWO.)

1. They will receive one bill for the accounts in the Organization.
2. The default service limits in all accounts will be increased.
3. They will receive a fixed discount for all usage across accounts.
4. They may benefit from lower unit pricing for aggregated usage.
5. They will be automatically enrolled in a business support plan.

Answer: 1, 4

Explanation:

You can use the consolidated billing feature in AWS Organizations to consolidate billing and payment for multiple AWS accounts. With consolidated billing you get:

- One bill for multiple accounts.
- Easy tracking or charges across accounts.
- Combined usage across accounts and sharing of volume pricing discounts, reserved instance discounts and savings plans.
- No extra fee.

CORRECT: "They will receive one bill for the accounts in the Organization" is a correct answer.

CORRECT: "They may benefit from lower unit pricing for aggregated usage" is also a correct answer.

INCORRECT: "The default service limits in all accounts will be increased" is incorrect. This is not true; service limit defaults are unaffected.

INCORRECT: "They will receive a fixed discount for all usage across accounts" is incorrect. There is no fixed usage discount applied for consolidated billing.

INCORRECT: "They will be automatically enrolled in a business support plan" is incorrect. This is not true; you must always pay for the business support plan.

References:

https://docs.aws.amazon.com/awsaccountbilling/latest/aboutv2/consolidated-billing.html

Save time with our exam-specific cheat sheets:

https://digitalcloud.training/certification-training/aws-certified-cloud-practitioner/aws-billing-and-pricing/

QUESTION 44

Which of the following represents a value proposition for using the AWS Cloud?

1. AWS is responsible for securing your applications.
2. It is not necessary to enter into long term contracts.
3. Customers can request specialized hardware.
4. AWS provides full access to their data centers.

Answer: 2

Explanation:

With AWS you can pay for what you use and there is no requirement to enter into long term contracts. However, there are opportunities to gain large discounts by committing to 1 or 3 years contracts for reserved instances and savings plans.

CORRECT: "It is not necessary to enter into long term contracts" is the correct answer.

INCORRECT: "AWS is responsible for securing your applications" is incorrect. AWS does not secure your applications.

INCORRECT: "Customers can request specialized hardware" is incorrect. This is not true; you have no say in what hardware AWS utilize.

INCORRECT: "AWS provides full access to their data centers" is incorrect. This is never the case; you cannot access the AWS data centers.

References:

https://docs.aws.amazon.com/whitepapers/latest/aws-overview/six-advantages-of-cloud-computing.html

Save time with our exam-specific cheat sheets:

https://digitalcloud.training/certification-training/aws-certified-cloud-practitioner/cloud-computing-concepts/

QUESTION 45

A company has many underutilized compute resources on-premises. Which AWS Cloud feature will help resolve this issue?

1. High availability
2. Elasticity
3. Global deployment
4. Fault tolerance

Answer: 2

Explanation:

Elasticity can resolve the issue of underutilization as you can easily and automatically adjust the resource allocations for your compute resources based on actual utilization. This ensures that you have the right amount of resources and do not pay for more than you need.

CORRECT: "Elasticity" is the correct answer.

INCORRECT: "High availability" is incorrect. This does not help with resolving underutilization.

INCORRECT: "Fault tolerance" is incorrect. This does not help with resolving underutilization.

INCORRECT: "Global deployment" is incorrect. This does not help with resolving underutilization.

References:

https://aws.amazon.com/aws-cost-management/aws-cost-optimization/right-sizing/

Save time with our exam-specific cheat sheets:

© 2022 Digital Cloud Training

https://digitalcloud.training/certification-training/aws-certified-cloud-practitioner/architecting-for-the-cloud/

QUESTION 46

What can a Cloud Practitioner use to categorize and track AWS costs by project?

1. Cost Allocation Tags
2. AWS Trusted Advisor
3. Consolidated billing
4. Multiple accounts

Answer: 1

Explanation:

Cost allocation tags can be used to tag and categorize your resources and then run view the billing in Cost Explorer and the cost allocation report. For example you can tag your resources by department or project and then view costs attributed to the resources used by those groups.

CORRECT: "Cost Allocation Tags" is the correct answer.

INCORRECT: "AWS Trusted Advisor" is incorrect. This service advises you on best practices for provisioning resources.

INCORRECT: "Consolidated billing" is incorrect. Consolidated billing will give you usage per account but not per project.

INCORRECT: "Multiple accounts" is incorrect. You do not need to split your usage across multiple accounts, you can instead use cost allocation tags.

References:

https://docs.aws.amazon.com/awsaccountbilling/latest/aboutv2/cost-alloc-tags.html

Save time with our exam-specific cheat sheets:

https://digitalcloud.training/certification-training/aws-certified-cloud-practitioner/aws-billing-and-pricing/

QUESTION 47

A company is deploying a MySQL database on AWS. The database must easily scale and have automatic backup enabled.

Which AWS service should the company?

1. Amazon Athena
2. Amazon DynamoDB
3. Amazon Aurora
4. Amazon DocumentDB

Answer: 3

Explanation:

Amazon Aurora is a relational database that is compatible with MySQL and PostgreSQL database engines. Aurora is extremely fast and scales up to 128 TB. You can also deploy replicas for read scaling within and across Regions. Aurora also offers automated backups.

CORRECT: "Amazon Aurora" is the correct answer.

INCORRECT: "Amazon DynamoDB" is incorrect. DynamoDB is a NoSQL (non-relational) database and you cannot deploy a MySQL database as it is a relational database type.

INCORRECT: "Amazon Athena" is incorrect. Athena is used for querying data in Amazon S3 using SQL.

INCORRECT: "Amazon DocumentDB" is incorrect. DocumentDB is a NoSQL database that supports document data structures.

References:

https://aws.amazon.com/rds/aurora/mysql-features/

Save time with our exam-specific cheat sheets:

https://digitalcloud.training/certification-training/aws-certified-cloud-practitioner/aws-databases/

QUESTION 48

A company plans to use reserved instances to get discounted pricing for Amazon EC2 instances. The company may need to change the EC2 instance type during the one year period.

Which instance purchasing option is the MOST cost-effective for this use case?

1. Standard Reserved Instances
2. Convertible Reserved Instances
3. Zonal Reserved Instances
4. Regional Reserved Instances

Answer: 2

Explanation:

A convertible reserved instance enables you to *exchange* one or more Convertible Reserved Instances for another Convertible Reserved Instance with a different configuration, including instance family, operating system, and tenancy.

CORRECT: "Convertible Reserved Instances" is the correct answer.

INCORRECT: "Standard Reserved Instances" is incorrect. With standard RIs you cannot change the instance type but you can change the instance size.

INCORRECT: "Regional Reserved Instances" is incorrect. Regional RIs apply to instance usage within any AZ in a specified Region.

INCORRECT: "Zonal Reserved Instances" is incorrect. Zonal RIs apply to instance usage within a specific AZ within an AWS Region.

References:

https://docs.aws.amazon.com/whitepapers/latest/cost-optimization-reservation-models/standard-vs.-convertible-offering-classes.html

Save time with our exam-specific cheat sheets:

https://digitalcloud.training/certification-training/aws-certified-cloud-practitioner/aws-billing-and-pricing/

QUESTION 49

Which of the following is a sole responsibility of AWS?

1. Application deployment
2. Patch management
3. Availability Zone management
4. Customer data access controls

Answer: 3

Explanation:

According to the shared responsibility model, AWS is responsible to the management of all AWS global infrastructure components including Regions, Availability Zones, Edge locations, Regional Edge Caches, and Local Zones.

CORRECT: "Availability Zone management" is the correct answer.

INCORRECT: "Application deployment" is incorrect. Applications are deployed by customers, not AWS.

INCORRECT: "Patch management" is incorrect. Patch management is a shared responsibility. Customers must patch instances databases running on EC2 and AWS will patch the underlying infrastructure and some managed services.

INCORRECT: "Customer data access controls" is incorrect. Customers are responsible for implementing access controls for their data.

References:

https://aws.amazon.com/compliance/shared-responsibility-model/

Save time with our exam-specific cheat sheets:

https://digitalcloud.training/certification-training/aws-certified-cloud-practitioner/aws-shared-responsibility-model/

QUESTION 50

Which AWS service provides a managed software version control system?

1. Amazon CodeDeploy
2. AWS CodePipeline
3. AWS DataSync
4. AWS CodeCommit

Answer: 4

Explanation:

AWS CodeCommit is a fully-managed source control service that hosts secure Git-based repositories. It makes it easy for teams to collaborate on code in a secure and highly scalable ecosystem.

CodeCommit eliminates the need to operate your own source control system or worry about scaling its infrastructure. You can use CodeCommit to securely store anything from source code to binaries, and it works seamlessly with your existing Git tools.

CORRECT: "AWS CodeCommit" is the correct answer.

INCORRECT: "Amazon CodeDeploy" is incorrect. CodeDeploy is a deployment service that deploys your application onto infrastructure.

INCORRECT: "AWS CodePipeline" is incorrect. CodePipeline is a continuous delivery service that automates release pipelines for code. CodeCommit can be used in a pipeline.

INCORRECT: "AWS DataSync" is incorrect. DataSync is used for replication and migrating data between storage systems and AWS.

References:

https://aws.amazon.com/codecommit/

Save time with our exam-specific cheat sheets:

https://digitalcloud.training/certification-training/aws-certified-cloud-practitioner/additional-aws-services-tools/

QUESTION 51

Which of the following deployments involves the reliability pillar of the AWS Well-Architected Framework?

1. Amazon RDS Multi-AZ deployment
2. Amazon EBS provisioned IOPS volume
3. Attach a WebACL to a CloudFront distribution
4. Use CloudFormation to deploy infrastructure

Answer: 1

Explanation:

An Amazon Relational Database Service (RDS) deployment across multiple availability zones is a good example of using the reliability pillar of the AWS Well-Architected Framework. The specific design principle being followed here is "Automatically recover from failure".

CORRECT: "Amazon RDS Multi-AZ deployment" is the correct answer.

INCORRECT: "Amazon EBS provisioned IOPS volume" is incorrect. This would be an example of performance efficiency.

INCORRECT: "Attach a WebACL to a CloudFront distribution" is incorrect. This would be an example of using the security pillar.

INCORRECT: "Use CloudFormation to deploy infrastructure" is incorrect. This would be an example of using the operational excellence pillar.

References:

https://aws.amazon.com/blogs/apn/the-5-pillars-of-the-aws-well-architected-framework/

Save time with our exam-specific cheat sheets:

https://digitalcloud.training/certification-training/aws-certified-cloud-practitioner/architecting-for-the-cloud/

QUESTION 52

A Cloud Practitioner needs to monitor a new Amazon EC2 instances CPU and network utilization. Which AWS service should be used?

1. Amazon Inspector
2. AWS CloudTrail
3. AWS Systems Manager
4. Amazon CloudWatch

Answer: 4

Explanation:

Amazon CloudWatch is a performance monitoring service. AWS services send metrics about their utilization to CloudWatch which collects the metrics. You can then view the results in CloudWatch and configure alarms.

CORRECT: "Amazon CloudWatch" is the correct answer.

INCORRECT: "AWS CloudTrail" is incorrect. CloudTrail is used for auditing, not performance monitoring.

INCORRECT: "Amazon Inspector" is incorrect. Inspector is an automated security service.

INCORRECT: "AWS Systems Manager" is incorrect. Systems Manager is used for managing EC2 instances such as installing patches and software.

References:

https://aws.amazon.com/cloudwatch/features/

Save time with our exam-specific cheat sheets:

https://digitalcloud.training/certification-training/aws-certified-cloud-practitioner/monitoring-and-logging-services/

QUESTION 53

AWS are able to continually reduce their pricing due to:

1. Economies of scale.
2. Pay-as-you go pricing.
3. Elastic compute services.
4. Compute savings plans.

Answer: 1

Explanation:

By using cloud computing, you can achieve a lower variable cost than you can get on your own. Because usage from hundreds of thousands of customers is aggregated in the cloud, providers such as AWS can achieve higher economies of scale, which translates into lower pay as-you-go prices.

CORRECT: "economies of scale" is the correct answer.

INCORRECT: "pay-as-you go pricing" is incorrect. This is a benefit to the customer but is not the reason the actual unit prices are continually being reduce.

INCORRECT: "elastic compute services" is incorrect. Elasticity is useful for scaling your resources and aligning costs with demand but is not why AWS prices are being lowered.

INCORRECT: "compute savings plans" is incorrect. This is another feature you can take advantage of for bigger discounts but is not the reason for prices being lowered.

References:

https://docs.aws.amazon.com/whitepapers/latest/aws-overview/six-advantages-of-cloud-computing.html

Save time with our exam-specific cheat sheets:

https://digitalcloud.training/certification-training/aws-certified-cloud-practitioner/cloud-computing-concepts/

QUESTION 54

Which AWS services can a company use to gather information about activity in their AWS account? (Select TWO.)

1. Amazon CloudFront
2. AWS CloudTrail
3. AWS Trusted Advisor
4. Amazon Connect
5. Amazon CloudWatch

Answer: 2, 5

Explanation:

Amazon CloudWatch is a performance monitoring service. AWS services send metrics about their utilization to CloudWatch which collects the metrics. Additionally, CloudWatch collects metrics about account activity such as billing information which can also be viewed.

AWS CloudTrail is an auditing service that monitors API activity in your account. Whenever you perform any operation in the account this results in an API action and this information is recorded to create an audit trail.

CORRECT: "AWS CloudTrail" is a correct answer.

CORRECT: "Amazon CloudWatch" is also a correct answer.

INCORRECT: "Amazon CloudFront" is incorrect. CloudFront is a content delivery network (CDN).

INCORRECT: "AWS Trusted Advisor" is incorrect. This service is used to assist with guidance on provisioning resources according to best practice.

INCORRECT: "Amazon Connect" is incorrect. This is a contact center service.

References:

https://aws.amazon.com/cloudwatch/

https://aws.amazon.com/cloudtrail/

Save time with our exam-specific cheat sheets:

https://digitalcloud.training/certification-training/aws-certified-cloud-practitioner/monitoring-and-logging-services/

QUESTION 55

A company is deploying an application in the AWS Cloud. How can they secure the application? (Select TWO.)

1. Enable encryption for the application data at rest.
2. Configure public access for the AWS services used by the application.
3. Enable monitoring by turning off encryption for data in transit.
4. Limit access privileges according to the principal of least privilege.
5. Provide full admin access to developer and operations staff.

Answer: 1, 4

Explanation:

In this scenario the company must apply best practice principals for securing their application. Enabling encryption for data at rest is definitely a good practice and data in transit should also be encrypted where possible as well. It is also a good practice to limit access privileges according to the principal of least privilege. This means limiting privileges to those required to perform a specific role.

CORRECT: "Enable encryption for the application data at rest" is a correct answer.

CORRECT: "Limit access privileges according to the principal of least privilege" is also a correct answer.

INCORRECT: "Configure public access for the AWS services used by the application" is incorrect. In some cases public access may be required and in that case only the front end service(s) should be configured for public access. Otherwise it would be best to not enable public access.

INCORRECT: "Enable monitoring by turning off encryption for data in transit" is incorrect. There is no need to turn off encryption in transit to enable monitoring and this would reduce security.

INCORRECT: "Provide full admin access to developer and operations staff" is incorrect. This is not a security best practice; it is better to assign permissions according to the principal of least privilege

References:

Save time with our exam-specific cheat sheets:

https://digitalcloud.training/certification-training/aws-certified-cloud-practitioner/cloud-security/

QUESTION 56

A Cloud Practitioner is developing a new application and wishes to integrate features of AWS services directly into the application.

Which of the following is the BEST tool for this purpose?

1. AWS Software Development Kit
2. AWS CodeDeploy
3. AWS Command Line Interface (CLI)
4. AWS CodePipeline

Answer: 1

Explanation:

A software development kit (SDK) is a collection of software development tools in one installable package. AWS provide SDKs for various programming languages and these can be used for integrating the features of AWS services directly into an application.

CORRECT: "AWS Software Development Kit" is the correct answer.

INCORRECT: "AWS Command Line Interface (CLI)" is incorrect. The AWS CLI is used for running commands but is not the best tool for integrating features of AWS services directly into an application.

INCORRECT: "AWS CodeDeploy" is incorrect. CodeDeploy is used for deploying code from a code repository and actually installing the application.

INCORRECT: "AWS CodePipeline" is incorrect. CodePipeline is used for automating the code release lifecycle.

References:

https://aws.amazon.com/tools/

QUESTION 57

A user needs to identify underutilized Amazon EC2 instances to reduce costs.

Which AWS service or feature will meet this requirement?

1. AWS CodeBuild
2. AWS Trusted Advisor
3. AWS Cost Explorer
4. AWS Personal Health Dashboard

Answer: 2

Explanation:

AWS Trusted Advisor offers a rich set of best practice checks and recommendations across five categories: cost optimization, security, fault tolerance, performance, and service limits.

The Trusted Advisor "low utilization Amazon EC2 instances" check, checks the Amazon Elastic Compute Cloud (Amazon EC2) instances that were running at any time during the last 14 days and alerts you if the daily CPU utilization was 10% or less and network I/O was 5 MB or less on 4 or more days.

CORRECT: "AWS Trusted Advisor" is the correct answer.

INCORRECT: "AWS CodeBuild" is incorrect. CodeBuild is used for compiling and testing code ahead of deployment.

INCORRECT: "AWS Cost Explorer" is incorrect. Cost Explorer can be used to view itemized costs but you cannot check resource utilization.

INCORRECT: "AWS Personal Health Dashboard" is incorrect. This dashboard will not warn you about underutilization of resources.

References:

Save time with our exam-specific cheat sheets:

https://digitalcloud.training/certification-training/aws-certified-cloud-practitioner/aws-cloud-management/

QUESTION 58

Which of the following can an AWS customer use to launch a new ElastiCache cluster? (Select TWO.)

1. AWS CloudFormation
2. AWS Concierge
3. AWS Systems Manager
4. AWS Management Console
5. AWS Data Pipeline

Answer: 1, 4

Explanation:

There are several ways to launch resources in AWS. You can use the AWS Management Console or Command Line Interface (CLI) or you can automate the process by using tools such as AWS CloudFormation.

With AWS CloudFormation you can deploy infrastructure such as Amazon ElastiCache clusters by defining your desired configuration state in code using a template file written in JSON or YAML. CloudFormation will then deploy the resources by creating a Stack according to the template file.

CORRECT: "AWS CloudFormation" is a correct answer.

CORRECT: "AWS Management Console" is also a correct answer.

INCORRECT: "AWS Concierge" is incorrect. The Concierge Support Team is available for customer who have an Enterprise level support plan. This team does not launch resources for you.

INCORRECT: "AWS Systems Manager" is incorrect. Systems Manager will not launch an ElastiCache cluster for you.

INCORRECT: "AWS Data Pipeline" is incorrect. AWS Data Pipeline is a web service that helps you reliably process and move data between different AWS compute and storage services.

References:

https://aws.amazon.com/cloudformation/

Save time with our exam-specific cheat sheets:

https://digitalcloud.training/certification-training/aws-certified-cloud-practitioner/additional-aws-services-tools/

QUESTION 59

A company is deploying a new web application in a single AWS Region that will be used by users globally.

Which AWS services will assist with lowering latency and improving transfer speeds for the global users? (Select TWO.)

1. AWS Direct Connect
2. AWS Global Accelerator
3. Amazon CloudFront
4. AWS Transfer Gateway
5. AWS Snowcone

Answer: 2, 3

Explanation:

Amazon CloudFront is a content delivery network (CDN) that caches content around the world for lower latency access. AWS Global Accelerator enables access to your application by leveraging the same Edge Locations as CloudFront and routing connections across the AWS global network.

Both of these services assist with lowering latency and improving transfer speeds for users who are distributed around the world.

CORRECT: "AWS Global Accelerator" is a correct answer.

CORRECT: "Amazon CloudFront" is also a correct answer.

INCORRECT: "AWS Direct Connect" is incorrect. This service provides private connections from data centers to AWS. It is not useful for distributed users as they will not be able to take advantage of it.

INCORRECT: "AWS Transfer Gateway" is incorrect. This service is used for optimizing the network topology of interconnected VPCs and on-premises networks.

INCORRECT: "AWS Snowcone" is incorrect. Snowcone is used as an edge device for transferring data.

References:

https://aws.amazon.com/global-accelerator/

https://aws.amazon.com/cloudfront/

Save time with our exam-specific cheat sheets:

https://digitalcloud.training/certification-training/aws-certified-cloud-practitioner/content-delivery-and-dns-services/

https://digitalcloud.training/certification-training/aws-certified-cloud-practitioner/aws-networking/

QUESTION 60

For what purpose would a Cloud Practitioner access AWS Artifact?

1. Download configuration details for all AWS resources.
2. Access training materials for AWS services.
3. Create a security assessment report for AWS services.
4. Gain access to AWS security and compliance documents.

Answer: 4

Explanation:

AWS Artifact is your go-to, central resource for compliance-related information that matters to you. It provides on-demand access to AWS' security and compliance reports and select online agreements.

Reports available in AWS Artifact include our Service Organization Control (SOC) reports, Payment Card Industry (PCI) reports, and certifications from accreditation bodies across geographies and compliance verticals that validate the implementation and operating effectiveness of AWS security controls.

CORRECT: "Gain access to AWS security and compliance documents" is the correct answer.

INCORRECT: "Download configuration details for all AWS resources" is incorrect. Artifact does not provide this capability.

INCORRECT: "Access training materials for AWS services" is incorrect. Artifact does not provide training materials.

INCORRECT: "Create a security assessment report for AWS services" is incorrect. Artifact cannot be used for this purpose.

References:

https://aws.amazon.com/artifact/

Save time with our exam-specific cheat sheets:

https://digitalcloud.training/certification-training/aws-certified-cloud-practitioner/cloud-security/

QUESTION 61

Which AWS Cloud service provides recommendations on how to optimize performance for AWS services?

1. Amazon Inspector
2. AWS Trusted Advisor
3. Amazon CloudWatch
4. AWS CloudTrail

Answer: 2

Explanation:

AWS Trusted Advisor can improve the performance of your service by checking your service limits, ensuring you take advantage of provisioned throughput, and monitoring for overutilized instances.

CORRECT: "AWS Trusted Advisor" is the correct answer.

INCORRECT: "Amazon Inspector" is incorrect. Inspector is an automated security assessment service that helps improve the security and compliance of applications deployed on AWS.

INCORRECT: "Amazon CloudWatch" is incorrect. CloudWatch monitors performance but does not provide recommendations for optimization.

INCORRECT: "AWS CloudTrail" is incorrect. CloudTrail is an auditing service.

References:

https://aws.amazon.com/premiumsupport/technology/trusted-advisor/

Save time with our exam-specific cheat sheets:

https://digitalcloud.training/certification-training/aws-certified-cloud-practitioner/cloud-security/

QUESTION 62

A company is migrating a monolithic application that does not scale well into the cloud and refactoring it into a microservices architecture.

Which best practice of the AWS Well-Architected Framework does this plan relate to?

1. Stop spending money on undifferentiated heavy lifting.
2. Implement loosely coupled services.
3. Manage change in automation.
4. Use multiple solutions to improve performance.

Answer: 2

Explanation:

A microservices architecture will help ensure that each component of the application can scale independently and be updated independently. Loose coupling further assists as it places reduces the dependencies between systems and ensures that messages and data being passed between application components can be reliably and durably stored.

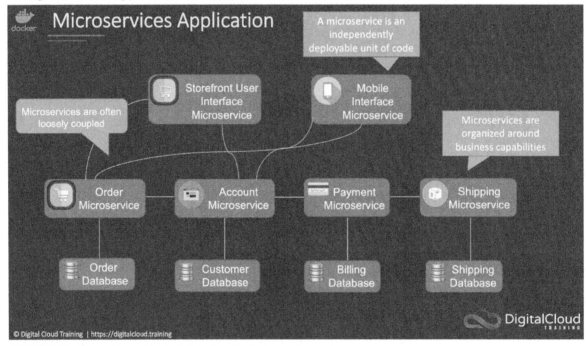

CORRECT: "Implement loosely coupled services" is the correct answer.

INCORRECT: "Stop spending money on undifferentiated heavy lifting" is incorrect. This is not the best practice being implemented by the company.

INCORRECT: "Manage change in automation" is incorrect. This is not the best practice being implemented by the company.

INCORRECT: "Use multiple solutions to improve performance" is incorrect. This is not the best practice being implemented by the company.

References:

https://aws.amazon.com/blogs/apn/the-5-pillars-of-the-aws-well-architected-framework/

Save time with our exam-specific cheat sheets:

https://digitalcloud.training/certification-training/aws-certified-cloud-practitioner/cloud-computing-concepts/

QUESTION 63

What are AWS Identity and Access Management (IAM) access keys used for?

1. Logging in to the AWS Management Console.
2. Ensuring the integrity of log files.
3. Making programmatic calls to AWS from AWS APIs.
4. Enabling encryption in transit for web servers.

Answer: 3

Explanation:

Access keys are long-term credentials for an IAM user or the AWS account root user. You can use access keys to sign programmatic requests to the AWS CLI or AWS API (directly or using the AWS SDK).

Access keys consist of two parts: an access key ID (for example, AKIAIOSFODNN7EXAMPLE) and a secret access key (for example, wJalrXUtnFEMI/K7MDENG/bPxRfiCYEXAMPLEKEY).

Like a user name and password, you must use both the access key ID and secret access key together to authenticate your requests. Manage your access keys as securely as you do your user name and password.

CORRECT: "Making programmatic calls to AWS from AWS APIs" is the correct answer.

INCORRECT: "Logging in to the AWS Management Console" is incorrect. You use a user name and password for the management console.

INCORRECT: "Ensuring the integrity of log files" is incorrect. This is not what access keys are used for.

INCORRECT: "Enabling encryption in transit for web servers" is incorrect. SSL/TLS certificates are used for creating encrypted channels using HTTPS.

References:

https://docs.aws.amazon.com/IAM/latest/UserGuide/id_credentials_access-keys.html

Save time with our exam-specific cheat sheets:

https://digitalcloud.training/certification-training/aws-certified-cloud-practitioner/identity-and-access-management/

QUESTION 64

What is the best practice for managing AWS IAM access keys?

1. There is no need to manage access keys.
2. Customers should rotate access keys regularly.
3. AWS rotate access keys on a schedule.
4. Never use access keys, always use IAM roles.

Answer: 2

Explanation:

It is a security best practice to rotate access keys regularly. This practice ensures that if access keys are compromised the security exposure is mitigated.

CORRECT: "Customers should rotate access keys regularly" is the correct answer.

INCORRECT: "There is no need to manage access keys" is incorrect. This is not true; you must rotate access keys.

INCORRECT: "AWS rotate access keys on a schedule" is incorrect. AWS do not rotate your access keys.

INCORRECT: "Never use access keys, always use IAM roles" is incorrect. It is often better and more secure to use IAM roles for some uses but it is certainly not the case that you should never use access keys.

References:

https://docs.aws.amazon.com/IAM/latest/UserGuide/id_credentials_access-keys.html

Save time with our exam-specific cheat sheets:

https://digitalcloud.training/certification-training/aws-certified-cloud-practitioner/identity-and-access-management/

QUESTION 65

According to the AWS shared responsibility model, which of the following is a responsibility of AWS?

1. Configuring network ACLs to block malicious attacks.
2. Patching software running on Amazon EC2 instances.
3. Updating the firmware on the underlying EC2 hosts.
4. Updating security group rules to enable connectivity.

Answer: 3

Explanation:

AWS are responsible for updating firmware on the physical Amazon EC2 host servers. Customers are then responsible for any patching of the EC2 operating system and any installed software.

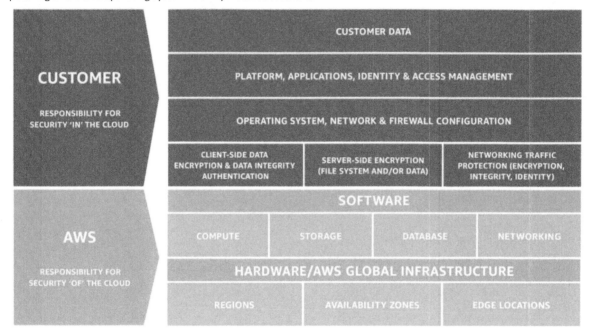

CORRECT: "Updating the firmware on the underlying EC2 hosts" is the correct answer.

INCORRECT: "Configuring network ACLs to block malicious attacks" is incorrect. This is a customer responsibility.

INCORRECT: "Patching software running on Amazon EC2 instances" is incorrect. This is a customer responsibility.

INCORRECT: "Updating security group rules to enable connectivity" is incorrect. This is a customer responsibility.

References:

https://aws.amazon.com/compliance/shared-responsibility-model/

Save time with our exam-specific cheat sheets:

https://digitalcloud.training/certification-training/aws-certified-cloud-practitioner/aws-shared-responsibility-model/

SET 2: PRACTICE QUESTIONS ONLY

For training purposes, go directly to *Set 2: Practice Questions, Answers & Explanations*

QUESTION 1

According to the shared responsibility mode, which security and compliance task is AWS responsible for?

1. Granting permissions to users and services
2. Updating Amazon EC2 host firmware
3. Encrypting data at rest
4. Updating operating systems

QUESTION 2

A company has a global user base and needs to deploy AWS services that can decrease network latency for their users. Which services may assist? (Select TWO.)

1. Amazon CloudFront
2. Amazon VPC
3. Application Auto Scaling
4. AWS Direct Connect
5. AWS Global Accelerator

QUESTION 3

What can be used to allow an application running on an Amazon EC2 instance to securely store data in an Amazon S3 bucket without using long-term credentials?

1. AWS Systems Manager
2. Amazon Connect
3. AWS IAM role
4. AWS IAM access key

QUESTION 4

Which AWS service does AWS Snowball Edge natively support?

1. AWS Server Migration Service (AWS SMS)
2. AWS Database Migration Service (AWS DMS)
3. AWS Trusted Advisor
4. Amazon EC2

QUESTION 5

AWS are able to continue to reduce their pricing due to:

1. Pay-as-you go pricing
2. The AWS global infrastructure
3. Economies of scale
4. Reserved instance pricing

QUESTION 6

According to the AWS shared responsibility model, which task is the customer's responsibility?

1. Maintaining the infrastructure needed to run Amazon DynamoDB.
2. Updating the operating system of AWS Lambda instances.
3. Maintaining Amazon API Gateway infrastructure.

4. Updating the guest operating system on Amazon EC2 instances.

QUESTION 7

A Cloud Practitioner noticed that IP addresses that are owned by AWS are being used to attempt to flood ports on some of the company's systems.

To whom should the issue be reported?

1. AWS Professional Services
2. AWS Partner Network (APN)
3. AWS Trust & Safety team
4. AWS Technical Account Manager (TAM)

QUESTION 8

Which on-premises costs must be included in a Total Cost of Ownership (TCO) calculation when comparing against the AWS Cloud? (Select TWO.)

1. Physical compute hardware
2. Operating system administration
3. Network infrastructure in the data center
4. Project management services
5. Database schema development

QUESTION 9

Which of the following can be used to identify a specific user who terminated an Amazon RDS DB instance?

1. AWS CloudTrail
2. Amazon Inspector
3. Amazon CloudWatch
4. AWS Trusted Advisor

QUESTION 10

Which AWS service can be used to perform data extract, transform, and load (ETL) operations so you can prepare data for analytics?

1. Amazon QuickSight
2. AWS Glue
3. Amazon Athena
4. Amazon S3 Select

QUESTION 11

Which of the following tasks can a user perform to optimize Amazon EC2 costs? (Select TWO.)

1. Implement Auto Scaling groups to add and remove instances based on demand.
2. Create a policy to restrict IAM users from accessing the Amazon EC2 console.
3. Set a budget to limit spending on Amazon EC2 instances using AWS Budgets.
4. Purchase Amazon EC2 Reserved Instances.
5. Create users in a single Region to reduce the spread of EC2 instances globally.

QUESTION 12

According to the shared responsibility model, which security-related task is the responsibility of the customer?

1. Maintaining server-side encryption.
2. Securing servers and racks at AWS data centers.

3. Maintaining firewall configurations at a hardware level.
4. Maintaining physical networking configuration.

QUESTION 13

A company plan to move the application development to AWS. Which benefits can they achieve when developing and running applications in the AWS Cloud compared to on-premises? (Select TWO.)

1. AWS automatically replicates all data globally.
2. AWS will fully manage the entire application.
3. AWS makes it easy to implement high availability.
4. AWS can accommodate large changes in application demand.
5. AWS takes care of application security patching.

QUESTION 14

Which AWS services offer compute capabilities? (Select TWO.)

1. Amazon DynamoDB
2. Amazon ECS
3. Amazon EFS
4. Amazon CloudHSM
5. AWS Lambda

QUESTION 15

A cloud practitioner needs to migrate a 70 TB of data from an on-premises data center into the AWS Cloud. The company has a slow and unreliable internet connection.

Which AWS service can the cloud practitioner leverage to transfer the data?

1. Amazon S3 Glacier
2. AWS Snowball
3. AWS Storage Gateway
4. AWS DataSync

QUESTION 16

Which AWS service is a fully-managed source control service that hosts secure Git-based repositories?

1. AWS CodeBuild
2. AWS CodeDeploy
3. AWS CodeCommit
4. AWS CodePipeline

QUESTION 17

A Cloud Practitioner is re-architecting a monolithic application. Which design principles for cloud architecture do AWS recommend? (Select TWO.)

1. Implement manual scalability.
2. Implement loose coupling.
3. Use self-managed servers.
4. Rely on individual components.
5. Design for scalability.

QUESTION 18

Which of the following a valid best practices for using the AWS Identity and Access Management (IAM) service? (Select TWO.)

1. Embed access keys in application code.
2. Create individual IAM users.
3. Use inline policies instead of customer managed policies.
4. Use groups to assign permissions to IAM users.
5. Grant maximum privileges to IAM users.

QUESTION 19

Which benefit of AWS enables companies to replace upfront fixed expenses with variable expenses when using on-demand technology services?

1. Pay-as-you-go pricing
2. Economies of scale
3. Global reach
4. High availability

QUESTION 20

A Service Control Policy (SCP) is used to manage the maximum available permissions and is associated with which of the following?

Service control policies (SCPs) manage permissions for which of the following?

1. AWS Global Infrastructure
2. AWS Regions
3. AWS Organizations
4. Availability Zones

QUESTION 21

What should a Cloud Practitioner ensure when designing a highly available architecture on AWS?

1. Servers have low-latency and high throughput network connectivity.
2. The failure of a single component should not affect the application.
3. There are enough servers to run at peak load available at all times.
4. A single monolithic application component handles all operations.

QUESTION 22

Which technology can automatically adjust compute capacity as demand for an application increases or decreases?

1. Load balancing
2. Auto Scaling
3. Fault tolerance
4. High availability

QUESTION 23

Which of the following is an advantage for a company running workloads in the AWS Cloud vs on-premises? (Select TWO.)

1. Less staff time is required to launch new workloads.
2. Increased time to market for new application features.
3. Higher acquisition costs to support elastic workloads.
4. Lower overall utilization of server and storage systems.
5. Increased productivity for application development teams.

QUESTION 24

Which cloud architecture design principle is supported by deploying workloads across multiple Availability Zones?

1. Automate infrastructure.
2. Design for agility.
3. Enable elasticity.
4. Design for failure.

QUESTION 25

A company requires a dashboard for reporting when using a business intelligence solution. Which AWS service can a Cloud Practitioner use?

1. Amazon Redshift
2. Amazon Kinesis
3. Amazon Athena
4. Amazon QuickSight

QUESTION 26

A Cloud Practitioner wants to configure the AWS CLI for programmatic access to AWS services. Which credential components are required? (Select TWO.)

1. An access key ID
2. A public key
3. A secret access key
4. An IAM Role
5. A private key

QUESTION 27

Which service can a Cloud Practitioner use to configure custom cost and usage limits and enable alerts for when defined thresholds are exceeded?

1. Consolidated billing
2. AWS Trusted Advisor
3. Cost Explorer
4. AWS Budgets

QUESTION 28

What is the function of Amazon EC2 Auto Scaling?

1. Scales the size of EC2 instances up or down automatically, based on demand.
2. Automatically updates the EC2 pricing model, based on demand.
3. Scales the number of EC2 instances in or out automatically, based on demand.
4. Automatically modifies the network throughput of EC2 instances, based on demand.

QUESTION 29

Which AWS service should a Cloud Practitioner use to establish a secure network connection between an on-premises network and AWS?

1. AWS Mobile Hub
2. AWS Web Application Firewall (WAF)
3. Amazon Virtual Private Cloud (VPC)
4. Virtual Private Network

QUESTION 30

Which AWS-managed service can be used to process vast amounts of data using a hosted Hadoop framework?

1. Amazon DynamoDB

2. Amazon Athena
3. Amazon EMR
4. Amazon Redshift

QUESTION 31

Which Amazon EC2 pricing model should be avoided if a workload cannot accept interruption if capacity becomes temporarily unavailable?

1. Spot Instances
2. On-Demand Instances
3. Standard Reserved Instances
4. Convertible Reserved Instances

QUESTION 32

A Cloud Practitioner requires a simple method to identify if unrestricted access to resources has been allowed by security groups. Which service can the Cloud Practitioner use?

1. AWS Trusted Advisor
2. Amazon CloudWatch
3. VPC Flow Logs
4. AWS CloudTrail

QUESTION 33

An eCommerce company plans to use the AWS Cloud to quickly deliver new functionality in an iterative manner, minimizing the time to market.

Which feature of the AWS Cloud provides this functionality?

1. Elasticity
2. Agility
3. Fault tolerance
4. Cost effectiveness

QUESTION 34

What can a Cloud Practitioner do with the AWS Cost Management tools? (Select TWO.)

1. Visualize AWS costs by day, service, and linked AWS account.
2. Terminate EC2 instances automatically if budget thresholds are exceeded.
3. Automatically modify EC2 instances to use Spot pricing to reduce costs.
4. Create budgets and receive notifications if current or forecasted usage exceeds the budgets.
5. Archive data to Amazon Glacier if it is not accessed for a configured period of time.

QUESTION 35

Which AWS dashboard displays relevant and timely information to help users manage events in progress, and provides proactive notifications to help plan for scheduled activities?

1. AWS Service Health Dashboard
2. AWS Personal Health Dashboard
3. AWS Trusted Advisor dashboard
4. Amazon CloudWatch dashboard

QUESTION 36

Which AWS service should a Cloud Practitioner use to automate configuration management using Puppet?

1. AWS Config
2. AWS OpsWorks
3. AWS CloudFormation
4. AWS Systems Manager

QUESTION 37

Which AWS service is used to send both text and email messages from distributed applications?

1. Amazon Simple Notification Service (Amazon SNS)
2. Amazon Simple Email Service (Amazon SES)
3. Amazon Simple Workflow Service (Amazon SWF)
4. Amazon Simple Queue Service (Amazon SQS)

QUESTION 38

Which AWS service or feature allows a company to receive a single monthly AWS bill when using multiple AWS accounts?

1. Consolidated billing
2. Amazon Cloud Directory
3. AWS Cost Explorer
4. AWS Cost and Usage report

QUESTION 39

A user needs an automated security assessment report that will identify unintended network access to Amazon EC2 instances and vulnerabilities on those instances.

Which AWS service will provide this assessment report?

1. EC2 security groups
2. AWS Config
3. Amazon Macie
4. Amazon Inspector

QUESTION 40

Which of the following best describes an Availability Zone in the AWS Cloud?

1. One or more physical data centers
2. A completely isolated geographic location
3. One or more edge locations based around the world
4. A subnet for deploying resources into

QUESTION 41

A company needs a consistent and dedicated connection between AWS resources and an on-premise system.

Which AWS service can fulfil this requirement?

1. AWS Direct Connect
2. AWS Managed VPN
3. Amazon Connect
4. AWS DataSync

QUESTION 42

Which AWS service helps customers meet corporate, contractual, and regulatory compliance requirements for data security by using dedicated hardware appliances within the AWS Cloud?

1. AWS Secrets Manager

2. AWS CloudHSM
3. AWS Key Management Service (AWS KMS)
4. AWS Directory Service

QUESTION 43

What can a Cloud Practitioner use the AWS Total Cost of Ownership (TCO) Calculator for?

1. Generate reports that break down AWS Cloud compute costs by duration, resource, or tags
2. Estimate savings when comparing the AWS Cloud to an on-premises environment
3. Estimate a monthly bill for the AWS Cloud resources that will be used
4. Enable billing alerts to monitor actual AWS costs compared to estimated costs

QUESTION 44

Which of the following should be used to improve the security of access to the AWS Management Console? (Select TWO.)

1. AWS Secrets Manager
2. AWS Certificate Manager
3. AWS Multi-Factor Authentication (AWS MFA)
4. Security group rules
5. Strong password policies

QUESTION 45

An application has highly dynamic usage patterns. Which characteristics of the AWS Cloud make it cost-effective for this type of workload? (Select TWO.)

1. High availability
2. Strict security
3. Elasticity
4. Pay-as-you-go pricing
5. Reliability

QUESTION 46

Which benefits can a company immediately realize using the AWS Cloud? (Select TWO.)

1. Variable expenses are replaced with capital expenses
2. Capital expenses are replaced with variable expenses
3. User control of physical infrastructure
4. Increased agility
5. No responsibility for security

QUESTION 47

Which AWS hybrid storage service enables a user's on-premises applications to seamlessly use AWS Cloud storage?

1. AWS Backup
2. Amazon Connect
3. AWS Direct Connect
4. AWS Storage Gateway

QUESTION 48

A user has limited knowledge of AWS services, but wants to quickly deploy a scalable Node.js application in an Amazon VPC.

Which service should be used to deploy the application?

1. AWS CloudFormation

2. AWS Elastic Beanstalk
3. Amazon EC2
4. Amazon LightSail

QUESTION 49

How can a security compliance officer retrieve AWS compliance documentation such as a SOC 2 report?

1. Using AWS Artifact
2. Using AWS Trusted Advisor
3. Using AWS Inspector
4. Using the AWS Personal Health Dashboard

QUESTION 50

Which AWS service can be used to run Docker containers?

1. AWS Lambda
2. Amazon ECR
3. Amazon ECS
4. Amazon AMI

QUESTION 51

What are the benefits of using the AWS Managed Services? (Select TWO.)

1. Alignment with ITIL processes
2. Managed applications so you can focus on infrastructure
3. Baseline integration with ITSM tools
4. Designed for small businesses
5. Support for all AWS services

QUESTION 52

Which services are involved with security? (Select TWO.)

1. AWS CloudHSM
2. AWS DMS
3. AWS KMS
4. AWS SMS
5. Amazon ELB

QUESTION 53

What are the names of two types of AWS Storage Gateway? (Select TWO.)

1. S3 Gateway
2. File Gateway
3. Block Gateway
4. Tape Gateway
5. Cached Gateway

QUESTION 54

An application stores images which will be retrieved infrequently, but must be available for retrieval immediately. Which is the most cost-effective storage option that meets these requirements?

1. Amazon Glacier with expedited retrievals
2. Amazon S3 Standard-Infrequent Access
3. Amazon EFS

4.   Amazon S3 Standard

QUESTION 55

Which AWS support plans provide support via email, chat and phone? (Select TWO.)

1.   Basic
2.   Developer
3.   Business
4.   Enterprise
5.   Global

QUESTION 56

Which AWS service can be used to host a static website?

1.   Amazon S3
2.   Amazon EBS
3.   AWS CloudFormation
4.   Amazon EFS

QUESTION 57

Which of the following are AWS recommended best practices in relation to IAM? (Select TWO.)

1.   Assign permissions to users
2.   Create individual IAM users
3.   Embed access keys in application code
4.   Enable MFA for all users
5.   Grant greatest privilege

QUESTION 58

Which of the following security operations tasks must be performed by AWS customers? (Select TWO.)

1.   Collecting syslog messages from physical firewalls
2.   Issuing data center access keycards
3.   Installing security updates on EC2 instances
4.   Enabling multi-factor authentication (MFA) for privileged users
5.   Installing security updates for server firmware

QUESTION 59

How can an organization assess applications for vulnerabilities and deviations from best practice?

1.   Use AWS Artifact
2.   Use AWS Inspector
3.   Use AWS Shield
4.   Use AWS WAF

QUESTION 60

Which AWS service protects against common exploits that could compromise application availability, compromise security or consume excessive resources?

1.   AWS WAF
2.   AWS Shield
3.   Security Group
4.   Network ACL

QUESTION 61

A new user is unable to access any AWS services, what is the most likely explanation?

1. The user needs to login with a key pair
2. The services are currently unavailable
3. By default new users are created without access to any AWS services
4. The default limit for user logons has been reached

QUESTION 62

Which of the following compliance programs allows the AWS environment to process, maintain, and store protected health information?

1. ISO 27001
2. PCI DSS
3. HIPAA
4. SOC 1

QUESTION 63

Which AWS service can be used to load data from Amazon S3, transform it, and move it to another destination?

1. Amazon RedShift
2. Amazon EMR
3. Amazon Kinesis
4. AWS Glue

QUESTION 64

How should an organization deploy an application running on multiple EC2 instances to ensure that a power failure does not cause an application outage?

1. Launch the EC2 instances in separate regions
2. Launch the EC2 instances into different VPCs
3. Launch the EC2 instances into different Availability Zones
4. Launch the EC2 instances into Edge Locations

QUESTION 65

Which of the statements below is correct in relation to Consolidated Billing? (Select TWO.)

1. You receive one bill per AWS account
2. You receive a single bill for multiple accounts
3. You pay a fee per linked account
4. You can combine usage and share volume pricing discounts
5. You are charged a fee per user

QUESTION 66

Amazon S3 is typically used for which of the following use cases? (Select TWO.)

1. Host a static website
2. Install an operating system
3. Media hosting
4. In-memory data cache
5. Message queue

SET 2: PRACTICE QUESTIONS AND ANSWERS

QUESTION 1

According to the shared responsibility mode, which security and compliance task is AWS responsible for?

1. Granting permissions to users and services
2. Updating Amazon EC2 host firmware
3. Encrypting data at rest
4. Updating operating systems

Answer: 2

Explanation:

According to the AWS shared responsibility model AWS are responsible for security "of" the cloud. This includes updating the firmware of the EC2 host servers on which instances run. All of the other answers are incorrect as they represent security "in" the cloud which is a customer responsibility.

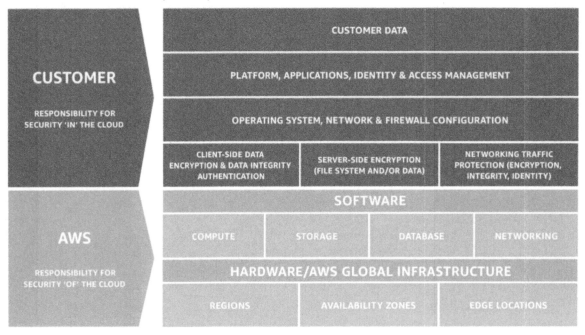

CORRECT: "Updating Amazon EC2 host firmware" is the correct answer.

INCORRECT: "Granting permissions to users and services" is incorrect as this is a customer responsibility.

INCORRECT: "Encrypting data at rest" is incorrect as this is a customer responsibility.

INCORRECT: "Updating operating systems" is incorrect as this is a customer responsibility.

References:

https://aws.amazon.com/compliance/shared-responsibility-model/

Save time with our exam-specific cheat sheets:

https://digitalcloud.training/certification-training/aws-certified-cloud-practitioner/aws-shared-responsibility-model/

QUESTION 2

A company has a global user base and needs to deploy AWS services that can decrease network latency for their users. Which services may assist? (Select TWO.)

1. Amazon CloudFront

2. Amazon VPC
3. Application Auto Scaling
4. AWS Direct Connect
5. AWS Global Accelerator

Answer: 1,5

Explanation:

Amazon CloudFront is a content delivery network (CDN) that caches media assets such as files, photos, and videos in Edge locations around the world. This gets your content closer to the user base which decreases latency.

AWS Global Accelerator is a service that can direct users to the nearest AWS Region that contains and endpoint for an application. The service utilizes Edge locations to decrease latency and then forwards all traffic on the AWS global network which also decreases latency.

CORRECT: "Amazon CloudFront" is a correct answer.

CORRECT: "AWS Global Accelerator" is also a correct answer.

INCORRECT: "Amazon VPC" is incorrect as this service does not decrease latency for global users.

INCORRECT: "Application Auto Scaling" is incorrect as this is used to scale applications based on workload, it does not decrease latency.

INCORRECT: "AWS Direct Connect" is incorrect as this service does decrease latency but not for a global user base.

References:

https://aws.amazon.com/global-accelerator/

https://aws.amazon.com/cloudfront/

Save time with our exam-specific cheat sheets:

https://digitalcloud.training/certification-training/aws-certified-cloud-practitioner/content-delivery-and-dns-services/

https://digitalcloud.training/certification-training/aws-certified-cloud-practitioner/aws-networking/

QUESTION 3

What can be used to allow an application running on an Amazon EC2 instance to securely store data in an Amazon S3 bucket without using long-term credentials?

1. AWS Systems Manager
2. Amazon Connect
3. AWS IAM role
4. AWS IAM access key

Answer: 3

Explanation:

An IAM *role* is an IAM identity that you can create in your account that has specific permissions. An IAM role is similar to an IAM user, in that it is an AWS identity with permission policies that determine what the identity can and cannot do in AWS. However, instead of being uniquely associated with one person, a role is intended to be assumable by anyone who needs it.

Also, a role does not have standard long-term credentials such as a password or access keys associated with it. Instead, when you assume a role, it provides you with temporary security credentials for your role session.

CORRECT: "AWS IAM role" is the correct answer.

INCORRECT: "AWS Systems Manager" is incorrect. This service manages Amazon EC2 instances.

INCORRECT: "Amazon Connect" is incorrect. This is a contact center service.

INCORRECT: "AWS IAM access key" is incorrect. Access keys are considered long-term credentials and therefore should not be embedded on EC2 instances in code. Using a role is more secure

References:

https://docs.aws.amazon.com/IAM/latest/UserGuide/id_roles.html

Save time with our exam-specific cheat sheets:

QUESTION 4

Which AWS service does AWS Snowball Edge natively support?
1.   AWS Server Migration Service (AWS SMS)
2.   AWS Database Migration Service (AWS DMS)
3.   AWS Trusted Advisor
4.   Amazon EC2

Answer: 4

Explanation:

You can run Amazon EC2 compute instances hosted on a Snowball Edge with the sbe1, sbe-c, and sbe-g instance types. The sbe1 instance type works on devices with the Snowball Edge Storage Optimized option. The sbe-c instance type works on devices with the Snowball Edge Compute Optimized option. Both the sbe-c and sbe-g instance types work on devices with the Snowball Edge Compute Optimized with GPU option.

CORRECT: "Amazon EC2" is the correct answer.

INCORRECT: "AWS Server Migration Service (AWS SMS)" is incorrect. AWS SMS does not integrate natively with Snowball Edge.

INCORRECT: "AWS Database Migration Service (AWS DMS)" is incorrect. AWS DMS does not integrate natively with Snowball Edge.

INCORRECT: "AWS Trusted Advisor" is incorrect. Trusted Advisor does not integrate natively with Snowball Edge.

References:

https://docs.aws.amazon.com/snowball/latest/developer-guide/using-ec2.html#ec2-overview-edge

Save time with our exam-specific cheat sheets:

https://digitalcloud.training/certification-training/aws-certified-cloud-practitioner/additional-aws-services-tools/

QUESTION 5

AWS are able to continue to reduce their pricing due to:
1.   Pay-as-you go pricing
2.   The AWS global infrastructure
3.   Economies of scale
4.   Reserved instance pricing

Answer: 3

Explanation:

By using cloud computing, you can achieve a lower variable cost than you can get on your own. Because usage from hundreds of thousands of customers is aggregated in the cloud, providers such as AWS can achieve higher economies of scale, which translates into lower pay as-you-go prices.

CORRECT: "Economies of scale" is the correct answer.

INCORRECT: "The AWS global infrastructure" is incorrect. The global infrastructure is the basis of the AWS platform but it is not the reason prices continue to reduce.

INCORRECT: "Pay-as-you go pricing" is incorrect. This pricing model is a benefit but not the reason unit prices are reducing.

INCORRECT: "Reserved instance pricing" is incorrect. This pricing model results in savings for customers in specific areas but not the reason for the overall reduction in prices.

References:

https://docs.aws.amazon.com/whitepapers/latest/aws-overview/six-advantages-of-cloud-computing.html

Save time with our exam-specific cheat sheets:

https://digitalcloud.training/certification-training/aws-certified-cloud-practitioner/cloud-computing-concepts/

QUESTION 6

According to the AWS shared responsibility model, which task is the customer's responsibility?

1. Maintaining the infrastructure needed to run Amazon DynamoDB.
2. Updating the operating system of AWS Lambda instances.
3. Maintaining Amazon API Gateway infrastructure.
4. Updating the guest operating system on Amazon EC2 instances.

Answer: 4

Explanation:

According to the AWS Shared Responsibility Model updating Amazon EC2 guest operating systems falls under the area of security "in" the cloud which is a customer responsibility. With EC2, AWS manage the underlying platform on which EC2 runs but you must launch and manage your operating systems.

CORRECT: "Updating the guest operating system on Amazon EC2 instances" is the correct answer.

INCORRECT: "Maintaining the infrastructure needed to run Amazon DynamoDB" is incorrect. This is a responsibility of AWS.

INCORRECT: "Updating the operating system of AWS Lambda instances" is incorrect. This is a responsibility of AWS.

INCORRECT: "Maintaining Amazon API Gateway infrastructure" is incorrect. This is a responsibility of AWS.

References:

https://aws.amazon.com/compliance/shared-responsibility-model/

Save time with our exam-specific cheat sheets:

https://digitalcloud.training/certification-training/aws-certified-cloud-practitioner/aws-shared-responsibility-model/

QUESTION 7

A Cloud Practitioner noticed that IP addresses that are owned by AWS are being used to attempt to flood ports on some of the company's systems.

To whom should the issue be reported?

1. AWS Professional Services
2. AWS Partner Network (APN)
3. AWS Trust & Safety team
4. AWS Technical Account Manager (TAM)

Answer: 3

Explanation:

If you suspect that AWS resources are used for abusive purposes, contact the AWS Trust & Safety team using the Report Amazon AWS abuse form, or by contacting abuse@amazonaws.com. Provide all the necessary information, including logs in plaintext, email headers, and so on, when you submit your request.

CORRECT: "AWS Trust & Safety team" is the correct answer.

INCORRECT: "AWS Professional Services" is incorrect. This is not the correct team.

INCORRECT: "AWS Partner Network (APN)" is incorrect. This is not the correct team.

INCORRECT: "AWS Technical Account Manager (TAM)" is incorrect. This is not the correct team.

References:

https://aws.amazon.com/premiumsupport/knowledge-center/report-aws-abuse/

Save time with our exam-specific cheat sheets:

https://digitalcloud.training/certification-training/aws-certified-cloud-practitioner/cloud-security/

QUESTION 8

Which on-premises costs must be included in a Total Cost of Ownership (TCO) calculation when comparing against the AWS Cloud? (Select TWO.)

1. Physical compute hardware
2. Operating system administration
3. Network infrastructure in the data center
4. Project management services
5. Database schema development

Answer: 1, 3

Explanation:

When performing a TCO analysis you must include all costs you are currently incurring in the on-premises environment that you will not pay for in the AWS Cloud. This should include labor costs for activities that will be reduced or eliminated. Labor costs that will continue to be incurred in the cloud need not be included.

CORRECT: "Physical compute hardware" is a correct answer.

CORRECT: "Network infrastructure in the data center" is also a correct answer.

INCORRECT: "Operating system administration" is incorrect. You don't need to include these costs as you will continue to incur them in the AWS Cloud.

INCORRECT: "Project management services" is incorrect. You don't need to include these costs as you will continue to incur them in the AWS Cloud.

INCORRECT: "Database schema development" is incorrect. You don't need to include these costs as you will continue to incur them in the AWS Cloud.

References:

https://docs.aws.amazon.com/whitepapers/latest/how-aws-pricing-works/aws-pricingtco-tools.html

Save time with our exam-specific cheat sheets:

https://digitalcloud.training/certification-training/aws-certified-cloud-practitioner/aws-billing-and-pricing/

QUESTION 9

Which of the following can be used to identify a specific user who terminated an Amazon RDS DB instance?

1. AWS CloudTrail
2. Amazon Inspector
3. Amazon CloudWatch
4. AWS Trusted Advisor

Answer: 1

Explanation:

AWS CloudTrail is a service that enables governance, compliance, operational auditing, and risk auditing of your AWS account. With CloudTrail, you can log, continuously monitor, and retain account activity related to actions across your AWS infrastructure.

CloudTrail provides event history of your AWS account activity, including actions taken through the AWS Management Console, AWS SDKs, command line tools, and other AWS services.

This event history simplifies security analysis, resource change tracking, and troubleshooting. In addition, you can use CloudTrail to detect unusual activity in your AWS accounts. These capabilities help simplify operational analysis and troubleshooting.

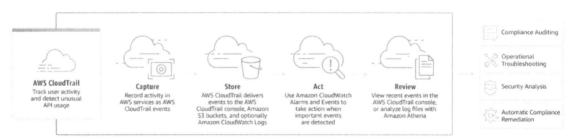

CORRECT: "AWS CloudTrail" is the correct answer.

INCORRECT: "Amazon Inspector" is incorrect. Inspector is used for running an automated security assessment service on cloud resources.

INCORRECT: "Amazon CloudWatch" is incorrect. CloudWatch is used for performance monitoring.

INCORRECT: "AWS Trusted Advisor" is incorrect. Trusted Advisor helps you to build your AWS resources in accordance with best practices.

References:

https://aws.amazon.com/cloudtrail/

Save time with our exam-specific cheat sheets:

https://digitalcloud.training/certification-training/aws-certified-cloud-practitioner/monitoring-and-logging-services/

QUESTION 10

Which AWS service can be used to perform data extract, transform, and load (ETL) operations so you can prepare data for analytics?

1.   Amazon QuickSight
2.   AWS Glue
3.   Amazon Athena
4.   Amazon S3 Select

Answer: 2

Explanation:

AWS Glue is a serverless data integration service that makes it easy to discover, prepare, and combine data for analytics, machine learning, and application development. AWS Glue provides all of the capabilities needed for data integration so that you can start analyzing your data and putting it to use in minutes instead of months.

AWS Glue provides both visual and code-based interfaces to make data integration easier. Users can easily find and access data using the AWS Glue Data Catalog. Data engineers and ETL (extract, transform, and load) developers can visually create, run, and monitor ETL workflows with a few clicks in AWS Glue Studio.

See how AWS Glue works with ETL workloads:

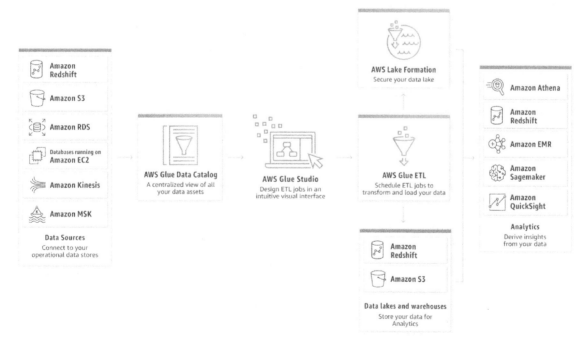

CORRECT: "AWS Glue" is the correct answer.

INCORRECT: "Amazon QuickSight" is incorrect. Amazon QuickSight is a cloud-native, serverless, business intelligence service.

INCORRECT: "Amazon Athena" is incorrect. Amazon Athena is a serverless, interactive query service to query data and analyze big data in Amazon S3 using standard SQL

INCORRECT: "Amazon S3 Select" is incorrect. This service enables applications to retrieve only a subset of data from an object by using simple SQL expressions.

References:

https://aws.amazon.com/glue/

Save time with our exam-specific cheat sheets:

https://digitalcloud.training/certification-training/aws-certified-cloud-practitioner/aws-analytics/

QUESTION 11

Which of the following tasks can a user perform to optimize Amazon EC2 costs? (Select TWO.)

1. Implement Auto Scaling groups to add and remove instances based on demand.
2. Create a policy to restrict IAM users from accessing the Amazon EC2 console.
3. Set a budget to limit spending on Amazon EC2 instances using AWS Budgets.
4. Purchase Amazon EC2 Reserved Instances.
5. Create users in a single Region to reduce the spread of EC2 instances globally.

Answer: 1, 4

Explanation:

Cost optimization can include using Auto Scaling groups to scale the number of EC2 instances according to actual demand. Also, using Amazon EC2 reserved instances for suitable workloads is a good way of optimizing costs over the longer term.

CORRECT: "Implement Auto Scaling groups to add and remove instances based on demand" is a correct answer.

CORRECT: "Purchase Amazon EC2 Reserved Instances" is also a correct answer.

INCORRECT: "Create a policy to restrict IAM users from accessing the Amazon EC2 console" is incorrect. This is not an optimization strategy; it will just prevent access completely which could be going too far.

INCORRECT: "Set a budget to limit spending on Amazon EC2 instances using AWS Budgets" is incorrect. You can use AWS Budgets to notify you of spend but not to actually limit spend.

INCORRECT: "Create users in a single Region to reduce the spread of EC2 instances globally" is incorrect. You cannot create users in a single Region, all IAM Users are global.

References:

https://aws.amazon.com/aws-cost-management/aws-cost-optimization/

Save time with our exam-specific cheat sheets:

https://digitalcloud.training/certification-training/aws-certified-cloud-practitioner/aws-billing-and-pricing/

QUESTION 12

According to the shared responsibility model, which security-related task is the responsibility of the customer?

1. Maintaining server-side encryption.
2. Securing servers and racks at AWS data centers.
3. Maintaining firewall configurations at a hardware level.
4. Maintaining physical networking configuration.

Answer: 1

Explanation:

All client-side and server-side encryption is a responsibility of the customer using the AWS Cloud. This can be clearly seen in the shared responsibility model infographic below:

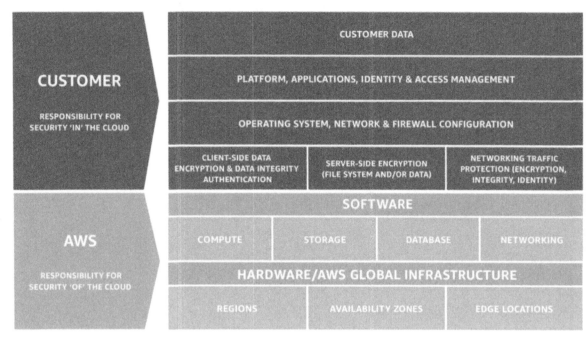

CORRECT: "Maintaining server-side encryption" is the correct answer.

INCORRECT: "Securing servers and racks at AWS data centers" is incorrect. This is an AWS responsibility.

INCORRECT: "Maintaining firewall configurations at a hardware level" is incorrect. This is an AWS responsibility.

INCORRECT: "Maintaining physical networking configuration" is incorrect. This is an AWS responsibility.

References:

https://aws.amazon.com/compliance/shared-responsibility-model/

Save time with our exam-specific cheat sheets:

https://digitalcloud.training/certification-training/aws-certified-cloud-practitioner/aws-shared-responsibility-model/

QUESTION 13

A company plan to move the application development to AWS. Which benefits can they achieve when developing and running applications in the AWS Cloud compared to on-premises? (Select TWO.)

1. AWS automatically replicates all data globally.
2. AWS will fully manage the entire application.
3. AWS makes it easy to implement high availability.
4. AWS can accommodate large changes in application demand.
5. AWS takes care of application security patching.

Answer: 3, 4

Explanation:

AWS provides many options for high availability including multiple availability zones within Regions and multiple Regions around the world. There are also many options to leverage durable data storage, message buses, databases.

AWS have a huge global infrastructure with massive amounts of capacity. It is therefore very easy to accommodate large changes in application demand and this can often be seamless to your application.

CORRECT: "AWS makes it easy to implement high availability" is a correct answer.

CORRECT: "AWS can accommodate large changes in application demand" is also a correct answer.

INCORRECT: "AWS automatically replicates all data globally" is incorrect. This is not true; data is not replicated globally unless you configure it do so.

INCORRECT: "AWS will fully manage the entire application" is incorrect. This is not true; AWS will not manage your application.

INCORRECT: "AWS takes care of application security patching" is incorrect. AWS take care of security patches for the underlying infrastructure but not your application.

References:

https://docs.aws.amazon.com/whitepapers/latest/aws-overview/six-advantages-of-cloud-computing.html

Save time with our exam-specific cheat sheets:

https://digitalcloud.training/certification-training/aws-certified-cloud-practitioner/cloud-computing-concepts/

QUESTION 14

Which AWS services offer compute capabilities? (Select TWO.)

1. Amazon DynamoDB
2. Amazon ECS
3. Amazon EFS
4. Amazon CloudHSM
5. AWS Lambda

Answer: 2, 5

Explanation:

The Amazon Elastic Container Service (ECS) is a compute service that allows you to run Docker containers as tasks on AWS. AWS Lambda is a function as a service offering that provides the ability to run compute functions in response to triggers.

CORRECT: "Amazon ECS" is a correct answer.

CORRECT: "AWS Lambda" is also a correct answer.

INCORRECT: "Amazon DynamoDB" is incorrect. DynamoDB is a database service.

INCORRECT: "Amazon EFS" is incorrect. The Elastic File System (EFS) is a file-based storage system.

INCORRECT: "Amazon CloudHSM" is incorrect. CloudHSM is a service that is used to securely store and manage encryption keys.

References:

https://aws.amazon.com/lambda/features/

https://aws.amazon.com/ecs/

Save time with our exam-specific cheat sheets:

https://digitalcloud.training/certification-training/aws-certified-cloud-practitioner/aws-compute/

QUESTION 15

A cloud practitioner needs to migrate a 70 TB of data from an on-premises data center into the AWS Cloud. The company has a slow and unreliable internet connection.

Which AWS service can the cloud practitioner leverage to transfer the data?

1. Amazon S3 Glacier
2. AWS Snowball
3. AWS Storage Gateway
4. AWS DataSync

Answer: 2

Explanation:

AWS Snowball is a method of transferring the data using a physical device. A Snowball Edge device can hold up to 80 TB so a single device can be used. This transfer method completely avoids the slow and unreliable internet connection.

CORRECT: "AWS Snowball" is the correct answer.

INCORRECT: "Amazon S3 Glacier" is incorrect. Glacier is used for archiving data in the cloud.

INCORRECT: "AWS Storage Gateway" is incorrect. Storage Gateway is a service that offers options for connecting on-premises storage to the cloud.

INCORRECT: "AWS DataSync" is incorrect. DataSync uses the internet to transfer data You can utilize Snowcone but that only holds up to 8 TB per device.

References:

https://docs.aws.amazon.com/snowball/latest/developer-guide/specifications.html#specs-v3s-optimized

Save time with our exam-specific cheat sheets:

https://digitalcloud.training/certification-training/aws-certified-cloud-practitioner/aws-storage/

QUESTION 16

Which AWS service is a fully-managed source control service that hosts secure Git-based repositories?

1. AWS CodeBuild
2. AWS CodeDeploy
3. AWS CodeCommit
4. AWS CodePipeline

Answer: 3

Explanation:

AWS CodeCommit is a fully-managed source control service that hosts secure Git-based repositories. It makes it easy for teams to collaborate on code in a secure and highly scalable ecosystem.

CodeCommit eliminates the need to operate your own source control system or worry about scaling its infrastructure. You can use CodeCommit to securely store anything from source code to binaries, and it works seamlessly with your existing Git tools.

CORRECT: "AWS CodeCommit" is the correct answer.

INCORRECT: "AWS CodeBuild" is incorrect. AWS CodeBuild is a fully managed continuous integration service that compiles source code, runs tests, and produces software packages that are ready to deploy.

INCORRECT: "AWS CodeDeploy" is incorrect. CodeDeploy is a deployment service that automates application deployments to Amazon EC2 instances, on-premises instances, serverless Lambda functions, or Amazon ECS services.

INCORRECT: "AWS CodePipeline" is incorrect. AWS CodePipeline is a fully managed continuous delivery service that helps you automate your release pipelines for fast and reliable application and infrastructure updates.

References:

https://aws.amazon.com/codecommit/features/

Save time with our exam-specific cheat sheets:

https://digitalcloud.training/certification-training/aws-certified-cloud-practitioner/additional-aws-services-tools/

QUESTION 17

A Cloud Practitioner is re-architecting a monolithic application. Which design principles for cloud architecture do AWS recommend? (Select TWO.)

1. Implement manual scalability.
2. Implement loose coupling.
3. Use self-managed servers.
4. Rely on individual components.
5. Design for scalability.

Answer: 2, 5

Explanation:

Dependencies such as queuing systems, streaming systems, workflows, and load balancers are loosely coupled. Loose coupling helps isolate behavior of a component from other components that depend on it, increasing resiliency and agility

AWS recommend that you architect applications that scale horizontally to increase aggregate workload availability. This scaling should be automatic where possible.

CORRECT: "Implement loose coupling" is a correct answer.

© 2022 Digital Cloud Training

CORRECT: "Design for scalability" is also a correct answer.

INCORRECT: "Implement manual scalability" is incorrect. AWS do not recommend manual processes. Everything should be automated as much as possible.

INCORRECT: "Use self-managed servers" is incorrect. AWS do not recommend using self-managed servers. They do recommend using serverless services if you can.

INCORRECT: "Rely on individual components" is incorrect. This is not a best practice; you should never rely on individual components. It is better to build redundancy into the system so the failure of an individual component does not affect the functioning of the application.

References:

https://aws.amazon.com/blogs/apn/the-5-pillars-of-the-aws-well-architected-framework/

Save time with our exam-specific cheat sheets:

https://digitalcloud.training/certification-training/aws-certified-cloud-practitioner/architecting-for-the-cloud/

QUESTION 18

Which of the following a valid best practices for using the AWS Identity and Access Management (IAM) service? (Select TWO.)
1. Embed access keys in application code.
2. Create individual IAM users.
3. Use inline policies instead of customer managed policies.
4. Use groups to assign permissions to IAM users.
5. Grant maximum privileges to IAM users.

Answer: 2, 4

Explanation:

This is the list of valid IAM best practices:

- Lock away your AWS account root user access keys
- Create individual IAM users
- Use groups to assign permissions to IAM users
- Grant least privilege
- Get started using permissions with AWS managed policies
- Use customer managed policies instead of inline policies
- Use access levels to review IAM permissions
- Configure a strong password policy for your users
- Enable MFA
- Use roles for applications that run on Amazon EC2 instances
- Use roles to delegate permissions
- Do not share access keys
- Rotate credentials regularly
- Remove unnecessary credentials
- Use policy conditions for extra security
- Monitor activity in your AWS account
- Video presentation about IAM best practices

CORRECT: "Create individual IAM users" is a correct answer.

CORRECT: "Use groups to assign permissions to IAM users" is also a correct answer.

INCORRECT: "Embed access keys in application code" is incorrect. This is not a best practice; you should always try and avoid embedding any secret credentials and access keys in application code. Instead, it is preferable to use IAM roles to delegate permission to applications.

INCORRECT: "Use inline policies instead of customer managed policies" is incorrect. This is not a best practice. You should use customer managed policies instead of inline policies.

INCORRECT: "Grant maximum privileges to IAM users" is incorrect. You should instead follow the principle of least privilege and grant the minimum permissions a user needs to perform their job role.

References:

https://docs.aws.amazon.com/IAM/latest/UserGuide/best-practices.html

Save time with our exam-specific cheat sheets:

https://digitalcloud.training/certification-training/aws-certified-cloud-practitioner/identity-and-access-management/

QUESTION 19

Which benefit of AWS enables companies to replace upfront fixed expenses with variable expenses when using on-demand technology services?

1. Pay-as-you-go pricing
2. Economies of scale
3. Global reach
4. High availability

Answer: 1

Explanation:

Pay-as-you-go-pricing is an example of the AWS advantage "Trade capital expense for variable expense". This is documented in the Six Advantages of Cloud Computing.

Instead of having to invest heavily in data centers and servers before you know how you're going to use them, you can pay only when you consume computing resources, and pay only for how much you consume.

CORRECT: "Pay-as-you-go pricing" is the correct answer.

INCORRECT: "Economies of scale" is incorrect. This is not an example of replacing fixed expenses with variable expenses. The benefit of economies of scale relates to achieving a lower variable cost than you can get on your own. Because usage from hundreds of thousands of customers is aggregated in the cloud, providers such as AWS can achieve higher economies of scale, which translates into lower pay as-you-go prices.

INCORRECT: "Global reach" is incorrect. This is most closely associated with the advantage "Go global in minutes". With AWS you can easily deploy your application in multiple regions around the world with just a few clicks. This means you can provide lower latency and a better experience for your customers at minimal cost.

INCORRECT: "High availability" is incorrect. High availability is not related to pricing. Instead, it means you can design your applications to be available with minimum downtime even when disruptions occur.

References:

https://docs.aws.amazon.com/whitepapers/latest/aws-overview/six-advantages-of-cloud-computing.html

Save time with our exam-specific cheat sheets:

https://digitalcloud.training/certification-training/aws-certified-cloud-practitioner/cloud-computing-concepts/

QUESTION 20

A Service Control Policy (SCP) is used to manage the maximum available permissions and is associated with which of the following?

Service control policies (SCPs) manage permissions for which of the following?

1. AWS Global Infrastructure
2. AWS Regions
3. AWS Organizations
4. Availability Zones

Answer: 3

Explanation:

Service control policies (SCPs) are a type of organization policy that you can use to manage permissions in your organization. SCPs offer central control over the maximum available permissions for all accounts in your organization. SCPs are associated with AWS Organizations and help you to ensure your accounts stay within your organization's access control guidelines. SCPs are available only in an organization that has all features enabled.

CORRECT: "AWS Organizations" is the correct answer.

INCORRECT: "AWS Global Infrastructure" is incorrect. SCPs are not associated with the AWS Global Infrastructure.

INCORRECT: "AWS Regions" is incorrect. SCPs are not associated with AWS Regions.

INCORRECT: "Availability Zones" is incorrect. SCPs are not associated with Availability Zones.

References:

https://docs.aws.amazon.com/organizations/latest/userguide/orgs_manage_policies_scps.html

Save time with our exam-specific cheat sheets:

https://digitalcloud.training/certification-training/aws-certified-cloud-practitioner/management-governance/

QUESTION 21

What should a Cloud Practitioner ensure when designing a highly available architecture on AWS?

1. Servers have low-latency and high throughput network connectivity.
2. The failure of a single component should not affect the application.
3. There are enough servers to run at peak load available at all times.
4. A single monolithic application component handles all operations.

Answer: 2

Explanation:

In a highly available system the failure of a single component should not affect the application. This means that if a single component such as an application server fails, there should be other applications servers available that can seamlessly take over operations and ensure the application continues to operate.

CORRECT: "The failure of a single component should not affect the application" is the correct answer.

INCORRECT: "Servers have low-latency and high throughput network connectivity" is incorrect. It is not necessary for all architectures to have low-latency and high throughput network connectivity and this does not ensure high availability.

INCORRECT: "There are enough servers to run at peak load available at all times" is incorrect. This would be wasteful in terms of resources and cost. There should be enough servers available to handle current load with adequate capacity to operate functionally in the event of a system failure. Additional servers can be launched automatically. as the application demand increases.

INCORRECT: "A single monolithic application component handles all operations" is incorrect. This is a bad design practice that reduces the availability of the system as the failure of update of any individual component can bring the whole system down.

References:

https://docs.aws.amazon.com/whitepapers/latest/real-time-communication-on-aws/high-availability-and-scalability-on-aws.html

Save time with our exam-specific cheat sheets:

https://digitalcloud.training/certification-training/aws-certified-cloud-practitioner/cloud-computing-concepts/

QUESTION 22

Which technology can automatically adjust compute capacity as demand for an application increases or decreases?

1. Load balancing
2. Auto Scaling
3. Fault tolerance
4. High availability

Answer: 2

Explanation:

Amazon EC2 Auto Scaling helps you maintain application availability and allows you to automatically add or remove EC2 instances according to conditions you define. You can use the fleet management features of EC2 Auto Scaling to maintain the health and availability of your fleet.

You can also use the dynamic and predictive scaling features of EC2 Auto Scaling to add or remove EC2 instances. Dynamic scaling responds to changing demand and predictive scaling automatically schedules the right number of EC2 instances based on predicted demand. Dynamic scaling and predictive scaling can be used together to scale faster.

The image below shows an example where an Auto Scaling group is configured to ensure the average CPU of instances in the ASG does not exceed 60%. An additional instance is being launched as the actual load is 71.5%.

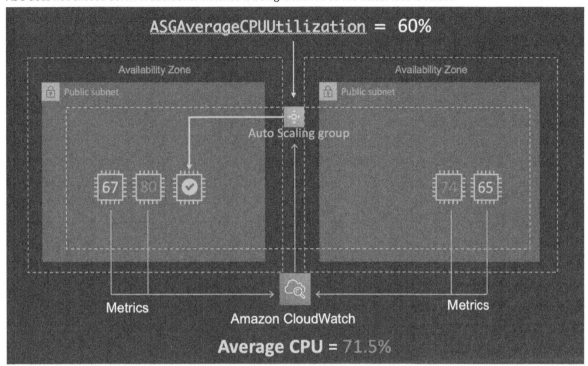

CORRECT: "Auto Scaling" is the correct answer.

INCORRECT: "Load balancing" is incorrect. Load balancing is not about compute capacity but ensuring connections are distributed across multiple instances.

INCORRECT: "Fault tolerance" is incorrect. Fault tolerance is related to the architecture of an application that ensures that the failure of any single component does not affect the application.

INCORRECT: "High availability" is incorrect. High availability ensures the maximum uptime for your application by designing the system to recover from failure.

References:

https://aws.amazon.com/ec2/autoscaling/

Save time with our exam-specific cheat sheets:

https://digitalcloud.training/certification-training/aws-certified-cloud-practitioner/aws-compute/

QUESTION 23

Which of the following is an advantage for a company running workloads in the AWS Cloud vs on-premises? (Select TWO.)

1. Less staff time is required to launch new workloads.
2. Increased time to market for new application features.
3. Higher acquisition costs to support elastic workloads.
4. Lower overall utilization of server and storage systems.
5. Increased productivity for application development teams.

Answer: 1, 5

Explanation:

Using AWS cloud services can help development teams to be more productive as they spend less time working on the infrastructure layer as it is provided for them. This additionally means launching new workloads requires less time as you can automate the implementation of the application and there is no underlying hardware layer to configure.

CORRECT: "Less staff time is required to launch new workloads" is a correct answer.

CORRECT: "Increased productivity for application development teams" is also a correct answer.

INCORRECT: "Increased time to market for new application features" is incorrect. AWS services should decrease time to market, not increase time.

INCORRECT: "Higher acquisition costs to support elastic workloads" is incorrect. The acquisition costs should be lower, not higher.

INCORRECT: "Lower overall utilization of server and storage systems" is incorrect. This is not a benefit of moving to the cloud.

References:

https://docs.aws.amazon.com/whitepapers/latest/aws-overview/six-advantages-of-cloud-computing.html

Save time with our exam-specific cheat sheets:

https://digitalcloud.training/certification-training/aws-certified-cloud-practitioner/cloud-computing-concepts/

QUESTION 24

Which cloud architecture design principle is supported by deploying workloads across multiple Availability Zones?

1. Automate infrastructure.
2. Design for agility.
3. Enable elasticity.
4. Design for failure.

Answer: 4

Explanation:

Amazon EC2 instances can be deployed in an Amazon VPC across multiple Availability Zones. You would then typically use an Elastic Load Balancer (ELB) to distribute load between the available instances. This architecture enables high availability as if a single instance fails or if something fails that causes an outage in an entire Availability Zone, the application still has available instances to continue to service demand.

CORRECT: "Design for failure" is the correct answer.

INCORRECT: "Design for agility" is incorrect. This is not an example of agility; it is an example of high availability and fault tolerance.

INCORRECT: "Automate infrastructure" is incorrect. This is not an example of automating.

INCORRECT: "Enable elasticity" is incorrect. This is not an example of elasticity. Elasticity would be enabled by using Amazon EC2 Auto Scaling.

References:

https://aws.amazon.com/architecture/well-architected/

Save time with our exam-specific cheat sheets:

https://digitalcloud.training/certification-training/aws-certified-cloud-practitioner/architecting-for-the-cloud/

QUESTION 25

A company requires a dashboard for reporting when using a business intelligence solution. Which AWS service can a Cloud Practitioner use?

1. Amazon Redshift
2. Amazon Kinesis
3. Amazon Athena
4. Amazon QuickSight

Answer: 4

Explanation:

Amazon QuickSight is a scalable, serverless, embeddable, machine learning-powered business intelligence (BI) service built for the cloud.

QuickSight lets you easily create and publish interactive BI dashboards that include Machine Learning-powered insights.

QuickSight dashboards can be accessed from any device, and seamlessly embedded into your applications, portals, and websites.

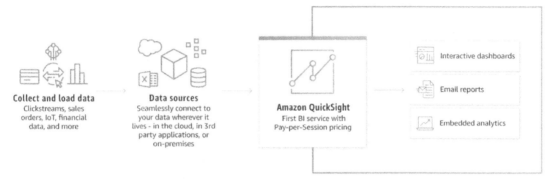

CORRECT: "Amazon QuickSight" is the correct answer.

INCORRECT: "Amazon Redshift" is incorrect. RedShift is a data warehouse solution not a dashboard. You can use QuickSight with RedShift.

INCORRECT: "Amazon Kinesis" is incorrect. This is a service for collecting streaming data.

INCORRECT: "Amazon Athena" is incorrect. Athena is used for running SQL queries on data in Amazon S3.

References:

https://aws.amazon.com/quicksight/

Save time with our exam-specific cheat sheets:

https://quicksight.aws.amazon.com/

QUESTION 26

A Cloud Practitioner wants to configure the AWS CLI for programmatic access to AWS services. Which credential components are required? (Select TWO.)

1. An access key ID
2. A public key
3. A secret access key
4. An IAM Role
5. A private key

Answer: 1,3

Explanation:

Access keys are long-term credentials for an IAM user or the AWS account root user. You can use access keys to sign programmatic requests to the AWS CLI or AWS API (directly or using the AWS SDK).

Access keys consist of two parts: an access key ID (for example, AKIAIOSFODNN7EXAMPLE) and a secret access key (for example, wJalrXUtnFEMI/K7MDENG/bPxRfiCYEXAMPLEKEY).

Like a user name and password, you must use both the access key ID and secret access key together to authenticate your requests. Manage your access keys as securely as you do your user name and password.

CORRECT: "An access key ID" is a correct answer.

CORRECT: "A secret access key" is also a correct answer.

INCORRECT: "A public key" is incorrect. Public/private keys are used for encryption and are also associated with the key pairs used to authenticate to EC2 instances.

INCORRECT: "A private key" is incorrect. Public/private keys are used for encryption and are also associated with the key pairs used to authenticate to EC2 instances.

INCORRECT: "An IAM Role" is incorrect. IAM Roles are not used for configuring the CLI for programmatic access. They can be used for delegating access to AWS services and cross-account access.

References:

https://docs.aws.amazon.com/IAM/latest/UserGuide/id_credentials_access-keys.html

Save time with our exam-specific cheat sheets:

https://digitalcloud.training/certification-training/aws-certified-cloud-practitioner/identity-and-access-management/

QUESTION 27

Which service can a Cloud Practitioner use to configure custom cost and usage limits and enable alerts for when defined thresholds are exceeded?

1. Consolidated billing
2. AWS Trusted Advisor
3. Cost Explorer
4. AWS Budgets

Answer: 4

Explanation:

AWS Budgets allows you to set custom budgets to track your cost and usage. With AWS Budgets, you can choose to be alerted by email or SNS notification when actual or forecasted cost and usage exceed your budget threshold, or when your actual RI and Savings Plans' utilization or coverage drops below your desired threshold.

CORRECT: "AWS Budgets" is the correct answer.

INCORRECT: "Consolidated billing" is incorrect. This is associated with AWS Organizations and provides a single bill across multiple member accounts.

INCORRECT: "AWS Trusted Advisor" is incorrect. This service provides guidance on AWS best practices.

INCORRECT: "Cost Explorer" is incorrect. This service is used for exploring the costs incurred within your account.

References:

https://aws.amazon.com/aws-cost-management/aws-budgets/

Save time with our exam-specific cheat sheets:

https://digitalcloud.training/certification-training/aws-certified-cloud-practitioner/aws-billing-and-pricing/

QUESTION 28

What is the function of Amazon EC2 Auto Scaling?

1. Scales the size of EC2 instances up or down automatically, based on demand.
2. Automatically updates the EC2 pricing model, based on demand.
3. Scales the number of EC2 instances in or out automatically, based on demand.
4. Automatically modifies the network throughput of EC2 instances, based on demand.

Answer: 3

Explanation:

Amazon EC2 Auto Scaling helps you maintain application availability and allows you to automatically add or remove EC2 instances according to conditions you define. You can use the fleet management features of EC2 Auto Scaling to maintain the health and availability of your fleet. You can also use the dynamic and predictive scaling features of EC2 Auto Scaling to add or remove EC2 instances.

CORRECT: "Scales the number of EC2 instances in or out automatically, based on demand." is the correct answer.

INCORRECT: "Scales the size of EC2 instances up or down automatically, based on demand." is incorrect. Auto Scaling adjusts the number of EC2 instances, not the size of EC2 instances.

INCORRECT: "Automatically updates the EC2 pricing model, based on demand." is incorrect. Auto Scaling does not change pricing models

INCORRECT: "Automatically modifies the network throughput of EC2 instances, based on demand." is incorrect. Auto Scaling does not modify network throughput for instances.

References:

https://aws.amazon.com/ec2/autoscaling/

Save time with our exam-specific cheat sheets:

https://digitalcloud.training/certification-training/aws-certified-cloud-practitioner/aws-compute/

QUESTION 29

Which AWS service should a Cloud Practitioner use to establish a secure network connection between an on-premises network and AWS?

1. AWS Mobile Hub
2. AWS Web Application Firewall (WAF)
3. Amazon Virtual Private Cloud (VPC)
4. Virtual Private Network

Answer: 4

Explanation:

AWS Virtual Private Network solutions establish secure connections between your on-premises networks, remote offices, client devices, and the AWS global network.

CORRECT: "Virtual Private Network" is the correct answer.

INCORRECT: "AWS Mobile Hub" is incorrect. This service is used for building, testing, and monitoring mobile applications that make use of one or more AWS services.

INCORRECT: "AWS Web Application Firewall (WAF)" is incorrect. This service is used for protecting against common web exploits.

INCORRECT: "Amazon Virtual Private Cloud (VPC)" is incorrect. This is a virtual network in the cloud. You connect your AWS VPN to your Amazon VPC.

References:

https://aws.amazon.com/vpn/

Save time with our exam-specific cheat sheets:

https://digitalcloud.training/certification-training/aws-certified-cloud-practitioner/aws-networking/

QUESTION 30

Which AWS-managed service can be used to process vast amounts of data using a hosted Hadoop framework?

1. Amazon DynamoDB
2. Amazon Athena
3. Amazon EMR
4. Amazon Redshift

Answer: 3

Explanation:

Amazon Elastic Map Reduce (EMR) is a web service that enables businesses, researchers, data analysts, and developers to easily and cost-effectively process vast amounts of data. EMR utilizes a hosted Hadoop framework running on Amazon EC2 and Amazon S3.

CORRECT: "Amazon EMR" is the correct answer.

INCORRECT: "Amazon DynamoDB" is incorrect. DynamoDB is not a hosted Hadoop framework, it is a no-SQL database.

INCORRECT: "Amazon Athena" is incorrect. Amazon Athena is a serverless, interactive query service to query data and analyze big data in Amazon S3 using standard SQL

INCORRECT: "Amazon Redshift" is incorrect. Amazon Redshift is a fast, simple, cost-effective data warehousing service.

References:

https://aws.amazon.com/emr/

Save time with our exam-specific cheat sheets:

https://digitalcloud.training/certification-training/aws-certified-cloud-practitioner/aws-databases/

QUESTION 31

Which Amazon EC2 pricing model should be avoided if a workload cannot accept interruption if capacity becomes temporarily unavailable?

1. Spot Instances
2. On-Demand Instances
3. Standard Reserved Instances
4. Convertible Reserved Instances

Answer: 1

Explanation:

Amazon EC2 Spot Instances let you take advantage of unused EC2 capacity in the AWS cloud. Spot Instances are available at up to a 90% discount compared to On-Demand prices.

The downside is that if capacity becomes temporarily unavailable, your instances may be terminated.

CORRECT: "Spot Instances" is the correct answer.

INCORRECT: "On-Demand Instances" is incorrect. On-demand instances are not subject to interruption if capacity becomes temporarily unavailable.

INCORRECT: "Standard Reserved Instances" is incorrect. Reserved instances are not subject to interruption if capacity becomes temporarily unavailable

INCORRECT: "Convertible Reserved Instances" is incorrect. Reserved instances are not subject to interruption if capacity becomes temporarily unavailable.

References:

https://aws.amazon.com/ec2/spot/

Save time with our exam-specific cheat sheets:

https://digitalcloud.training/certification-training/aws-certified-cloud-practitioner/aws-billing-and-pricing/

QUESTION 32

A Cloud Practitioner requires a simple method to identify if unrestricted access to resources has been allowed by security groups. Which service can the Cloud Practitioner use?

1. AWS Trusted Advisor
2. Amazon CloudWatch
3. VPC Flow Logs
5. AWS CloudTrail

Answer: 1

Explanation:

AWS Trusted Advisor checks security groups for rules that allow unrestricted access (0.0.0.0/0) to specific ports. Unrestricted access increases opportunities for malicious activity (hacking, denial-of-service attacks, loss of data). The ports with highest risk are flagged red, and those with less risk are flagged yellow. Ports flagged green are typically used by applications that require unrestricted access, such as HTTP and SMTP.

The following image shows the results of the security group checks in an AWS account:

	Region	Security Group Name	Security Group ID	Protocol	From Port	To Port
☐ ❶	ap-southeast-1	Web-Access	sg-07436d56194786bb4	tcp	3389	3389
☐ ❶	ap-southeast-2	default	sg-d0af14ad	tcp	3306	3306
☐ ❶	ap-southeast-2	launch-wizard-3	sg-0dcf0c1a7e7a2789d	tcp	3389	3389
☐ ❶	ap-southeast-2	Web-Access	sg-0f3f8f4ec27acd22e	tcp	3389	3389
☐ ❶	ap-southeast-2	launch-wizard-2	sg-08b07bd99e6a0167b	tcp	3389	3389
☐ ❶	eu-west-1	Web-Access	sg-0099a305fbdabd462	tcp	3389	3389
☐ ❶	eu-west-2	Web-Access	sg-01d0a779c7a03e940	tcp	3389	3389
☐ ❶	us-east-1	Web-Access	sg-026d3dc0b93925646	tcp	3389	3389
☐ ❶	us-west-1	Web-Access	sg-0f6b746076130845f	tcp	3389	3389
☐ ❶	us-west-2	Web-Access	sg-0709de13300816496	tcp	3389	3389
☐ ❶	ap-northeast-2	Web-Access	sg-035ae49310a074dac	tcp	3389	3389
☐ ❶	ap-south-1	Web-Access	sg-0b958ef76e13ca576	tcp	3389	3389
☐ ❶	eu-central-1	Web-Access	sg-0f361cd8ed3c33c02	tcp	3389	3389
☐ ❶	eu-west-3	Web-Access	sg-056e9c19d2210f1bc	tcp	3389	3389
☐ ❶	us-east-2	Web-Access	sg-045e88cf0bd4223f8	tcp	3389	3389
☐ ⚠	ap-southeast-1	launch-wizard-1	sg-0c60b93df73bd8a3c	tcp	22	22
☐ ⚠	ap-southeast-1	Web-Access	sg-07436d56194786bb4	tcp	22	22
☐ ⚠	ap-southeast-2	launch-wizard-1	sg-00169f4e4adaa6d34	tcp	22	22
☐ ⚠	ap-southeast-2	Web-Access	sg-098ad3c1eb4c6ae68	tcp	22	22
☐ ⚠	ap-southeast-2	Web-Access	sg-0d3b8dc769032330c	tcp	22	22

CORRECT: "AWS Trusted Advisor" is the correct answer.

INCORRECT: "Amazon CloudWatch" is incorrect. CloudWatch is used for performance monitoring.

INCORRECT: "VPC Flow Logs" is incorrect. VPC Flow Logs are used to capture network traffic information, they will not easily identify unrestricted security groups.

INCORRECT: "AWS CloudTrail" is incorrect. This service is used for auditing API actions

References:

https://aws.amazon.com/premiumsupport/technology/trusted-advisor/

Save time with our exam-specific cheat sheets:

https://digitalcloud.training/certification-training/aws-certified-cloud-practitioner/cloud-security/

QUESTION 33

An eCommerce company plans to use the AWS Cloud to quickly deliver new functionality in an iterative manner, minimizing the time to market.

Which feature of the AWS Cloud provides this functionality?

1. Elasticity
2. Agility
3. Fault tolerance
4. Cost effectiveness

Answer: 2

Explanation:

In a cloud computing environment, new IT resources are only a click away, which means that you reduce the time to make those resources available to your developers from weeks to just minutes.

This results in a dramatic increase in agility for the organization, since the cost and time it takes to experiment and develop is significantly lower.

CORRECT: "Agility" is the correct answer.

INCORRECT: "Elasticity" is incorrect. Elasticity enables infrastructure to scale based on demand and helps applications perform and be cost effective. It does not reduce time to market.

INCORRECT: "Fault tolerance" is incorrect as this is involved with ensuring applications stay available in the event of a fault.

INCORRECT: "Cost effectiveness" is incorrect. The AWS Cloud can be cost effective but this is not the benefit that allows faster time to market.

References:

https://docs.aws.amazon.com/whitepapers/latest/aws-overview/six-advantages-of-cloud-computing.html

Save time with our exam-specific cheat sheets:

https://digitalcloud.training/certification-training/aws-certified-cloud-practitioner/cloud-computing-concepts/

QUESTION 34

What can a Cloud Practitioner do with the AWS Cost Management tools? (Select TWO.)

1. Visualize AWS costs by day, service, and linked AWS account.
2. Terminate EC2 instances automatically if budget thresholds are exceeded.
3. Automatically modify EC2 instances to use Spot pricing to reduce costs.
4. Create budgets and receive notifications if current or forecasted usage exceeds the budgets.
5. Archive data to Amazon Glacier if it is not accessed for a configured period of time.

Answer: 1,4

Explanation:

AWS Cost Explorer has an easy-to-use interface that lets you visualize, understand, and manage your AWS costs and usage over time. It can be used to visualize AWS costs by day, service, and linked AWS account.

AWS Budgets can be used to receive notifications if current or forecasted usage exceeds the budgets.

CORRECT: "Visualize AWS costs by day, service, and linked AWS account" is a correct answer.

CORRECT: "Create budgets and receive notifications if current or forecasted usage exceeds the budgets" is also a correct answer.

INCORRECT: "Terminate EC2 instances automatically if budget thresholds are exceeded" is incorrect. The cost management tools can alert on budget breaches but they do not directly terminate instances.

INCORRECT: "Automatically modify EC2 instances to use Spot pricing to reduce costs" is incorrect. The cost management tools cannot modify the pricing model of EC2 instances.

INCORRECT: "Archive data to Amazon Glacier if it is not accessed for a configured period of time" is incorrect. Use lifecycle rules in Amazon S3 to automatically move data between storage classes.

References:

https://aws.amazon.com/aws-cost-management/aws-cost-explorer/

https://aws.amazon.com/aws-cost-management/aws-budgets/

Save time with our exam-specific cheat sheets:

https://digitalcloud.training/certification-training/aws-certified-cloud-practitioner/aws-billing-and-pricing/

QUESTION 35

Which AWS dashboard displays relevant and timely information to help users manage events in progress, and provides proactive notifications to help plan for scheduled activities?

1. AWS Service Health Dashboard
2. AWS Personal Health Dashboard
3. AWS Trusted Advisor dashboard
4. Amazon CloudWatch dashboard

Answer: 2

Explanation:

AWS Personal Health Dashboard provides alerts and remediation guidance when AWS is experiencing events that may impact you. While the Service Health Dashboard displays the general status of AWS services, Personal Health Dashboard gives you a personalized view into the performance and availability of the AWS services underlying your AWS resources.

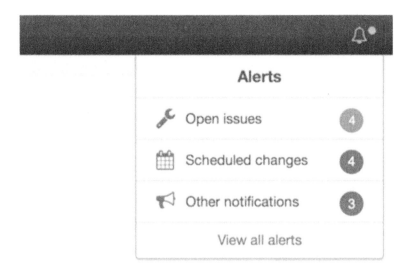

The dashboard displays relevant and timely information to help you manage events in progress, and provides proactive notification to help you plan for scheduled activities. With Personal Health Dashboard, alerts are triggered by changes in the health of AWS resources, giving you event visibility, and guidance to help quickly diagnose and resolve issues.

CORRECT: "AWS Personal Health Dashboard" is the correct answer.

INCORRECT: "AWS Service Health Dashboard" is incorrect. This shows the current status of services across regions. However, it does not provide proactive notifications of scheduled activities or guidance of any kind.

INCORRECT: "AWS Trusted Advisor dashboard" is incorrect. AWS Trusted Advisor is an online tool that provides you real time guidance to help you provision your resources following AWS best practices.

INCORRECT: "Amazon CloudWatch dashboard" is incorrect as this service is used for monitoring performance related information for your infrastructure and resources, not the underlying AWS resources.

References:

https://aws.amazon.com/premiumsupport/technology/personal-health-dashboard/

Save time with our exam-specific cheat sheets:

https://digitalcloud.training/certification-training/aws-certified-cloud-practitioner/cloud-security/

QUESTION 36

Which AWS service should a Cloud Practitioner use to automate configuration management using Puppet?

1. AWS Config
2. AWS OpsWorks
3. AWS CloudFormation
4. AWS Systems Manager

Answer: 2

Explanation:

AWS OpsWorks is a configuration management service that provides managed instances of Chef and Puppet. Chef and Puppet are automation platforms that allow you to use code to automate the configurations of your servers.

OpsWorks lets you use Chef and Puppet to automate how servers are configured, deployed, and managed across your Amazon EC2 instances or on-premises compute environments,

CORRECT: "AWS OpsWorks" is the correct answer.

INCORRECT: "AWS Config" is incorrect. AWS Config is a service that enables you to assess, audit, and evaluate the configurations of your AWS resources.

INCORRECT: "AWS CloudFormation" is incorrect. AWS CloudFormation provides a common language for you to model and provision AWS and third party application resources in your cloud environment.

INCORRECT: "AWS Systems Manager" is incorrect. AWS Systems Manager gives you visibility and control of your infrastructure on AWS. Systems Manager provides a unified user interface so you can view operational data from multiple AWS services and allows you to automate operational tasks across your AWS resources.

References:

https://aws.amazon.com/opsworks/

Save time with our exam-specific cheat sheets:

https://digitalcloud.training/certification-training/aws-certified-cloud-practitioner/additional-aws-services-tools/

QUESTION 37

Which AWS service is used to send both text and email messages from distributed applications?

1. Amazon Simple Notification Service (Amazon SNS)
2. Amazon Simple Email Service (Amazon SES)
3. Amazon Simple Workflow Service (Amazon SWF)
4. Amazon Simple Queue Service (Amazon SQS)

Answer: 1

Explanation:

Amazon Simple Notification Service (SNS) is a highly available, durable, secure, fully managed pub/sub messaging service that enables you to decouple microservices, distributed systems, and serverless applications.

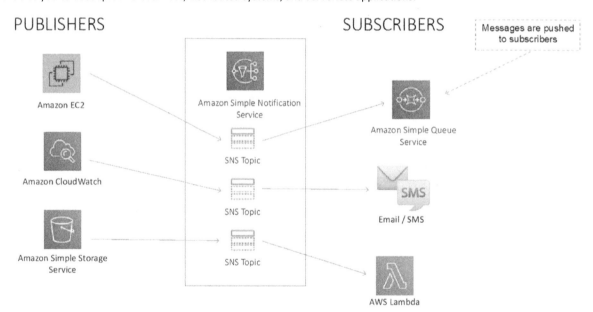

Amazon SNS provides topics for high-throughput, push-based, many-to-many messaging. Using Amazon SNS topics, your publisher systems can fan out messages to a large number of subscriber endpoints for parallel processing, including Amazon SQS queues, AWS Lambda functions, and HTTP/S webhooks.

Additionally, SNS can be used to fan out notifications to end users using mobile push, SMS, and email.

CORRECT: "Amazon Simple Notification Service (Amazon SNS)" is the correct answer.

INCORRECT: "Amazon Simple Email Service (Amazon SES)" is incorrect. This service is used for sending email but not SMS text messages.

INCORRECT: "Amazon Simple Workflow Service (Amazon SWF)" is incorrect. Amazon SWF helps developers build, run, and scale background jobs that have parallel or sequential steps. You can think of Amazon SWF as a fully-managed state tracker and task coordinator in the Cloud.

INCORRECT: "Amazon Simple Queue Service (Amazon SQS)" is incorrect. Amazon Simple Queue Service (SQS) is a fully managed message queuing service that enables you to decouple and scale microservices, distributed systems, and serverless applications.

References:

https://aws.amazon.com/sns/

Save time with our exam-specific cheat sheets:

https://digitalcloud.training/certification-training/aws-certified-cloud-practitioner/notification-services/

QUESTION 38

Which AWS service or feature allows a company to receive a single monthly AWS bill when using multiple AWS accounts?

1. Consolidated billing
2. Amazon Cloud Directory
3. AWS Cost Explorer
4. AWS Cost and Usage report

Answer: 1

Explanation:

You can use the consolidated billing feature in AWS Organizations to consolidate billing and payment for multiple AWS accounts or multiple Amazon Internet Services Pvt. Ltd (AISPL) accounts. Every organization in AWS Organizations has a *master (payer) account* that pays the charges of all the *member (linked) accounts*.

Consolidated billing has the following benefits:

- **One bill** – You get one bill for multiple accounts.
- **Easy tracking** – You can track the charges across multiple accounts and download the combined cost and usage data.
- **Combined usage** – You can combine the usage across all accounts in the organization to share the volume pricing discounts, Reserved Instance discounts, and Savings Plans. This can result in a lower charge for your project, department, or company than with individual standalone accounts.
- **No extra fee** – Consolidated billing is offered at no additional cost.

CORRECT: "Consolidated billing" is the correct answer.

INCORRECT: "Amazon Cloud Directory" is incorrect. Cloud Directory is used for creating cloud-native directories. This is not related to billing.

INCORRECT: "AWS Cost Explorer" is incorrect. AWS Cost Explorer has an easy-to-use interface that lets you visualize, understand, and manage your AWS costs and usage over time. It does not centralize billing.

INCORRECT: "AWS Cost and Usage report" is incorrect. The AWS Cost & Usage Report lists AWS usage for each service category used by an account and its IAM users in hourly or daily line items, as well as any tags that you have activated for cost allocation purposes.

References:

https://docs.aws.amazon.com/awsaccountbilling/latest/aboutv2/consolidated-billing.html

Save time with our exam-specific cheat sheets:

https://digitalcloud.training/certification-training/aws-certified-cloud-practitioner/aws-billing-and-pricing/

QUESTION 39

A user needs an automated security assessment report that will identify unintended network access to Amazon EC2 instances and vulnerabilities on those instances.

Which AWS service will provide this assessment report?

1. EC2 security groups
2. AWS Config
3. Amazon Macie
4. Amazon Inspector

Answer: 4

Explanation:

Amazon Inspector is an automated security assessment service that helps improve the security and compliance of applications deployed on AWS. Amazon Inspector automatically assesses applications for exposure, vulnerabilities, and deviations from best practices.

After performing an assessment, Amazon Inspector produces a detailed list of security findings prioritized by level of severity. These findings can be reviewed directly or as part of detailed assessment reports which are available via the Amazon Inspector console or API.

CORRECT: "Amazon Inspector" is the correct answer.

INCORRECT: "EC2 security groups" is incorrect. Security groups are instance-level firewalls used for controlling network traffic reaching and leaving EC2 instances.

INCORRECT: "AWS Config" is incorrect. AWS Config is a service that enables you to assess, audit, and evaluate the configurations of your AWS resources.

INCORRECT: "Amazon Macie" is incorrect. Amazon Macie is a fully managed data security and data privacy service that uses machine learning and pattern matching to discover and protect sensitive data in AWS.

References:

https://aws.amazon.com/inspector/

Save time with our exam-specific cheat sheets:

https://digitalcloud.training/certification-training/aws-certified-cloud-practitioner/cloud-security/

QUESTION 40

Which of the following best describes an Availability Zone in the AWS Cloud?

1. One or more physical data centers
2. A completely isolated geographic location
3. One or more edge locations based around the world
4. A subnet for deploying resources into

Answer: 1

Explanation:

An Availability Zone (AZ) is one or more discrete data centers with redundant power, networking, and connectivity in an AWS Region. AZ's give customers the ability to operate production applications and databases that are more highly available, fault tolerant, and scalable than would be possible from a single data center.

The diagram below shows how AZs relate to AWS Regions:

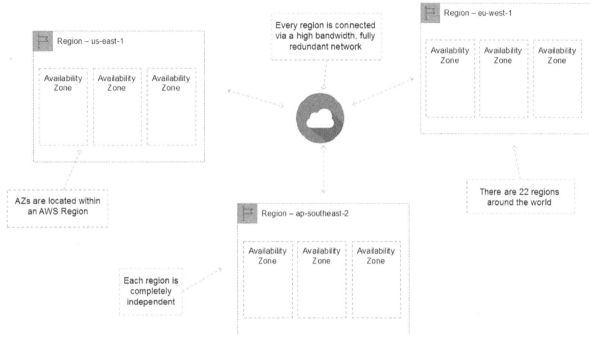

CORRECT: "One or more physical data centers" is the correct answer.

INCORRECT: "A completely isolated geographic location" is incorrect. This is a description of an AWS Region.

INCORRECT: "One or more edge locations based around the world" is incorrect. Edge locations are used by Amazon CloudFront for caching content.

INCORRECT: "A subnet for deploying resources into" is incorrect. Subnets are created within AZs.

References:

https://aws.amazon.com/about-aws/global-infrastructure/regions_az/

Save time with our exam-specific cheat sheets:

https://digitalcloud.training/certification-training/aws-certified-cloud-practitioner/aws-global-infrastructure/

QUESTION 41

A company needs a consistent and dedicated connection between AWS resources and an on-premise system.

Which AWS service can fulfil this requirement?

1. AWS Direct Connect
2. AWS Managed VPN
3. Amazon Connect
4. AWS DataSync

Answer: 1

Explanation:

An AWS Direct Connect connection is a private, dedicated link to AWS. As it does not use the internet, performance is consistent.

The following diagram shows how a corporate data center is connected to AWS using a Direct Connect link via an AWS Direct Connect location:

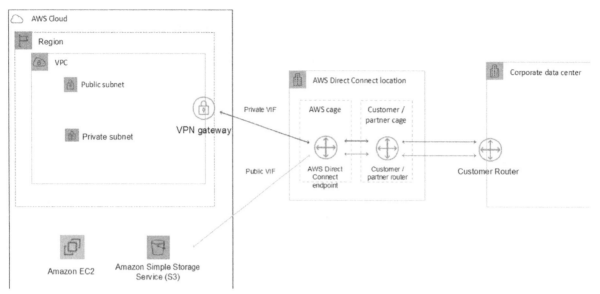

CORRECT: "AWS Direct Connect" is the correct answer.

INCORRECT: "AWS Managed VPN" is incorrect. This services uses the public internet so it is not a dedicated link and performance will not be consistent.

INCORRECT: "Amazon Connect" is incorrect. Amazon Connect is an easy to use omnichannel cloud contact center that helps companies provide superior customer service at a lower cost

INCORRECT: "AWS DataSync" is incorrect. AWS DataSync makes it simple and fast to move large amounts of data online between on-premises storage and Amazon S3, Amazon Elastic File System (Amazon EFS), or Amazon FSx for Windows File Server.

References:

https://aws.amazon.com/directconnect/

Save time with our exam-specific cheat sheets:

https://digitalcloud.training/certification-training/aws-certified-cloud-practitioner/aws-networking/

QUESTION 42

Which AWS service helps customers meet corporate, contractual, and regulatory compliance requirements for data security by using dedicated hardware appliances within the AWS Cloud?

1. AWS Secrets Manager
2. AWS CloudHSM
3. AWS Key Management Service (AWS KMS)
4. AWS Directory Service

Answer: 2

Explanation:

The AWS CloudHSM service helps you meet corporate, contractual, and regulatory compliance requirements for data security by using dedicated Hardware Security Module (HSM) instances within the AWS cloud. AWS CloudHSM enables you to easily generate and use your own encryption keys on the AWS Cloud.

CORRECT: "AWS CloudHSM" is the correct answer.

INCORRECT: "AWS Secrets Manager" is incorrect. AWS Secrets Manager enables you to easily rotate, manage, and retrieve database credentials, API keys, and other secrets throughout their lifecycle.

INCORRECT: "AWS Key Management Service (AWS KMS)" is incorrect. This service is also involved with creating and managing encryption keys but does not use dedicated hardware.

INCORRECT: "AWS Directory Service" is incorrect. AWS Directory Service for Microsoft Active Directory, also known as AWS

Managed Microsoft AD, enables your directory-aware workloads and AWS resources to use managed Active Directory in the AWS Cloud.

References:

https://aws.amazon.com/cloudhsm/features/

Save time with our exam-specific cheat sheets:

https://digitalcloud.training/certification-training/aws-certified-cloud-practitioner/cloud-security/

QUESTION 43

What can a Cloud Practitioner use the AWS Total Cost of Ownership (TCO) Calculator for?

1. Generate reports that break down AWS Cloud compute costs by duration, resource, or tags
2. Estimate savings when comparing the AWS Cloud to an on-premises environment
3. Estimate a monthly bill for the AWS Cloud resources that will be used
4. Enable billing alerts to monitor actual AWS costs compared to estimated costs

Answer: 2

Explanation:

The TCO calculators allow you to estimate the cost savings when using AWS, compared to on-premises, and provide a detailed set of reports that can be used in executive presentations. The calculators also give you the option to modify assumptions that best meet your business needs.

CORRECT: "Estimate savings when comparing the AWS Cloud to an on-premises environment" is the correct answer.

INCORRECT: "Generate reports that break down AWS Cloud compute costs by duration, resource, or tags" is incorrect. This describes the AWS Cost & Usage Report.

INCORRECT: "Estimate a monthly bill for the AWS Cloud resources that will be used" is incorrect. This describes the AWS Pricing Calculator (or Simple Monthly Calculator).

INCORRECT: "Enable billing alerts to monitor actual AWS costs compared to estimated costs" is incorrect. Billing alerts can be enabled using Amazon CloudWatch.

References:

https://aws.amazon.com/tco-calculator/

Save time with our exam-specific cheat sheets:

https://digitalcloud.training/certification-training/aws-certified-cloud-practitioner/aws-billing-and-pricing/

QUESTION 44

Which of the following should be used to improve the security of access to the AWS Management Console? (Select TWO.)

1. AWS Secrets Manager
2. AWS Certificate Manager
3. AWS Multi-Factor Authentication (AWS MFA)
4. Security group rules
5. Strong password policies

Answer: 3, 5

Explanation:

For extra security, AWS recommends that you require multi-factor authentication (MFA) for all users in your account. With MFA, users have a device that generates a response to an authentication challenge.

Both the user's credentials (something you know) and the device-generated response (something you have) are required to complete the sign-in process. If a user's password or access keys are compromised, your account resources are still secure because of the additional authentication requirement.

Something you know:

Something you have:

IAM User

EJPx!*21p9%

Password

MFA Virtual MFA

e.g. Google Authenticator on
your smart phone

MFA Physical MFA

704 688

040 683

308 396

800 652

Additionally, strong password policies should be used to enforce measures including minimum password length, complexity, and password reuse restrictions.

CORRECT: "AWS Multi-Factor Authentication (AWS MFA)" is a correct answer.

CORRECT: "Strong password policies" is also a correct answer.

INCORRECT: "AWS Secrets Manager" is incorrect. This service enables you to easily rotate, manage, and retrieve database credentials, API keys, and other secrets throughout their lifecycle.

INCORRECT: "AWS Certificate Manager" is incorrect. This service is used for creating SSL/TLS certificates for use with HTTPS connections.

INCORRECT: "Security group rules" is incorrect as these are used to restrict traffic to/from your EC2 instances.

References:

https://docs.aws.amazon.com/IAM/latest/UserGuide/best-practices.html

Save time with our exam-specific cheat sheets:

https://digitalcloud.training/certification-training/aws-certified-cloud-practitioner/identity-and-access-management/

QUESTION 45

An application has highly dynamic usage patterns. Which characteristics of the AWS Cloud make it cost-effective for this type of workload? (Select TWO.)

1. High availability
2. Strict security
3. Elasticity
4. Pay-as-you-go pricing
5. Reliability

Answer: 3, 4

Explanation:

AWS is a cost-effective for dynamic workloads because it is elastic, meaning your workload can scale based on demand. And because you only pay for what you use (pay-as-you-go pricing).

CORRECT: "Elasticity" is the correct answer.

CORRECT: "Pay-as-you-go pricing" is the correct answer.

INCORRECT: "High availability" is incorrect. This is not a characteristic that results in cost-effectiveness.

INCORRECT: "Strict security" is incorrect. This is not a characteristic that results in cost-effectiveness.

INCORRECT: "Reliability" is incorrect. This is not a characteristic that results in cost-effectiveness.

References:

https://aws.amazon.com/architecture/

QUESTION 46

Which benefits can a company immediately realize using the AWS Cloud? (Select TWO.)

1. Variable expenses are replaced with capital expenses
2. Capital expenses are replaced with variable expenses
3. User control of physical infrastructure
4. Increased agility
5. No responsibility for security

Answer: 2, 4

Explanation:

A couple of the benefits that companies will realize immediately when using the AWS Cloud are increased agility and a change from capital expenditure to variable operational expenditure.

Agility is enabled through the flexibility of cloud services and the ease with which applications can be deployed, scaled, and managed. When using cloud services you pay for what you use and this is a variable, operational expense which can be beneficial to company cashflow.

CORRECT: "Capital expenses are replaced with variable expenses" is a correct answer.

CORRECT: "Increased agility" is also a correct answer.

INCORRECT: "Variable expenses are replaced with capital expenses" is incorrect. This is the wrong way around, capital expenses are replaced with variable expenses.

INCORRECT: "User control of physical infrastructure" is incorrect. This is not true, you do not get control of the physical infrastructure.

INCORRECT: "No responsibility for security" is incorrect. This is not true, you are still responsible for "security in the cloud".

References:

https://docs.aws.amazon.com/whitepapers/latest/aws-overview/six-advantages-of-cloud-computing.html

QUESTION 47

Which AWS hybrid storage service enables a user's on-premises applications to seamlessly use AWS Cloud storage?

1. AWS Backup
2. Amazon Connect
3. AWS Direct Connect
4. AWS Storage Gateway

Answer: 4

Explanation:

AWS Storage Gateway is a hybrid cloud storage service that gives you on-premises access to virtually unlimited cloud storage. Customers use Storage Gateway to simplify storage management and reduce costs for key hybrid cloud storage use cases.

These include moving tape backups to the cloud, reducing on-premises storage with cloud-backed file shares, providing low latency access to data in AWS for on-premises applications, as well as various migration, archiving, processing, and disaster recovery use cases.

CORRECT: "AWS Storage Gateway" is the correct answer.

INCORRECT: "AWS Backup" is incorrect. AWS Backup is a fully managed backup service that makes it easy to centralize and automate the backup of data across AWS services. It is not used for connecting on-premises storage to cloud storage.

INCORRECT: "Amazon Connect" is incorrect. Amazon Connect is an easy to use omnichannel cloud contact center that helps companies provide superior customer service at a lower cost. It has nothing to do with storing data.

INCORRECT: "AWS Direct Connect" is incorrect. AWS Direct Connect is a cloud service solution that makes it easy to establish a dedicated network connection from your premises to AWS. It is not related to storage of data.

References:

https://aws.amazon.com/storagegateway/?whats-new-cards.sort-by=item.additionalFields.postDateTime&whats-new-cards.sort-order=desc

Save time with our exam-specific cheat sheets:

https://digitalcloud.training/certification-training/aws-certified-cloud-practitioner/additional-aws-services-tools/

QUESTION 48

A user has limited knowledge of AWS services, but wants to quickly deploy a scalable Node.js application in an Amazon VPC.

Which service should be used to deploy the application?

1. AWS CloudFormation
2. AWS Elastic Beanstalk
3. Amazon EC2
4. Amazon LightSail

Answer: 2

Explanation:

AWS Elastic Beanstalk is an easy-to-use service for deploying and scaling web applications and services developed with Java, .NET, PHP, Node.js, Python, Ruby, Go, and Docker on familiar servers such as Apache, Nginx, Passenger, and IIS.

You can simply upload your code and Elastic Beanstalk automatically handles the deployment, from capacity provisioning, load balancing, auto-scaling to application health monitoring. At the same time, you retain full control over the AWS resources powering your application and can access the underlying resources at any time.

CORRECT: "AWS Elastic Beanstalk" is the correct answer.

INCORRECT: "Amazon LightSail" is incorrect. LightSail is a good service to use when you don't have good knowledge of AWS. However, you cannot deploy a scalable node.js application into a VPC.

INCORRECT: "AWS CloudFormation" is incorrect. CloudFormation is used for automating the deployment of infrastructure resources in AWS.

INCORRECT: "Amazon EC2" is incorrect. This would require more expertise that using Elastic Beanstalk.

References:

https://aws.amazon.com/elasticbeanstalk/

Save time with our exam-specific cheat sheets:

https://digitalcloud.training/certification-training/aws-certified-cloud-practitioner/additional-aws-services-tools/

QUESTION 49

How can a security compliance officer retrieve AWS compliance documentation such as a SOC 2 report?

1. Using AWS Artifact
2. Using AWS Trusted Advisor
3. Using AWS Inspector
4. Using the AWS Personal Health Dashboard

Answer: 1

Explanation:

AWS Artifact, available in the console, is a self-service audit artifact retrieval portal that provides our customers with on-demand access to AWS' compliance documentation and AWS agreements.

You can use AWS Artifact Reports to download AWS security and compliance documents, such as AWS ISO certifications, Payment Card Industry (PCI), and System and Organization Control (SOC) reports.

CORRECT: "Using AWS Artifact" is the correct answer.

INCORRECT: "Using AWS Trusted Advisor" is incorrect. AWS Trusted Advisor is an online resource to help you reduce cost, increase performance, and improve security by optimizing your AWS environment.

INCORRECT: "Using AWS Inspector" is incorrect. Inspector is an automated security assessment service that helps improve the security and compliance of applications deployed on AWS.

INCORRECT: "Using the AWS Personal Health Dashboard" is incorrect. AWS Personal Health Dashboard provides alerts and remediation guidance when AWS is experiencing events that may impact you.

References:

https://aws.amazon.com/artifact/

Save time with our exam-specific cheat sheets:

https://digitalcloud.training/certification-training/aws-certified-cloud-practitioner/cloud-security/

QUESTION 50

Which AWS service can be used to run Docker containers?

1. AWS Lambda
2. Amazon ECR
3. Amazon ECS
4. Amazon AMI

Answer: 3

Explanation:

Amazon Elastic Container Service (ECS) is a highly scalable, high performance container management service that supports Docker containers and allows you to easily run applications on a managed cluster of Amazon EC2 instances.

CORRECT: "Amazon ECS" is the correct answer.

INCORRECT: "AWS Lambda" is incorrect. AWS Lambda is a serverless technology that lets you run code in response to events as functions

INCORRECT: "Amazon ECR" is incorrect. Amazon Elastic Container Registry (ECR) is a fully-managed Docker container registry that makes it easy for developers to store, manage, and deploy Docker container images

INCORRECT: "Amazon AMI" is incorrect. Amazon Machine Images (AMI) store configuration information for Amazon EC2 instances.

References:

https://aws.amazon.com/ecs/

Save time with our exam-specific cheat sheets:

https://digitalcloud.training/certification-training/aws-certified-cloud-practitioner/aws-compute/

QUESTION 51

What are the benefits of using the AWS Managed Services? (Select TWO.)

1. Alignment with ITIL processes
2. Managed applications so you can focus on infrastructure
3. Baseline integration with ITSM tools
4. Designed for small businesses
5. Support for all AWS services

Answer: 1,3

Explanation:

AWS Managed Services manages the daily operations of your AWS infrastructure in alignment with ITIL processes. AWS Managed Services provides a baseline integration with IT Service Management (ITSM) tools such as the ServiceNow platform.

AWS Managed Services provides ongoing **management of your AWS infrastructure so you can focus on your applications**. By implementing best practices to maintain your infrastructure, AWS Managed Services helps to reduce your operational overhead and risk.

AWS Managed Services currently supports the 20+ services most critical for Enterprises, and will continue to expand our list of integrated AWS services.

AWS Managed Services is **designed to meet the needs of Enterprises** that require stringent SLAs, adherence to corporate compliance, and integration with their systems and ITIL®-based processes.

CORRECT: "Alignment with ITIL processes" is a correct answer.

CORRECT: "Baseline integration with ITSM tools" is also a correct answer.

INCORRECT: "Managed applications so you can focus on infrastructure" is incorrect as this is not offered by AWS Managed Services.

INCORRECT: "Designed for small businesses" is incorrect as the service is designed for enterprises.

INCORRECT: "Support for all AWS services" is incorrect as the service does not support all AWS services.

References:

https://aws.amazon.com/managed-services/

QUESTION 52

Which services are involved with security? (Select TWO.)

1. AWS CloudHSM
2. AWS DMS
3. AWS KMS
4. AWS SMS
5. Amazon ELB

Answer: 1,3

Explanation:

AWS Key Management Service (KMS) gives you centralized control over the encryption keys used to protect your data. AWS CloudHSM is a cloud-based hardware security module (HSM) that enables you to easily generate and use your own encryption keys on the AWS Cloud.

CORRECT: "AWS CloudHSM" is a correct answer.

CORRECT: "AWS KMS" is also a correct answer.

INCORRECT: "AWS DMS" is incorrect. AWS Database Migration Service is used for migration of databases.

INCORRECT: "AWS SMS" is incorrect. AWS Server Migration Service is used for migration of virtual machines.

INCORRECT: "Amazon ELB" is incorrect. Amazon Elastic Load Balancing is used for distributing incoming connections to pools of EC2 instances

References:

https://aws.amazon.com/cloudhsm/

https://aws.amazon.com/kms/

Save time with our exam-specific cheat sheets:

https://digitalcloud.training/certification-training/aws-certified-cloud-practitioner/cloud-security/

QUESTION 53

What are the names of two types of AWS Storage Gateway? (Select TWO.)

1. S3 Gateway
2. File Gateway
3. Block Gateway
4. Tape Gateway
5. Cached Gateway

Answer: 2,4

Explanation:

The AWS Storage Gateway service enables hybrid storage between on-premises environments and the AWS Cloud. It provides low-latency performance by caching frequently accessed data on premises, while storing data securely and durably in Amazon cloud storage services. AWS Storage Gateway supports three storage interfaces: file, volume, and tape

File gateway provides a virtual on-premises file server, which enables you to store and retrieve files as objects in Amazon S3

The volume gateway represents the family of gateways that support block-based volumes, previously referred to as gateway-cached and gateway-stored modes

Tape Gateway (formerly known as Gateway Virtual Tape Library) is used for backup with popular backup software.

The diagram below depicts a File Gateway.

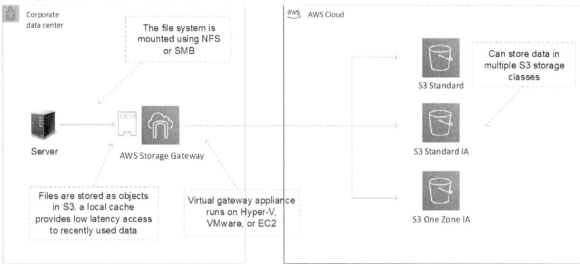

All other answers are bogus and use terms that are associated with Storage Gateways (S3, block, cached)

CORRECT: "File Gateway" is a correct answer.

CORRECT: "Tape Gateway" is also a correct answer.

INCORRECT: "S3 Gateway" is incorrect as explained above.

INCORRECT: "Block Gateway" is incorrect as explained above.

INCORRECT: "Cached Gateway" is incorrect as explained above.

References:

https://aws.amazon.com/storagegateway/

Save time with our exam-specific cheat sheets:

https://digitalcloud.training/certification-training/aws-certified-cloud-practitioner/additional-aws-services-tools/

QUESTION 54

An application stores images which will be retrieved infrequently, but must be available for retrieval immediately. Which is the most cost-effective storage option that meets these requirements?

1. Amazon Glacier with expedited retrievals
2. Amazon S3 Standard-Infrequent Access
3. Amazon EFS
4. Amazon S3 Standard

Answer: 2

Explanation:

Amazon S3 Standard-Infrequent Access is the most cost-effective choice. It provides immediate access and is suitable for this use case as it is lower cost than S3 standard. Note that you must pay a fee for retrievals which is why you would only use this tier for infrequent access use cases.

	S3 Standard	S3 Intelligent-Tiering*	S3 Standard-IA	S3 One Zone-IA†	S3 Glacier	S3 Glacier Deep Archive
Designed for durability	99.999999999% (11 9's)	99.999999999% (11 9's)	99.999999999% (11 9's)	99.999999999% (11 9's)	99.999999999% (11 9's)	99.999999999% (11 9's)
Designed for availability	99.99%	99.9%	99.9%	99.5%	99.99%	99.99%
Availability SLA	99.9%	99%	99%	99%	99.9%	99.9%
Availability Zones	≥3	≥3	≥3	1	≥3	≥3
Minimum capacity charge per object	N/A	N/A	128KB	128KB	40KB	40KB
Minimum storage duration charge	N/A	30 days	30 days	30 days	90 days	180 days
Retrieval fee	N/A	N/A	per GB retrieved	per GB retrieved	per GB retrieved	per GB retrieved
First byte latency	milliseconds	milliseconds	milliseconds	milliseconds	select minutes or hours	select hours
Storage type	Object	Object	Object	Object	Object	Object
Lifecycle transitions	Yes	Yes	Yes	Yes	Yes	Yes

CORRECT: "Amazon S3 Standard-Infrequent Access" is the correct answer.

INCORRECT: "Amazon Glacier with expedited retrievals" is incorrect. Amazon Glacier with expedited retrievals is fast (1-5 minutes) but not immediate.

INCORRECT: "Amazon EFS" is incorrect. Amazon EFS is a high-performance file system and not ideally suited to this scenario, it is also not the most cost-effective option.

INCORRECT: "Amazon S3 Standard" is incorrect. Amazon S3 Standard provides immediate retrieval but is not less cost-effective compared to Standard-Infrequent access.

References:

https://aws.amazon.com/s3/storage-classes/

Save time with our exam-specific cheat sheets:

https://digitalcloud.training/certification-training/aws-certified-cloud-practitioner/aws-storage/

QUESTION 55

Which AWS support plans provide support via email, chat and phone? (Select TWO.)

1. Basic
2. Developer
3. Business
4. Enterprise
5. Global

Answer: 3,4

Explanation:

Only the business and enterprise plans provide support via email, chat and phone.

	Developer	Business	Enterprise
Enhanced Technical Support	Business hours** email access to Cloud Support Associates Unlimited cases / 1 primary contact	24x7 phone, email, and chat access to Cloud Support Engineers Unlimited cases / unlimited contacts (IAM supported)	24x7 phone, email, and chat access to Cloud Support Engineers Unlimited cases / unlimited contacts (IAM supported)

CORRECT: "Business" is the correct answer.

CORRECT: "Enterprise" is the correct answer.

INCORRECT: "Basic" is incorrect does not provide support via email, chat and phone.

INCORRECT: "Developer" is incorrect only provides email support.

INCORRECT: "Global" is incorrect is not a support plan offered by AWS.

References:

https://aws.amazon.com/premiumsupport/plans/

Save time with our exam-specific cheat sheets:

https://digitalcloud.training/certification-training/aws-certified-cloud-practitioner/aws-billing-and-pricing/

QUESTION 56

Which AWS service can be used to host a static website?

1. Amazon S3
2. Amazon EBS
3. AWS CloudFormation
4. Amazon EFS

Answer: 1

Explanation:

You can use Amazon S3 to host a static website. On a *static* website, individual webpages include static content. They might also contain client-side scripts.

By contrast, a *dynamic* website relies on server-side processing, including server-side scripts such as PHP, JSP, or ASP.NET. Amazon S3 does not support server-side scripting, but AWS has other resources for hosting dynamic websites.

CORRECT: "Amazon S3" is the correct answer.

INCORRECT: "Amazon EBS" is incorrect as it cannot be used to host a static website.

INCORRECT: "AWS CloudFormation" is incorrect as it cannot be used to host a static website.

INCORRECT: "Amazon EFS" is incorrect as it cannot be used to host a static website.

References:

https://docs.aws.amazon.com/AmazonS3/latest/dev/WebsiteHosting.html

Save time with our exam-specific cheat sheets:

https://digitalcloud.training/certification-training/aws-certified-cloud-practitioner/aws-storage/

QUESTION 57

Which of the following are AWS recommended best practices in relation to IAM? (Select TWO.)

1. Assign permissions to users
2. Create individual IAM users
3. Embed access keys in application code
4. Enable MFA for all users
5. Grant greatest privilege

Answer: 2,4

Explanation:

AWS recommends that you create individual IAM users rather than sharing IAM user accounts.

For extra security, AWS recommends that you require multi-factor authentication (MFA) for all users in your account. For privileged IAM users who are allowed to access sensitive resources or API operations, AWS recommend using U2F or hardware MFA devices.

CORRECT: "Create individual IAM users" is the correct answer.

CORRECT: "Enable MFA for all users" is the correct answer.

INCORRECT: "Assign permissions to users" is incorrect. You should use groups to assign permissions to IAM users and should avoid embedding access keys in application code.

INCORRECT: "Embed access keys in application code" is incorrect as this is against best practice as it is highly insecure.

INCORRECT: "Grant greatest privilege" is incorrect. AWS recommend creating individual IAM users and assigning the **least** privilege necessary for them to perform their role.

References:

https://docs.aws.amazon.com/IAM/latest/UserGuide/best-practices.html

Save time with our exam-specific cheat sheets:

https://digitalcloud.training/certification-training/aws-certified-cloud-practitioner/identity-and-access-management/

QUESTION 58

Which of the following security operations tasks must be performed by AWS customers? (Select TWO.)

1. Collecting syslog messages from physical firewalls
2. Issuing data center access keycards
3. Installing security updates on EC2 instances
4. Enabling multi-factor authentication (MFA) for privileged users
5. Installing security updates for server firmware

Answer: 3,4

Explanation:

The customer is responsible for installing security updates on EC2 instances and enabling MFA. AWS is responsible for security of the physical data center and the infrastructure upon which customer services run.

CORRECT: "Installing security updates on EC2 instances" is a correct answer.

CORRECT: "Enabling multi-factor authentication (MFA) for privileged users" is also a correct answer.

INCORRECT: "Collecting syslog messages from physical firewalls" is incorrect as this is an AWS responsibility.

INCORRECT: "Issuing data center access keycards" is incorrect as this is an AWS responsibility.

INCORRECT: "Installing security updates for server firmware" is incorrect as this is an AWS responsibility.

References:

https://aws.amazon.com/compliance/shared-responsibility-model/

Save time with our exam-specific cheat sheets:

https://digitalcloud.training/certification-training/aws-certified-cloud-practitioner/aws-shared-responsibility-model/

QUESTION 59

How can an organization assess applications for vulnerabilities and deviations from best practice?

1. Use AWS Artifact
2. Use AWS Inspector
3. Use AWS Shield
4. Use AWS WAF

Answer: 2

Explanation:

Inspector is an automated security assessment service that helps improve the security and compliance of applications deployed on AWS. Inspector automatically assesses applications for vulnerabilities or deviations from best practices.

CORRECT: "Use AWS Inspector" is the correct answer.

INCORRECT: "Use AWS Artifact" is incorrect. AWS Artifact is your go-to, central resource for compliance-related information that matters to you.

INCORRECT: "Use AWS Shield" is incorrect. AWS Shield is a managed Distributed Denial of Service (DDoS) protection service.

INCORRECT: "Use AWS WAF" is incorrect. AWS Web application Firewall (WAF) is a firewall service, it is not used for assessing best practice.

References:

https://aws.amazon.com/inspector/

Save time with our exam-specific cheat sheets:

https://digitalcloud.training/certification-training/aws-certified-cloud-practitioner/cloud-security/

QUESTION 60

Which AWS service protects against common exploits that could compromise application availability, compromise security or consume excessive resources?

1. AWS WAF
2. AWS Shield
3. Security Group
4. Network ACL

Answer: 1

Explanation:

AWS WAF is a web application firewall that protects against common exploits that could compromise application availability, compromise security or consume excessive resources.

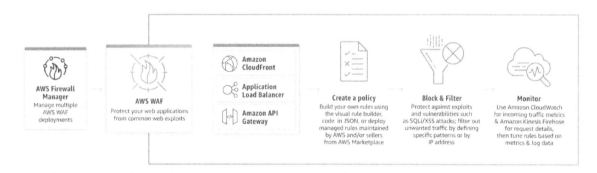

CORRECT: "AWS WAF" is the correct answer.

INCORRECT: "AWS Shield" is incorrect. AWS Shield is a managed Distributed Denial of Service (DDoS) protection service.

INCORRECT: "Security Group" is incorrect. Security groups are firewalls applied at the instance level.

INCORRECT: "Network ACL" is incorrect. Network ACLs are firewalls applied at the subnet level.

References:

https://aws.amazon.com/waf/

Save time with our exam-specific cheat sheets:

https://digitalcloud.training/certification-training/aws-certified-cloud-practitioner/cloud-security/

QUESTION 61

A new user is unable to access any AWS services, what is the most likely explanation?

1. The user needs to login with a key pair
2. The services are currently unavailable
3. By default new users are created without access to any AWS services
4. The default limit for user logons has been reached

Answer: 3

Explanation:

By default new users are created with NO access to any AWS services – they can only login to the AWS console. You must apply permissions to users to allow them to access services.

The recommended way to do this is to organize users into groups and then apply permissions policies to the group.

CORRECT: "By default new users are created without access to any AWS services" is the correct answer.

INCORRECT: "The user needs to login with a key pair" is incorrect. Key pairs are used for programmatic access using the API so they are required for API access only.

INCORRECT: "The services are currently unavailable" is incorrect as it is far more likely that the user just doesn't have permissions.

INCORRECT: "The default limit for user logons has been reached" is incorrect as there is no limit for user logons.

References:

https://docs.aws.amazon.com/IAM/latest/UserGuide/id_users_create.html

Save time with our exam-specific cheat sheets:

https://digitalcloud.training/certification-training/aws-certified-cloud-practitioner/identity-and-access-management/

QUESTION 62

Which of the following compliance programs allows the AWS environment to process, maintain, and store protected health information?

1. ISO 27001
2. PCI DSS
3. HIPAA
4. SOC 1

Answer: 3

Explanation:

AWS enables covered entities and their business associates subject to the U.S. Health Insurance Portability and Accountability Act of 1996 (HIPAA) to use the secure AWS environment to process, maintain, and store protected health information.

CORRECT: "HIPAA" is the correct answer.

INCORRECT: "ISO 27001" is incorrect as ISO/IEC 27001 is an information security standard.

INCORRECT: "PCI DSS" is incorrect as PCI DSS is related to the security of credit card payments.

INCORRECT: "SOC 1" is incorrect as this relates to financial reporting.

References:

https://aws.amazon.com/compliance/programs/

https://aws.amazon.com/compliance/hipaa-compliance/

QUESTION 63

Which AWS service can be used to load data from Amazon S3, transform it, and move it to another destination?

1. Amazon RedShift
2. Amazon EMR
3. Amazon Kinesis
4. AWS Glue

Answer: 4

Explanation:

AWS Glue is an Extract, Transform, and Load (ETL) service. You can use AWS Glue with data sources on Amazon S3, RedShift and other databases. With AWS Glue you transform and move the data to various destinations. It is used to prepare and load data for analytics.

CORRECT: "AWS Glue" is the correct answer.

INCORRECT: "Amazon RedShift" is incorrect. Amazon RedShift is a data warehouse. With a data warehouse you load data from other databases such as transactional SQL databases and run analysis. You can analyze data using SQL and Business Intelligence tools.

INCORRECT: "Amazon EMR" is incorrect. Amazon EMR is a managed Hadoop framework running on EC2 and S3. It is used for analyzing data, not for ETL.

INCORRECT: "Amazon Kinesis" is incorrect. Amazon Kinesis is used for collecting, processing and analyzing real-time streaming data.

References:

https://aws.amazon.com/glue/

Save time with our exam-specific cheat sheets:

https://digitalcloud.training/certification-training/aws-certified-cloud-practitioner/aws-analytics/

QUESTION 64

How should an organization deploy an application running on multiple EC2 instances to ensure that a power failure does not cause an application outage?

1. Launch the EC2 instances in separate regions
2. Launch the EC2 instances into different VPCs
3. Launch the EC2 instances into different Availability Zones
4. Launch the EC2 instances into Edge Locations

Answer: 3

Explanation:

If you have multiple EC2 instances that are part of an application, you should deploy them into separate availability zones (AZs). Each AZ has redundant power and is also fed from a different grid. AZs also have low-latency network links which is often advantageous for most applications.

You do not need to deploy into separate regions to prevent a power outage bringing your application down. AZs have redundant power and grids so you are safe deploying your applications into multiple AZs. If you split your applications across regions you introduce latency which may impact your application. You may also run into data sovereignty issues in some cases.

Deploying your EC2 instances into different VPCs is not required and would complicate your application deployment. Also, bear in mind that VPCs within a region use the same underlying infrastructure so deploying into different VPCs may still result in your EC2 instances being deployed into the same AZs. It is a best practice to deploy into separate AZs.

CORRECT: "Launch the EC2 instances into different Availability Zones" is the correct answer.

INCORRECT: "Launch the EC2 instances in separate regions" is incorrect as described above.

INCORRECT: "Launch the EC2 instances into different VPCs" is incorrect as described above.

INCORRECT: "Launch the EC2 instances into Edge Locations" is incorrect. You cannot deploy EC2 instances into Edge Locations.

References:

https://aws.amazon.com/about-aws/global-infrastructure/

Save time with our exam-specific cheat sheets:

https://digitalcloud.training/certification-training/aws-certified-cloud-practitioner/aws-global-infrastructure/

QUESTION 65

Which of the statements below is correct in relation to Consolidated Billing? (Select TWO.)

1. You receive one bill per AWS account
2. You receive a single bill for multiple accounts
3. You pay a fee per linked account
4. You can combine usage and share volume pricing discounts
5. You are charged a fee per user

Answer: 2,4

Explanation:

Consolidated billing has the following benefits:

One bill – You get one bill for multiple accounts.

Easy tracking – You can track the charges across multiple accounts and download the combined cost and usage data.

Combined usage – You can combine the usage across all accounts in the organization to share the volume pricing discounts and Reserved Instance discounts. This can result in a lower charge for your project, department, or company than with individual standalone accounts.

CORRECT: "You receive a single bill for multiple accounts" is a correct answer.

CORRECT: "You can combine usage and share volume pricing discounts" is also a correct answer.

INCORRECT: "You receive one bill per AWS account" is incorrect as you receive a single bill for multiple accounts.

INCORRECT: "You pay a fee per linked account" is incorrect as you do not pay a fee.

INCORRECT: "You are charged a fee per user" is incorrect as you do not pay a fee.

References:

https://docs.aws.amazon.com/awsaccountbilling/latest/aboutv2/consolidated-billing.html

Save time with our exam-specific cheat sheets:

https://digitalcloud.training/certification-training/aws-certified-cloud-practitioner/aws-billing-and-pricing/

QUESTION 66

Amazon S3 is typically used for which of the following use cases? (Select TWO.)

1. Host a static website
2. Install an operating system
3. Media hosting
4. In-memory data cache
5. Message queue

Answer: 1,3

Explanation:

Amazon S3 is an object storage system. Typical use cases include: Backup and storage, application hosting, media hosting, software delivery and hosting a static website.

CORRECT: "Host a static website" is the correct answer.

CORRECT: "Media hosting" is the correct answer.

INCORRECT: "Install an operating system" is incorrect. You cannot install an operating system on an object-based storage system. Instead, you need a block-based storage system such as Amazon EBS.

INCORRECT: "In-memory data cache" is incorrect. You cannot use Amazon S3 as an in-memory data cache; for this you need a service such as Amazon ElastiCache.

INCORRECT: "Message queue" is incorrect. You cannot use Amazon S3 as a message queue (or at least it is not a typical use case). You should use a services such as Amazon SQS or Amazon MQ.

References:

https://docs.aws.amazon.com/AmazonS3/latest/gsg/S3-gsg-CommonUseScenarios.html

Save time with our exam-specific cheat sheets:

https://digitalcloud.training/certification-training/aws-certified-cloud-practitioner/aws-storage/

SET 3: PRACTICE QUESTIONS ONLY

For training purposes, go directly to <u>Set 3: Practice Questions, Answers & Explanations</u>

QUESTION 1

Which AWS service or feature can be used to restrict the individual API actions that users and roles in each member account can access?

1. Amazon Macie
2. AWS Organizations
3. AWS Shield
4. AWS IAM

QUESTION 2

Which AWS service can be used to track the activity of users on AWS?

1. AWS CloudTrail
2. AWS Directory Service
3. Amazon Inspector
4. Amazon CloudWatch

QUESTION 3

A company needs to optimize costs and resource usage through monitoring of operational health for all resources running on AWS.

Which AWS service will meet these requirements?

1. AWS Control Tower
2. Amazon CloudWatch
3. AWS CloudTrail
4. AWS Config

QUESTION 4

A user needs a quick way to determine if any Amazon EC2 instances have ports that allow unrestricted access.

Which AWS service will support this requirement?

1. VPC Flow Logs
2. AWS Shield
3. AWS Trusted Advisor
4. AWS CloudWatch Logs

QUESTION 5

A company has a website that delivers static content from an Amazon S3 bucket to users from around the world. Which AWS service will deliver the content with low latency?

1. AWS Lambda
2. Amazon CloudFront
3. AWS Elastic Beanstalk
4. AWS Global Accelerator

QUESTION 6

Which AWS service or component allows inbound traffic from the internet to access a VPC?

1. NAT Gateway
2. Internet gateway
3. VPC Route Table
4. Virtual Private Gateway

QUESTION 7

A company plans to connect their on-premises data center to the AWS Cloud and requires consistent bandwidth and performance.

Which AWS service should the company choose?

1. AWS VPN
2. Amazon Connect
3. AWS Direct Connect
4. Amazon CloudFront

QUESTION 8

A manager is planning to migrate applications to the AWS Cloud and needs to obtain AWS compliance reports.

How can these reports be generated?

1. Download the reports from AWS Secrets Manager.
2. Contact the AWS Compliance team.
3. Create a support ticket with AWS Support.
4. Download the reports from AWS Artifact.

QUESTION 9

A company has been using an AWS managed IAM policy for granting permissions to users but needs to add some permissions.

How can this be achieved?

1. Create a rule in AWS WAF.
2. Create a custom IAM policy.
3. Edit the AWS managed policy.
4. Create a Service Control Policy.

QUESTION 10

Which AWS service or feature can be used to capture information about inbound and outbound IP traffic on network interfaces in a VPC?

1. Internet gateway
2. AWS CloudTrail
3. VPC Endpoint
4. VPC Flow Logs

QUESTION 11

Which AWS services can be used as infrastructure automation tools? (Select TWO.)

1. AWS CloudFormation
2. Amazon CloudFront
3. AWS Batch
4. AWS OpsWorks
5. Amazon QuickSight

QUESTION 12

What technology enables compute capacity to adjust as loads change?

1. Load balancing
2. Automatic failover
3. Round robin
4. Auto Scaling

QUESTION 13

How can a company separate costs for storage, Amazon EC2, Amazon S3, and other AWS services by department?

1. Add department-specific tags to each resource
2. Create a separate VPC for each department
3. Create a separate AWS account for each department
4. Use AWS Organizations

QUESTION 14

Which AWS Support plan provides access to architectural and operational reviews, as well as 24/7 access to Cloud Support Engineers through email, online chat, and phone?

1. Basic
2. Business
3. Developer
4. Enterprise

QUESTION 15

Under the AWS shared responsibility model, which of the following is an example of security in the AWS Cloud?

1. Managing edge locations
2. Physical security
3. Firewall configuration
4. Global infrastructure

QUESTION 16

Which AWS service provides on-demand downloads of AWS security and compliance reports?

1. AWS Directory Service
2. AWS Artifact
3. AWS Trusted Advisor
4. Amazon Inspector

QUESTION 17

Which Amazon EC2 pricing model is the most cost-effective for an always-up, right-sized database server running a project that will last 1 year?

1. On-Demand Instances
2. Convertible Reserved Instances
3. Spot Instances
4. Standard Reserved Instances

QUESTION 18

Which feature enables fast, easy, and secure transfers of files over long distances between a client and an Amazon S3 bucket?

1. S3 Static Websites
2. S3 Copy
3. Multipart Upload
4. S3 Transfer Acceleration

QUESTION 19

Under the AWS shared responsibility model what is AWS responsible for? (Select TWO.)

1. Physical security of the data center
2. Replacement and disposal of disk drives
3. Configuration of security groups
4. Patch management of operating systems
5. Encryption of customer data

QUESTION 20

Which AWS service is known as a "serverless" service and runs code as functions triggered by events?

1. Amazon ECS
2. AWS Lambda
3. Amazon CodeDeploy
4. Amazon Cognito

QUESTION 21

Which statement best describes Amazon Route 53?

1. Amazon Route 53 is a service that enables routing within VPCs in an account
2. Amazon Route 53 is a highly available and scalable Domain Name System (DNS) service
3. Amazon Route 53 enables hybrid cloud models by extending an organization's on-premise networks into the AWS cloud
4. Amazon Route 53 is a service for distributing incoming connections between a fleet of registered EC2 instances

QUESTION 22

Which service provides a way to convert video and audio files from their source format into versions that will playback on devices like smartphones, tablets and PCs?

1. Amazon Elastic Transcoder
2. AWS Glue
3. Amazon Rekognition
4. Amazon Comprehend

QUESTION 23

When using AWS Organizations with consolidated billing what are two valid best practices? (Select TWO.)

1. Always enable multi-factor authentication (MFA) on the root account
2. Always use a straightforward password on the root account
3. The paying account should be used for billing purposes only
4. Use the paying account for deploying resources
5. Never exceed the limit of 20 linked accounts

QUESTION 24

Which AWS support plan comes with a Technical Account Manager (TAM)?

1. Basic
2. Developer

3. Business
4. Enterprise

QUESTION 25

Which service provides the ability to simply upload applications and have AWS handle the deployment details of capacity provisioning, load balancing, auto-scaling, and application health monitoring?

1. Amazon EC2
2. AWS Elastic Beanstalk
3. Amazon EC2 Auto Scaling
4. AWS OpsWorks

QUESTION 26

You are concerned that you may be getting close to some of the default service limits for several AWS services. What AWS tool can be used to display current usage and limits?

1. AWS CloudWatch
2. AWS Personal Health Dashboard
3. AWS Trusted Advisor
4. AWS Systems Manager

QUESTION 27

You need to run a production process that will use several EC2 instances and run constantly on an ongoing basis. The process cannot be interrupted or restarted without issue. What EC2 pricing model would be best for this workload?

1. Reserved instances
2. Spot instances
3. On-demand instances
4. Flexible instances

QUESTION 28

Which AWS service does API Gateway integrate with to enable users from around the world to achieve the lowest possible latency for API requests and responses?

1. AWS Direct Connect
2. Amazon S3 Transfer Acceleration
3. Amazon CloudFront
4. AWS Lambda

QUESTION 29

Which service can an organization use to track API activity within their account?

1. AWS CloudTrail
2. Amazon CloudWatch
3. AWS IAM
4. AWS CloudHSM

QUESTION 30

What tool provides real time guidance to help you provision your resources following best practices in the areas of cost optimization, performance, security and fault tolerance?

1. AWS Inspector
2. AWS Trusted Advisor
3. AWS Personal Health Dashboard

4. AWS IAM

QUESTION 31

What is the best way for an organization to transfer hundreds of terabytes of data from their on-premise data center into Amazon S3 with limited bandwidth available?

1. Use S3 Transfer Acceleration
2. Apply compression before uploading
3. Use AWS Snowball
4. Use Amazon CloudFront

QUESTION 32

Which database allows you to scale at the push of a button without incurring any downtime?

1. Amazon RDS
2. Amazon EMR
3. Amazon DynamoDB
4. Amazon RedShift

QUESTION 33

What are the charges for using Amazon Glacier? (Select TWO.)

1. Data transferred into Glacier
2. Retrieval requests
3. Data storage
4. Enhanced networking
5. Number of Availability Zones

QUESTION 34

Which of the following statements are correct about the benefits of AWS Direct Connect? (Select TWO.)

1. Quick to implement
2. Increased reliability (predictable performance)
3. Lower cost than a VPN
4. Increased bandwidth (predictable bandwidth)
5. Uses redundant paths across the Internet

QUESTION 35

Which AWS service lets you use Chef and Puppet to automate how servers are configured, deployed, and managed across your Amazon EC2 instances or on-premises compute environments?

1. AWS Elastic Beanstalk
2. AWS CloudFormation
3. AWS Systems Manager
4. AWS OpsWorks

QUESTION 36

Which AWS database service provides a fully managed data warehouse that can be analyzed using SQL tools and business intelligence tools?

1. Amazon RDS
2. Amazon DynamoDB
3. Amazon RedShift
4. Amazon ElastiCache

QUESTION 37

Which service can be used to create sophisticated, interactive graph applications?

1. Amazon RedShift
2. Amazon Neptune
3. AWS X-Ray
4. Amazon Athena

QUESTION 38

When using Amazon IAM, what authentication methods are available to use? (Select TWO.)

1. Client certificates
2. Access keys
3. AWS KMS
4. Server certificates
5. AES 256

QUESTION 39

How does the consolidated billing feature of AWS Organizations treat Reserved Instances that were purchased by another account in the organization?

1. All accounts in the organization are treated as one account so any account can receive the hourly cost benefit
2. Only the master account can benefit from the hourly cost benefit of the reserved instances
3. All accounts in the organization are treated as one account for volume discounts but not for reserved instances
4. AWS Organizations does not support any volume or reserved instance benefits across accounts, it is just a method of aggregating bills

QUESTION 40

Which of the below AWS services supports automated backups as a default configuration?

1. Amazon S3
2. Amazon RDS
3. Amazon EC2
4. Amazon EBS

QUESTION 41

What are the advantages of Availability Zones? (Select TWO.)

1. They allow regional disaster recovery
2. They provide fault isolation
3. They enable the caching of data for faster delivery to end users
4. They are connected by low-latency network connections
5. They enable you to connect your on-premises networks to AWS to form a hybrid cloud

QUESTION 42

Which of the options below are recommendations in the cost optimization pillar of the well-architected framework? (Select TWO.)

1. Adopt a consumption model
2. Adopt a capital expenditure model
3. Start spending money on data center operations
4. Analyze and attribute expenditure
5. Manage your services independently

QUESTION 43

What are Edge locations used for?

1. They are used for terminating VPN connections
2. They are used by CloudFront for caching content
3. They are the public-facing APIs for Amazon S3
4. They are used by regions for inter-region connectivity

QUESTION 44

To ensure the security of your AWS account, what are two AWS best practices for managing access keys? (Select TWO.)

1. Don't create any access keys, use IAM roles instead
2. Don't generate an access key for the root account user
3. Where possible, use IAM roles with temporary security credentials
4. Rotate access keys daily
5. Use MFA for access keys

QUESTION 45

An Amazon EC2 instance running the Amazon Linux 2 AMI is billed in what increment?

1. Per second
2. Per hour
3. Per CPU
4. Per GB

QUESTION 46

To gain greater discounts, which services can be reserved? (Select TWO.)

1. Amazon RedShift
2. Amazon S3
3. AWS Lambda
4. Amazon DynamoDB
5. Amazon CloudWatch

QUESTION 47

Which service allows an organization to view operational data from multiple AWS services through a unified user interface and automate operational tasks?

1. AWS Config
2. AWS OpsWorks
3. AWS Systems Manager
4. Amazon CloudWatch

QUESTION 48

How can an organization track resource inventory and configuration history for the purpose of security and regulatory compliance?

1. Configure AWS Config with the resource types
2. Create an Amazon CloudTrail trail
3. Implement Amazon GuardDuty
4. Run a report with AWS Artifact

QUESTION 49

A security operations engineer needs to implement threat detection and monitoring for malicious or unauthorized behavior. Which service should be used?

1. AWS Shield
2. AWS KMS
3. AWS CloudHSM
4. AWS GuardDuty

QUESTION 50

Which authentication method is used to authenticate programmatic calls to AWS services?

1. Console password
2. Server certificate
3. Key pair
4. Access keys

QUESTION 51

What is a benefit of moving an on-premises database to Amazon Relational Database Service (RDS)?

1. There is no need to manage operating systems
2. You can scale vertically without downtime
3. There is no database administration required
4. You can run any database engine

QUESTION 52

What are the benefits of using Amazon Rekognition with image files?

1. Can be used to resize images
2. Can be used to identify objects in an image
3. Can be used to transcode audio
4. Can help with image compression

QUESTION 53

Which IAM entity is associated with an access key ID and secret access key?

1. IAM Group
2. IAM Role
3. IAM Policy
4. IAM User

QUESTION 54

Which IAM entity can be used for assigning permissions to multiple users?

1. IAM User
2. IAM Group
3. IAM Role
4. IAM password policy

QUESTION 55

Which service can be used to cost-effectively move exabytes of data into AWS?

1. AWS Snowmobile

2. AWS Snowball
3. S3 Transfer Acceleration
4. S3 Cross-Region Replication (CRR)

QUESTION 56

Which AWS services are associated with Edge Locations? (Select TWO.)

1. Amazon CloudFront
2. AWS Direct Connect
3. AWS Shield
4. Amazon EBS
5. AWS Config

QUESTION 57

Which service can be used to easily create multiple accounts?

1. AWS IAM
2. AWS CloudFormation
3. AWS Organizations
4. Amazon Connect

QUESTION 58

What is a specific benefit of an Enterprise Support plan?

1. Included Technical Support Manager
2. Included AWS Solutions Architect
3. Included Cloud Support Associate
4. Included Technical Account Manager

QUESTION 59

You have been running an on-demand Amazon EC2 instance running Linux for 4hrs, 5 minutes and 6 seconds. How much time will you be billed for?

1. 5hrs
2. 4hrs, 6mins
3. 4hrs, 5mins, and 6 seconds
4. 4hrs

QUESTION 60

Which of the below is an example of an architectural benefit of moving to the cloud?

1. Elasticity
2. Monolithic services
3. Proprietary hardware
4. Vertical scalability

QUESTION 61

What are the benefits of using reserved instances? (Select TWO.)

1. Reduced cost
2. More flexibility
3. Reserve capacity
4. Uses dedicated hardware
5. High availability

QUESTION 62

Which AWS tools can be used for automation? (Select TWO.)

1. AWS Elastic Beanstalk
2. Elastic Load Balancing
3. AWS CloudFormation
4. Amazon Elastic File System (EFS)
5. AWS Lambda

QUESTION 63

Which IAM entity can be used for assigning permissions to AWS services?

1. IAM Access Key ID and Secret Access Key
2. IAM Policy
3. IAM Role
4. Security Token Service (STS)

QUESTION 64

How does Amazon EC2 Auto Scaling help with resiliency?

1. By distributing connections to EC2 instances
2. By launching and terminating instances as needed
3. By changing instance types to increase capacity
4. By automating the failover of applications

QUESTION 65

Your CTO wants to move to cloud. What cost advantages are there to moving to cloud?

1. You provision only what you need and adjust to peak load
2. You can reduce your marketing costs
3. You don't need to pay for application licensing
4. You get free data transfer into and out of the cloud

SET 3: PRACTICE QUESTIONS AND ANSWERS

QUESTION 1

Which AWS service or feature can be used to restrict the individual API actions that users and roles in each member account can access?

1. Amazon Macie
2. AWS Organizations
3. AWS Shield
4. AWS IAM

Answer: 2

Explanation:

AWS Organizations offers Service control policies (SCPs) which are a type of organization policy that you can use to manage permissions in your organization. SCPs offer central control over the maximum available permissions (API actions) for all accounts in your organization. SCPs help you to ensure your accounts stay within your organization's access control guidelines. SCPs are available only in an organization that has all features enabled.

CORRECT: "AWS Organizations" is the correct answer.

INCORRECT: "Amazon Macie" is incorrect. Amazon Macie is a fully managed data security and data privacy service that uses machine learning and pattern matching to discover and protect your sensitive data in AWS

INCORRECT: "AWS Shield" is incorrect. AWS Shield a service that protects workloads against distributed denial of service (DDoS) attacks.

INCORRECT: "AWS IAM" is incorrect. AWS IAM is used for assigning permissions but SCPs in AWS Organizations are used to control which API actions are allowed in an account. You need to be granted permission in IAM and have the API allowed to be able to use the API successfully.

References:

https://docs.aws.amazon.com/organizations/latest/userguide/orgs_manage_policies_scps.html

Save time with our exam-specific cheat sheets:

https://digitalcloud.training/certification-training/aws-certified-cloud-practitioner/management-governance/

QUESTION 2

Which AWS service can be used to track the activity of users on AWS?

1. AWS CloudTrail
2. AWS Directory Service
3. Amazon Inspector
4. Amazon CloudWatch

Answer: 1

Explanation:

AWS CloudTrail is a service that enables governance, compliance, operational auditing, and risk auditing of your AWS account. With CloudTrail, you can log, continuously monitor, and retain account activity related to actions across your AWS infrastructure.

Think of CloudTrail is an auditing service (who did what and when), and CloudWatch as a performance monitoring service (how much resource was used).

CORRECT: "AWS CloudTrail" is the correct answer.

INCORRECT: "AWS Directory Service" is incorrect. This service provides several options for running directory services on AWS and connecting to directory services on-premises.

INCORRECT: "Amazon Inspector" is incorrect. Amazon Inspector is an automated security assessment service that helps improve the security and compliance of applications deployed on AWS

INCORRECT: "Amazon CloudWatch" is incorrect. CloudWatch is used for performance monitoring, not auditing.

References:

https://aws.amazon.com/cloudtrail/

Save time with our exam-specific cheat sheets:

https://digitalcloud.training/certification-training/aws-certified-cloud-practitioner/monitoring-and-logging-services/

QUESTION 3

A company needs to optimize costs and resource usage through monitoring of operational health for all resources running on AWS.

Which AWS service will meet these requirements?

1. AWS Control Tower
2. Amazon CloudWatch
3. AWS CloudTrail
4. AWS Config

Answer: 2

Explanation:

Amazon CloudWatch is a performance monitoring tool that receives metrics from AWS services. This data can be used for monitoring the operational health of resources as well as being used to optimize costs through ensuring systems are right-sized and just enough capacity is provisioned.

CORRECT: "Amazon CloudWatch" is the correct answer.

INCORRECT: "AWS Control Tower" is incorrect. AWS Control Tower is a service that is intended for organizations with multiple accounts and teams who are looking for the easiest way to set up their new multi-account AWS environment and govern at scale

INCORRECT: "AWS CloudTrail" is incorrect. CloudTrail is used for auditing (who did what and when), it is not used for monitoring operational health.

INCORRECT: "AWS Config" is incorrect. Config is used for managing compliance for AWS services.

References:

https://aws.amazon.com/cloudwatch/

Save time with our exam-specific cheat sheets:

https://digitalcloud.training/certification-training/aws-certified-cloud-practitioner/monitoring-and-logging-services/

QUESTION 4

A user needs a quick way to determine if any Amazon EC2 instances have ports that allow unrestricted access.

Which AWS service will support this requirement?

1. VPC Flow Logs
2. AWS Shield
3. AWS Trusted Advisor
4. AWS CloudWatch Logs

Answer: 3

Explanation:

Access to the ports on an Amazon EC2 instance is controlled through security groups. AWS Trusted Advisor scans the security groups in your account to see if any security groups allow unrestricted access to any ports. This information is then presented to you in the console and you can then act on this information to secure the ports through editing the rules in the security group.

CORRECT: "AWS Trusted Advisor" is the correct answer.

INCORRECT: "VPC Flow Logs" is incorrect. VPC Flow Logs capture information about the IP traffic going to and from network interfaces in your VPC.

INCORRECT: "AWS Shield" is incorrect. AWS Shield is a managed service for mitigating distributed denial of service (DDoS) attacks.

INCORRECT: "AWS CloudWatch Logs" is incorrect. CloudWatch Logs captures logging information from applications and AWS services.

References:

https://aws.amazon.com/premiumsupport/technology/trusted-advisor/

Save time with our exam-specific cheat sheets:

https://digitalcloud.training/certification-training/aws-certified-cloud-practitioner/cloud-security/

QUESTION 5

A company has a website that delivers static content from an Amazon S3 bucket to users from around the world. Which AWS service will deliver the content with low latency?

1. AWS Lambda
2. Amazon CloudFront
3. AWS Elastic Beanstalk
4. AWS Global Accelerator

Answer: 2

Explanation:

Amazon CloudFront is a content delivery network (CDN) and can use an Amazon S3 bucket configured as a static website as an origin for the content is caches globally. CloudFront reduces latency for global users by serving the requested content from a local cache.

CORRECT: "Amazon CloudFront" is the correct answer.

INCORRECT: "AWS Lambda" is incorrect. Lambda is a serverless compute service that runs code in response to triggers.

INCORRECT: "AWS Elastic Beanstalk" is incorrect. Elastic Beanstalk is a platform as a service offering that is used to run applications on a managed platform.

INCORRECT: "AWS Global Accelerator" is incorrect. Global Accelerator is used to direct traffic to application endpoints in different Regions using the AWS global network. It does not cache content and would not be used in front of an S3 bucket.

References:

https://aws.amazon.com/cloudfront/

QUESTION 6

Which AWS service or component allows inbound traffic from the internet to access a VPC?

1. NAT Gateway
2. Internet gateway
3. VPC Route Table
4. Virtual Private Gateway

Answer: 2

Explanation:

An Internet gateway is attached to a VPC and allows inbound traffic from the internet to access the VPC. It is also used as a target in route tables for outbound internet traffic.

CORRECT: "Internet gateway" is the correct answer.

INCORRECT: "NAT Gateway" is incorrect. A NAT gateway is used for outbound internet access for instances running in a private subnet.

INCORRECT: "VPC Route Table" is incorrect. The route table is used within a VPC for directing traffic.

INCORRECT: "Virtual Private Gateway" is incorrect. A VGW is used for IPSec VPN connections to access a VPC.

References:

https://docs.aws.amazon.com/vpc/latest/userguide/VPC_Internet_Gateway.html

QUESTION 7

A company plans to connect their on-premises data center to the AWS Cloud and requires consistent bandwidth and performance.

Which AWS service should the company choose?

1. AWS VPN
2. Amazon Connect
3. AWS Direct Connect
4. Amazon CloudFront

Answer: 3

Explanation:

AWS Direct Connect is a cloud service solution that makes it easy to establish a dedicated network connection from your premises to AWS. Using AWS Direct Connect, you can establish private connectivity between AWS and your datacenter, office, or colocation environment, which in many cases can reduce your network costs, increase bandwidth throughput, and provide a more consistent network experience than Internet-based connections.

CORRECT: "AWS Direct Connect" is the correct answer.

INCORRECT: "AWS VPN" is incorrect. A virtual private network (VPN) uses the internet and does not offer consistent network bandwidth or performance.

INCORRECT: "Amazon Connect" is incorrect. This is contact centre solution, not a networking technology.

INCORRECT: "Amazon CloudFront" is incorrect. CloudFront is a CDN used for caching content. It is not used for connecting from on-premises data centers to the AWS Cloud.

References:

https://aws.amazon.com/directconnect/

QUESTION 8

A manager is planning to migrate applications to the AWS Cloud and needs to obtain AWS compliance reports.

How can these reports be generated?

1. Download the reports from AWS Secrets Manager.
2. Contact the AWS Compliance team.
3. Create a support ticket with AWS Support.
4. Download the reports from AWS Artifact.

Answer: 4

Explanation:

AWS Artifact is your go-to, central resource for compliance-related information that matters to you. It provides on-demand access to AWS' security and compliance reports and select online agreements.

Reports available in AWS Artifact include Service Organization Control (SOC) reports, Payment Card Industry (PCI) reports, and certifications from accreditation bodies across geographies and compliance verticals that validate the implementation and operating effectiveness of AWS security controls.

Agreements available in AWS Artifact include the Business Associate Addendum (BAA) and the Nondisclosure Agreement (NDA).

CORRECT: "Download the reports from AWS Artifact" is the correct answer.

INCORRECT: "Contact the AWS Compliance team" is incorrect. You do not need to contact anyone at AWS, you can simply download this information.

INCORRECT: "Download the reports from AWS Secrets Manager" is incorrect. AWS Secrets Manager is used for storing secrets such as database authentication credentials or license codes. It is not used for storing compliance reports.

INCORRECT: "Create a support ticket with AWS Support" is incorrect. You do not need to contact anyone at AWS, you can simply download this information.

References:

https://aws.amazon.com/artifact/

Save time with our exam-specific cheat sheets:

https://digitalcloud.training/certification-training/aws-certified-cloud-practitioner/cloud-security/

QUESTION 9

A company has been using an AWS managed IAM policy for granting permissions to users but needs to add some permissions.

How can this be achieved?

1. Create a rule in AWS WAF.
2. Create a custom IAM policy.
3. Edit the AWS managed policy.
4. Create a Service Control Policy.

Answer: 2

Explanation:

AWS managed policies cannot be edited so if you need to add permissions to users that are not granted in the policy you must create your own custom IAM policy.

CORRECT: "Create a custom IAM policy" is the correct answer.

INCORRECT: "Edit the AWS managed policy" is incorrect. You cannot edit AWS managed policies.

INCORRECT: "Create a Service Control Policy" is incorrect. SCPs are used in AWS Organizations to restrict available permissions. They do not grant permissions.

INCORRECT: "Create a rule in AWS WAF" is incorrect. WAF is a web application firewall used for protecting resources from web-based attacks.

References:

https://docs.aws.amazon.com/IAM/latest/UserGuide/access_policies_create.html

Save time with our exam-specific cheat sheets:

https://digitalcloud.training/certification-training/aws-certified-cloud-practitioner/cloud-security/

QUESTION 10

Which AWS service or feature can be used to capture information about inbound and outbound IP traffic on network interfaces in a VPC?

1. Internet gateway
2. AWS CloudTrail
3. VPC Endpoint
4. VPC Flow Logs

Answer: 4

Explanation:

VPC Flow Logs is a feature that enables you to capture information about the IP traffic going to and from network interfaces in your VPC. Flow log data can be published to Amazon CloudWatch Logs or Amazon S3. After you've created a flow log, you can retrieve and view its data in the chosen destination.

Flow logs can help you with a number of tasks, such as:

- Diagnosing overly restrictive security group rules
- Monitoring the traffic that is reaching your instance
- Determining the direction of the traffic to and from the network interfaces

Flow log data is collected outside of the path of your network traffic, and therefore does not affect network throughput or latency. You can create or delete flow logs without any risk of impact to network performance.

CORRECT: "VPC Flow Logs" is the correct answer.

INCORRECT: "Internet gateway" is incorrect. An internet gateway is attached to a VPC and used for sending and receiving data from the internet.

INCORRECT: "AWS CloudTrail" is incorrect. CloudTrail is used for auditing API activity.

INCORRECT: "VPC Endpoint" is incorrect. VPC endpoints are used for connecting to public AWS services using private IP addresses.

References:

https://docs.aws.amazon.com/vpc/latest/userguide/flow-logs.html

Save time with our exam-specific cheat sheets:

https://digitalcloud.training/certification-training/aws-certified-cloud-practitioner/aws-networking/

QUESTION 11

Which AWS services can be used as infrastructure automation tools? (Select TWO.)

1. AWS CloudFormation
2. Amazon CloudFront
3. AWS Batch
4. AWS OpsWorks
5. Amazon QuickSight

Answer: 1, 4

Explanation:

AWS CloudFormation provides a common language for you to model and provision AWS and third party application resources in your cloud environment. AWS CloudFormation allows you to use programming languages or a simple text file to model and provision, in an automated and secure manner, all the resources needed for your applications across all regions and accounts.

AWS OpsWorks is a configuration management service that provides managed instances of Chef and Puppet. Chef and Puppet are automation platforms that allow you to use code to automate the configurations of your servers. OpsWorks lets you use Chef and Puppet to automate how servers are configured, deployed, and managed across your Amazon EC2 instances or on-premises compute environments.

CORRECT: "AWS CloudFormation" is a correct answer.

CORRECT: "AWS OpsWorks" is also a correct answer.

INCORRECT: "Amazon CloudFront" is incorrect. Amazon CloudFront is a fast content delivery network (CDN) service that securely delivers data, videos, applications, and APIs to customers globally with low latency, high transfer speeds.

INCORRECT: "AWS Batch" is incorrect. AWS Batch enables developers, scientists, and engineers to easily and efficiently run hundreds of thousands of batch computing jobs on AWS.

INCORRECT: "Amazon QuickSight" is incorrect. Amazon QuickSight is a fast, cloud-powered business intelligence service that makes it easy to deliver insights to everyone in your organization.

References:

https://aws.amazon.com/cloudformation/

https://aws.amazon.com/opsworks/

Save time with our exam-specific cheat sheets:

https://digitalcloud.training/certification-training/aws-certified-cloud-practitioner/additional-aws-services-tools/

QUESTION 12

What technology enables compute capacity to adjust as loads change?

1. Load balancing
2. Automatic failover
3. Round robin
4. Auto Scaling

Answer: 4

Explanation:

Auto Scaling allows the dynamic adjustment of provisioned resources based on demand. For instance, you can use Amazon EC2 Auto Scaling to launch additional EC2 instances when CloudWatch metrics report the CPU utilization has reached a certain threshold.

CORRECT: "Auto Scaling" is the correct answer.

INCORRECT: "Load balancing" is incorrect. This technology is more focused on high availability by distributing connections to multiple instances.

INCORRECT: "Automatic failover" is incorrect. This is a technology that enables high availability by failing over to standby resources in the event of a service disruption.

INCORRECT: "Round robin" is incorrect. This is typically associated with the Domain Name Service (DNS) where responses are provided from a pool of addresses in a sequential and circular fashion.

References:

https://aws.amazon.com/autoscaling/

Save time with our exam-specific cheat sheets:

https://digitalcloud.training/certification-training/aws-certified-cloud-practitioner/elastic-load-balancing-and-auto-scaling/

QUESTION 13

How can a company separate costs for storage, Amazon EC2, Amazon S3, and other AWS services by department?

1. Add department-specific tags to each resource
2. Create a separate VPC for each department
3. Create a separate AWS account for each department
4. Use AWS Organizations

Answer: 1

Explanation:

A tag is a label that you or AWS assigns to an AWS resource. Each tag consists of a *key* and a *value*. For each resource, each tag key must be unique, and each tag key can have only one value.

You can use tags to organize your resources, and cost allocation tags to track your AWS costs on a detailed level. After you activate cost allocation tags, AWS uses the cost allocation tags to organize your resource costs on your cost allocation report, to make it easier for you to categorize and track your AWS costs.

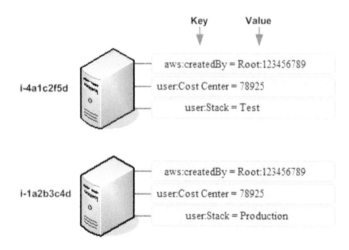

AWS provides two types of cost allocation tags, an *AWS generated tags* and *user-defined tags*. AWS defines, creates, and applies the AWS generated tags for you, and you define, create, and apply user-defined tags. You must activate both types of tags separately before they can appear in Cost Explorer or on a cost allocation report.

CORRECT: "Add department-specific tags to each resource" is the correct answer.

INCORRECT: "Create a separate VPC for each department" is incorrect. This is unnecessary and would not help with separating costs.

INCORRECT: "Create a separate AWS account for each department" is incorrect. This is overly complex and unnecessary.

INCORRECT: "Use AWS Organizations" is incorrect. Consolidated billing can separate bills by account but for department based cost separation cost allocation tags should be used.

References:

https://docs.aws.amazon.com/awsaccountbilling/latest/aboutv2/cost-alloc-tags.html

Save time with our exam-specific cheat sheets:

https://digitalcloud.training/certification-training/aws-certified-cloud-practitioner/aws-billing-and-pricing/

QUESTION 14

Which AWS Support plan provides access to architectural and operational reviews, as well as 24/7 access to Cloud Support Engineers through email, online chat, and phone?

1. Basic
2. Business
3. Developer
4. Enterprise

Answer: 4

Explanation:

Only the enterprise plan provides Well-Architected Reviews and Operational Reviews. 24/7 access to Cloud Support Engineers through email, online chat, and phone is offered on the business and enterprise plans.

CORRECT: "Enterprise" is the correct answer.

INCORRECT: "Basic" is incorrect. Basic only includes: 24x7 access to customer service, documentation, whitepapers, and support forums.

INCORRECT: "Business" is incorrect as it does not provide access to architectural and operational reviews.

INCORRECT: "Developer" is incorrect as you get support from Cloud Support Associates, not Engineers and also do not get access to architectural and operational reviews.

References:

https://aws.amazon.com/premiumsupport/plans/

Save time with our exam-specific cheat sheets:

https://digitalcloud.training/certification-training/aws-certified-cloud-practitioner/aws-billing-and-pricing/

QUESTION 15

Under the AWS shared responsibility model, which of the following is an example of security in the AWS Cloud?

1. Managing edge locations
2. Physical security
3. Firewall configuration
4. Global infrastructure

Answer: 3

Explanation:

Firewall configuration is an example of "security in the cloud". This is the customer's responsibility, not an AWS responsibility.

CORRECT: "Firewall configuration" is the correct answer.

INCORRECT: "Managing edge locations" is incorrect. This is an example of "security of the cloud" and is an AWS responsibility.

INCORRECT: "Physical security" is incorrect. This is an example of "security of the cloud" and is an AWS responsibility.

INCORRECT: "Global infrastructure" is incorrect. This is an example of "security of the cloud" and is an AWS responsibility.

References:

https://aws.amazon.com/compliance/shared-responsibility-model/

Save time with our exam-specific cheat sheets:

https://digitalcloud.training/certification-training/aws-certified-cloud-practitioner/aws-shared-responsibility-model/

QUESTION 16

Which AWS service provides on-demand downloads of AWS security and compliance reports?

1. AWS Directory Service
2. AWS Artifact
3. AWS Trusted Advisor
4. Amazon Inspector

Answer: 2

Explanation:

AWS Artifact is the go-to, central resource for compliance-related information that matters to you. It provides on-demand access to AWS' security and compliance reports and select online agreements.

Reports available in AWS Artifact include Service Organization Control (SOC) reports, Payment Card Industry (PCI) reports, and certifications from accreditation bodies across geographies and compliance verticals that validate the implementation and operating effectiveness of AWS security controls.

CORRECT: "AWS Artifact" is the correct answer.

INCORRECT: "AWS Directory Service" is incorrect. AWS Directory Service for Microsoft Active Directory, also known as AWS Managed Microsoft AD, is an AWS-managed directory service built on actual Microsoft Active Directory and powered by Windows Server 2012 R2.

INCORRECT: "AWS Trusted Advisor" is incorrect. AWS Trusted Advisor is an online tool that provides you real time guidance to help you provision your resources following AWS best practices.

INCORRECT: "Amazon Inspector" is incorrect. Amazon Inspector is an automated security assessment service that helps improve the security and compliance of applications deployed on AWS.

References:

https://aws.amazon.com/artifact/

Save time with our exam-specific cheat sheets:

https://digitalcloud.training/certification-training/aws-certified-cloud-practitioner/cloud-security/

QUESTION 17

Which Amazon EC2 pricing model is the most cost-effective for an always-up, right-sized database server running a project that will last 1 year?

1. On-Demand Instances
2. Convertible Reserved Instances
3. Spot Instances
4. Standard Reserved Instances

Answer: 4

Explanation:

Reserved Instances (RIs) provide you with a significant discount (up to 72%) compared to On-Demand instance pricing. Standard reserved instances offer the most cost savings. RIs are based on a 1 or 3 year contract so they are suitable for workloads that will run for the duration of the contract period.

CORRECT: "Standard Reserved Instances" is the correct answer.

INCORRECT: "Convertible Reserved Instances" is incorrect. You have the flexibility to change families, OS types, and tenancies while benefitting from RI pricing when you use Convertible RIs. However, this is not required for a right-sized server.

INCORRECT: "On-Demand Instances" is incorrect. This pricing model offers not discounts.

INCORRECT: "Spot Instances" is incorrect. Though you can achieve greater cost savings with Spot instances, the instances can be terminated when AWS need the capacity back.

References:

https://aws.amazon.com/ec2/pricing/reserved-instances/

Save time with our exam-specific cheat sheets:

https://digitalcloud.training/certification-training/aws-certified-cloud-practitioner/aws-billing-and-pricing/

QUESTION 18

Which feature enables fast, easy, and secure transfers of files over long distances between a client and an Amazon S3 bucket?

1. S3 Static Websites
2. S3 Copy
3. Multipart Upload
4. S3 Transfer Acceleration

Answer: 4

Explanation:

Amazon S3 Transfer Acceleration enables fast, easy, and secure transfers of files over long distances between your client and your Amazon S3 bucket. S3 Transfer Acceleration leverages Amazon CloudFront's globally distributed AWS Edge Locations.

CORRECT: "S3 Transfer Acceleration" is the correct answer.

INCORRECT: "S3 Static Websites" is incorrect. S3 can also be used to host static websites but this does not assist with the performance of uploads to S3.

INCORRECT: "S3 Copy" is incorrect. With S3 copy you can create a copy of objects up to 5GB in size in a single atomic operation.

INCORRECT: "Multipart Upload" is incorrect. Multipart upload can be used to speed up uploads to S3.

References:

https://docs.aws.amazon.com/AmazonS3/latest/dev/transfer-acceleration.html

Save time with our exam-specific cheat sheets:

https://digitalcloud.training/certification-training/aws-certified-cloud-practitioner/aws-storage/

QUESTION 19

Under the AWS shared responsibility model what is AWS responsible for? (Select TWO.)

1. Physical security of the data center
2. Replacement and disposal of disk drives
3. Configuration of security groups
4. Patch management of operating systems
5. Encryption of customer data

Answer: 1,2

Explanation:

AWS are responsible for "Security **of** the Cloud" and customers are responsible for "Security **in** the Cloud".

AWS are responsible for items such as the physical security of the DC, replacement of old disk drives, and patch management of the infrastructure.

Customers are responsible for items such as configuring security groups, network ACLs, patching their operating systems and encrypting their data

CORRECT: "Physical security of the data center" is the correct answer.

CORRECT: "Replacement and disposal of disk drives" is the correct answer.

INCORRECT: "Configuration of security groups" is incorrect as this is a customer responsibility.

INCORRECT: "Patch management of operating systems" is incorrect as this is a customer responsibility.

INCORRECT: "Encryption of customer data" is incorrect as this is a customer responsibility.

References:

https://aws.amazon.com/compliance/shared-responsibility-model/

Save time with our exam-specific cheat sheets:

https://digitalcloud.training/certification-training/aws-certified-cloud-practitioner/aws-shared-responsibility-model/

QUESTION 20

Which AWS service is known as a "serverless" service and runs code as functions triggered by events?

1. Amazon ECS
2. AWS Lambda
3. Amazon CodeDeploy
4. Amazon Cognito

Answer: 2

Explanation:

AWS Lambda lets you run code as functions without provisioning or managing servers. Lambda-based applications (also referred to as serverless applications) are composed of functions triggered by events. With serverless computing, your application still runs on servers, but all the server management is done by AWS.

CORRECT: "AWS Lambda" is the correct answer.

INCORRECT: "Amazon ECS" is incorrect. Amazon Elastic Container Service (ECS) is a highly scalable, high performance container management service that supports Docker containers and allows you to easily run applications on a managed cluster of Amazon EC2 instances.

INCORRECT: "Amazon CodeDeploy" is incorrect. AWS CodeDeploy is a fully managed deployment service that automates software deployments to a variety of compute services such as Amazon EC2, AWS Lambda, and your on-premises servers.

INCORRECT: "Amazon Cognito" is incorrect. Amazon Cognito lets you add user sign-up, sign-in, and access control to your web and mobile apps quickly and easily.

References:

https://aws.amazon.com/lambda/features/

Save time with our exam-specific cheat sheets:

https://digitalcloud.training/certification-training/aws-certified-cloud-practitioner/aws-compute/

QUESTION 21

Which statement best describes Amazon Route 53?

1. Amazon Route 53 is a service that enables routing within VPCs in an account
2. Amazon Route 53 is a highly available and scalable Domain Name System (DNS) service
3. Amazon Route 53 enables hybrid cloud models by extending an organization's on-premise networks into the AWS cloud
4. Amazon Route 53 is a service for distributing incoming connections between a fleet of registered EC2 instances

Answer: 2

Explanation:

Amazon Route 53 is a highly available and scalable cloud Domain Name System (DNS) web service. It is designed to give developers and businesses an extremely reliable and cost effective way to route end users to Internet applications by translating names like www.example.com into the numeric IP addresses like 192.0.2.1 that computers use to connect to each other. Amazon Route 53 is fully compliant with IPv6 as well.

CORRECT: "Amazon Route 53 is a highly available and scalable Domain Name System (DNS) service" is the correct answer.

INCORRECT: "Amazon Route 53 is a service that enables routing within VPCs in an account" is incorrect. The VPC router performs routing within a VPC.

INCORRECT: "Amazon Route 53 enables hybrid cloud models by extending an organization's on-premise networks into the AWS cloud" is incorrect. Direct Connect enables hybrid cloud models by extending an organization's on-premise networks into the AWS cloud.

INCORRECT: "Amazon Route 53 is a service for distributing incoming connections between a fleet of registered EC2 instances" is incorrect. Auto Scaling is a service for distributing incoming connections between a fleet of registered EC2 instances.

References:

https://aws.amazon.com/route53/

Save time with our exam-specific cheat sheets:

https://digitalcloud.training/certification-training/aws-certified-cloud-practitioner/content-delivery-and-dns-services/

QUESTION 22

Which service provides a way to convert video and audio files from their source format into versions that will playback on devices like smartphones, tablets and PCs?

1. Amazon Elastic Transcoder
2. AWS Glue
3. Amazon Rekognition
4. Amazon Comprehend

Answer: 1

Explanation:

Amazon Elastic Transcoder is a highly scalable, easy to use and cost-effective way for developers and businesses to convert (or "transcode") video and audio files from their source format into versions that will playback on devices like smartphones, tablets and PCs.

CORRECT: "Amazon Elastic Transcoder" is the correct answer.

INCORRECT: "AWS Glue" is incorrect. AWS Glue is a fully managed extract, transform, and load (ETL) service that makes it easy for customers to prepare and load their data for analytics.

INCORRECT: "Amazon Rekognition" is incorrect. Amazon Rekognition makes it easy to add image and video analysis to your applications.

INCORRECT: "Amazon Comprehend" is incorrect. Amazon Comprehend is a natural language processing (NLP) service that uses machine learning to find insights and relationships in text.

References:

https://aws.amazon.com/elastictranscoder/

Save time with our exam-specific cheat sheets:

https://digitalcloud.training/certification-training/aws-certified-cloud-practitioner/additional-aws-services-tools/

QUESTION 23

When using AWS Organizations with consolidated billing what are two valid best practices? (Select TWO.)
1. Always enable multi-factor authentication (MFA) on the root account
2. Always use a straightforward password on the root account
3. The paying account should be used for billing purposes only
4. Use the paying account for deploying resources
5. Never exceed the limit of 20 linked accounts

Answer: 1,3

Explanation:

When using AWS Organizations with consolidated billing, best practices include:

– Always enable multi-factor authentication (MFA) on the root account.

– Always use a strong and complex password on the root account.

– The Paying account should be used for billing purposes only. Do not deploy resources into the Paying account.

There is a default limit of 20 linked accounts but this can be extended and there is no reason why you should stick to a maximum of 20 accounts.

CORRECT: "Always enable multi-factor authentication (MFA) on the root account" is a correct answer.

CORRECT: "The paying account should be used for billing purposes only" is also a correct answer.

INCORRECT: "Always use a straightforward password on the root account" is incorrect as you should use a complex password.

INCORRECT: "Use the paying account for deploying resources" is incorrect as you should deploy resources in the linked accounts.

INCORRECT: "Never exceed the limit of 20 linked accounts" is incorrect as you can extend the default limit.

References:

https://aws.amazon.com/organizations/

Save time with our exam-specific cheat sheets:

https://digitalcloud.training/certification-training/aws-certified-cloud-practitioner/aws-billing-and-pricing/

QUESTION 24

Which AWS support plan comes with a Technical Account Manager (TAM)?
1. Basic
2. Developer
3. Business
4. Enterprise

Answer: 4

Explanation:

Only the Enterprise plan comes with a TAM.

	Developer	Business	Enterprise
Proactive Programs		Access to Infrastructure Event Management for additional fee.	Infrastructure Event Management Well-Architected Reviews Operations Reviews Technical Account Manager (TAM) coordinates access to programs and other AWS experts as needed.
Technical Account Management			Designated Technical Account Manager (TAM) to proactively monitor your environment and assist with optimization.

CORRECT: "Enterprise" is the correct answer.

INCORRECT: "Basic" is incorrect as this plan does not come with a TAM.

INCORRECT: "Developer" is incorrect as this plan does not come with a TAM.

INCORRECT: "Business" is incorrect as this plan does not come with a TAM.

References:

https://aws.amazon.com/premiumsupport/plans/

Save time with our exam-specific cheat sheets:

https://digitalcloud.training/certification-training/aws-certified-cloud-practitioner/aws-billing-and-pricing/

QUESTION 25

Which service provides the ability to simply upload applications and have AWS handle the deployment details of capacity provisioning, load balancing, auto-scaling, and application health monitoring?

1. Amazon EC2
2. AWS Elastic Beanstalk
3. Amazon EC2 Auto Scaling
4. AWS OpsWorks

Answer: 2

Explanation:

AWS Elastic Beanstalk can be used to quickly deploy and manage applications in the AWS Cloud. Developers upload applications and Elastic Beanstalk handles the deployment details of capacity provisioning, load balancing, auto-scaling, and application health monitoring. Considered a Platform as a Service (PaaS) solution. Supports Java, .NET, PHP, Node.js, Python, Ruby, Go, and Docker web applications.

CORRECT: "AWS Elastic Beanstalk" is the correct answer.

INCORRECT: "Amazon EC2" is incorrect. Amazon EC2 is an IaaS solution that provides unmanaged instances that you can deploy with a variety of operating systems.

INCORRECT: "Amazon EC2 Auto Scaling" is incorrect. Amazon EC2 Auto Scaling provides elasticity for your applications by automatically launching or terminating EC2 instances according to application load or schedules you define.

INCORRECT: "AWS OpsWorks" is incorrect. AWS OpsWorks provides a managed service for Chef and Puppet. This service is involved with automation and configuration management.

References:

https://aws.amazon.com/elasticbeanstalk/

Save time with our exam-specific cheat sheets:

https://digitalcloud.training/certification-training/aws-certified-cloud-practitioner/additional-aws-services-tools/

QUESTION 26

You are concerned that you may be getting close to some of the default service limits for several AWS services. What AWS tool can be used to display current usage and limits?

1. AWS CloudWatch
2. AWS Personal Health Dashboard
3. AWS Trusted Advisor
4. AWS Systems Manager

Answer: 3

Explanation:

Trusted Advisor is an online resource to help you reduce cost, increase performance, and improve security by optimizing your AWS environment. Trusted Advisor provides real time guidance to help you provision your resources following AWS best practices. Offers a Service Limits check (in the Performance category) that displays your usage and limits for some aspects of some services.

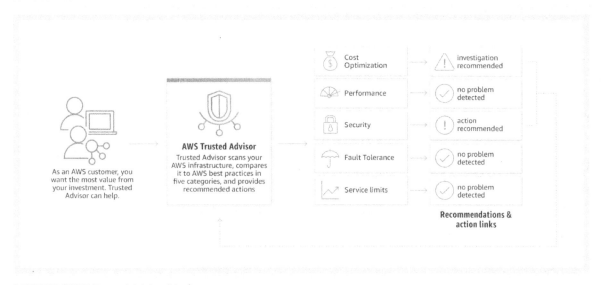

CORRECT: "AWS Trusted Advisor" is the correct answer.

INCORRECT: "AWS CloudWatch" is incorrect. Amazon CloudWatch is a monitoring and management service built for developers, system operators, site reliability engineers (SRE), and IT managers.

INCORRECT: "AWS Personal Health Dashboard" is incorrect. AWS Personal Health Dashboard provides alerts and remediation guidance when AWS is experiencing events that may impact you.

INCORRECT: "AWS Systems Manager" is incorrect. AWS Systems Manager gives you visibility and control of your infrastructure on AWS.

References:

https://docs.aws.amazon.com/general/latest/gr/aws_service_limits.html

Save time with our exam-specific cheat sheets:

https://digitalcloud.training/certification-training/aws-certified-cloud-practitioner/additional-aws-services-tools/

QUESTION 27

You need to run a production process that will use several EC2 instances and run constantly on an ongoing basis. The process cannot be interrupted or restarted without issue. What EC2 pricing model would be best for this workload?

1. Reserved instances
2. Spot instances
3. On-demand instances
4. Flexible instances

Answer: 1

Explanation:

Reserved Instance (RIs) provide you with a significant discount (up to 75%) compared to On-Demand instance pricing. You have the flexibility to change families, OS types, and tenancies while benefitting from RI pricing when you use Convertible RIs.

In this scenario for a stable process that will run constantly on an ongoing basis RIs will be the most affordable solution.

CORRECT: "Reserved instances" is the correct answer.

INCORRECT: "Spot instances" is incorrect as the instance cannot be terminated.

INCORRECT: "On-demand instances" is incorrect as this would not be the most cost-effective option.

INCORRECT: "Flexible instances" is incorrect as there's no such thing.

References:

https://aws.amazon.com/ec2/pricing/reserved-instances/

Save time with our exam-specific cheat sheets:

https://digitalcloud.training/certification-training/aws-certified-cloud-practitioner/aws-billing-and-pricing/

QUESTION 28

Which AWS service does API Gateway integrate with to enable users from around the world to achieve the lowest possible latency for API requests and responses?

1. AWS Direct Connect
2. Amazon S3 Transfer Acceleration
3. Amazon CloudFront
4. AWS Lambda

Answer: 3

Explanation:

Amazon CloudFront is used as the public endpoint for API Gateway. Provides reduced latency and distributed denial of service protection through the use of CloudFront.

CORRECT: "Amazon CloudFront" is the correct answer.

INCORRECT: "AWS Direct Connect" is incorrect. AWS Direct Connect is a cloud service solution that makes it easy to establish a dedicated network connection from your premises to AWS.

INCORRECT: "Amazon S3 Transfer Acceleration" is incorrect. Amazon S3 Transfer Acceleration is a bucket-level feature that enables faster data transfers to and from Amazon S3.

INCORRECT: "AWS Lambda" is incorrect. AWS Lambda lets you run code without provisioning or managing servers.

References:

https://aws.amazon.com/cloudfront/

Save time with our exam-specific cheat sheets:

https://digitalcloud.training/certification-training/aws-certified-cloud-practitioner/additional-aws-services-tools/

QUESTION 29

Which service can an organization use to track API activity within their account?

1. AWS CloudTrail
2. Amazon CloudWatch
3. AWS IAM
4. AWS CloudHSM

Answer: 1

Explanation:

AWS CloudTrail is a web service that records activity made on your account and delivers log files to an Amazon S3 bucket. CloudTrail is for auditing (CloudWatch is for performance monitoring).

CloudTrail is about logging and saves a history of API calls for your AWS account. Provides visibility into user activity by recording actions taken on your account. API history enables security analysis, resource change tracking, and compliance auditing

CORRECT: "AWS CloudTrail" is the correct answer.

INCORRECT: "Amazon CloudWatch" is incorrect. Amazon CloudWatch is a monitoring service for AWS cloud resources and the applications you run on AWS. CloudWatch is for performance monitoring (CloudTrail is for auditing). Used to collect and track metrics, collect and monitor log files, and set alarms.

INCORRECT: "AWS IAM" is incorrect. AWS Identity and Access Management is an identity service that provide authentication and authorization services

INCORRECT: "AWS CloudHSM" is incorrect. AWS CloudHSM is a cloud-based hardware security module (HSM) that enables you to easily generate and use your own encryption keys on the AWS Cloud.

References:

https://aws.amazon.com/cloudtrail/

Save time with our exam-specific cheat sheets:

https://digitalcloud.training/certification-training/aws-certified-cloud-practitioner/monitoring-and-logging-services/

QUESTION 30

What tool provides real time guidance to help you provision your resources following best practices in the areas of cost optimization, performance, security and fault tolerance?

1. AWS Inspector
2. AWS Trusted Advisor
3. AWS Personal Health Dashboard
4. AWS IAM

Answer: 2

Explanation:

Trusted Advisor is an online resource that helps to reduce cost, increase performance and improve security by optimizing your AWS environment. Trusted Advisor provides real time guidance to help you provision your resources following best practices. Advisor will advise you on Cost Optimization, Performance, Security, and Fault Tolerance

CORRECT: "AWS Trusted Advisor" is the correct answer.

INCORRECT: "AWS Inspector" is incorrect. Inspector is an automated security assessment service that helps improve the security and compliance of applications deployed on AWS.

INCORRECT: "AWS Personal Health Dashboard" is incorrect. AWS Personal Health Dashboard provides alerts and remediation guidance when AWS is experiencing events that may impact you.

INCORRECT: "AWS IAM" is incorrect. AWS Identity and Access Management is an identity service that provide authentication and authorization services.

References:

https://aws.amazon.com/premiumsupport/technology/trusted-advisor/

Save time with our exam-specific cheat sheets:

https://digitalcloud.training/certification-training/aws-certified-cloud-practitioner/cloud-security/

QUESTION 31

What is the best way for an organization to transfer hundreds of terabytes of data from their on-premise data center into Amazon S3 with limited bandwidth available?

1. Use S3 Transfer Acceleration
2. Apply compression before uploading
3. Use AWS Snowball
4. Use Amazon CloudFront

Answer: 3

Explanation:

Snowball is a petabyte-scale data transport solution that uses devices designed to be secure to transfer large amounts of data into and out of the AWS Cloud. Using Snowball addresses common challenges with large-scale data transfers including high network costs, long transfer times, and security concerns

CORRECT: "Use AWS Snowball" is the correct answer.

INCORRECT: "Use S3 Transfer Acceleration" is incorrect. Amazon S3 Transfer Acceleration enables fast, easy, and secure transfers of files over long distances between your client and an S3 bucket. Transfer Acceleration takes advantage of Amazon CloudFront's globally distributed edge locations. However, for these volumes of data Snowball is a better choice.

INCORRECT: "Apply compression before uploading" is incorrect as for this volume of data Snowball should be used.

INCORRECT: "Use Amazon CloudFront" is incorrect as this cannot be used for uploading large quantities of data to Amazon S3.

References:

https://aws.amazon.com/snowball/

Save time with our exam-specific cheat sheets:

https://digitalcloud.training/certification-training/aws-certified-cloud-practitioner/aws-storage/

QUESTION 32

Which database allows you to scale at the push of a button without incurring any downtime?

1. Amazon RDS
2. Amazon EMR
3. Amazon DynamoDB
4. Amazon RedShift

Answer: 3

Explanation:

Amazon Dynamo DB is a fully managed NoSQL database service that provides fast and predictable performance with seamless scalability. Push button scaling means that you can scale the DB at any time without incurring downtime.

All other databases are based on EC2 instances and therefore you must increase the instance size to scale which will incur downtime.

CORRECT: "Amazon DynamoDB" is the correct answer.

INCORRECT: "Amazon RDS" is incorrect as explained above.

INCORRECT: "Amazon EMR" is incorrect as explained above.

INCORRECT: "Amazon RedShift" is incorrect as explained above.

References:

https://aws.amazon.com/dynamodb/

Save time with our exam-specific cheat sheets:

https://digitalcloud.training/certification-training/aws-certified-cloud-practitioner/aws-databases/

QUESTION 33

What are the charges for using Amazon Glacier? (Select TWO.)

1. Data transferred into Glacier
2. Retrieval requests
3. Data storage
4. Enhanced networking
5. Number of Availability Zones

Answer: 2,3

Explanation:

With Amazon Glacier you pay for storage on a per GB / month basis, retrieval requests and quantity (based on expedited, standard, or bulk), and data transfer out of Glacier.

	S3 Standard	S3 Intelligent-Tiering*	S3 Standard-IA	S3 One Zone-IA†	S3 Glacier	S3 Glacier Deep Archive
Designed for durability	99.999999999% (11 9's)	99.999999999% (11 9's)	99.999999999% (11 9's)	99.999999999% (11 9's)	99.999999999% (11 9's)	99.999999999% (11 9's)
Designed for availability	99.99%	99.9%	99.9%	99.5%	99.99%	99.99%
Availability SLA	99.9%	99%	99%	99%	99.9%	99.9%
Availability Zones	≥3	≥3	≥3	1	≥3	≥3
Minimum capacity charge per object	N/A	N/A	128KB	128KB	40KB	40KB
Minimum storage duration charge	N/A	30 days	30 days	30 days	90 days	180 days
Retrieval fee	N/A	N/A	per GB retrieved	per GB retrieved	per GB retrieved	per GB retrieved
First byte latency	milliseconds	milliseconds	milliseconds	milliseconds	select minutes or hours	select hours
Storage type	Object	Object	Object	Object	Object	Object
Lifecycle transitions	Yes	Yes	Yes	Yes	Yes	Yes

CORRECT: "Retrieval requests" is the correct answer.

CORRECT: "Data storage" is the correct answer.

INCORRECT: "Data transferred into Glacier" is incorrect. You do not pay for data transferred in and there are no minimum storage fees.

INCORRECT: "Enhanced networking" is incorrect. Enhanced networking is a feature of EC2.

INCORRECT: "Number of Availability Zones" is incorrect. You do not pay for the number of AZs.

References:

https://aws.amazon.com/s3/storage-classes/

https://aws.amazon.com/glacier/pricing/

Save time with our exam-specific cheat sheets:

https://digitalcloud.training/certification-training/aws-certified-cloud-practitioner/aws-billing-and-pricing/

QUESTION 34

Which of the following statements are correct about the benefits of AWS Direct Connect? (Select TWO.)
1. Quick to implement
2. Increased reliability (predictable performance)
3. Lower cost than a VPN
4. Increased bandwidth (predictable bandwidth)
5. Uses redundant paths across the Internet

Answer: 2,4

Explanation:

AWS Direct Connect is a network service that provides an alternative to using the Internet to connect customers' on premise sites to AWS.

Data is transmitted through a private network connection between AWS and a customer's data center or corporate network.

Benefits of AWS Direct Connect:

– Reduce cost when using large volumes of traffic.

– Increase reliability (predictable performance).

– Increase bandwidth (predictable bandwidth).

– Decrease latency.

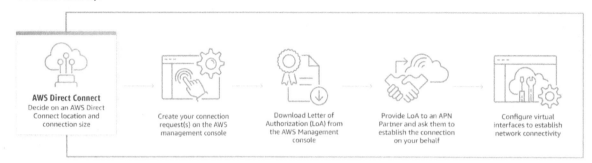

AWS Direct Connect
Decide on an AWS Direct Connect location and connection size

Create your connection request(s) on the AWS management console

Download Letter of Authorization (LoA) from the AWS Management console

Provide LoA to an APN Partner and ask them to establish the connection on your behalf

Configure virtual interfaces to establish network connectivity

CORRECT: "Increased reliability (predictable performance)" is a correct answer.

CORRECT: "Increased bandwidth (predictable bandwidth)" is also a correct answer.

INCORRECT: "Quick to implement" is incorrect. Direct Connect is not fast to implement as it can take weeks to months to setup (use VPN for fast deployment times).

INCORRECT: "Lower cost than a VPN" is incorrect. Direct Connect is more expensive than VPN.

INCORRECT: "Uses redundant paths across the Internet" is incorrect. Direct Connect uses private network connections, it does not use redundant paths over the Internet.

References:

https://aws.amazon.com/directconnect/

Save time with our exam-specific cheat sheets:

https://digitalcloud.training/certification-training/aws-certified-cloud-practitioner/aws-networking/

QUESTION 35

Which AWS service lets you use Chef and Puppet to automate how servers are configured, deployed, and managed across your Amazon EC2 instances or on-premises compute environments?

1. AWS Elastic Beanstalk
2. AWS CloudFormation
3. AWS Systems Manager
4. AWS OpsWorks

Answer: 4

Explanation:

AWS OpsWorks is a configuration management service that provides managed instances of Chef and Puppet. OpsWorks lets you use Chef and Puppet to automate how servers are configured, deployed, and managed across your Amazon EC2 instances or on-premises compute environments.

CORRECT: "AWS OpsWorks" is the correct answer.

INCORRECT: "AWS Elastic Beanstalk" is incorrect. This service does not use Chef or Puppet.

INCORRECT: "AWS CloudFormation" is incorrect. This service does not use Chef or Puppet.

INCORRECT: "AWS Systems Manager" is incorrect. This service does not use Chef or Puppet.

References:

https://aws.amazon.com/opsworks/

Save time with our exam-specific cheat sheets:

https://digitalcloud.training/certification-training/aws-certified-cloud-practitioner/additional-aws-services-tools/

QUESTION 36

Which AWS database service provides a fully managed data warehouse that can be analyzed using SQL tools and business intelligence tools?

1. Amazon RDS
2. Amazon DynamoDB
3. Amazon RedShift
4. Amazon ElastiCache

Answer: 3

Explanation:

Amazon RedShift is a fully managed data warehouse service designed to handle petabytes of data for analysis. Data can be analyzed with standard SQL tools and business intelligence tools. RedShift allows you to run complex analytic queries against petabytes of structured data.

CORRECT: "Amazon RedShift" is the correct answer.

INCORRECT: "Amazon RDS" is incorrect. RDS is Amazon's transactional relational database.

INCORRECT: "Amazon DynamoDB" is incorrect. DynamoDB is Amazon's non-relational database service.

INCORRECT: "Amazon ElastiCache" is incorrect. ElastiCache is a data caching service that is used to help improve the speed/performance of web applications running on AWS.

References:

https://aws.amazon.com/redshift/

Save time with our exam-specific cheat sheets:

https://digitalcloud.training/certification-training/aws-certified-cloud-practitioner/aws-databases/

QUESTION 37

Which service can be used to create sophisticated, interactive graph applications?

1. Amazon RedShift
2. Amazon Neptune
3. AWS X-Ray
4. Amazon Athena

Answer: 2

Explanation:

Amazon Neptune is a fast, reliable, fully-managed graph database service that makes it easy to build and run applications that work with highly connected datasets. With Amazon Neptune, you can create sophisticated, interactive graph applications that can query billions of relationships in milliseconds.

CORRECT: "Amazon Neptune" is the correct answer.

INCORRECT: "Amazon RedShift" is incorrect. Amazon Redshift is a fast, scalable data warehouse that makes it simple and cost-effective to analyze all your data across your data warehouse and data lake.

INCORRECT: "AWS X-Ray" is incorrect. AWS X-Ray helps developers analyze and debug production, distributed applications, such as those built using a microservices architecture.

INCORRECT: "Amazon Athena" is incorrect. Amazon Athena is an interactive query service that makes it easy to analyze data in Amazon S3 using standard SQL.

References:

https://aws.amazon.com/neptune/

Save time with our exam-specific cheat sheets:

https://digitalcloud.training/certification-training/aws-certified-cloud-practitioner/additional-aws-services-tools/

QUESTION 38

When using Amazon IAM, what authentication methods are available to use? (Select TWO.)

1. Client certificates
2. Access keys
3. AWS KMS
4. Server certificates
5. AES 256

Answer: 2,4

Explanation:

Supported authentication methods include console passwords, access keys and server certificates.

Access keys are a combination of an access key ID and a secret access key and can be used to make programmatic calls to AWS.

Server certificates are SSL/TLS certificates that you can use to authenticate with some AWS services.

CORRECT: "Access keys" is a correct answer.

CORRECT: "Server certificates" is also a correct answer.

INCORRECT: "Client certificates" is incorrect. Client certificates are not a valid IAM authentication method.

INCORRECT: "AWS KMS" is incorrect. AWS Key Management Service (KMS) is used for managing encryption keys and is not used for authentication..

INCORRECT: "AES 256" is incorrect. AES 256 is an encryption algorithm, not an authentication method.

References:

https://docs.aws.amazon.com/IAM/latest/UserGuide/introduction.html

Save time with our exam-specific cheat sheets:

https://digitalcloud.training/certification-training/aws-certified-cloud-practitioner/identity-and-access-management/

QUESTION 39

How does the consolidated billing feature of AWS Organizations treat Reserved Instances that were purchased by another account in the organization?

1. All accounts in the organization are treated as one account so any account can receive the hourly cost benefit
2. Only the master account can benefit from the hourly cost benefit of the reserved instances
3. All accounts in the organization are treated as one account for volume discounts but not for reserved instances
4. AWS Organizations does not support any volume or reserved instance benefits across accounts, it is just a method of aggregating bills

Answer: 1

Explanation:

For billing purposes, the consolidated billing feature of AWS Organizations treats all the accounts in the organization as one account. This means that all accounts in the organization can receive the hourly cost benefit of Reserved Instances that are purchased by any other account.

CORRECT: "All accounts in the organization are treated as one account so any account can receive the hourly cost benefit" is the correct answer.

INCORRECT: "Only the master account can benefit from the hourly cost benefit of the reserved instances" is incorrect as explained above.

INCORRECT: "All accounts in the organization are treated as one account for volume discounts but not for reserved instances" is incorrect as explained above..

INCORRECT: "AWS Organizations does not support any volume or reserved instance benefits across accounts, it is just a method of aggregating bills" is incorrect as explained above.

References:

https://aws.amazon.com/organizations/

QUESTION 40

Which of the below AWS services supports automated backups as a default configuration?

1. Amazon S3
2. Amazon RDS
3. Amazon EC2
4. Amazon EBS

Answer: 2

Explanation:

Amazon RDS automated backups allow point in time recovery to any point within the retention period down to a second. When automated backups are turned on for your DB Instance, Amazon RDS automatically performs a full daily snapshot of your data (during your preferred backup window) and captures transaction logs (as updates to your DB Instance are made). Automated backups are enabled by default and data is stored on S3 and is equal to the size of the DB

CORRECT: "Amazon RDS" is the correct answer.

INCORRECT: "Amazon S3" is incorrect. Amazon S3 objects are replicated across multiple facilities. You can also archive data onto Amazon Glacier and use versioning to maintain copies of older versions of objects

INCORRECT: "Amazon EC2" is incorrect. EC2 instances using EBS volumes can be backed up by creating a snapshot of the EBS volume.

INCORRECT: "Amazon EBS" is incorrect. EC2 instances using EBS volumes can be backed up by creating a snapshot of the EBS volume.

References:

https://docs.aws.amazon.com/AmazonRDS/latest/UserGuide/USER_WorkingWithAutomatedBackups.html

QUESTION 41

What are the advantages of Availability Zones? (Select TWO.)

1. They allow regional disaster recovery
2. They provide fault isolation
3. They enable the caching of data for faster delivery to end users
4. They are connected by low-latency network connections
5. They enable you to connect your on-premises networks to AWS to form a hybrid cloud

Answer: 2,4

Explanation:

Each AWS region contains multiple distinct locations called Availability Zones (AZs). Each AZ is engineered to be isolated from failures in other AZs. An AZ is a data center, and in some cases, an AZ consists of multiple data centers.

AZs within a region provide inexpensive, low-latency network connectivity to other zones in the same region. This allows you to replicate your data across data centers in a synchronous manner so that failover can be automated and be transparent for your users.

CORRECT: "They provide fault isolation" is a correct answer.

CORRECT: "They are connected by low-latency network connections" is also a correct answer.

INCORRECT: "They allow regional disaster recovery" is incorrect. An AZ enables fault tolerance and high availability for your applications within a region not across regions.

INCORRECT: "They enable the caching of data for faster delivery to end users" is incorrect. CloudFront is the technology that is used to enable caching of data for faster delivery to end users.

INCORRECT: "They enable you to connect your on-premises networks to AWS to form a hybrid cloud" is incorrect. Direct Connect is the technology that is used to connect your on-premises network to AWS to form a hybrid cloud.

References:

https://aws.amazon.com/about-aws/global-infrastructure/

Save time with our exam-specific cheat sheets:

https://digitalcloud.training/certification-training/aws-certified-cloud-practitioner/architecting-for-the-cloud/

QUESTION 42

Which of the options below are recommendations in the cost optimization pillar of the well-architected framework? (Select TWO.)

1. Adopt a consumption model
2. Adopt a capital expenditure model
3. Start spending money on data center operations
4. Analyze and attribute expenditure
5. Manage your services independently

Answer: 1,4

Explanation:

The cost optimization pillar includes the ability to avoid or eliminate unneeded cost or suboptimal resource.

There are five design principles for cost optimization in the cloud:

– Adopt a consumption model.

– Measure overall efficiency.

– Stop spending money on data center operations.

– Analyze and attribute expenditure.

– Use managed services to reduce cost of ownership.

CORRECT: "Adopt a consumption model" is the correct answer.

CORRECT: "Analyze and attribute expenditure" is the correct answer.

INCORRECT: "Adopt a capital expenditure model" is incorrect. Please refer to the design principles above.

INCORRECT: "Start spending money on data center operations" is incorrect. Please refer to the design principles above.

INCORRECT: "Manage your services independently" is incorrect. Please refer to the design principles above.

References:

https://aws.amazon.com/blogs/apn/the-5-pillars-of-the-aws-well-architected-framework/

Save time with our exam-specific cheat sheets:

https://digitalcloud.training/certification-training/aws-certified-cloud-practitioner/architecting-for-the-cloud/

QUESTION 43

What are Edge locations used for?

1. They are used for terminating VPN connections
2. They are used by CloudFront for caching content
3. They are the public-facing APIs for Amazon S3
4. They are used by regions for inter-region connectivity

Answer: 2

Explanation:

An edge location is used by CloudFront and is the location where content is cached (separate to AWS regions/AZs). Requests are automatically routed to the nearest edge location. Edge locations are not tied to Availability Zones or regions

CORRECT: "They are used by CloudFront for caching content" is the correct answer.

INCORRECT: "They are used for terminating VPN connections" is incorrect. They have nothing to do with VPN connections.

INCORRECT: "They are the public-facing APIs for Amazon S3" is incorrect. Amazon S3 does not run from Edge Locations.

INCORRECT: "They are used by regions for inter-region connectivity" is incorrect. They are not used for connectivity between regions.

References:

https://wa.aws.amazon.com/wat.concept.edge-location.en.html

Save time with our exam-specific cheat sheets:

https://digitalcloud.training/certification-training/aws-certified-cloud-practitioner/content-delivery-and-dns-services/

QUESTION 44

To ensure the security of your AWS account, what are two AWS best practices for managing access keys? (Select TWO.)

1. Don't create any access keys, use IAM roles instead
2. Don't generate an access key for the root account user
3. Where possible, use IAM roles with temporary security credentials
4. Rotate access keys daily
5. Use MFA for access keys

Answer: 2,3

Explanation:

Best practices include:

– Don't generate an access key for the root account user.

– Use Temporary Security Credentials (IAM Roles) Instead of Long-Term Access Keys.

– Manage IAM User Access Keys Properly.

CORRECT: "Don't generate an access key for the root account user" is a correct answer.

CORRECT: "Where possible, use IAM roles with temporary security credentials" is also a correct answer.

INCORRECT: "Don't create any access keys, use IAM roles instead" is incorrect. You should use IAM roles where possible, but AWS do not recommend that you don't create any access keys as they also have a purpose

INCORRECT: "Rotate access keys daily" is incorrect. Rotating access keys is a recommended practice, but doing it daily would be excessive and hard to manage.

INCORRECT: "Use MFA for access keys" is incorrect. You can use MFA for securing accounts, but it does not secure access keys

References:

https://docs.aws.amazon.com/general/latest/gr/aws-access-keys-best-practices.html

Save time with our exam-specific cheat sheets:

https://digitalcloud.training/certification-training/aws-certified-cloud-practitioner/identity-and-access-management/

QUESTION 45

An Amazon EC2 instance running the Amazon Linux 2 AMI is billed in what increment?

1. Per second
2. Per hour
3. Per CPU
4. Per GB

Answer: 1

Explanation:

Amazon EC2 instances running Linux are billed in one second increments, with a minimum of 60 seconds.

CORRECT: "Per second" is the correct answer.

INCORRECT: "Per hour" is incorrect. You do not pay per hour.

INCORRECT: "Per CPU" is incorrect. You do not pay per CPU.

INCORRECT: "Per GB" is incorrect. You pay for Amazon EBS on a per GB of provisioned storage basis.

References:

https://aws.amazon.com/about-aws/whats-new/2017/10/announcing-amazon-ec2-per-second-billing/

https://d1.awsstatic.com/whitepapers/aws_pricing_overview.pdf

Save time with our exam-specific cheat sheets:

https://digitalcloud.training/certification-training/aws-certified-cloud-practitioner/aws-billing-and-pricing/

QUESTION 46

To gain greater discounts, which services can be reserved? (Select TWO.)

1. Amazon RedShift
2. Amazon S3
3. AWS Lambda
4. Amazon DynamoDB
5. Amazon CloudWatch

Answer: 1,4

Explanation:

Reservations provide you with greater discounts, up to 75%, by paying for capacity ahead of time. Some of the services you can reserve include: EC2, DynamoDB, ElastiCache, RDS, and RedShift.

CORRECT: "Amazon RedShift" is a correct answer.

CORRECT: "Amazon DynamoDB" is also a correct answer.

INCORRECT: "Amazon S3" is incorrect. You cannot reserve Amazon S3, you pay for what you use.

INCORRECT: "AWS Lambda" is incorrect. AWS Lambda is a service that provides functions and cannot be reserved.

INCORRECT: "Amazon CloudWatch" is incorrect. You cannot reserve Amazon CloudWatch which is a monitoring service.

References:

https://d1.awsstatic.com/whitepapers/aws_pricing_overview.pdf

Save time with our exam-specific cheat sheets:

https://digitalcloud.training/certification-training/aws-certified-cloud-practitioner/aws-billing-and-pricing/

QUESTION 47

Which service allows an organization to view operational data from multiple AWS services through a unified user interface and automate operational tasks?

1. AWS Config
2. AWS OpsWorks
3. AWS Systems Manager
4. Amazon CloudWatch

Answer: 3

Explanation:

AWS Systems Manager gives you visibility and control of your infrastructure on AWS. Systems Manager provides a unified user interface so you can view operational data from multiple AWS services and allows you to automate operational tasks across your AWS resources.

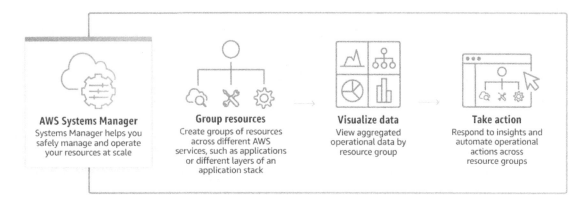

CORRECT: "AWS Systems Manager" is the correct answer.

INCORRECT: "AWS Config" is incorrect. AWS Config is a fully-managed service that provides you with an AWS resource inventory, configuration history, and configuration change notifications to enable security and regulatory compliance.

INCORRECT: "AWS OpsWorks" is incorrect. AWS OpsWorks is a configuration management service that provides managed instances of Chef and Puppet.

INCORRECT: "Amazon CloudWatch" is incorrect. Amazon CloudWatch is a monitoring service for AWS cloud resources and the applications you run on AWS. You use CloudWatch for performance monitoring, not automating operational tasks.

References:

https://aws.amazon.com/systems-manager/

Save time with our exam-specific cheat sheets:

https://digitalcloud.training/certification-training/aws-certified-cloud-practitioner/additional-aws-services-tools/

QUESTION 48

How can an organization track resource inventory and configuration history for the purpose of security and regulatory compliance?

1. Configure AWS Config with the resource types
2. Create an Amazon CloudTrail trail
3. Implement Amazon GuardDuty
4. Run a report with AWS Artifact

Answer: 1

Explanation:

AWS Config is a fully-managed service that provides you with an AWS resource inventory, configuration history, and configuration change notifications to enable security and regulatory compliance.

CORRECT: "Configure AWS Config with the resource types" is the correct answer.

INCORRECT: "Create an Amazon CloudTrail trail" is incorrect. CloudTrail tracks API activity. This means it is used to monitor who does what on Amazon. It does not provide a resource inventory or configuration history.

INCORRECT: "Implement Amazon GuardDuty" is incorrect. Amazon GuardDuty offers threat detection and continuous security monitoring for malicious or unauthorized behavior to help you protect your AWS accounts and workloads.

INCORRECT: "Run a report with AWS Artifact" is incorrect. AWS Artifact is used for obtaining on-demand security and compliance reports and select online agreements. This service provides access to AWS security and compliance reports such as SOC and PCI. You don't use Artifact to track your own resource inventory and configuration history.

References:

https://docs.aws.amazon.com/config/latest/developerguide/gs-console.html

Save time with our exam-specific cheat sheets:

https://digitalcloud.training/certification-training/aws-certified-cloud-practitioner/cloud-security/

QUESTION 49

A security operations engineer needs to implement threat detection and monitoring for malicious or unauthorized behavior. Which service should be used?

1. AWS Shield
2. AWS KMS
3. AWS CloudHSM
4. AWS GuardDuty

Answer: 4

Explanation:

Amazon GuardDuty offers threat detection and continuous security monitoring for malicious or unauthorized behavior to help you protect your AWS accounts and workloads.

CORRECT: "AWS GuardDuty" is the correct answer.

INCORRECT: "AWS Shield" is incorrect. AWS Shield is a managed Distributed Denial of Service (DDoS) protection service.

INCORRECT: "AWS KMS" is incorrect. AWS Key Management Service gives you centralized control over the encryption keys used to protect your data.

INCORRECT: "AWS CloudHSM" is incorrect. AWS CloudHSM is a cloud-based hardware security module (HSM) that enables you to easily generate and use your own encryption keys on the AWS Cloud.

References:

https://aws.amazon.com/guardduty/

Save time with our exam-specific cheat sheets:

https://digitalcloud.training/certification-training/aws-certified-cloud-practitioner/cloud-security/

QUESTION 50

Which authentication method is used to authenticate programmatic calls to AWS services?

1. Console password
2. Server certificate
3. Key pair
4. Access keys

Answer: 4

Explanation:

Access keys are a combination of an access key ID and a secret access key. They are used to make programmatic calls to AWS using the API.

CORRECT: "Access keys" is the correct answer.

INCORRECT: "Console password" is incorrect. Console passwords are used for signing users into the AWS Management Console, not for making programmatic calls to AWS services.

INCORRECT: "Server certificate" is incorrect. Server certificates can be used to authenticate to some AWS services using HTTPS.

INCORRECT: "Key pair" is incorrect. Key pairs should not be confused with access keys. Key pairs are used for authenticating to Amazon EC2 instances.

References:

https://docs.aws.amazon.com/IAM/latest/UserGuide/id_credentials_access-keys.html

Save time with our exam-specific cheat sheets:

https://digitalcloud.training/certification-training/aws-certified-cloud-practitioner/identity-and-access-management/

QUESTION 51

What is a benefit of moving an on-premises database to Amazon Relational Database Service (RDS)?

1. There is no need to manage operating systems
2. You can scale vertically without downtime
3. There is no database administration required
4. You can run any database engine

Answer: 1

Explanation:

With Amazon RDS, which is a managed service, you do not need to manage operating systems. This reduces operational costs.

CORRECT: "There is no need to manage operating systems" is the correct answer.

INCORRECT: "You can scale vertically without downtime" is incorrect. You cannot scale vertically without downtime. When scaling with RDS you must change the instance type, and this requires a short period of downtime while the instances' operating system reboots.

INCORRECT: "There is no database administration required" is incorrect. There is still database administration required in the cloud. You don't manage the underlying operating system but still need to manage your own tables and data within the DB.

INCORRECT: "You can run any database engine" is incorrect. You cannot run any database engine with RDS. The options are MySQL, Microsoft SQL, MariaDB, Oracle, PostgreSQL and Aurora.

References:

https://aws.amazon.com/rds/features/

Save time with our exam-specific cheat sheets:

https://digitalcloud.training/certification-training/aws-certified-cloud-practitioner/aws-databases/

QUESTION 52

What are the benefits of using Amazon Rekognition with image files?

1. Can be used to resize images
2. Can be used to identify objects in an image
3. Can be used to transcode audio
4. Can help with image compression

Answer: 2

Explanation:

Rekognition Image is a deep learning powered image recognition service that detects objects, scenes, and faces; extracts text; recognizes celebrities; and identifies inappropriate content in images. It also allows you to search and compare faces.

CORRECT: "Can be used to identify objects in an image" is the correct answer.

INCORRECT: "Can be used to resize images" is incorrect. You cannot use Rekognition to resize images.

INCORRECT: "Can be used to transcode audio" is incorrect. You should use the Elastic Transcoder service to transcode audio.

INCORRECT: "Can help with image compression" is incorrect. You cannot use Rekognition to compress images.

References:

https://aws.amazon.com/rekognition/image-features/

Save time with our exam-specific cheat sheets:

https://digitalcloud.training/certification-training/aws-certified-cloud-practitioner/additional-aws-services-tools/

QUESTION 53

Which IAM entity is associated with an access key ID and secret access key?

1. IAM Group
2. IAM Role
3. IAM Policy
4. IAM User

Answer: 4

Explanation:

An access key ID and secret access key are used to sign programmatic requests to AWS. They are associated with an IAM user.

You cannot associate an access key ID and secret access key with an IAM Group, Role or Policy.

CORRECT: "IAM User" is the correct answer.

INCORRECT: "IAM Group" is incorrect as explained above.

INCORRECT: "IAM Role" is incorrect as explained above.

INCORRECT: "IAM Policy" is incorrect as explained above.

References:

https://docs.aws.amazon.com/general/latest/gr/aws-sec-cred-types.html#access-keys-and-secret-access-keys

Save time with our exam-specific cheat sheets:

https://digitalcloud.training/certification-training/aws-certified-cloud-practitioner/identity-and-access-management/

QUESTION 54

Which IAM entity can be used for assigning permissions to multiple users?

1. IAM User
2. IAM Group
3. IAM Role
4. IAM password policy

Answer: 2

Explanation:

Groups are collections of users and have policies attached to them. You can use groups to assign permissions to multiple users. To do this place the users in the group and then create an IAM policy with the correct permissions and attach it to the group.

You do not use an IAM User, Role, or password policy to assign permissions to multiple users.

CORRECT: "IAM Group" is the correct answer.

INCORRECT: "IAM User" is incorrect as explained above.

INCORRECT: "IAM Role" is incorrect as explained above.

INCORRECT: "IAM password policy" is incorrect as explained above.

References:

https://docs.aws.amazon.com/IAM/latest/UserGuide/id_groups.html

Save time with our exam-specific cheat sheets:

https://digitalcloud.training/certification-training/aws-certified-cloud-practitioner/identity-and-access-management/

QUESTION 55

Which service can be used to cost-effectively move exabytes of data into AWS?

1. AWS Snowmobile
2. AWS Snowball
3. S3 Transfer Acceleration
4. S3 Cross-Region Replication (CRR)

Answer: 1

Explanation:

With AWS Snowmobile you can move 100PB per snowmobile. AWS call this an "Exabyte-scale data transfer service".

CORRECT: "AWS Snowmobile" is the correct answer.

INCORRECT: "AWS Snowball" is incorrect. With AWS Snowball you can move up to 80TB per device. AWS call this a "petabyte-scale data transfer service".

INCORRECT: "S3 Transfer Acceleration" is incorrect. S3 Transfer Acceleration is meant speed up uploads to Amazon S3 but would not be used for exabytes of data.

INCORRECT: "S3 Cross-Region Replication (CRR)" is incorrect. S3 Cross-Region Replication is used for copying data between regions, not into AWS. It is also unsuitable for moving such as huge amount of data.

References:

https://aws.amazon.com/snowmobile/

Save time with our exam-specific cheat sheets:

https://digitalcloud.training/certification-training/aws-certified-cloud-practitioner/aws-storage/

QUESTION 56

Which AWS services are associated with Edge Locations? (Select TWO.)

1. Amazon CloudFront
2. AWS Direct Connect
3. AWS Shield
4. Amazon EBS
5. AWS Config

Answer: 1,3

Explanation:

Edge Locations are parts of the Amazon CloudFront content delivery network (CDN) that are all around the world and are used to get content closer to end-users for better performance.

AWS Shield which protects against Distributed Denial of Service (DDoS) attacks is available globally on Amazon CloudFront Edge Locations.

CORRECT: "Amazon CloudFront" is a correct answer.

CORRECT: "AWS Shield" is also a correct answer.

INCORRECT: "AWS Direct Connect" is incorrect. AWS Direct Connect is a networking service used for creating a hybrid cloud between on-premises and AWS Cloud using a private network connection

INCORRECT: "Amazon EBS" is incorrect. Amazon EBS is a storage service.

INCORRECT: "AWS Config" is incorrect. AWS Config is used for evaluating the configuration state of AWS resources.

References:

https://aws.amazon.com/shield/

https://aws.amazon.com/cloudfront/

Save time with our exam-specific cheat sheets:

https://digitalcloud.training/certification-training/aws-certified-cloud-practitioner/content-delivery-and-dns-services/

QUESTION 57

Which service can be used to easily create multiple accounts?

1. AWS IAM
2. AWS CloudFormation
3. AWS Organizations
4. Amazon Connect

Answer: 3

Explanation:

AWS Organizations can be used for automating AWS account creation via the Organizations API.

CORRECT: "AWS Organizations" is the correct answer.

INCORRECT: "AWS IAM" is incorrect. You cannot use IAM for creating accounts.

INCORRECT: "AWS CloudFormation" is incorrect. You could theoretically use AWS CloudFormation to automate the account creation along with some scripting, but that is certainly not an easy way to reach this result.

INCORRECT: "Amazon Connect" is incorrect. Amazon Connect is a self-service, cloud-based contact center service that makes it easy for businesses to deliver better customer service at a lower cost.

References:

https://docs.aws.amazon.com/organizations/latest/userguide/orgs_manage_accounts_create.html

https://aws.amazon.com/blogs/security/how-to-use-aws-organizations-to-automate-end-to-end-account-creation/

Save time with our exam-specific cheat sheets:

https://digitalcloud.training/certification-training/aws-certified-cloud-practitioner/aws-billing-and-pricing/

QUESTION 58

What is a specific benefit of an Enterprise Support plan?

1. Included Technical Support Manager
2. Included AWS Solutions Architect
3. Included Cloud Support Associate
4. Included Technical Account Manager

Answer: 4

Explanation:

Only the Enterprise Support plan gets a Technical Account Manager (TAM).

You do not get an AWS Solutions Architect with any plan.

Cloud Support Associates are provided in the Developer plan.

There's no such thing as a Technical Support Manager in the AWS support plans.

CORRECT: "Included Technical Account Manager" is the correct answer.

INCORRECT: "Included Technical Support Manager" is incorrect as explained above.

INCORRECT: "Included AWS Solutions Architect" is incorrect as explained above.

INCORRECT: "Included Cloud Support Associate" is incorrect as explained above.

References:

https://aws.amazon.com/premiumsupport/plans/

Save time with our exam-specific cheat sheets:

https://digitalcloud.training/certification-training/aws-certified-cloud-practitioner/aws-billing-and-pricing/

QUESTION 59

You have been running an on-demand Amazon EC2 instance running Linux for 4hrs, 5 minutes and 6 seconds. How much time will you be billed for?

1. 5hrs
2. 4hrs, 6mins
3. 4hrs, 5mins, and 6 seconds
4. 4hrs

Answer: 3

Explanation:

On-demand, Reserved and Spot Amazon EC2 Linux instances are charged per second with a minimum charge of 1 minute. Therefore, as the minimum has been exceeded, exactly 4hrs, 5mins and 6 seconds will be charged.

CORRECT: "4hrs, 5mins, and 6 seconds" is the correct answer.

INCORRECT: "5hrs" is incorrect as explained above.

INCORRECT: "4hrs, 6mins" is incorrect as explained above.

INCORRECT: "4hrs" is incorrect as explained above.

References:

Save time with our exam-specific cheat sheets:

https://digitalcloud.training/certification-training/aws-certified-cloud-practitioner/aws-billing-and-pricing/

QUESTION 60

Which of the below is an example of an architectural benefit of moving to the cloud?

1. Elasticity
2. Monolithic services
3. Proprietary hardware
4. Vertical scalability

Answer: 1

Explanation:

A key architectural benefit of moving to the cloud is that you get elasticity. This means your applications can scale as demand increases and scale back as demand decreases. This reduces cost as you only pay for what you use, when you need it.

CORRECT: "Elasticity" is the correct answer.

INCORRECT: "Monolithic services" is incorrect. Monolithic services are not a design patter of the public cloud. Developers and architects prefer service oriented or micro-service architectures instead.

INCORRECT: "Proprietary hardware" is incorrect. You do not get to choose your hardware in AWS as the infrastructure on which your services run is managed and operated by AWS. So you cannot use proprietary hardware.

INCORRECT: "Vertical scalability" is incorrect. Vertical scalability is not unique to the cloud, nor is it something we aspire to as architects. Most of the time horizontal scalability is preferred and is something that the AWS cloud provides for many services.

References:

https://aws.amazon.com/architecture/

Save time with our exam-specific cheat sheets:

https://digitalcloud.training/certification-training/aws-certified-cloud-practitioner/architecting-for-the-cloud/

QUESTION 61

What are the benefits of using reserved instances? (Select TWO.)

1. Reduced cost
2. More flexibility
3. Reserve capacity
4. Uses dedicated hardware
5. High availability

Answer: 1,3

Explanation:

With reserved instances you commit to a 1- or 3-year term and get a significant discount from the on-demand rate. You can also reserve capacity in an availability zone with reserved instances.

CORRECT: "Reduced cost" is a correct answer.

CORRECT: "Reserve capacity" is also a correct answer.

INCORRECT: "More flexibility" is incorrect. You don't get more flexibility with reserved instances. If you need flexibility on-demand is better but more costly.

INCORRECT: "Uses dedicated hardware" is incorrect. Reserved instances are different to dedicated instances. Dedicates instances and dedicates hosts use dedicated hardware but reserved instances do not.

INCORRECT: "High availability" is incorrect. You do not get high availability with reserved instances; this is a pricing model.

References:

https://aws.amazon.com/ec2/pricing/reserved-instances/

QUESTION 62

Which AWS tools can be used for automation? (Select TWO.)

1. AWS Elastic Beanstalk
2. Elastic Load Balancing
3. AWS CloudFormation
4. Amazon Elastic File System (EFS)
5. AWS Lambda

Answer: 1,3

Explanation:

AWS Elastic Beanstalk and AWS CloudFormation are both examples of automation. Beanstalk is a platform service that leverages the automation capabilities of CloudFormation to build out application architectures.

CORRECT: "AWS Elastic Beanstalk" is a correct answer.

CORRECT: "AWS CloudFormation" is also a correct answer.

INCORRECT: "Elastic Load Balancing" is incorrect. Elastic Load Balancing (ELB) is used for distributing incoming connections to Amazon EC2 instances. This is not an example of automation; it is load balancing.

INCORRECT: "Amazon Elastic File System (EFS)" is incorrect. Amazon EFS is a file system.

INCORRECT: "AWS Lambda" is incorrect. AWS Lambda is a compute service, not an automation service.

References:

https://aws.amazon.com/elasticbeanstalk/

https://aws.amazon.com/cloudformation/

QUESTION 63

Which IAM entity can be used for assigning permissions to AWS services?

1. IAM Access Key ID and Secret Access Key
2. IAM Policy
3. IAM Role
4. Security Token Service (STS)

Answer: 3

Explanation:

With IAM Roles you can delegate permissions to resources for users and services without using permanent credentials (e.g. username and password). To do so you can create a role and assign an IAM policy to the role that has the permissions required.

CORRECT: "IAM Role" is the correct answer.

INCORRECT: "IAM Access Key ID and Secret Access Key" is incorrect. An access key ID and secret access key are assigned to IAM users and used for programmatic access using the API or CLI.

INCORRECT: "IAM Policy" is incorrect. An IAM policy is a policy document that is used to define permissions that can be applied to users, groups and roles. You don't apply the policy to the service, you apply it to the role. The role is then used to assign permissions to the AWS service.

INCORRECT: "Security Token Service (STS)" is incorrect. This service is used for gaining temporary security credentials.

References:

https://docs.aws.amazon.com/IAM/latest/UserGuide/id_roles_create_for-service.html

https://digitalcloud.training/certification-training/aws-certified-cloud-practitioner/identity-and-access-management/

QUESTION 64

How does Amazon EC2 Auto Scaling help with resiliency?

1. By distributing connections to EC2 instances
2. By launching and terminating instances as needed
3. By changing instance types to increase capacity
4. By automating the failover of applications

Answer: 2

Explanation:

Amazon EC2 Auto Scaling launches and terminates instances as demand changes. This helps with resiliency and high availability as it can also be set to ensure a minimum number of instances are always available.

CORRECT: "By launching and terminating instances as needed" is the correct answer.

INCORRECT: "By distributing connections to EC2 instances" is incorrect. Auto Scaling is not responsible for distributing connections to EC2 instances, that is a job for an Elastic Load Balancer (ELB).

INCORRECT: "By changing instance types to increase capacity" is incorrect. Auto Scaling does not change the instance type. You have to create a new launch configuration if you need to increase your instance size, this is not automatic.

INCORRECT: "By automating the failover of applications" is incorrect. Auto Scaling does not do application failover.

References:

https://aws.amazon.com/ec2/autoscaling/

Save time with our exam-specific cheat sheets:

https://digitalcloud.training/certification-training/aws-certified-cloud-practitioner/elastic-load-balancing-and-auto-scaling/

QUESTION 65

Your CTO wants to move to cloud. What cost advantages are there to moving to cloud?

1. You provision only what you need and adjust to peak load
2. You can reduce your marketing costs
3. You don't need to pay for application licensing
4. You get free data transfer into and out of the cloud

Answer: 1

Explanation:

One of the best benefits of cloud is that you can launch what you need to and automatically adjust your resources as demand changes. This means you only ever pay for what you're using.

CORRECT: "You provision only what you need and adjust to peak load" is the correct answer.

INCORRECT: "You can reduce your marketing costs" is incorrect. You don't reduce marketing costs when moving to the cloud, your organization still needs to do the same amount of marketing.

INCORRECT: "You don't need to pay for application licensing" is incorrect. It is not true that you don't need to pay for application licensing in the cloud. You still pay for your application licenses when running on Amazon EC2.

INCORRECT: "You get free data transfer into and out of the cloud" is incorrect. You do not get free bi-directional data transfer into and out of the cloud. AWS charge for outbound data transfer.

References:

https://aws.amazon.com/pricing/

Save time with our exam-specific cheat sheets:

https://digitalcloud.training/certification-training/aws-certified-cloud-practitioner/aws-billing-and-pricing/

SET 4: PRACTICE QUESTIONS ONLY

For training purposes, go directly to Set 4: Practice Questions, Answers & Explanations

QUESTION 1

Which AWS service should be used to create a billing alarm?

1. AWS Trusted Advisor
2. AWS CloudTrail
3. Amazon CloudWatch
4. Amazon QuickSight

QUESTION 2

How can consolidated billing within AWS Organizations help lower overall monthly expenses?

1. By providing a consolidated view of monthly billing across multiple accounts
2. By pooling usage across multiple accounts to achieve a pricing tier discount
3. By automating the creation of new accounts through APIs
4. By leveraging service control policies (SCP) for centralized service management

QUESTION 3

Which Amazon EC2 pricing model should be used to comply with per-core software license requirements?

1. Dedicated Hosts
2. On-Demand Instances
3. Spot Instances
4. Reserved Instances

QUESTION 4

Which of the following are advantages of the AWS Cloud? (Select TWO.)

1. AWS manages the maintenance of the cloud infrastructure
2. AWS manages the security of applications built on AWS
3. AWS manages capacity planning for physical servers
4. AWS manages the development of applications on AWS
5. AWS manages cost planning for virtual servers

QUESTION 5

The ability to horizontally scale Amazon EC2 instances based on demand is an example of which concept?

1. Economy of scale
2. Elasticity
3. High availability
4. Agility

QUESTION 6

Which AWS service provides a quick and automated way to create and manage AWS accounts?

1. AWS QuickSight
2. Amazon LightSail
3. AWS Organizations
4. Amazon Connect

QUESTION 7

Which tool can be used to create alerts when the actual or forecasted cost of AWS services exceed a certain threshold?

1. AWS Cost Explorer
2. AWS Budgets
3. AWS Cost and Usage report
4. AWS CloudTrail

QUESTION 8

A user has an AWS account with a Business-level AWS Support plan and needs assistance with handling a production service disruption.

Which action should the user take?

1. Contact the dedicated Technical Account Manager
2. Contact the dedicated AWS Concierge Support team
3. Open a business-critical system down support case
4. Open a production system down support case

QUESTION 9

Which type of AWS Storage Gateway can be used to backup data with popular backup software?

1. File Gateway
2. Volume Gateway
3. Gateway Virtual Tape Library
4. Backup Gateway

QUESTION 10

You would like to collect custom metrics from a production application every 1 minute. What type of monitoring should you use?

1. CloudWatch with detailed monitoring
2. CloudTrail with basic monitoring
3. CloudWatch with basic monitoring
4. CloudTrail with detailed monitoring

QUESTION 11

What billing timeframes are available for Amazon EC2 on-demand instances? (Select TWO.)

1. Per week
2. Per day
3. Per hour
4. Per minute
5. Per second

QUESTION 12

Which Amazon EC2 pricing option provides significant discounts for fixed term contracts?

1. Reserved Instances
2. Spot Instances
3. Dedicated Instances
4. Dedicated Hosts

QUESTION 13

When using Amazon RDS databases, which items are you charged for? (Select TWO.)

1. Inbound data transfer
2. Multi AZ
3. Single AZ
4. Backup up to the DB size
5. Outbound data transfer

QUESTION 14

How are AWS Lambda functions triggered?

1. Events
2. Schedules
3. Metrics
4. Counters

QUESTION 15

Which tool can be used to provide real time guidance on provisioning resources following AWS best practices?

1. AWS Trusted Advisor
2. AWS Simple Monthly Calculator
3. AWS Inspector
4. AWS Personal Health Dashboard

QUESTION 16

When performing a total cost of ownership (TCO) analysis between on-premises and the AWS Cloud, which factors are only relevant to on-premises deployments? (Select TWO.)

1. Hardware procurement teams
2. Operating system licensing
3. Facility operations costs
4. Database administration
5. Application licensing

QUESTION 17

How does "elasticity" benefit an application design?

1. By reducing interdependencies between application components
2. By automatically scaling resources based on demand
3. By selecting the correct storage tier for your workload
4. By reserving capacity to reduce cost

QUESTION 18

What is the benefit of using fully managed services compared to deploying 3rd party software on EC2?

1. You don't need to back-up your data
2. Improved security
3. Reduced operational overhead
4. You have greater control and flexibility

QUESTION 19

What are the fundamental charges for an Amazon EC2 instance? (Select TWO.)

1. Basic monitoring
2. Data storage
3. Server uptime
4. AMI
5. Private IP address

QUESTION 20

Which AWS service uses a highly secure hardware storage device to store encryption keys?

1. AWS CloudHSM
2. AWS IAM
3. Amazon Cloud Directory
4. AWS WAF

QUESTION 21

Which type of security control can be used to deny network access from a specific IP address?

1. AWS Shield
2. AWS WAF
3. Network ACL
4. Security Group

QUESTION 22

Which service can be used to manage configuration versions?

1. AWS Service Catalog
2. AWS Artifact
3. Amazon Inspector
4. AWS Config

QUESTION 23

Which aspects of security on AWS are customer responsibilities? (Select TWO.)

1. Setting up account password policies
2. Physical access controls
3. Server-side encryption
4. Patching of storage systems
5. Availability of AWS regions

QUESTION 24

Which of the following are architectural best practices for the AWS Cloud? (Select TWO.)

1. Deploy into multiple Availability Zones
2. Deploy into a single availability zone
3. Close coupling
4. Design for fault tolerance
5. Create monolithic architectures

QUESTION 25

To reduce the price of your Amazon EC2 instances, which term lengths are available for reserved instances? (Select TWO.)

1. 4 years
2. 1 year
3. 5 years

4. 2 years
5. 3 years

QUESTION 26

What are the fundamental charges for Elastic Block Store (EBS) volumes? (Select TWO.)

1. The amount of data storage provisioned
2. The amount of data storage consumed
3. Number of snapshots
4. Provisioned IOPS
5. Inbound data transfer

QUESTION 27

What is the most cost-effective Amazon S3 storage tier for data that is not often accessed but requires high availability?

1. Amazon S3 Standard-IA
2. Amazon S3 Standard
3. Amazon S3 One Zone-IA
4. Amazon Glacier

QUESTION 28

What is the main benefit of the principle of "loose coupling"?

1. Reduce operational complexity
2. Reduce interdependencies so a failure in one component does not cascade to other components
3. Automate the deployment of infrastructure using code
4. Enables applications to scale automatically based on current demand

QUESTION 29

Which Amazon EC2 billing option gives you low cost, maximum flexibility, no upfront costs or commitment, and you only pay for what you use?

1. Dedicated Host
2. Spot Instances
3. Reserved Instances
4. On-Demand Instances

QUESTION 30

Where can resources be launched when configuring Amazon EC2 Auto Scaling?

1. A single subnet
2. Multiple AZs within a region
3. Multiple AZs and multiple regions
4. Multiple VPCs

QUESTION 31

Which service can be used to improve performance for users around the world?

1. AWS LightSail
2. Amazon CloudFront
3. Amazon Connect
4. Amazon ElastiCache

QUESTION 32

Which of the below are components that can be configured in the VPC section of the AWS management console? (Select TWO.)

1. EBS volumes
2. Subnet
3. Endpoints
4. DNS records
5. Elastic Load Balancer

QUESTION 33

Which of the following is a benefit of moving to the AWS Cloud?

1. Outsource all IT operations
2. Pay for what you use
3. Capital purchases
4. Long term commitments

QUESTION 34

In addition to DNS services, what other services does Amazon Route 53 provide? (Select TWO.)

1. DHCP
2. Caching
3. Domain registration
4. IP Routing
5. Traffic flow

QUESTION 35

What can be assigned to an IAM user? (Select TWO.)

1. An access key ID and secret access key
2. An SSL/TLS certificate
3. A key pair
4. A password for logging into Linux
5. A password for access to the management console

QUESTION 36

The AWS acceptable use policy for penetration testing allows?

1. Customers to carry out security assessments or penetration tests against their AWS infrastructure without prior approval for selected services
2. Customers to carry out security assessments or penetration tests against their AWS infrastructure after obtaining authorization from AWS
3. AWS to perform penetration testing against customer resources without notification
4. Authorized security assessors to perform penetration tests against any AWS customer without authorization

QUESTION 37

Which type of connection should be used to connect an on-premises data center with the AWS cloud that is high speed, low latency and does not use the Internet?

1. Direct Connect
2. VPC Endpoints
3. AWS Managed VPN
4. Client VPN

QUESTION 38

Which of the advantages of cloud listed below is most closely addressed by the capabilities of AWS Auto Scaling?

1. Benefit from massive economies of scale
2. Stop guessing about capacity
3. Stop spending money running and maintaining data centers
4. Go global in minutes

QUESTION 39

Which statement is correct in relation to the AWS Shared Responsibility Model?

1. AWS are responsible for the security of regions and availability zones
2. Customers are responsible for patching storage systems
3. AWS are responsible for encrypting customer data
4. Customers are responsible for security of the cloud

QUESTION 40

Which of the following is an advantage of cloud computing compared to deploying your own infrastructure on-premise?

1. Flexibility to choose your own hardware
2. Spend using a CAPEX model
3. Paying only for what you use
4. Ability to choose bespoke infrastructure configurations

QUESTION 41

Which service can be added to a database to provide improved performance for some requests?

1. Amazon RedShift
2. Amazon EFS
3. Amazon ElastiCache
4. Amazon RDS

QUESTION 42

Which service can be used to assign a policy to a group?

1. AWS IAM
2. Amazon Cognito
3. Amazon STS
4. AWS Shield

QUESTION 43

Which AWS service lets you add user sign up, sign-in and access control to web and mobile apps?

1. AWS Artifact
2. Amazon Cognito
3. AWS CloudHSM
4. AWS Directory Service

QUESTION 44

What is the difference between an EBS volume and an Instance store?

1. EBS volumes are object storage devices whereas Instance store volume are block based
2. Instance store volumes are ephemeral whereas EBS volumes are persistent storage

3. Instance store volumes can be used with all EC2 instance types whereas EBS cannot
4. EBS volumes are file-level storage devices whereas Instance store volumes are object-based

QUESTION 45

What are two components of Amazon S3? (Select TWO.)

1. Buckets
2. Directories
3. Objects
4. Block devices
5. File systems

QUESTION 46

Which of the below are good use cases for a specific Amazon EC2 pricing model? (Select TWO.)

1. Reserved instances for steady state predictable usage
2. On-demand for regulatory requirements that do not allow multi-tenant virtualization
3. On-demand for ad-hoc requirements that cannot be interrupted
4. Spot for consistent load over a long term
5. Reserved instances for applications with flexible start and end times

QUESTION 47

Which of the following security related activities are AWS customers responsible for? (Select TWO.)

1. Secure disposal of faulty disk drives
2. Implementing data center access controls
3. Installing patches on network devices
4. Installing patches on Windows operating systems
5. Implementing IAM password policies

QUESTION 48

An organization has an on-premises cloud and accesses their AWS Cloud over the Internet. How can they create a private hybrid cloud connection that avoids the internet?

1. AWS Direct Connect
2. AWS Managed VPN
3. AWS VPN CloudHub
4. AWS VPC Endpoint

QUESTION 49

Which team is available to support AWS customers on an Enterprise support plan with account issues?

1. AWS Technical Support
2. AWS Billing and Accounts
3. AWS Concierge
4. AWS Technical Account Manager

QUESTION 50

What are two examples of the advantages of cloud computing? (Select TWO.)

1. Increase speed and agility
2. Trade operating costs for capital costs
3. Secure data centers
4. Benefit from massive economies of scale

5. Trade variable expense for capital expense

QUESTION 51

Which of the following is an architectural best practice recommended by AWS?

1. Design for success
2. Design for failure
3. Think servers, not services
4. Use manual operational processes

QUESTION 52

What is the scope of an Amazon Virtual Private Cloud (VPC)?

1. It spans a single CIDR block
2. It spans all Availability Zones within a region
3. It spans multiple subnets
4. It spans all Availability Zones in all regions

QUESTION 53

Which AWS service allows you to automate the evaluation of recorded configurations against desired configuration?

1. AWS OpsWorks
2. AWS Service Catalog
3. AWS CloudFormation
4. AWS Config

QUESTION 54

Which of the options below are recommendations in the reliability pillar of the well-architected framework? (Select TWO.)

1. Test recovery procedures
2. Manually recover from failure
3. Manage change in manual processes
4. Stop guessing about capacity
5. Scale vertically using big systems

QUESTION 55

Which storage type can be mounted using the NFS protocol to many EC2 instances simultaneously?

1. Amazon Instance Store
2. Amazon EBS
3. Amazon S3
4. Amazon EFS

QUESTION 56

Which Amazon RDS deployment type is best used to enable fault tolerance in the event of the failure of an availability zone?

1. Multiple Regions
2. Read Replicas
3. Write Replicas
4. Multiple Availability Zones

QUESTION 57

Which feature of AWS IAM enables you to identify unnecessary permissions that have been assigned to users?

1. Role Advisor
2. Access Advisor
3. Permissions Advisor
4. Group Advisor

QUESTION 58

What types of monitoring can Amazon CloudWatch be used for? (Select TWO.)

1. Infrastructure
2. Data center
3. Operational health
4. API access
5. Application performance

QUESTION 59

Which AWS service enables hybrid cloud storage between on-premises and the AWS Cloud?

1. Amazon S3 Cross Region Replication (CRR)
2. AWS Storage Gateway
3. Amazon Elastic File System (EFS)
4. Amazon CloudFront

QUESTION 60

What does an organization need to do to move to another AWS region?

1. Just start deploying resources in the additional region
2. Create a separate IAM account for that region
3. Apply for another AWS account in that region
4. Submit an application to extend their account to the additional region

QUESTION 61

Which Compute service should be used for running a Linux operating system upon which you will install custom software?

1. Amazon EC2
2. Amazon ECS
3. Amazon EKS
4. AWS Lambda

QUESTION 62

Which of the following need to be included in a total cost of ownership (TCO) analysis? (Select TWO.)

1. IT Manager salary
2. Facility equipment installation
3. Application development
4. Company-wide marketing
5. Data center security costs

QUESTION 63

What does an organization need to do in Amazon IAM to enable user access to services being launched in new region?

1. Nothing, IAM is global
2. Enable global mode in IAM to provision the required access
3. Update the user accounts to allow access from another region
4. Create new user accounts in the new region

© 2022 Digital Cloud Training

QUESTION 64

Which statement is true in relation to data stored within an AWS Region?

1. Data is not replicated outside of a region unless you configure it
2. Data is always replicated to another region
3. Data is automatically archived after 90 days
4. Data is always automatically replicated to at least one other availability zone

QUESTION 65

An organization has multiple AWS accounts and uses a mixture of on-demand and reserved instances. One account has a considerable amount of unused reserved instances. How can the organization reduce their costs? (Select TWO.)

1. Create an AWS Organization configuration linking the accounts
2. Use Spot instances instead
3. Redeem their reserved instances
4. Setup consolidated billing between the accounts
5. Switch to using placement groups

SET 4: PRACTICE QUESTIONS AND ANSWERS

QUESTION 1

Which AWS service should be used to create a billing alarm?

1. AWS Trusted Advisor
2. AWS CloudTrail
3. Amazon CloudWatch
4. Amazon QuickSight

Answer: 3

Explanation:

You can monitor your estimated AWS charges by using Amazon CloudWatch. When you enable the monitoring of estimated charges for your AWS account, the estimated charges are calculated and sent several times daily to CloudWatch as metric data.

Billing metric data is stored in the US East (N. Virginia) Region and represents worldwide charges. This data includes the estimated charges for every service in AWS that you use, in addition to the estimated overall total of your AWS charges.

The alarm triggers when your account billing exceeds the threshold you specify. It triggers only when actual billing exceeds the threshold. It doesn't use projections based on your usage so far in the month.

CORRECT: "Amazon CloudWatch" is the correct answer.

INCORRECT: "AWS Trusted Advisor" is incorrect. AWS Trusted Advisor is an online tool that provides you real time guidance to help you provision your resources following AWS best practices.

INCORRECT: "AWS CloudTrail" is incorrect. CloudTrail logs API activity, not performance or billing metrics.

INCORRECT: "Amazon QuickSight" is incorrect. Amazon QuickSight is a fast, cloud-powered business intelligence service that makes it easy to deliver insights to everyone in your organization.

References:

https://docs.aws.amazon.com/AmazonCloudWatch/latest/monitoring/monitor_estimated_charges_with_cloudwatch.html

Save time with our exam-specific cheat sheets:

https://digitalcloud.training/certification-training/aws-certified-cloud-practitioner/monitoring-and-logging-services/

QUESTION 2

How can consolidated billing within AWS Organizations help lower overall monthly expenses?

1. By providing a consolidated view of monthly billing across multiple accounts
2. By pooling usage across multiple accounts to achieve a pricing tier discount
3. By automating the creation of new accounts through APIs
4. By leveraging service control policies (SCP) for centralized service management

Answer: 2

Explanation:

You can use the consolidated billing feature in AWS Organizations to consolidate billing and payment for multiple AWS accounts or multiple Amazon Internet Services Pvt. Ltd (AISPL) accounts. Every organization in AWS Organizations has a *master (payer) account* that pays the charges of all the *member (linked) accounts*.

Consolidated billing has the following benefits:

- **One bill** – You get one bill for multiple accounts.
- **Easy tracking** – You can track the charges across multiple accounts and download the combined cost and usage data.
- **Combined usage** – You can combine the usage across all accounts in the organization to share the volume pricing discounts, Reserved Instance discounts, and Savings Plans. This can result in a lower charge for your project, department, or company than with individual standalone accounts.
- **No extra fee** – Consolidated billing is offered at no additional cost.

CORRECT: "By pooling usage across multiple accounts to achieve a pricing tier discount" is the correct answer.

INCORRECT: "By providing a consolidated view of monthly billing across multiple accounts" is incorrect. This is useful, but doesn't lower costs.

INCORRECT: "By automating the creation of new accounts through APIs" is incorrect as this does not lower costs.

INCORRECT: "By leveraging service control policies (SCP) for centralized service management" is incorrect. SCPs are used for controlling the API actions you can use, not for lowering costs.

References:

https://docs.aws.amazon.com/awsaccountbilling/latest/aboutv2/consolidated-billing.html

Save time with our exam-specific cheat sheets:

https://digitalcloud.training/certification-training/aws-certified-cloud-practitioner/aws-billing-and-pricing/

QUESTION 3

Which Amazon EC2 pricing model should be used to comply with per-core software license requirements?

1. Dedicated Hosts
2. On-Demand Instances
3. Spot Instances
4. Reserved Instances

Answer: 1

Explanation:

Amazon EC2 Dedicated Hosts allow you to use your eligible software licenses from vendors such as Microsoft and Oracle on Amazon EC2, so that you get the flexibility and cost effectiveness of using your own licenses, but with the resiliency, simplicity and elasticity of AWS. An Amazon EC2 Dedicated Host is a physical server fully dedicated for your use, so you can help address corporate compliance requirements.

CORRECT: "Dedicated Hosts" is the correct answer.

INCORRECT: "On-Demand Instances" is incorrect. This is a standard pricing model and does not offer the advantages requested.

INCORRECT: "Spot Instances" is incorrect. This is used to obtain discounted pricing for short-term requirements that can be interrupted.

INCORRECT: "Reserved Instances" is incorrect. This is used to lower cost by reserving usage of an instance for a term of 1 or 3 years.

References:

https://aws.amazon.com/ec2/dedicated-hosts/

Save time with our exam-specific cheat sheets:

https://digitalcloud.training/certification-training/aws-certified-cloud-practitioner/aws-billing-and-pricing/

QUESTION 4

Which of the following are advantages of the AWS Cloud? (Select TWO.)

1. AWS manages the maintenance of the cloud infrastructure
2. AWS manages the security of applications built on AWS
3. AWS manages capacity planning for physical servers
4. AWS manages the development of applications on AWS
5. AWS manages cost planning for virtual servers

Answer: 1, 3

Explanation:

AWS is responsible for security of the AWS Cloud as well as capacity planning and maintenance of the AWS infrastructure. This includes physical infrastructure such as data centers, servers, storage systems, and networking equipment.

CORRECT: "AWS manages the maintenance of the cloud infrastructure" is a correct answer.

CORRECT: "AWS manages capacity planning for physical servers" is also a correct answer.

INCORRECT: "AWS manages the security of applications built on AWS" is incorrect. This is the responsibility of the customer.

INCORRECT: "AWS manages the development of applications on AWS" is incorrect. This is the responsibility of the customer.

INCORRECT: "AWS manages cost planning for virtual servers" is incorrect. This is the responsibility of the customer.

References:

https://aws.amazon.com/compliance/shared-responsibility-model/

Save time with our exam-specific cheat sheets:

https://digitalcloud.training/certification-training/aws-certified-cloud-practitioner/aws-shared-responsibility-model/

QUESTION 5

The ability to horizontally scale Amazon EC2 instances based on demand is an example of which concept?

1. Economy of scale
2. Elasticity
3. High availability
4. Agility

Answer: 2

Explanation:

Elasticity is the ability to dynamically adjust the capacity of a service or resource based on demand. Scaling can be vertical (e.g. increase instance size) or horizontal (e.g. add more EC2 instances).

CORRECT: "Elasticity" is the correct answer.

INCORRECT: "Economy of scale" is incorrect. This refers to pricing benefits based on AWS purchasing large amounts of resources.

INCORRECT: "High availability" is incorrect. This is an example of resilience.

INCORRECT: "Agility" is incorrect. This is an example of flexibility and speed of implementation.

References:

https://d1.awsstatic.com/whitepapers/architecture/AWS_Well-Architected_Framework.pdf

Save time with our exam-specific cheat sheets:

https://digitalcloud.training/certification-training/aws-certified-cloud-practitioner/architecting-for-the-cloud/

QUESTION 6

Which AWS service provides a quick and automated way to create and manage AWS accounts?

1. AWS QuickSight
2. Amazon LightSail
3. AWS Organizations
4. Amazon Connect

Answer: 3

Explanation:

AWS Organizations is a web service that enables you to consolidate your multiple AWS accounts into an *organization* and centrally manage your accounts and their resources. The AWS Organizations API can be used to create AWS accounts and this can be automated through code.

CORRECT: "AWS Organizations" is the correct answer.

INCORRECT: "AWS QuickSight" is incorrect. Amazon QuickSight is a fast, cloud-powered business intelligence service that makes it easy to deliver insights to everyone in your organization.

INCORRECT: "Amazon LightSail" is incorrect. LightSail offers virtual servers (instances) that are easy to set up and backed by the power and reliability of AWS.

INCORRECT: "Amazon Connect" is incorrect. Amazon Connect is an easy to use omnichannel cloud contact center that helps companies provide superior customer service at a lower cost

References:

https://docs.aws.amazon.com/organizations/latest/APIReference/Welcome.html

Save time with our exam-specific cheat sheets:

https://digitalcloud.training/certification-training/aws-certified-cloud-practitioner/cloud-security/

QUESTION 7

Which tool can be used to create alerts when the actual or forecasted cost of AWS services exceed a certain threshold?

1. AWS Cost Explorer
2. AWS Budgets
3. AWS Cost and Usage report
4. AWS CloudTrail

Answer: 2

Explanation:

AWS Budgets gives you the ability to set custom budgets that alert you when your costs or usage exceed (or are forecasted to exceed) your budgeted amount.

You can also use AWS Budgets to set reservation utilization or coverage targets and receive alerts when your utilization drops below the threshold you define. Reservation alerts are supported for Amazon EC2, Amazon RDS, Amazon Redshift, Amazon ElastiCache, and Amazon Elasticsearch reservations.

CORRECT: "AWS Budgets" is the correct answer.

INCORRECT: "AWS Cost Explorer" is incorrect. Cost Explorer lets you visualize and understand your costs but AWS Budgets should be used for alerting based on forecast or actual usage.

INCORRECT: "AWS Cost and Usage report" is incorrect. This is another tool that can be used to view usage for AWS services by category but AWS Budgets should be used for alerting based on forecast or actual usage.

INCORRECT: "AWS CloudTrail" is incorrect. CloudTrail is used for logging API activity, it will not alert you based on usage of AWS services.

References:

https://aws.amazon.com/aws-cost-management/aws-budgets/

Save time with our exam-specific cheat sheets:

https://digitalcloud.training/certification-training/aws-certified-cloud-practitioner/aws-billing-and-pricing/

QUESTION 8

A user has an AWS account with a Business-level AWS Support plan and needs assistance with handling a production service disruption.

Which action should the user take?

1. Contact the dedicated Technical Account Manager
2. Contact the dedicated AWS Concierge Support team
3. Open a business-critical system down support case
4. Open a production system down support case

Answer: 4

Explanation:

The Business support plan provides a service level agreement (SLA) of < 1 hour for production system down support cases.

CORRECT: "Open a production system down support case" is the correct answer.

INCORRECT: "Contact the dedicated Technical Account Manager" is incorrect. The dedicated TAM only comes with the Enterprise support plan.

INCORRECT: "Contact the dedicated AWS Concierge Support team" is incorrect. The concierge support team only comes with the Enterprise support plan.

INCORRECT: "Open a business-critical system down support case" is incorrect. The business-critical system down support only comes with the Enterprise support plan.

References:

https://aws.amazon.com/premiumsupport/plans/

Save time with our exam-specific cheat sheets:

https://digitalcloud.training/certification-training/aws-certified-cloud-practitioner/aws-billing-and-pricing/

QUESTION 9

Which type of AWS Storage Gateway can be used to backup data with popular backup software?

1. File Gateway
2. Volume Gateway
3. Gateway Virtual Tape Library
4. Backup Gateway

Answer: 3

Explanation:

The AWS Storage Gateway service enables hybrid storage between on-premises environments and the AWS Cloud.

The Gateway Virtual Tape Library can be used with popular backup software such as NetBackup, Backup Exec and Veeam. Uses a virtual media changer and tape drives.

CORRECT: "Gateway Virtual Tape Library" is the correct answer.

INCORRECT: "File Gateway" is incorrect. File gateway provides a virtual on-premises file server, which enables you to store and retrieve files as objects in Amazon S3.

INCORRECT: "Volume Gateway" is incorrect. The volume gateway represents the family of gateways that support block-based volumes, previously referred to as gateway-cached and gateway-stored modes.

INCORRECT: "Backup Gateway" is incorrect. There is no such thing as a Backup Gateway in the AWS products.

References:

https://docs.aws.amazon.com/storagegateway/latest/userguide/WhatIsStorageGateway.html

Save time with our exam-specific cheat sheets:

https://digitalcloud.training/certification-training/aws-certified-cloud-practitioner/additional-aws-services-tools/

QUESTION 10

You would like to collect custom metrics from a production application every 1 minute. What type of monitoring should you use?

1. CloudWatch with detailed monitoring
2. CloudTrail with basic monitoring
3. CloudWatch with basic monitoring
4. CloudTrail with detailed monitoring

Answer: 1

Explanation:

Amazon CloudWatch is a monitoring service for AWS cloud resources and the applications you run on AWS. CloudWatch is for performance monitoring (CloudTrail is for auditing).

It is used to collect and track metrics, collect and monitor log files, and set alarms. Basic monitoring collects metrics every 5 minutes whereas detailed monitoring collects metrics every 1 minute

AWS CloudTrail is a web service that records activity made on your account and delivers log files to an Amazon S3 bucket. CloudTrail is for auditing, whereas CloudWatch is for performance monitoring. CloudTrail is about logging and saves a history of API calls for your AWS account

CORRECT: "CloudWatch with detailed monitoring" is the correct answer.

INCORRECT: "CloudTrail with basic monitoring" is incorrect as explained above.

INCORRECT: "CloudWatch with basic monitoring" is incorrect as explained above.

INCORRECT: "CloudTrail with detailed monitoring" is incorrect as explained above.

References:

https://docs.aws.amazon.com/AWSEC2/latest/UserGuide/using-cloudwatch-new.html

Save time with our exam-specific cheat sheets:

https://digitalcloud.training/certification-training/aws-certified-cloud-practitioner/monitoring-and-logging-services/

QUESTION 11

What billing timeframes are available for Amazon EC2 on-demand instances? (Select TWO.)

1. Per week
2. Per day
3. Per hour
4. Per minute
5. Per second

Answer: 3,5

Explanation:

With EC2 you are billed either by the second, for some Linux instances, or by the hour for all other instance types.

CORRECT: "Per second" is a correct answer.

CORRECT: "Per hour" is also a correct answer.

INCORRECT: "Per week" is incorrect as explained above.

INCORRECT: "Per day" is incorrect as explained above.

INCORRECT: "Per minute" is incorrect as explained above.

References:

https://aws.amazon.com/premiumsupport/knowledge-center/ec2-instance-hour-billing/

Save time with our exam-specific cheat sheets:

https://digitalcloud.training/certification-training/aws-certified-cloud-practitioner/aws-billing-and-pricing/

QUESTION 12

Which Amazon EC2 pricing option provides significant discounts for fixed term contracts?

1. Reserved Instances
2. Spot Instances
3. Dedicated Instances
4. Dedicated Hosts

Answer: 1

Explanation:

Reserved instances provide significant discounts, up to 75% compared to On-Demand pricing, by paying for capacity ahead of time.

CORRECT: "Reserved Instances" is the correct answer.

INCORRECT: "Spot Instances" is incorrect. Spot Instances allow you to purchase spare computing capacity with no upfront commitment at discounted hourly rates. This is not used for long-term requirements.

INCORRECT: "Dedicated Instances" is incorrect. Dedicated Instances are Amazon EC2 instances that run in a VPC on hardware that's dedicated to a single customer.

INCORRECT: "Dedicated Hosts" is incorrect. Dedicated hosts are EC2 servers dedicated to a single customer.

References:

https://aws.amazon.com/ec2/pricing/reserved-instances/

Save time with our exam-specific cheat sheets:

https://digitalcloud.training/certification-training/aws-certified-cloud-practitioner/aws-billing-and-pricing/

QUESTION 13

When using Amazon RDS databases, which items are you charged for? (Select TWO.)

1. Inbound data transfer
2. Multi AZ
3. Single AZ
4. Backup up to the DB size
5. Outbound data transfer

Answer: 2,5

Explanation:

With Amazon RDS you are charged for the type and size of database, the uptime, any additional storage of backup (above the DB size), requests, deployment type (e.g. you pay for multi AZ), and data transfer outbound.

CORRECT: "Multi AZ" is a correct answer.

CORRECT: "Outbound data transfer" is also a correct answer.

INCORRECT: "Inbound data transfer" is incorrect as you do not pay for inbound data.

INCORRECT: "Single AZ" is incorrect as this is not something you pay an additional charge for.

INCORRECT: "Backup up to the DB size" is incorrect as you do not pay for backup storage up to the size of the database. You only pay for backup storage in excess of the database size.

References:

https://aws.amazon.com/rds/pricing/

Save time with our exam-specific cheat sheets:

https://digitalcloud.training/certification-training/aws-certified-cloud-practitioner/aws-billing-and-pricing/

QUESTION 14

How are AWS Lambda functions triggered?

1. Events
2. Schedules
3. Metrics
4. Counters

Answer: 1

Explanation:

AWS Lambda lets you run code as functions without provisioning or managing server. Lambda-based applications (also referred to as serverless applications) are composed of functions triggered by events.

For instance, you can trigger a Lambda function to run when an object is uploaded to an Amazon S3 bucket or a message is added to an Amazon SQS queue.

CORRECT: "Events" is the correct answer.

INCORRECT: "Schedules" is incorrect as functions are triggered by events.

INCORRECT: "Metrics" is incorrect as functions are triggered by events.

INCORRECT: "Counters" is incorrect as functions are triggered by events.

References:

https://docs.aws.amazon.com/lambda/latest/dg/lambda-invocation.html

Save time with our exam-specific cheat sheets:

https://digitalcloud.training/certification-training/aws-certified-cloud-practitioner/aws-compute/

QUESTION 15

Which tool can be used to provide real time guidance on provisioning resources following AWS best practices?

1. AWS Trusted Advisor
2. AWS Simple Monthly Calculator
3. AWS Inspector
4. AWS Personal Health Dashboard

Answer: 1

Explanation:

Trusted Advisor is an online resource that helps to reduce cost, increase performance and improve security by optimizing your AWS environment. Trusted Advisor provides real time guidance to help you provision your resources following best practices.

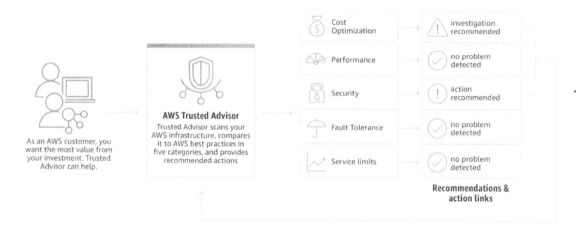

CORRECT: "AWS Trusted Advisor" is the correct answer.

INCORRECT: "AWS Simple Monthly Calculator" is incorrect. The AWS Simple Monthly Calculator helps you to estimate the cost of using AWS services.

INCORRECT: "AWS Inspector" is incorrect. Inspector is an automated security assessment service that helps improve the security and compliance of applications deployed on AWS

INCORRECT: "AWS Personal Health Dashboard" is incorrect. AWS Personal Health Dashboard provides alerts and remediation guidance when AWS is experiencing events that may impact you.

References:

https://aws.amazon.com/premiumsupport/technology/trusted-advisor/

Save time with our exam-specific cheat sheets:

https://digitalcloud.training/certification-training/aws-certified-cloud-practitioner/cloud-security/

QUESTION 16

When performing a total cost of ownership (TCO) analysis between on-premises and the AWS Cloud, which factors are only relevant to on-premises deployments? (Select TWO.)

1. Hardware procurement teams
2. Operating system licensing
3. Facility operations costs
4. Database administration
5. Application licensing

Answer: 1,3

Explanation:

Facility operations and hardware procurement costs are something you no longer need to pay for in the AWS Cloud. These factors therefore must be included as an on-premise cost so you can understand the cost of staying in your own data centers.

Database administration, operating system licensing and application licensing will still be required in the AWS Cloud.

CORRECT: "Hardware procurement teams" is a correct answer.

CORRECT: "Facility operations costs" is also a correct answer.

INCORRECT: "Operating system licensing" is incorrect as these are factors that are relevant to both on-premise and the cloud.

INCORRECT: "Database administration" is incorrect as these are factors that are relevant to both on-premise and the cloud.

INCORRECT: "Application licensing" is incorrect as these are factors that are relevant to both on-premise and the cloud.

References:

https://media.amazonwebservices.com/AWS_TCO_Web_Applications.pdf

Save time with our exam-specific cheat sheets:

https://digitalcloud.training/certification-training/aws-certified-cloud-practitioner/aws-billing-and-pricing/

QUESTION 17

How does "elasticity" benefit an application design?

1. By reducing interdependencies between application components
2. By automatically scaling resources based on demand
3. By selecting the correct storage tier for your workload
4. By reserving capacity to reduce cost

Answer: 2

Explanation:

Elasticity refers to the automatic scaling of resources based on demand. The benefit is that you provision only the necessary resources at a given time (optimizing cost) and don't have to worry about absorbing spikes in demand.

CORRECT: "By automatically scaling resources based on demand" is the correct answer.

INCORRECT: "By reducing interdependencies between application components" is incorrect. Elasticity does not reduce interdependencies between systems – this is known as loose coupling.

INCORRECT: "By selecting the correct storage tier for your workload" is incorrect. Selecting the correct storage tier would be an example of right-sizing, not elasticity.

INCORRECT: "By reserving capacity to reduce cost" is incorrect. Reserving capacity to reduce cost refers to using reservations such as EC2 Reserved Instances.

References:

https://wa.aws.amazon.com/wat.concept.elasticity.en.html

Save time with our exam-specific cheat sheets:

https://digitalcloud.training/certification-training/aws-certified-cloud-practitioner/architecting-for-the-cloud/

QUESTION 18

What is the benefit of using fully managed services compared to deploying 3rd party software on EC2?

1. You don't need to back-up your data
2. Improved security
3. Reduced operational overhead
4. You have greater control and flexibility

Answer: 3

Explanation:

Fully managed services reduce your operational overhead as AWS manage not just the infrastructure layer but the service layers above it. Examples are Amazon Aurora and Amazon ElastiCache where the database is managed for you.

CORRECT: "Reduced operational overhead" is the correct answer.

INCORRECT: "You don't need to back-up your data" is incorrect. You do still need to backup your data. For instance, with Amazon ElastiCache it's up to you to configure backups to S3.

INCORRECT: "Improved security" is incorrect. Security is not necessarily improved by managing your own software stack. AWS are extremely good at securing their services and there is arguably less chance that they will expose vulnerabilities than a customer who deploys their own applications.

INCORRECT: "You have greater control and flexibility" is incorrect. You do not have greater control and flexibility with fully managed services. AWS take more responsibility for providing the service and you therefore have fewer options. For example you may not be able to configure the performance parameters of a database as you'd like to or use your own backup or operational software.

Save time with our exam-specific cheat sheets:

https://digitalcloud.training/certification-training/aws-certified-cloud-practitioner/architecting-for-the-cloud/

QUESTION 19

What are the fundamental charges for an Amazon EC2 instance? (Select TWO.)

1. Basic monitoring
2. Data storage
3. Server uptime
4. AMI
5. Private IP address

Answer: 2,3

Explanation:

When using EC2 instances you are charged for the compute uptime of the instance based on the family and type you chose. You are also charged for the amount of data provisioned.

CORRECT: "Data storage" is a correct answer.

CORRECT: "Server uptime" is also a correct answer.

INCORRECT: "Basic monitoring" is incorrect. Basic monitoring is free for EC2, detailed monitoring is charged.

INCORRECT: "AMI" is incorrect. Amazon Machine Images (AMIs) are not chargeable. You can purchase chargeable AMIs via the marketplace but you are not charged for any you create.

INCORRECT: "Private IP address" is incorrect. You do not pay for private IP addresses.

References:

https://aws.amazon.com/ec2/pricing/

Save time with our exam-specific cheat sheets:

https://digitalcloud.training/certification-training/aws-certified-cloud-practitioner/aws-billing-and-pricing/

QUESTION 20

Which AWS service uses a highly secure hardware storage device to store encryption keys?

1. AWS CloudHSM
2. AWS IAM
3. Amazon Cloud Directory
4. AWS WAF

Answer: 1

Explanation:

AWS CloudHSM is a cloud-based hardware security module (HSM) that allows you to easily add secure key storage and high-performance crypto operations to your AWS applications

CORRECT: "AWS CloudHSM" is the correct answer.

INCORRECT: "AWS IAM" is incorrect. AWS Identity and Access Management (IAM) is used for managing users, groups, and roles in AWS.

INCORRECT: "Amazon Cloud Directory" is incorrect. Amazon Cloud Directory enables you to build flexible cloud-native directories for organizing hierarchies of data along multiple dimensions.

INCORRECT: "AWS WAF" is incorrect. AWS WAF is a web application firewall that helps protect your web applications from common web exploits.

References:

https://aws.amazon.com/cloudhsm/features/

Save time with our exam-specific cheat sheets:

https://digitalcloud.training/certification-training/aws-certified-cloud-practitioner/cloud-security/

QUESTION 21

Which type of security control can be used to deny network access from a specific IP address?

1. AWS Shield
2. AWS WAF
3. Network ACL
4. Security Group

Answer: 3

Explanation:

A Network ACL supports allow and deny rules. You can create a deny rule specifying a specific IP address that you would like to block.

Security Group	Network ACL
Operates at the instance (interface) level	Operates at the subnet level
Supports allow rules only	Supports allow and deny rules
Stateful	Stateless
Evaluates all rules	Processes rules in order
Applies to an instance only if associated with a group	Automatically applies to all instances in the subnets its associated with

CORRECT: "Network ACL" is the correct answer.

INCORRECT: "AWS Shield" is incorrect. AWS Shield is a managed Distributed Denial of Service (DDoS) protection service

INCORRECT: "AWS WAF" is incorrect. AWS WAF is a web application firewall

INCORRECT: "Security Group" is incorrect. A Security Group only supports allow rules

References:

https://docs.aws.amazon.com/vpc/latest/userguide/vpc-network-acls.html

Save time with our exam-specific cheat sheets:

https://digitalcloud.training/certification-training/aws-certified-cloud-practitioner/aws-networking/

QUESTION 22

Which service can be used to manage configuration versions?

1. AWS Service Catalog
2. AWS Artifact
3. Amazon Inspector
4. AWS Config

Answer: 4

Explanation:

AWS Config is a fully-managed service that provides you with an AWS resource inventory, configuration history, and configuration change notifications to enable security and regulatory compliance.

CORRECT: "AWS Config" is the correct answer.

INCORRECT: "AWS Service Catalog" is incorrect. AWS Service Catalog is used to create and manage catalogs of IT services that you have approved for use on AWS, including virtual machine images, servers, software, and databases to complete multi-tier application architectures.

INCORRECT: "AWS Artifact" is incorrect. AWS Artifact is a central resource for compliance-related information. This service can be used to get compliance information related to AWS' certifications/attestations.

INCORRECT: "Amazon Inspector" is incorrect. Inspector is an automated security assessment service that helps improve the security and compliance of applications deployed on AWS.

References:

https://docs.aws.amazon.com/config/latest/developerguide/how-does-config-work.html

Save time with our exam-specific cheat sheets:

QUESTION 23

Which aspects of security on AWS are customer responsibilities? (Select TWO.)

1. Setting up account password policies
2. Physical access controls
3. Server-side encryption
4. Patching of storage systems
5. Availability of AWS regions

Answer: 1,3

Explanation:

AWS are responsible for the "security of the cloud". This includes protecting the infrastructure that runs all of the services offered in the AWS Cloud. This infrastructure is composed of the hardware, software, networking, and facilities that run AWS Cloud services.

The customer is responsible for "security in the cloud". Customer responsibility depends on the service consumed but includes aspects such as Identity and Access Management (includes password policies), encryption of data, protection of network traffic, and operating system, network and firewall configuration.

CORRECT: "Setting up account password policies" is a correct answer.

CORRECT: "Server-side encryption" is also a correct answer.

INCORRECT: "Physical access controls" is incorrect as explained above.

INCORRECT: "Patching of storage systems" is incorrect as explained above.

INCORRECT: "Availability of AWS regions" is incorrect as explained above.

References:

https://aws.amazon.com/compliance/shared-responsibility-model/

Save time with our exam-specific cheat sheets:

https://digitalcloud.training/certification-training/aws-certified-cloud-practitioner/aws-shared-responsibility-model/

QUESTION 24

Which of the following are architectural best practices for the AWS Cloud? (Select TWO.)

1. Deploy into multiple Availability Zones
2. Deploy into a single availability zone
3. Close coupling
4. Design for fault tolerance
5. Create monolithic architectures

Answer: 1,4

Explanation:

It is an architectural best practice to deploy your resources into multiple availability zones and design for fault tolerance. These both ensure that if resources or infrastructure fails, your application continues to run.

CORRECT: "Deploy into multiple Availability Zones" is a correct answer.

CORRECT: "Design for fault tolerance" is also a correct answer.

INCORRECT: "Deploy into a single availability zone" is incorrect. You should not deploy all of your resources into a single availability zone as any infrastructure failure will take down access to your resources.

INCORRECT: "Close coupling" is incorrect. Close coupling is not an architectural best practice – loose coupling is. With loose coupling you reduce interdependencies between components of an application and often put a middle layer such as a message bus between components.

INCORRECT: "Create monolithic architectures" is incorrect. You should not create monolithic architectures. With monolithic architectures you have a single instance running multiple components of the application, if any of these components fails, your application fails. It is better to design microservices architectures where components are spread across more instances.

References:

https://aws.amazon.com/architecture/well-architected/

Save time with our exam-specific cheat sheets:

https://digitalcloud.training/certification-training/aws-certified-cloud-practitioner/architecting-for-the-cloud/

QUESTION 25

To reduce the price of your Amazon EC2 instances, which term lengths are available for reserved instances? (Select TWO.)

1. 4 years
2. 1 year
3. 5 years
4. 2 years
5. 3 years

Answer: 2,5

Explanation:

Reserved instances provide significant discounts, up to 75% compared to On-Demand pricing, by paying for capacity ahead of time. They are good for applications that have predictable usage, that need reserved capacity, and for customers who can commit to a 1 or 3-year term.

CORRECT: "1 year" is a correct answer.

CORRECT: "3 years" is also a correct answer.

INCORRECT: "4 years" is incorrect as only 1 and 3 year options are available.

INCORRECT: "5 years" is incorrect as only 1 and 3 year options are available.

INCORRECT: "2 years" is incorrect as only 1 and 3 year options are available.

References:

https://aws.amazon.com/ec2/pricing/reserved-instances/

Save time with our exam-specific cheat sheets:

https://digitalcloud.training/certification-training/aws-certified-cloud-practitioner/aws-billing-and-pricing/

QUESTION 26

What are the fundamental charges for Elastic Block Store (EBS) volumes? (Select TWO.)

1. The amount of data storage provisioned
2. The amount of data storage consumed
3. Number of snapshots
4. Provisioned IOPS
5. Inbound data transfer

Answer: 1,4

Explanation:

With EBS volumes you are charged for the amount of data provisioned (not consumed) per month. This means you can have empty space within a volume and you still pay for it. With provisioned IOPS volumes you are also charged for the amount you provision in IOPS

CORRECT: "The amount of data storage provisioned" is a correct answer.

CORRECT: "Provisioned IOPS" is also a correct answer.

INCORRECT: "The amount of data storage consumed" is incorrect as you pay for the amount provisioned.

INCORRECT: "Number of snapshots" is incorrect. You pay for the storage consumed by snapshots, not by the number of snapshots.

INCORRECT: "Inbound data transfer" is incorrect as you do not pay for data ingress.

QUESTION 27

What is the most cost-effective Amazon S3 storage tier for data that is not often accessed but requires high availability?

1. Amazon S3 Standard-IA
2. Amazon S3 Standard
3. Amazon S3 One Zone-IA
4. Amazon Glacier

Answer: 1

Explanation:

S3 Standard-IA is for data that is accessed less frequently, but requires rapid access when needed. S3 Standard-IA offers the high durability, high throughput, and low latency of S3 Standard with 99.9% availability

CORRECT: "Amazon S3 Standard-IA" is the correct answer.

INCORRECT: "Amazon S3 Standard" is incorrect as this class will cost more and is designed for data that requires regular access.

INCORRECT: "Amazon S3 One Zone-IA" is incorrect. S3 One Zone-IA is for data that is accessed less frequently, but requires rapid access when needed. Unlike other S3 Storage Classes which store data in a minimum of three Availability Zones (AZs), S3 One Zone-IA stores data in a single AZ and offers lower availability.

INCORRECT: "Amazon Glacier" is incorrect. Glacier is a data archiving solution so not suitable for a storage tier that requires infrequent access.

References:

https://aws.amazon.com/s3/storage-classes/

QUESTION 28

What is the main benefit of the principle of "loose coupling"?

1. Reduce operational complexity
2. Reduce interdependencies so a failure in one component does not cascade to other components
3. Automate the deployment of infrastructure using code
4. Enables applications to scale automatically based on current demand

Answer: 2

Explanation:

As application complexity increases, a desirable attribute of an IT system is that it can be broken into smaller, loosely coupled components. This means that IT systems should be designed in a way that reduces interdependencies—a change or a failure in one component should not cascade to other components.

CORRECT: "Reduce interdependencies so a failure in one component does not cascade to other components" is the correct answer.

INCORRECT: "Reduce operational complexity" is incorrect. Loose coupling does not reduce operational complexity. In fact, it may increase complexity as you have more services running and more interactions.

INCORRECT: "Automate the deployment of infrastructure using code" is incorrect. This is an example of "Infrastructure as code" – services such as CloudFormation provide this functionality.

INCORRECT: "Enables applications to scale automatically based on current demand" is incorrect. This is an example of Elasticity.

References:

Save time with our exam-specific cheat sheets:

https://digitalcloud.training/certification-training/aws-certified-cloud-practitioner/architecting-for-the-cloud/

QUESTION 29

Which Amazon EC2 billing option gives you low cost, maximum flexibility, no upfront costs or commitment, and you only pay for what you use?

1. Dedicated Host
2. Spot Instances
3. Reserved Instances
4. On-Demand Instances

Answer: 4

Explanation:

With On-Demand instances you pay for hours used with no commitment. There are no upfront costs so you have maximum flexibility.

CORRECT: "On-Demand Instances" is the correct answer.

INCORRECT: "Dedicated Host" is incorrect. Dedicated hosts use physically dedicated EC2 servers to isolate your workloads and are expensive

INCORRECT: "Spot Instances" is incorrect. Spot instances are used for getting a very low price which you bid on. You lose some flexibility as you are constrained by market prices and your workloads can be terminated if the market price exceeds your bid price

INCORRECT: "Reserved Instances" is incorrect. Reserved instances are based on a commitment to 1 or 3 years in exchange for a large discount.

References:

https://aws.amazon.com/ec2/pricing/

Save time with our exam-specific cheat sheets:

https://digitalcloud.training/certification-training/aws-certified-cloud-practitioner/aws-compute/

QUESTION 30

Where can resources be launched when configuring Amazon EC2 Auto Scaling?

1. A single subnet
2. Multiple AZs within a region
3. Multiple AZs and multiple regions
4. Multiple VPCs

Answer: 2

Explanation:

Amazon EC2 Auto Scaling is configured within the EC2 console and can launch instances within a VPC across multiple AZs. It cannot launch resources into another AWS Region.

CORRECT: "Multiple AZs within a region" is the correct answer.

INCORRECT: "Multiple AZs and multiple regions" is incorrect as you cannot launch resources into another Region.

INCORRECT: "A single subnet" is incorrect as instances can be launched in multiple subnets.

INCORRECT: "Multiple VPCs" is incorrect as you cannot use a single Auto Scaling group to launch resources into multiple subnets.

References:

https://aws.amazon.com/ec2/autoscaling/

Save time with our exam-specific cheat sheets:

QUESTION 31

Which service can be used to improve performance for users around the world?

1. AWS LightSail
2. Amazon CloudFront
3. Amazon Connect
4. Amazon ElastiCache

Answer: 2

Explanation:

Amazon CloudFront is a content delivery network (CDN) that caches content at Edge Locations around the world. This gets the content closer to users which improves performance.

CORRECT: "Amazon CloudFront" is the correct answer.

INCORRECT: "AWS LightSail" is incorrect. AWS LightSail is a compute service that offers a lower cost and easier to use alternative to Amazon EC2.

INCORRECT: "Amazon Connect" is incorrect. Amazon Connect Amazon Connect is a self-service, cloud-based contact center service that makes it easy for any business to deliver better customer service at lower cost.

INCORRECT: "Amazon ElastiCache" is incorrect. Amazon ElastiCache is a caching service for databases. Though it does improve read performance for database queries, it is not a global service that is designed to improve performance for users around the world.

References:

https://aws.amazon.com/cloudfront/faqs/

Save time with our exam-specific cheat sheets:

https://digitalcloud.training/certification-training/aws-certified-cloud-practitioner/content-delivery-and-dns-services/

QUESTION 32

Which of the below are components that can be configured in the VPC section of the AWS management console? (Select TWO.)

1. EBS volumes
2. Subnet
3. Endpoints
4. DNS records
5. Elastic Load Balancer

Answer:

Explanation:

You can configure subnets and endpoints within the VPC section of AWS management console.

EBS volumes and ELB must be configured in the EC2 section of the AWS management console and DNS records must be configured in Amazon Route 53.

CORRECT: "Subnet" is a correct answer.

CORRECT: "Endpoints" is also a correct answer.

INCORRECT: "EBS volumes" is incorrect as explained above.

INCORRECT: "DNS records" is incorrect as explained above.

INCORRECT: "Elastic Load Balancer" is incorrect as explained above.

References:

https://aws.amazon.com/vpc/

Save time with our exam-specific cheat sheets:

https://digitalcloud.training/certification-training/aws-certified-cloud-practitioner/aws-networking/

QUESTION 33

Which of the following is a benefit of moving to the AWS Cloud?

1. Outsource all IT operations
2. Pay for what you use
3. Capital purchases
4. Long term commitments

Answer:

Explanation:

With the AWS cloud you pay for what you use. This is a significant advantage compared to on-premises infrastructure where you need to purchase more equipment than you need to allow for peak capacity. You also need to pay for that equipment upfront.

CORRECT: "Pay for what you use" is the correct answer.

INCORRECT: "Outsource all IT operations" is incorrect. You do not outsource all IT operations when moving to the AWS Cloud. AWS provide some higher-level managed services which reduces your operations effort but does not eliminate it.

INCORRECT: "Capital purchases" is incorrect. Capital purchases are not a benefit of moving to the cloud. The AWS Cloud is mostly an operational expenditure which is favored by many CFOs.

INCORRECT: "Long term commitments" is incorrect. You do not need to enter into long term commitments with the AWS Cloud. There are options for 1 or 3 year commitments to lower prices with some services but this is not an advantage of the cloud.

References:

https://aws.amazon.com/pricing/

Save time with our exam-specific cheat sheets:

https://digitalcloud.training/certification-training/aws-certified-cloud-practitioner/aws-billing-and-pricing/

QUESTION 34

In addition to DNS services, what other services does Amazon Route 53 provide? (Select TWO.)

1. DHCP
2. Caching
3. Domain registration
4. IP Routing
5. Traffic flow

Answer: 3,5

Explanation:

Amazon Route 53 features include domain registration, DNS, traffic flow, health checking, and failover. .Route 53 does not support DHCP, IP routing or caching.

CORRECT: "Domain registration" is the correct answer.

CORRECT: "Traffic flow" is the correct answer.

INCORRECT: "DHCP" is incorrect as explained above.

INCORRECT: "Caching" is incorrect as explained above.

INCORRECT: " IP Routing" is incorrect. The DNS features of Route 53 are called "routing policies", however this is not traditional IP routing which is performed by routers. It is intelligent DNS that responds with different results based on certain factors such as latency, weight, or failover configuration.

References:

https://aws.amazon.com/route53/

Save time with our exam-specific cheat sheets:

https://digitalcloud.training/certification-training/aws-certified-cloud-practitioner/content-delivery-and-dns-services/

QUESTION 35

What can be assigned to an IAM user? (Select TWO.)

1. An access key ID and secret access key
2. An SSL/TLS certificate
3. A key pair
4. A password for logging into Linux
5. A password for access to the management console

Answer: 1,5

Explanation:

An IAM user is an entity that represents a person or service. Users can be assigned an access key ID and secret access key for programmatic access to the AWS API, CLI, SDK, and other development tools and a password for access to the management console.

CORRECT: "An access key ID and secret access key" is the correct answer.

CORRECT: "A password for access to the management console" is the correct answer.

INCORRECT: "An SSL/TLS certificate" is incorrect. You cannot assign an SSL/TLS certificate to a user.

INCORRECT: "A key pair" is incorrect. Key pairs are used with Amazon EC2 as a method of using public key encryption to securely access EC2 instances.

INCORRECT: "A password for logging into Linux" is incorrect. You cannot assign an IAM user with a password for logging into a Linux instance.

References:

https://docs.aws.amazon.com/IAM/latest/UserGuide/id_users.html

Save time with our exam-specific cheat sheets:

https://digitalcloud.training/certification-training/aws-certified-cloud-practitioner/identity-and-access-management/

QUESTION 36

The AWS acceptable use policy for penetration testing allows?

1. Customers to carry out security assessments or penetration tests against their AWS infrastructure without prior approval for selected services
2. Customers to carry out security assessments or penetration tests against their AWS infrastructure after obtaining authorization from AWS
3. AWS to perform penetration testing against customer resources without notification
4. Authorized security assessors to perform penetration tests against any AWS customer without authorization

Answer: 1

Explanation:

AWS customers are welcome to carry out security assessments or penetration tests against their AWS infrastructure without prior approval for the following eight services:

- Amazon EC2 instances, NAT Gateways, and Elastic Load Balancers.
- Amazon RDS.
- Amazon CloudFront.
- Amazon Aurora.
- Amazon API Gateways.
- AWS Lambda and Lambda Edge functions.
- Amazon LightSail resources.
- Amazon Elastic Beanstalk environments.

CORRECT: "Customers to carry out security assessments or penetration tests against their AWS infrastructure without prior approval for selected services" is the correct answer.

INCORRECT: "Customers to carry out security assessments or penetration tests against their AWS infrastructure after obtaining authorization from AWS" is incorrect as you do not need authorization.

INCORRECT: "AWS to perform penetration testing against customer resources without notification" is incorrect as AWS will not perform penetration testing on customer resources.

INCORRECT: "Authorized security assessors to perform penetration tests against any AWS customer without authorization" is incorrect. This is not something that is authorized

References:

https://aws.amazon.com/security/penetration-testing/

Save time with our exam-specific cheat sheets:

https://digitalcloud.training/certification-training/aws-certified-cloud-practitioner/cloud-security/

QUESTION 37

Which type of connection should be used to connect an on-premises data center with the AWS cloud that is high speed, low latency and does not use the Internet?

1. Direct Connect
2. VPC Endpoints
3. AWS Managed VPN
4. Client VPN

Answer: 1

Explanation:

AWS Direct Connect is a network service that provides an alternative to using the Internet to connect a customer's on premise sites to AWS. Data is transmitted through a private network connection between AWS and a customer's datacenter or corporate network. Direct Connect is high bandwidth, and low latency.

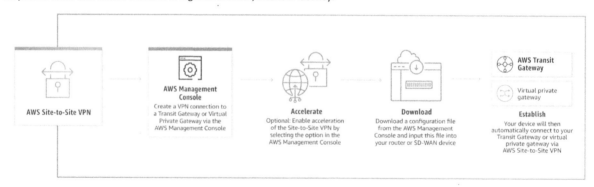

CORRECT: "Direct Connect" is the correct answer.

INCORRECT: "VPC Endpoints" is incorrect. VPC endpoint enable private connectivity to services hosted in AWS, from within your VPC without using an Internet Gateway, VPN, Network Address Translation (NAT) devices, or firewall proxies.

INCORRECT: "AWS Managed VPN" is incorrect. The AWS Managed VPN (which is a type of IPSec VPN) is fast to setup but uses the public Internet and therefore latency is not as good and is unpredictable.

INCORRECT: "Client VPN" is incorrect. A site-to-site VPN should be used rather than a client VPN to connect two sites together.

References:

https://aws.amazon.com/vpn/

Save time with our exam-specific cheat sheets:

https://digitalcloud.training/certification-training/aws-certified-cloud-practitioner/aws-networking/

QUESTION 38

Which of the advantages of cloud listed below is most closely addressed by the capabilities of AWS Auto Scaling?

1. Benefit from massive economies of scale
2. Stop guessing about capacity
3. Stop spending money running and maintaining data centers
4. Go global in minutes

Answer: 2

Explanation:

AWS Auto Scaling helps you to adapt to the demand for you application and scale up and down as needed. This means you don't have to guess capacity upfront as you can provision what you need and allows Auto Scaling to manage the scaling.

CORRECT: "Stop guessing about capacity" is the correct answer.

INCORRECT: "Benefit from massive economies of scale" is incorrect. This is a cost advantage of cloud.

INCORRECT: "Stop spending money running and maintaining data centers" is incorrect. This is a cost advantage of moving to cloud.

INCORRECT: "Go global in minutes" is incorrect. This is a benefit of deploying cloud services globally.

References:

https://aws.amazon.com/autoscaling/

Save time with our exam-specific cheat sheets:

https://digitalcloud.training/certification-training/aws-certified-cloud-practitioner/cloud-computing-concepts/

QUESTION 39

Which statement is correct in relation to the AWS Shared Responsibility Model?
1. AWS are responsible for the security of regions and availability zones
2. Customers are responsible for patching storage systems
3. AWS are responsible for encrypting customer data
4. Customers are responsible for security of the cloud

Answer: 1

Explanation:

AWS are responsible for "Security of the Cloud". AWS is responsible for protecting the infrastructure that runs all of the services offered in the AWS Cloud. This infrastructure is composed of the hardware, software, networking, and facilities that run AWS Cloud services, and this includes regions, availability zones and edge locations.

Customers are responsible for "Security in the Cloud". This includes encrypting customer data, patching operating systems but not patching or maintaining the underlying infrastructure.

CORRECT: "AWS are responsible for the security of regions and availability zones" is the correct answer.

INCORRECT: "Customers are responsible for patching storage systems" is incorrect as this is an AWS responsibility.

INCORRECT: "AWS are responsible for encrypting customer data" is incorrect as this is a customer responsibility.

INCORRECT: "Customers are responsible for security of the cloud" is incorrect as this is an AWS responsibility.

References:

https://aws.amazon.com/compliance/shared-responsibility-model/

Save time with our exam-specific cheat sheets:

https://digitalcloud.training/certification-training/aws-certified-cloud-practitioner/aws-shared-responsibility-model/

QUESTION 40

Which of the following is an advantage of cloud computing compared to deploying your own infrastructure on-premise?
1. Flexibility to choose your own hardware
2. Spend using a CAPEX model
3. Paying only for what you use
4. Ability to choose bespoke infrastructure configurations

Answer: 3

Explanation:

With AWS you only pay for what you use. However, you cannot choose your own hardware/infrastructure and the payment model is operational (OPEX) not capital (CAPEX).

CORRECT: "Paying only for what you use" is the correct answer.

INCORRECT: "Flexibility to choose your own hardware" is incorrect as explained above.

INCORRECT: "Spend using a CAPEX model" is incorrect as explained above.

INCORRECT: "Ability to choose bespoke infrastructure configurations" is incorrect as explained above.

References:

https://docs.aws.amazon.com/whitepapers/latest/aws-overview/six-advantages-of-cloud-computing.html

Save time with our exam-specific cheat sheets:

https://digitalcloud.training/certification-training/aws-certified-cloud-practitioner/cloud-computing-concepts/

QUESTION 41

Which service can be added to a database to provide improved performance for some requests?

1. Amazon RedShift
2. Amazon EFS
3. Amazon ElastiCache
4. Amazon RDS

Answer: 3

Explanation:

Amazon ElastiCache provides in-memory caching which improves performance for read requests when the data is cached in ElastiCache. ElastiCache can be placed in front of your database.

CORRECT: "Amazon ElastiCache" is the correct answer.

INCORRECT: "Amazon RedShift" is incorrect. Amazon RedShift is a data warehouse that is used for performing analytics on data.

INCORRECT: "Amazon EFS" is incorrect. Amazon EFS is an Elastic File System, not a caching service.

INCORRECT: "Amazon RDS" is incorrect. Amazon RDS is a relational SQL type of database. It is not a service that you place in front of another database to improve performance. Instead you might use RDS as your back-end database and use ElastiCache in front of it to improve performance through its in-memory caching.

References:

https://aws.amazon.com/elasticache/

Save time with our exam-specific cheat sheets:

https://digitalcloud.training/certification-training/aws-certified-cloud-practitioner/aws-databases/

QUESTION 42

Which service can be used to assign a policy to a group?

1. AWS IAM
2. Amazon Cognito
3. Amazon STS
4. AWS Shield

Answer: 1

Explanation:

IAM is used to securely control individual and group access to AWS resources. Groups are collections of users and have policies attached to them. You can use IAM to attach a policy to a group

CORRECT: "AWS IAM" is the correct answer.

INCORRECT: "Amazon Cognito" is incorrect. Amazon Cognito is used for authentication using mobile apps

INCORRECT: "AWS STS" is incorrect. The AWS Security Token Service (STS) is a web service that enables you to request temporary, limited-privilege credentials for IAM users or for users that you authenticate (federated users)

INCORRECT: "AWS Shield" is incorrect. AWS Shield is a managed Distributed Denial of Service (DDoS) protection service that safeguards applications running on AWS.

References:

https://docs.aws.amazon.com/IAM/latest/UserGuide/introduction.html

Save time with our exam-specific cheat sheets:

https://digitalcloud.training/certification-training/aws-certified-cloud-practitioner/identity-and-access-management/

QUESTION 43

Which AWS service lets you add user sign up, sign-in and access control to web and mobile apps?

1. AWS Artifact
2. Amazon Cognito
3. AWS CloudHSM
4. AWS Directory Service

Answer: 2

Explanation:

Amazon Cognito lets you add user sign-up, sign-in, and access control to your web and mobile apps quickly and easily. Amazon Cognito scales to millions of users and supports sign-in with social identity providers, such as Facebook, Google, and Amazon, and enterprise identity providers via SAML 2.0.

CORRECT: "AWS Cognito" is the correct answer.

INCORRECT: "AWS Artifact" is incorrect. AWS Artifact is your go-to, central resource for compliance-related information that matters to you.

INCORRECT: "AWS CloudHSM" is incorrect. AWS CloudHSM is a cloud-based hardware security module (HSM) that enables you to easily generate and use your own encryption keys on the AWS Cloud

INCORRECT: "AWS Directory Service" is incorrect. AWS Directory Service for Microsoft Active Directory, also known as AWS Managed Microsoft AD, enables your directory-aware workloads and AWS resources to use managed Active Directory in the AWS Cloud.

References:

https://aws.amazon.com/cognito/

Save time with our exam-specific cheat sheets:

https://digitalcloud.training/certification-training/aws-certified-cloud-practitioner/additional-aws-services-tools/

QUESTION 44

What is the difference between an EBS volume and an Instance store?

1. EBS volumes are object storage devices whereas Instance store volume are block based
2. Instance store volumes are ephemeral whereas EBS volumes are persistent storage
3. Instance store volumes can be used with all EC2 instance types whereas EBS cannot
4. EBS volumes are file-level storage devices whereas Instance store volumes are object-based

Answer: 2

Explanation:

EBS-backed means the root volume is an EBS volume and storage is persistent. Instance store-backed means the root volume is an instance store volume and storage is not persistent. Both EBS and Instance store volumes are block-based storage devices.

EBS volumes can be used with all EC2 instance types whereas Instance store volumes are more limited in compatibility

CORRECT: "Instance store volumes are ephemeral whereas EBS volumes are persistent storage" is the correct answer.

INCORRECT: "EBS volumes are object storage devices whereas Instance store volume are block based" is incorrect as both are block-based storage devices.

INCORRECT: "Instance store volumes can be used with all EC2 instance types whereas EBS cannot" is incorrect as this is not true.

INCORRECT: "EBS volumes are file-level storage devices whereas Instance store volumes are object-based" is incorrect as both are block-based storage devices.

References:

https://aws.amazon.com/premiumsupport/knowledge-center/instance-store-vs-ebs/

Save time with our exam-specific cheat sheets:

https://digitalcloud.training/certification-training/aws-certified-cloud-practitioner/aws-storage/

QUESTION 45

What are two components of Amazon S3? (Select TWO.)

1. Buckets
2. Directories
3. Objects
4. Block devices
5. File systems

Answer: 1,3

Explanation:

Amazon S3 is an object-based storage system that is accessed using a RESTful API over HTTP(S). It consists of buckets, which are root level folders, and objects, which are the files, images etc. that you upload

The terms directory, file system and block device do not apply to Amazon S3.

CORRECT: "Buckets" is a correct answer.

CORRECT: "Objects" is also a correct answer.

INCORRECT: "Directories" is incorrect as explained above.

INCORRECT: "Block devices" is incorrect as explained above.

INCORRECT: "File systems" is incorrect as explained above.

References:

https://docs.aws.amazon.com/AmazonS3/latest/dev/Welcome.html

Save time with our exam-specific cheat sheets:

https://digitalcloud.training/certification-training/aws-certified-cloud-practitioner/aws-storage/

QUESTION 46

Which of the below are good use cases for a specific Amazon EC2 pricing model? (Select TWO.)

1. Reserved instances for steady state predictable usage
2. On-demand for regulatory requirements that do not allow multi-tenant virtualization
3. On-demand for ad-hoc requirements that cannot be interrupted
4. Spot for consistent load over a long term
5. Reserved instances for applications with flexible start and end times

Answer: 1,3

Explanation:

Typical use cases for the pricing models listed are:

On-demand: Good for users that want the low cost and flexibility of EC2 without any up-front payment or long-term commitment. Applications with short term, spiky, or unpredictable workloads that cannot be interrupted

Reserved: Applications with steady state or predictable usage or that require reserved capacity

Spot: Applications that have flexible start and end times and that are only feasible at very low compute prices. May be terminated

Dedicated hosts: Useful for regulatory requirements that may not support multi-tenant virtualization. Great for licensing which does not support multi-tenancy or cloud deployments

CORRECT: "Reserved instances for steady state predictable usage" is a correct answer.

CORRECT: "On-demand for ad-hoc requirements that cannot be interrupted" is also a correct answer.

INCORRECT: "On-demand for regulatory requirements that do not allow multi-tenant virtualization" is incorrect. Please refer to the typical use cases above.

INCORRECT: "Spot for consistent load over a long term" is incorrect. Please refer to the typical use cases above.

INCORRECT: "Reserved instances for applications with flexible start and end times" is incorrect. Please refer to the typical use cases above.

References:

https://aws.amazon.com/ec2/pricing/

Save time with our exam-specific cheat sheets:

https://digitalcloud.training/certification-training/aws-certified-cloud-practitioner/aws-compute/

QUESTION 47

Which of the following security related activities are AWS customers responsible for? (Select TWO.)

1. Secure disposal of faulty disk drives
2. Implementing data center access controls
3. Installing patches on network devices
4. Installing patches on Windows operating systems
5. Implementing IAM password policies

Answer: 4,5

Explanation:

Customers are responsible for configuring their own IAM password policies and installing operating system patches on Amazon EC2 instances

AWS are responsible for installing patches on physical hardware devices, data center access controls and secure disposal of disk drives

CORRECT: "Installing patches on Windows operating systems" is the correct answer.

CORRECT: "Implementing IAM password policies" is the correct answer.

INCORRECT: "Secure disposal of faulty disk drives" is incorrect as this is an AWS responsibility.

INCORRECT: "Implementing data center access controls" is incorrect as this is an AWS responsibility.

© 2022 Digital Cloud Training

INCORRECT: "Installing patches on network devices" is incorrect as this is an AWS responsibility.

References:

https://aws.amazon.com/compliance/shared-responsibility-model/

Save time with our exam-specific cheat sheets:

https://digitalcloud.training/certification-training/aws-certified-cloud-practitioner/aws-shared-responsibility-model/

QUESTION 48

An organization has an on-premises cloud and accesses their AWS Cloud over the Internet. How can they create a private hybrid cloud connection that avoids the internet?

1. AWS Direct Connect
2. AWS Managed VPN
3. AWS VPN CloudHub
4. AWS VPC Endpoint

Answer: 1

Explanation:

AWS Direct Connect is a low-latency, high-bandwidth, private connection to AWS. This can be used to create a private hybrid cloud connection between on-premises and the AWS Cloud.

CORRECT: "AWS Direct Connect" is the correct answer.

INCORRECT: "AWS Managed VPN" is incorrect. AWS Managed VPN uses the Internet for network connections, so it is not creating a private connection. The connection is secured but uses the Internet.

INCORRECT: "AWS VPN CloudHub" is incorrect. AWS VPN CloudHub uses the Internet for network connections, so it is not creating a private connection. The connection is secured but uses the Internet.

INCORRECT: "AWS VPC Endpoint" is incorrect. An AWS VPC Endpoint is a PrivateLink connection that connects an AWS public service to a VPC using a private connection. This does not connect on-premises environments to AWS.

References:

https://aws.amazon.com/directconnect/faqs/

Save time with our exam-specific cheat sheets:

https://digitalcloud.training/certification-training/aws-certified-cloud-practitioner/aws-networking/

QUESTION 49

Which team is available to support AWS customers on an Enterprise support plan with account issues?

1. AWS Technical Support
2. AWS Billing and Accounts
3. AWS Concierge
4. AWS Technical Account Manager

Answer: 3

Explanation:

Included as part of the Enterprise Support plan, the Support Concierge Team are AWS billing and account experts that specialize in working with enterprise accounts.

CORRECT: "AWS Concierge" is the correct answer.

INCORRECT: "AWS Technical Support" is incorrect as this is not the name of the team.

INCORRECT: "AWS Billing and Accounts" is incorrect as the Support Concierge Team fulfil this role.

INCORRECT: "AWS Technical Account Manager" is incorrect. The Technical Account Manager provides expert monitoring and optimization for your environment and coordinates access to other programs and experts.

References:

https://aws.amazon.com/premiumsupport/features/

QUESTION 50

What are two examples of the advantages of cloud computing? (Select TWO.)

1. Increase speed and agility
2. Trade operating costs for capital costs
3. Secure data centers
4. Benefit from massive economies of scale
5. Trade variable expense for capital expense

Answer: 1,4

Explanation:

The 6 advantages of cloud computing are:

– Trade capital expense for variable expense.

– Benefit from massive economies of scale.

– Stop guessing about capacity.

– Increase speed and agility.

– Stop spending money running and maintaining data centers.

– Go global in minutes.

CORRECT: "Increase speed and agility" is a correct answer.

CORRECT: "Benefit from massive economies of scale" is also a correct answer.

INCORRECT: "Trade operating costs for capital costs" is incorrect as this is backwards.

INCORRECT: "Secure data centers" is incorrect. Secure data centers are not a reason to move to the cloud. Your on-premises data centers should also be secure.

INCORRECT: "Trade variable expense for capital expense" is incorrect as this is backwards.

References:

https://docs.aws.amazon.com/whitepapers/latest/aws-overview/six-advantages-of-cloud-computing.html

QUESTION 51

Which of the following is an architectural best practice recommended by AWS?

1. Design for success
2. Design for failure
3. Think servers, not services
4. Use manual operational processes

Answer: 2

Explanation:

It is recommended that you design for failure. This means always considering what would happen if a component of an application fails and ensuring there is resilience in the architecture.

CORRECT: "Design for failure" is the correct answer.

INCORRECT: "Design for success" is incorrect. Design for success sounds good, but this is not an architectural best practice. As much as we want our applications to be successful, we should always be cognizant of the potential failures that might occur and ensure we are prepared for them.

INCORRECT: "Think servers, not services" is incorrect. AWS do not recommend that you "think servers, not services". What they do recommend is that you "think services, not servers". This means that you should consider using managed services and serverless services rather than just using Amazon EC2.

INCORRECT: "Use manual operational processes" is incorrect. You should not use manual operational processes; this is not an architectural best practice. You should automate as much as possible in the cloud.

References:

https://aws.amazon.com/architecture/well-architected/

Save time with our exam-specific cheat sheets:

https://digitalcloud.training/certification-training/aws-certified-cloud-practitioner/architecting-for-the-cloud/

QUESTION 52

What is the scope of an Amazon Virtual Private Cloud (VPC)?

1. It spans a single CIDR block
2. It spans all Availability Zones within a region
3. It spans multiple subnets
4. It spans all Availability Zones in all regions

Answer: 2

Explanation:

A virtual private cloud (VPC) is a virtual network dedicated to your AWS account. A VPC spans all the Availability Zones in the region.

CORRECT: "It spans all Availability Zones within a region" is the correct answer.

INCORRECT: "It spans a single CIDR block" is incorrect. You can have multiple CIDR blocks in a VPC.

INCORRECT: "It spans multiple subnets" is incorrect. A VPC spans AZs, subnets are created within AZs

INCORRECT: "It spans all Availability Zones in all regions" is incorrect as it is within a single Region.

References:

https://docs.aws.amazon.com/vpc/latest/userguide/what-is-amazon-vpc.html

Save time with our exam-specific cheat sheets:

https://digitalcloud.training/certification-training/aws-certified-cloud-practitioner/aws-networking/

QUESTION 53

Which AWS service allows you to automate the evaluation of recorded configurations against desired configuration?

1. AWS OpsWorks
2. AWS Service Catalog
3. AWS CloudFormation
4. AWS Config

Answer: 4

Explanation:

AWS Config is a service that enables you to assess, audit, and evaluate the configurations of your AWS resources. Config continuously monitors and records your AWS resource configurations and allows you to automate the evaluation of recorded configurations against desired configurations.

CORRECT: "AWS Config" is the correct answer.

INCORRECT: "AWS OpsWorks" is incorrect. AWS OpsWorks is a configuration management service that provides managed instances of Chef and Puppet.

INCORRECT: "AWS Service Catalog" is incorrect. AWS Service Catalog allows organizations to create and manage catalogs of IT services that are approved for use on AWS.

INCORRECT: "AWS CloudFormation" is incorrect. AWS CloudFormation provides a common language for you to describe and provision all the infrastructure resources in your cloud environment.

References:

https://aws.amazon.com/config/

Save time with our exam-specific cheat sheets:

https://digitalcloud.training/certification-training/aws-certified-cloud-practitioner/additional-aws-services-tools/

QUESTION 54

Which of the options below are recommendations in the reliability pillar of the well-architected framework? (Select TWO.)

1. Test recovery procedures
2. Manually recover from failure
3. Manage change in manual processes
4. Stop guessing about capacity
5. Scale vertically using big systems

Answer: 1,4

Explanation:

The reliability pillar includes the ability of a system to recover from infrastructure or service disruptions, dynamically acquire computing resources to meet demand, and mitigate disruptions such as misconfigurations or transient network issues

There are five design principles for reliability in the cloud:

– Test recovery procedures.

– Automatically recover from failure.

– Scale horizontally to increase aggregate system availability.

– Stop guessing capacity.

– Manage change in automation.

CORRECT: "Test recovery procedures" is a correct answer.

CORRECT: "Stop guessing about capacity" is also a correct answer.

INCORRECT: "Manually recover from failure" is incorrect as applications should automatically recover from failure.

INCORRECT: "Manage change in manual processes" is incorrect as you should manage change in automation.

INCORRECT: "Scale vertically using big systems" is incorrect as you should scale applications horizontally.

References:

https://aws.amazon.com/blogs/apn/the-5-pillars-of-the-aws-well-architected-framework/

Save time with our exam-specific cheat sheets:

https://digitalcloud.training/certification-training/aws-certified-cloud-practitioner/architecting-for-the-cloud/

QUESTION 55

Which storage type can be mounted using the NFS protocol to many EC2 instances simultaneously?

1. Amazon Instance Store
2. Amazon EBS
3. Amazon S3
4. Amazon EFS

Answer: 4

Explanation:

EFS is a fully-managed service that makes it easy to set up and scale file storage in the Amazon Cloud. EFS uses the NFSv4.1 protocol. Can concurrently connect 1 to 1000s of EC2 instances, from multiple AZs.

CORRECT: "Amazon EFS" is the correct answer.

INCORRECT: "Amazon Instance Store" is incorrect. Amazon Instance Store is a type of ephemeral block-based volume that can be attached to a single EC2 instance at a time.

INCORRECT: "Amazon EBS" is incorrect. EBS volumes can only be attached to a single EC2 instance at a time and are block devices (not NFS).

INCORRECT: "Amazon S3" is incorrect. Amazon S3 is an object store and is connected to using a RESTful protocol over HTTP.

References:

https://aws.amazon.com/efs/

Save time with our exam-specific cheat sheets:

https://digitalcloud.training/certification-training/aws-certified-cloud-practitioner/aws-storage/

QUESTION 56

Which Amazon RDS deployment type is best used to enable fault tolerance in the event of the failure of an availability zone?

1.   Multiple Regions
2.   Read Replicas
3.   Write Replicas
4.   Multiple Availability Zones

Answer: 4

Explanation:

Multi AZ provides a mechanism to failover the RDS database to another synchronously replicated copy in the event of the failure of an AZ. The endpoint address for the RDS instances gets remapped to the standby instance as can be seen in the image below:

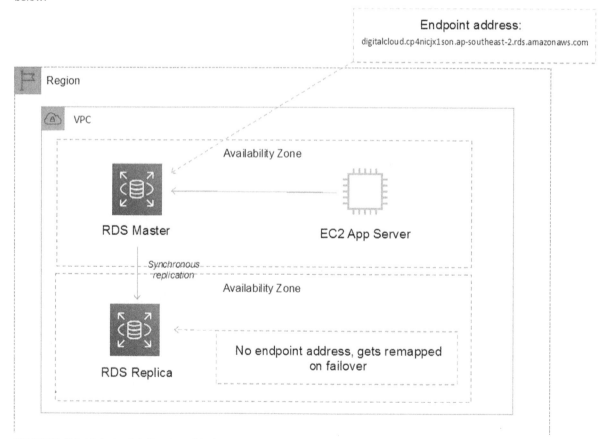

CORRECT: "Multiple Availability Zones" is the correct answer.

INCORRECT: "Multiple Regions" is incorrect. There is no option for multiple region failover of Amazon RDS.

INCORRECT: "Read Replicas" is incorrect. Read replicas are used for offloading read traffic from a primary database but cannot be used for writing. You can failover the DB by promoting a read replica in a DR situation but this is not the best answer as the multi-AZ feature is preferred.

INCORRECT: "Write Replicas" is incorrect. There is no such thing as write replicas.

References:

https://aws.amazon.com/rds/features/multi-az/

Save time with our exam-specific cheat sheets:

https://digitalcloud.training/certification-training/aws-certified-cloud-practitioner/aws-databases/

QUESTION 57

Which feature of AWS IAM enables you to identify unnecessary permissions that have been assigned to users?

1. Role Advisor
2. Access Advisor
3. Permissions Advisor
4. Group Advisor

Answer: 2

Explanation:

The IAM console provides information about when IAM users and roles last attempted to access AWS services. This information is called *service last accessed data*. This data can help you identify unnecessary permissions so that you can refine your IAM policies to better adhere to the principle of "least privilege."

That means granting the minimum permissions required to perform a specific task. You can find the data on the **Access Advisor** tab in the IAM console by examining the detail view for any IAM user, group, role, or managed policy.

CORRECT: "Access Advisor" is the correct answer.

INCORRECT: "Role Advisor" is incorrect as this is not a valid feature.

INCORRECT: "Permissions Advisor" is incorrect as this is not a valid feature.

INCORRECT: "Group Advisor" is incorrect as this is not a valid feature.

References:

https://docs.aws.amazon.com/IAM/latest/UserGuide/access_policies_access-advisor.html

Save time with our exam-specific cheat sheets:

https://digitalcloud.training/certification-training/aws-certified-cloud-practitioner/identity-and-access-management/

QUESTION 58

What types of monitoring can Amazon CloudWatch be used for? (Select TWO.)

1. Infrastructure
2. Data center
3. Operational health
4. API access
5. Application performance

Answer: 3,5

Explanation:

Amazon CloudWatch is a monitoring service for AWS cloud resources and the applications you run on AWS. CloudWatch performs performance monitoring and can monitor custom metrics generated by applications and the operational health of your AWS resources

Infrastructure and data center monitoring is not accessible to AWS customers

CORRECT: "Operational health" is a correct answer.

CORRECT: "Application performance" is also a correct answer.

INCORRECT: "Infrastructure" is incorrect as this monitoring is not accessible to AWS customers.

INCORRECT: "Data center" is incorrect as this monitoring is not accessible to AWS customers.

INCORRECT: "API access" is incorrect. AWS CloudTrail monitors API access

References:

https://docs.aws.amazon.com/AmazonCloudWatch/latest/monitoring/WhatIsCloudWatch.html

Save time with our exam-specific cheat sheets:

https://digitalcloud.training/certification-training/aws-certified-cloud-practitioner/monitoring-and-logging-services/

QUESTION 59

Which AWS service enables hybrid cloud storage between on-premises and the AWS Cloud?

1. Amazon S3 Cross Region Replication (CRR)
2. AWS Storage Gateway
3. Amazon Elastic File System (EFS)
4. Amazon CloudFront

Answer: 2

Explanation:

The AWS Storage Gateway service enables hybrid cloud storage between on-premises environments and the AWS Cloud. It seamlessly integrates on-premises enterprise applications and workflows with Amazon's block and object cloud storage services through industry standard storage protocols.

CORRECT: "AWS Storage Gateway" is the correct answer.

INCORRECT: "Amazon S3 Cross Region Replication (CRR)" is incorrect. Amazon S3 CRR is used for copying data from one S3 bucket to another S3 bucket in another region. That is not an examples of hybrid cloud.

INCORRECT: "Amazon Elastic File System (EFS)" is incorrect. Amazon EFS is not a hybrid cloud storage solution. With EFS you can mount file systems from on-premises servers, however it does not offer a local cache or method of moving data into the cloud.

INCORRECT: "Amazon CloudFront" is incorrect. Amazon CloudFront is a content delivery network. It is used to get content closer to users, it is not a hybrid cloud storage solution.

References:

https://docs.aws.amazon.com/storagegateway/latest/userguide/WhatIsStorageGateway.html

Save time with our exam-specific cheat sheets:

https://digitalcloud.training/certification-training/aws-certified-cloud-practitioner/aws-storage/

QUESTION 60

What does an organization need to do to move to another AWS region?

1. Just start deploying resources in the additional region
2. Create a separate IAM account for that region
3. Apply for another AWS account in that region
4. Submit an application to extend their account to the additional region

Answer: 1

Explanation:

You don't need to do anything except start deploying resources in the new region. With the AWS cloud you can use any region around the world at any time. There is no need for a separate account, and IAM is a global service.

CORRECT: "Just start deploying resources in the additional region" is the correct answer.

INCORRECT: "Create a separate IAM account for that region" is incorrect as IAM is a global service.

INCORRECT: "Apply for another AWS account in that region" is incorrect as you can use IAM across Regions and do not need another account.

INCORRECT: "Submit an application to extend their account to the additional region" is incorrect as you do not need to extend accounts across Regions.

References:

https://aws.amazon.com/iam/faqs/

Save time with our exam-specific cheat sheets:

https://digitalcloud.training/certification-training/aws-certified-cloud-practitioner/identity-and-access-management/

https://digitalcloud.training/certification-training/aws-certified-cloud-practitioner/aws-global-infrastructure/

QUESTION 61

Which Compute service should be used for running a Linux operating system upon which you will install custom software?

1. Amazon EC2
2. Amazon ECS
3. Amazon EKS
4. AWS Lambda

Answer: 1

Explanation:

Amazon EC2 should be used when you need access to a full operating system instance that you can manage.

Amazon Elastic Container Service (ECS) and Amazon Elastic Container Service for Kubernetes (EKS) are used for running software containers, not full operating system instances.

AWS Lambda runs code as functions in response to events.

CORRECT: "Amazon EC2" is the correct answer.

INCORRECT: "Amazon ECS" is incorrect as explained above.

INCORRECT: "Amazon EKS" is incorrect as explained above.

INCORRECT: "AWS Lambda" is incorrect as explained above.

References:

https://aws.amazon.com/ec2/

Save time with our exam-specific cheat sheets:

https://digitalcloud.training/certification-training/aws-certified-cloud-practitioner/aws-compute/

QUESTION 62

Which of the following need to be included in a total cost of ownership (TCO) analysis? (Select TWO.)

1. IT Manager salary
2. Facility equipment installation
3. Application development
4. Company-wide marketing
5. Data center security costs

Answer: 2,5

Explanation:

To perform a TCO you need to document all of the costs you're incurring today to run your IT operations. That includes facilities equipment installation and data center security costs. That way you get to compare the full cost of running your IT on-premises today, to running it in the cloud.

CORRECT: "Facility equipment installation" is a correct answer.

CORRECT: "Data center security costs" is also a correct answer.

INCORRECT: "IT Manager salary" is incorrect. The IT manager's salary should not be included, as it will still need to be paid when the organization moves to the cloud.

INCORRECT: "Application development" is incorrect. Application development still needs to continue as you will still have applications running in the cloud.

INCORRECT: "Company-wide marketing" is incorrect. Company-wide marketing campaigns are unaffected by moving to the cloud

References:

https://aws.amazon.com/tco-calculator/

Save time with our exam-specific cheat sheets:

https://digitalcloud.training/certification-training/aws-certified-cloud-practitioner/aws-billing-and-pricing/

QUESTION 63

What does an organization need to do in Amazon IAM to enable user access to services being launched in new region?

1. Nothing, IAM is global
2. Enable global mode in IAM to provision the required access
3. Update the user accounts to allow access from another region
4. Create new user accounts in the new region

Answer: 1

Explanation:

IAM is used to securely control individual and group access to AWS resources. IAM is universal (global) and does not apply to regions.

CORRECT: "Nothing, IAM is global" is the correct answer.

INCORRECT: "Enable global mode in IAM to provision the required access" is incorrect as you do not need to do anything to use IAM globally.

INCORRECT: "Update the user accounts to allow access from another region" is incorrect as you don't need to update user accounts.

INCORRECT: "Create new user accounts in the new region" is incorrect as IAM is global.

References:

https://docs.aws.amazon.com/IAM/latest/UserGuide/introduction.html

Save time with our exam-specific cheat sheets:

https://digitalcloud.training/certification-training/aws-certified-cloud-practitioner/identity-and-access-management/

QUESTION 64

Which statement is true in relation to data stored within an AWS Region?

1. Data is not replicated outside of a region unless you configure it
2. Data is always replicated to another region
3. Data is automatically archived after 90 days
4. Data is always automatically replicated to at least one other availability zone

Answer: 1

Explanation:

Data stored within an AWS region is not replicated outside of that region automatically. It is up to customers of AWS to determine whether they want to replicate their data to other regions. You must always consider compliance and network latency when making this decision.

CORRECT: "Data is not replicated outside of a region unless you configure it" is the correct answer.

INCORRECT: "Data is always replicated to another region" is incorrect. Data is never replicated outside of a region unless you configure it.

INCORRECT: "Data is automatically archived after 90 days" is incorrect. Data is never automatically archived. You must configure data to be archived.

INCORRECT: "Data is always automatically replicated to at least one other availability zone" is incorrect. Data is not automatically replicated to at least one availability zone – this is specific to each service and you must check how your data is stored and whether the availability and durability is acceptable.

References:

https://d1.awsstatic.com/whitepapers/Security/AWS_Security_Best_Practices.pdf

Save time with our exam-specific cheat sheets:

https://digitalcloud.training/certification-training/aws-certified-cloud-practitioner/aws-storage/

QUESTION 65

An organization has multiple AWS accounts and uses a mixture of on-demand and reserved instances. One account has a considerable amount of unused reserved instances. How can the organization reduce their costs? (Select TWO.)

1.   Create an AWS Organization configuration linking the accounts
2.   Use Spot instances instead
3.   Redeem their reserved instances
4.   Setup consolidated billing between the accounts
5.   Switch to using placement groups

Answer: 1,4

Explanation:

AWS organizations allow you to consolidate multiple AWS accounts into an organization that you create and centrally manage. Unused reserved instances (RIs) for EC2 are applied across the group so the organization can utilize their unused reserved instance instead of consuming on-demand instances which will lower their costs.

CORRECT: "Create an AWS Organization configuration linking the accounts" is the correct answer.

CORRECT: "Setup consolidated billing between the accounts" is the correct answer.

INCORRECT: "Use Spot instances instead" is incorrect. Spot instance pricing is variable so it is not guaranteed to lower the cost and it is not suitable for workloads that cannot be unexpectedly terminated by AWS.

INCORRECT: "Redeem their reserved instances" is incorrect. You cannot redeem your reserved instances. You can sell them on the AWS marketplace, however.

INCORRECT: "Switch to using placement groups" is incorrect. Using placement groups will not lower their costs.

References:

https://docs.aws.amazon.com/organizations/latest/userguide/orgs_introduction.html

Save time with our exam-specific cheat sheets:

https://digitalcloud.training/certification-training/aws-certified-cloud-practitioner/aws-billing-and-pricing/

SET 5: PRACTICE QUESTIONS ONLY

For training purposes, go directly to Set 5: Practice Questions, Answers & Explanations

QUESTION 1

Which AWS service can be used to prepare and load data for analytics using an extract, transform and load (ETL) process?

1. AWS Lambda
2. AWS Glue
3. Amazon EMR
4. Amazon Athena

QUESTION 2

Which AWS service can be used to send automated notifications to HTTP endpoints?

1. Amazon SQS
2. Amazon SWF
3. Amazon SNS
4. Amazon SES

QUESTION 3

Which of the following constitute the five pillars for the AWS Well-Architected Framework? (Select TWO.)

1. Operational excellence, security, and reliability
2. Operational excellence, elasticity and scalability
3. Cost prioritization, and cost optimization
4. Data consistency, and cost optimization
5. Performance efficiency, and cost optimization

QUESTION 4

Assuming you have configured them correctly, which AWS services can scale automatically without intervention? (Select TWO.)

1. Amazon RDS
2. Amazon EC2
3. Amazon S3
4. Amazon DynamoDB
5. Amazon EBS

QUESTION 5

Which AWS components aid in the construction of fault-tolerant applications? (Select TWO.)

1. Elastic IP addresses
2. ARNs
3. AMIs
4. Tags
5. Block device mappings

QUESTION 6

A company wants to utilize a pay as you go cloud model for all of their applications without CAPEX costs and which is highly elastic. Which cloud delivery model will suit them best?

1. Public
2. Private

3. Hybrid
4. On-premise

QUESTION 7

Which of the following are advantages of using the AWS cloud computing over legacy IT? (Select TWO.)

1. You are able to pass responsibility for the availability of your application to AWS
2. You don't need to worry about over provisioning as you can elastically scale
3. You don't need to patch your operating systems
4. You can bring new applications to market faster
5. You can bring services closer to your end users

QUESTION 8

Which AWS services form the app-facing services of the AWS serverless infrastructure? (Select TWO.)

1. AWS Step Functions
2. AWS Lambda
3. Amazon API Gateway
4. Amazon DynamoDB
5. Amazon EFS

QUESTION 9

What is the name of the AWS managed Docker registry service used by the Amazon Elastic Container Service (ECS)?

1. Elastic Container Registry
2. ECS Container Registry
3. Docker Container Registry
4. Docker Image Repository

QUESTION 10

What are two benefits of using AWS Lambda? (Select TWO.)

1. No servers to manage
2. Integrated snapshots
3. Continuous scaling (scale out)
4. Flexible operating system choices
5. Open source software

QUESTION 11

With which service can a developer upload code using a ZIP or WAR file and have the service handle the end-to-end deployment of the resources?

1. AWS CodeDeploy
2. AWS Elastic Beanstalk
3. Amazon ECS
4. AWS CodeCommit

QUESTION 12

Which service can you use to monitor, store and access log files generated by EC2 instances and on-premises servers?

1. AWS CloudTrail
2. AWS OpsWorks
3. Amazon CloudWatch Logs
4. Amazon Kinesis

QUESTION 13

What offerings are included in the Amazon Lightsail product set? (Select TWO.)

1. Virtual Private Server
2. NoSQL database
3. Managed MySQL database
4. Object storage
5. Serverless functions

QUESTION 14

Which AWS service is part of the suite of "serverless" services and runs code as functions?

1. Amazon ECS
2. Amazon EKS
3. AWS Lambda
4. AWS CodeCommit

QUESTION 15

To reward customers for using their services, what are two ways AWS reduce prices? (Select TWO.)

1. Volume based discounts when you use more services
2. Reduction in inbound data transfer charges
3. Reduced cost for reserved capacity
4. Discounts for using a wider variety of services
5. Removal of termination fees for customers who spend more

QUESTION 16

Which type of Amazon RDS automated backup allows you to restore the database with a granularity of as little as 5 minutes?

1. Snapshot backup
2. Full backup
3. Incremental backup
4. Point-in-time recovery

QUESTION 17

Which DynamoDB feature provides in-memory acceleration to tables that result in significant performance improvements?

1. Amazon ElastiCache
2. Amazon DynamoDB Accelerator (DAX)
3. Amazon EFS
4. Amazon CloudFront

QUESTION 18

Which AWS service lets connected devices easily and securely interact with cloud applications and other devices?

1. Amazon Workspaces
2. AWS Directory Service
3. AWS IoT Core
4. AWS Server Migration Service (SMS)

QUESTION 19

Which AWS service enables developers and data scientists to build, train, and deploy machine learning models?

1. Amazon Rekognition
2. Amazon Comprehend
3. Amazon SageMaker
4. Amazon MQ

QUESTION 20

Which service provides alerts and remediation guidance when AWS is experiencing events that may impact you?

1. AWS Trusted Advisor
2. AWS Inspector
3. AWS Personal Health Dashboard
4. AWS Shield

QUESTION 21

What are the primary benefits of using AWS Elastic Load Balancing? (Select TWO.)

1. High availability
2. Elasticity
3. Automation
4. Caching
5. Regional resilience

QUESTION 22

What is an Edge location?

1. A public endpoint for Amazon S3
2. A content delivery network (CDN) endpoint for CloudFront
3. A virtual private gateway for VPN
4. A VPC peering connection endpoint

QUESTION 23

What is the relationship between subnets and availability zones?

1. You can create one or more subnets within each availability zone
2. Subnets span across multiple availability zones
3. You can create one subnet per availability zone
4. Subnets contain one or more availability zones

QUESTION 24

How can you configure Amazon Route 53 to monitor the health and performance of your application?

1. Using DNS lookups
2. Using Route 53 health checks
3. Using the Route 53 API
4. Using CloudWatch

QUESTION 25

A developer needs a way to automatically provision a collection of AWS resources. Which AWS service is primarily used for deploying infrastructure as code?

1. AWS Elastic Beanstalk
2. AWS CloudFormation
3. AWS CodeDeploy
4. Jenkins

QUESTION 26

How can a company connect from their on-premises network to VPCs in multiple regions using private connections?

1. AWS Managed VPN
2. AWS Direct Connect Gateway
3. Amazon CloudFront
4. Inter-Region VPC Peering

QUESTION 27

Which of the following descriptions is incorrect in relation to the design of Availability Zones?

1. AZ's have direct, low-latency, high throughput and redundant network connections between each other
2. Each AZ is designed as an independent failure zone
3. AZs are physically separated within a typical metropolitan region and are located in lower risk flood plains
4. Each subnet in a VPC is mapped to all AZs in the region

QUESTION 28

When designing a VPC, what is the purpose of an Internet Gateway?

1. Provides Internet access for EC2 instances in private subnets
2. Enables Internet communications for instances in public subnets
3. It's a bastion host for inbound management connections
4. It's used for making VPN connections to a VPC

QUESTION 29

What is the name of the online, self-service portal that AWS provides to enable customers to view reports and, such as PCI reports, and accept agreements?

1. AWS Compliance Portal
2. AWS Documentation Portal
3. AWS Artifact
4. AWS DocuFact

QUESTION 30

What are two correct statements about AWS Organizations with consolidated billing? (Select TWO.)

1. Multiple bills are provided per organization
2. One bill provided for multiple accounts
3. Linked accounts lose their management independence
4. Volume pricing discounts applied across multiple accounts
5. CloudTrail can be configured per organization

QUESTION 31

Which AWS IAM best practice recommends applying the minimum permissions necessary to perform a task when creating IAM policies?

1. Create individual IAM users
2. Use roles to delegate permissions
3. Grant least privilege
4. Enable MFA for privileged users

QUESTION 32

What are the benefits of using IAM roles for applications that run on EC2 instances? (Select TWO.)

1. Easier to configure than using storing access keys within the EC2 instance
2. More secure than storing access keys within applications
3. Can apply multiple roles to a single instance
4. It is easier to manage IAM roles
5. Role credentials are permanent

QUESTION 33

Under the AWS Shared Responsibility Model, which of the following is the customer NOT responsible for?

1. Adding firewall rules to security groups and network ACLs
2. Applying encryption to data stored on an EBS volume
3. Applying bucket policies to share Amazon S3 data
4. Installing firmware updates on host servers

QUESTION 34

Which type of storage stores objects comprised of key, value pairs?

1. Amazon DynamoDB
2. Amazon EBS
3. Amazon EFS
4. Amazon S3

QUESTION 35

Which type of EBS volumes can be encrypted?

1. Non-root volumes only
2. Both non-root and root volumes
3. Only non-root volumes created from snapshots
4. Only root volumes can have encryption applied at launch time

QUESTION 36

What feature of Amazon S3 enables you to set rules to automatically transfer objects between different storage classes at defined time intervals?

1. Elastic Data Management
2. Object Lifecycle Management
3. Auto Lifecycle Scaling
4. S3 Archiving

QUESTION 37

What charges are applicable to Amazon S3 Standard storage class? (Select TWO.)

1. Per GB/month storage fee
2. Retrieval fee
3. Minimum capacity charge per object
4. Data ingress
5. Data egress

QUESTION 38

How can a company protect their Amazon S3 data from a regional disaster?

1. Archive to Amazon Glacier
2. Use Cross-Region Replication (CRR) to copy to another region
3. Use lifecycle actions to move to another S3 storage class

4.   Enable Multi-Factor Authentication (MFA) delete

QUESTION 39

Which AWS support plan provides email only support by Cloud Support Associates?

1.   Basic
2.   Developer
3.   Business
4.   Enterprise

QUESTION 40

Which support plan is the lowest cost option that allows unlimited cases to be open?

1.   Basic
2.   Developer
3.   Business
4.   Enterprise

QUESTION 41

Which service allows an organization to bring their own licensing on host hardware that is physically isolated from other AWS accounts?

1.   EC2 Dedicated Instances
2.   EC2 Spot Instances
3.   EC2 Dedicated Hosts
4.   EC2 Reserved Instances

QUESTION 42

Which of the below is an example of optimizing for cost?

1.   Choosing the fastest EC2 instance to ensure performance
2.   Provision extra capacity to allow for growth
3.   Replace an EC2 compute instance with AWS Lambda
4.   Deploy resources with AWS CloudFormation

QUESTION 43

Which service is used for caching data?

1.   Amazon Simple Queue Service (SQS)
2.   Amazon DynamoDB DAX
3.   AWS Key Management Service (KMS)
4.   Amazon Elastic File System (EFS)

QUESTION 44

Which service is used introduce fault tolerance into an application architecture?

1.   Amazon CloudFront
2.   Amazon ElastiCache
3.   Amazon Elastic Load Balancing
4.   Amazon DynamoDB

QUESTION 45

Which tools can you use to manage identities in IAM? (choose 2)

1. Amazon CloudWatch API
2. AWS Management Console
3. AWS Command Line Tools
4. EC2 Management Console
5. EC2 Management Console
6. Amazon Workspaces

QUESTION 46

Which of the following would be good reasons to move from on-premises to the AWS Cloud? (Select TWO.)

1. Gain access to free technical support services
2. Reduce costs through easier right-sizing of workloads
3. Improve agility and elasticity
4. Gain end-to-end operational management of the entire infrastructure stack
5. Outsource all security responsibility

QUESTION 47

Which service runs your application code only when needed without needing to run servers?

1. Amazon EC2
2. Amazon ECS
3. AWS Lambda
4. AWS LightSail

QUESTION 48

Which AWS feature of Amazon EC2 allows an administrator to create a standardized image that can be used for launching new instances?

1. Amazon Golden Image
2. Amazon Block Template
3. Amazon Machine Image
4. Amazon EBS Mount Point

QUESTION 49

What information must be entered into the AWS TCO Calculator?

1. The number of end users in your company
2. The number of applications in your company
3. The number of storage systems in your company
4. The number of servers in your company

QUESTION 50

An Elastic IP Address can be remapped between EC2 instances across which boundaries?

1. Regions
2. Edge Locations
3. Availability Zones
4. DB Subnets

QUESTION 51

Which AWS service can assist with providing recommended actions on cost optimization?

1. AWS Inspector
2. AWS Trusted Advisor

3. AWS Artifact
4. Amazon CloudWatch Events

QUESTION 52

How can an online education company ensure their video courses play with minimal latency for their users around the world?

1. Use Amazon S3 Transfer Acceleration to speed up downloads
2. Use Amazon EBS Cross Region Replication to get the content close to the users
3. Use Amazon Aurora Global Database
4. Use Amazon CloudFront to get the content closer to users

QUESTION 53

Which AWS security service provides a firewall at the subnet level within a VPC?

1. Security Group
2. IAM Policy
3. Bucket Policy
4. Network Access Control List

QUESTION 54

Which services allow you to store files on AWS? (Select TWO.)

1. AWS Lambda
2. Amazon LightSail
3. Amazon EBS
4. Amazon EFS
5. Amazon SQS

QUESTION 55

Which AWS program can help an organization to design, build, and manage their workloads on AWS?

1. APN Consulting Partners
2. APN Technology Consultants
3. AWS Business Development Manager
4. AWS Technical Account Manager

QUESTION 56

Which of the following statements is correct about Amazon S3 cross-region replication?

1. Both source and destination S3 buckets must have versioning disabled
2. The source and destination S3 buckets cannot be in different AWS Regions
3. S3 buckets configured for cross-region replication can be owned by a single AWS account or by different accounts
4. The source S3 bucket owner must have the source and destination AWS Regions disabled for their account

QUESTION 57

Which of the following Amazon EC2 pricing models allows customers to use existing server-bound software licenses?

1. Spot Instances
2. Reserved Instances
3. Dedicated Hosts
4. On-Demand Instances

QUESTION 58

A company has deployed several relational databases on Amazon RDS. Every month, the database software vendor releases new security patches that need to be applied to the database.

What is the MOST efficient way to apply the security patches?

1. Connect to each database instance on a monthly basis, and download and apply the necessary security patches from the vendor
2. Enable automatic patching for the instances using the Amazon RDS console
3. In AWS Config, configure a rule for the instances and the required patch level
4. Use AWS Systems Manager to automate database patching according to a schedule

QUESTION 59

A Cloud Practitioner needs to rapidly deploy a popular IT solution and start using it immediately.

What should the Cloud Practitioner use?

1. AWS Well-Architected Framework documentation
2. Amazon CloudFront
3. AWS Elastic Beanstalk
4. AWS Quick Start reference deployments

QUESTION 60

A cloud practitioner needs to decrease application latency and increase performance for globally distributed users.

Which services can assist? (Select TWO.)

1. Amazon ECS
2. Amazon S3
3. Amazon AppStream 2.0
4. Amazon ElastiCache
5. Amazon CloudFront

QUESTION 61

A company needs protection from distributed denial of service (DDoS) attacks on its website and assistance from AWS experts during such events.

Which AWS managed service will meet these requirements?

1. AWS Shield Advanced
2. AWS Firewall Manager
3. AWS Web Application Firewall
4. Amazon GuardDuty

QUESTION 62

Which of the following must be used together to gain programmatic access to an AWS account? (Select TWO.)

1. An access key ID
2. A primary key
3. A secret access key
4. A user ID
5. A secondary key

QUESTION 63

An application that is deployed across multiple Availability Zones could be described as:

1. Being highly available

2. Having global reach
3. Being secure
4. Having elasticity

QUESTION 64

A Cloud Practitioner is developing a disaster recovery plan and intends to replicate data between multiple geographic areas.

Which of the following meets these requirements?

1. AWS Accounts
2. AWS Regions
3. Availability Zones
4. Edge locations

QUESTION 65

A user deploys an Amazon Aurora database instance in multiple Availability Zones.

This strategy involves which pillar of the AWS Well-Architected Framework?

1. Performance efficiency
2. Reliability
3. Cost optimization
4. Security

SET 5: PRACTICE QUESTIONS AND ANSWERS

QUESTION 1

Which AWS service can be used to prepare and load data for analytics using an extract, transform and load (ETL) process?

1. AWS Lambda
2. AWS Glue
3. Amazon EMR
4. Amazon Athena

Answer: 2

Explanation:

AWS Glue is a fully managed extract, transform, and load (ETL) service that makes it easy for customers to prepare and load their data for analytics.

You can point AWS Glue to data stored on AWS, and AWS Glue discovers the data and stores the associated metadata (e.g. table definition and schema) in the AWS Glue Data Catalog. Once cataloged, the data is immediately searchable, queryable, and available for ETL.

CORRECT: "AWS Glue" is the correct answer.

INCORRECT: "AWS Lambda" is incorrect. AWS Lambda is a serverless application that runs code as functions in response to events

INCORRECT: "Amazon EMR" is incorrect. Amazon Elastic Map Reduce (EMR) provides a managed Hadoop framework that makes it easy, fast, and cost-effective to process vast amounts of data across dynamically scalable Amazon EC2 instances

INCORRECT: "Amazon Athena" is incorrect. Amazon Athena is an interactive query service that makes it easy to analyze data in Amazon S3 using standard SQL.

References:

https://aws.amazon.com/glue/

Save time with our exam-specific cheat sheets:

https://digitalcloud.training/certification-training/aws-certified-cloud-practitioner/additional-aws-services-tools/

QUESTION 2

Which AWS service can be used to send automated notifications to HTTP endpoints?

1. Amazon SQS
2. Amazon SWF
3. Amazon SNS
4. Amazon SES

Answer: 3

Explanation:

Amazon Simple Notification Service (Amazon SNS) is a web service that makes it easy to set up, operate, and send notifications from the cloud. SNS can be used to send automated or manual notifications to email, mobile (SMS), SQS, and HTTP endpoints.

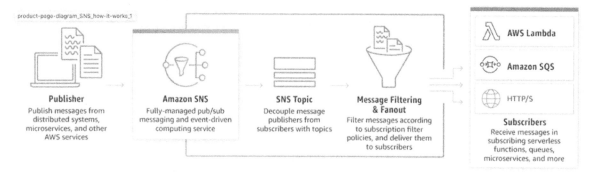

CORRECT: "Amazon SNS" is the correct answer.

INCORRECT: "Amazon SQS" is incorrect. Amazon Simple Queue Service (SQS) is a fully managed message queuing service that enables you to decouple and scale microservices, distributed systems, and serverless applications. This is a message bus, not a notification service.

INCORRECT: "Amazon SWF" is incorrect. Amazon SWF helps developers build, run, and scale background jobs that have parallel or sequential step. It is not a notification service.

INCORRECT: "Amazon SES" is incorrect. Amazon Simple Email Service (Amazon SES) is a cloud-based email sending service designed to help digital marketers and application developers send marketing, notification, and transactional emails. It is limited to sending email.

References:

https://aws.amazon.com/sns/

Save time with our exam-specific cheat sheets:

https://digitalcloud.training/certification-training/aws-certified-cloud-practitioner/notification-services/

QUESTION 3

Which of the following constitute the five pillars for the AWS Well-Architected Framework? (Select TWO.)

1. Operational excellence, security, and reliability
2. Operational excellence, elasticity and scalability
3. Cost prioritization, and cost optimization
4. Data consistency, and cost optimization
5. Performance efficiency, and cost optimization

Answer: 1, 5

Explanation:

The five pillars of the AWS Well-Architected Framework are operational excellence, security, reliability, performance efficiency, and cost optimization

CORRECT: "Operational excellence, security, and reliability" is the correct answer.

CORRECT: "Performance efficiency, and cost optimization" is the correct answer.

INCORRECT: "Operational excellence, elasticity and scalability" is incorrect as elasticity and scalability are not included.

INCORRECT: "Cost prioritization, and cost optimization" is incorrect as cost prioritization is not included.

INCORRECT: "Data consistency, and cost optimization" is incorrect as data consistency is not included.

References:

https://aws.amazon.com/blogs/apn/the-5-pillars-of-the-aws-well-architected-framework/

Save time with our exam-specific cheat sheets:

https://digitalcloud.training/certification-training/aws-certified-cloud-practitioner/architecting-for-the-cloud/

QUESTION 4

Assuming you have configured them correctly, which AWS services can scale automatically without intervention? (Select TWO.)

1. Amazon RDS
2. Amazon EC2
3. Amazon S3
4. Amazon DynamoDB
5. Amazon EBS

Answer: 3, 4

Explanation:

Both S3 and DynamoDB automatically scale as demand dictates. In the case of DynamoDB you can either configure the on-demand or provisioned capacity mode. With on-demand capacity mode DynamoDB automatically adjusts the read and write throughput for you.

EBS and RDS do not scale automatically. You must intervene to adjust volume sizes and database instance types to scale these resources

CORRECT: "Amazon S3" is a correct answer.

CORRECT: "Amazon DynamoDB" is also a correct answer.

INCORRECT: "Amazon RDS" is incorrect as explained above.

INCORRECT: "Amazon EC2" is incorrect. EC2 cannot scale automatically. You need to use Auto Scaling to scale the number of EC2 instances deployed.

INCORRECT: "Amazon EBS" is incorrect as explained above.

References:

https://aws.amazon.com/blogs/architecture/tag/scalability/

Save time with our exam-specific cheat sheets:

https://digitalcloud.training/certification-training/aws-certified-cloud-practitioner/aws-databases/

QUESTION 5

Which AWS components aid in the construction of fault-tolerant applications? (Select TWO.)

1. Elastic IP addresses
2. ARNs
3. AMIs
4. Tags
5. Block device mappings

Answer: 1, 3

Explanation:

Elastic IP addresses can be easily remapped between EC2 instances in the event of a failure. Amazon Machine Images (AMIs) can be used to quickly launch replacement instances when there is a failure

Amazon Resource Names (ARNs), tags and block device mappings don't really help with fault tolerance

CORRECT: "Elastic IP addresses" is a correct answer.

CORRECT: "AMIs" is also a correct answer.

INCORRECT: "ARNs" is incorrect as explained above.

INCORRECT: "Tags" is incorrect as explained above.

INCORRECT: "Block device mappings" is incorrect as explained above.

References:

https://aws.amazon.com/whitepapers/designing-fault-tolerant-applications/

Save time with our exam-specific cheat sheets:

https://digitalcloud.training/certification-training/aws-certified-cloud-practitioner/architecting-for-the-cloud/

QUESTION 6

A company wants to utilize a pay as you go cloud model for all of their applications without CAPEX costs and which is highly elastic. Which cloud delivery model will suit them best?

1. Public
2. Private
3. Hybrid
4. On-premise

Answer: 1

Explanation:

The public cloud is offered under a purely pay as you go model (unless you choose to reserve), and allows companies to completely avoid CAPEX costs. The public cloud is also highly elastic so companies can grow and shrink the applications as demand changes.

Private and on-premise clouds are essentially the same, though both could be managed by a third party and even could be delivered under an OPEX model by some vendors. However, they are typically more CAPEX heavy and the elasticity is limited.

A hybrid model combines public and private and this company wants to go all in on a single model.

CORRECT: "Public" is the correct answer.

INCORRECT: "Private" is incorrect as explained above.

INCORRECT: "Hybrid" is incorrect as explained above.

INCORRECT: "On-premise" is incorrect as explained above.

References:

https://aws.amazon.com/types-of-cloud-computing/

Save time with our exam-specific cheat sheets:

https://digitalcloud.training/certification-training/aws-certified-cloud-practitioner/cloud-computing-concepts/

QUESTION 7

Which of the following are advantages of using the AWS cloud computing over legacy IT? (Select TWO.)

1. You are able to pass responsibility for the availability of your application to AWS
2. You don't need to worry about over provisioning as you can elastically scale
3. You don't need to patch your operating systems
4. You can bring new applications to market faster
5. You can bring services closer to your end users

Answer: 2, 4

Explanation:

With cloud computing you no longer need to guess about capacity as you can elastically scale. This means you don't end up overprovisioning but instead react to the load on your servers. You can also be faster and more agile with development and release of applications.

CORRECT: "You don't need to worry about over provisioning as you can elastically scale" is a correct answer.

CORRECT: "You can bring new applications to market faster" is also a correct answer.

INCORRECT: "You are able to pass responsibility for the availability of your application to AWS" is incorrect. You do not pass responsibility for your application to AWS. AWS runs the infrastructure but you still manage the application

INCORRECT: "You don't need to patch your operating systems" is incorrect. You still need to patch your own operating systems.

INCORRECT: "You can bring services closer to your end users" is incorrect. The cloud is centralized so you won't necessarily bring services closer to your end users.

References:

https://docs.aws.amazon.com/whitepapers/latest/aws-overview/six-advantages-of-cloud-computing.html

Save time with our exam-specific cheat sheets:

QUESTION 8

Which AWS services form the app-facing services of the AWS serverless infrastructure? (Select TWO.)

1. AWS Step Functions
2. AWS Lambda
3. Amazon API Gateway
4. Amazon DynamoDB
5. Amazon EFS

Answer: 2, 3

Explanation:

AWS Lambda and Amazon API Gateway are both app-facing components of the AWS Serverless infrastructure

AWS Step Functions is an orchestration service

CORRECT: "AWS Lambda" is a correct answer.

CORRECT: "Amazon API Gateway" is also a correct answer.

INCORRECT: "AWS Step Functions" is incorrect. This is a serverless orchestration service.

INCORRECT: Amazon DynamoDB" is incorrect. Amazon DynamoDB is a serverless database service. Databases are backend, not app-facing.

INCORRECT: "Amazon EFS" is incorrect. EFS is a filesystem. Typically, EFS is mounted by Amazon EC2 instances.

References:

https://aws.amazon.com/serverless/

Save time with our exam-specific cheat sheets:

https://digitalcloud.training/certification-training/aws-certified-cloud-practitioner/aws-compute/

https://digitalcloud.training/certification-training/aws-certified-cloud-practitioner/aws-networking/

QUESTION 9

What is the name of the AWS managed Docker registry service used by the Amazon Elastic Container Service (ECS)?

1. Elastic Container Registry
2. ECS Container Registry
3. Docker Container Registry
4. Docker Image Repository

Answer: 1

Explanation:

Amazon Elastic Container Registry (ECR) is a fully-managed Docker container registry that makes it easy for developers to store, manage, and deploy Docker container images.

Amazon ECR is integrated with Amazon Elastic Container Service (ECS). Amazon ECR eliminates the need to operate your own container repositories or worry about scaling the underlying infrastructure.

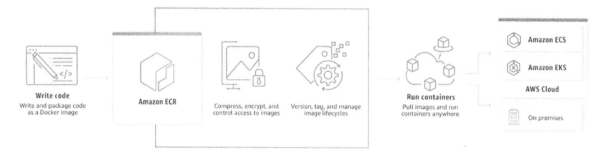

CORRECT: "Elastic Container Registry" is the correct answer.

INCORRECT: "ECS Container Registry" is incorrect as this is the wrong name.

INCORRECT: "Docker Container Registry" is incorrect as this is not an AWS registry.

INCORRECT: "Docker Image Repository" is incorrect as this is not an AWS registry.

References:

https://aws.amazon.com/ecr/

Save time with our exam-specific cheat sheets:

https://digitalcloud.training/certification-training/aws-certified-cloud-practitioner/aws-compute/

QUESTION 10

What are two benefits of using AWS Lambda? (Select TWO.)

1. No servers to manage
2. Integrated snapshots
3. Continuous scaling (scale out)
4. Flexible operating system choices
5. Open source software

Answer: 1, 3

Explanation:

With AWS Lambda you don't have any servers to manage (serverless). Lambda functions scale out rather than up running multiple invocations of the function in parallel.

CORRECT: "No servers to manage" is a correct answer.

CORRECT: "Continuous scaling (scale out)" is also a correct answer.

INCORRECT: "Integrated snapshots" is incorrect. You do not have integrated snapshots (or any persistent storage) with Lambda.

INCORRECT: "Flexible operating system choices" is incorrect. You do not manage the operating system on which the functions run so have no choice of software.

INCORRECT: "Open source software" is incorrect. Lambda is AWS proprietary not open source.

References:

https://aws.amazon.com/lambda/

Save time with our exam-specific cheat sheets:

https://digitalcloud.training/certification-training/aws-certified-cloud-practitioner/aws-compute/

QUESTION 11

With which service can a developer upload code using a ZIP or WAR file and have the service handle the end-to-end deployment of the resources?

1. AWS CodeDeploy
2. AWS Elastic Beanstalk

3. Amazon ECS
4. AWS CodeCommit

Answer: 2

Explanation:

AWS Elastic Beanstalk can be used to quickly deploy and manage applications in the AWS Cloud. Developers upload applications and Elastic Beanstalk handles the deployment details of capacity provisioning, load balancing, auto-scaling, and application health monitoring.

You can upload code directly using a ZIP or WAR file. You can also use a Git archive.

CORRECT: "AWS Elastic Beanstalk" is the correct answer.

INCORRECT: "AWS CodeDeploy" is incorrect. AWS CodeDeploy is a fully managed deployment service that automates software deployments to a variety of compute services such as Amazon EC2, AWS Lambda, and on-premises servers.

INCORRECT: "Amazon ECS" is incorrect. Amazon Elastic Container Service is a managed service for running Docker containers.

INCORRECT: "AWS CodeCommit" is incorrect. AWS CodeCommit is a fully-managed source control service that hosts secure Git-based repositories. It does not actually automate the build of the code or infrastructure on which it runs.

References:

https://docs.aws.amazon.com/elasticbeanstalk/latest/dg/applications-sourcebundle.html

Save time with our exam-specific cheat sheets:

https://digitalcloud.training/certification-training/aws-certified-cloud-practitioner/aws-compute/

QUESTION 12

Which service can you use to monitor, store and access log files generated by EC2 instances and on-premises servers?

1. AWS CloudTrail
2. AWS OpsWorks
3. Amazon CloudWatch Logs
4. Amazon Kinesis

Answer: 3

Explanation:

You can use Amazon CloudWatch Logs to monitor, store, and access your log files from Amazon Elastic Compute Cloud (Amazon EC2) instances, AWS CloudTrail, Route 53, and other sources. You can then retrieve the associated log data from CloudWatch Logs.

CORRECT: "Amazon CloudWatch Logs" is the correct answer.

INCORRECT: "AWS CloudTrail" is incorrect. AWS CloudTrail is used for recording a history of API actions taken on your account.

INCORRECT: "AWS OpsWorks" is incorrect. OpsWorks is a configuration management service.

INCORRECT: "Amazon Kinesis" is incorrect. Amazon Kinesis is a set of services used for collecting, processing and analyzing streaming data.

References:

https://docs.aws.amazon.com/AmazonCloudWatch/latest/logs/WhatIsCloudWatchLogs.html

Save time with our exam-specific cheat sheets:

https://docs.aws.amazon.com/AmazonCloudWatch/latest/logs/WhatIsCloudWatchLogs.html

QUESTION 13

What offerings are included in the Amazon Lightsail product set? (Select TWO.)

1. Virtual Private Server
2. NoSQL database
3. Managed MySQL database
4. Object storage

5. Serverless functions

Answer: 1, 3

Explanation:

Amazon LightSail provides an easy, low cost way to consume cloud services without needing the skill set for using VPC resources. The product set includes virtual private servers (instances), managed MySQL databases, HA storage, and load balancing

You can connect to other AWS services such as S3, DynamoDB, and CloudFront, however these are not part of the LightSail product range

CORRECT: "Virtual Private Server" is a correct answer.

CORRECT: "Managed MySQL database" is also a correct answer.

INCORRECT: "NoSQL database" is incorrect as explained above.

INCORRECT: "Object storage" is incorrect as explained above.

INCORRECT: "Serverless functions" is incorrect as explained above.

References:

https://aws.amazon.com/lightsail/features/

Save time with our exam-specific cheat sheets:

https://digitalcloud.training/certification-training/aws-certified-cloud-practitioner/aws-compute/

QUESTION 14

Which AWS service is part of the suite of "serverless" services and runs code as functions?

1. Amazon ECS
2. Amazon EKS
3. AWS Lambda
4. AWS CodeCommit

Answer: 3

Explanation:

AWS Lambda is a serverless compute service that runs your code in response to events and automatically manages the underlying compute resources for you. The code you run on AWS Lambda is called a "Lambda function".

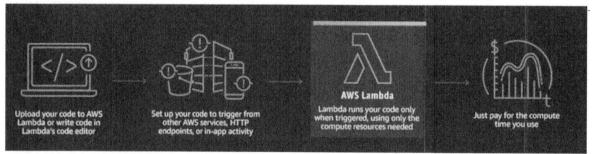

CORRECT: "AWS Lambda" is the correct answer.

INCORRECT: "Amazon ECS" is incorrect. Amazon ECS is used for running software containers such as Docker containers.

INCORRECT: "Amazon EKS" is incorrect. Amazon EKS is used for managing software containers such as Docker containers.

INCORRECT: "AWS CodeCommit" is incorrect. AWS CodeCommit is a fully-managed source control service that hosts secure Git-based repositories.

References:

https://aws.amazon.com/lambda/

https://aws.amazon.com/lambda/features/

Save time with our exam-specific cheat sheets:

QUESTION 15

To reward customers for using their services, what are two ways AWS reduce prices? (Select TWO.)

1. Volume based discounts when you use more services
2. Reduction in inbound data transfer charges
3. Reduced cost for reserved capacity
4. Discounts for using a wider variety of services
5. Removal of termination fees for customers who spend more

Answer: 1, 3

Explanation:

AWS provide volume based discount so that when you use more services you reduce the cost per service. You can also reserve capacity by locking in to fixed 1 or 3 year contracts to get significant discounts

You never pay for inbound data transfer

You don't get discounts for using a variety of services, only when you use more services

There are never termination fees with AWS

CORRECT: "Volume based discounts when you use more services" is the correct answer.

CORRECT: "Reduced cost for reserved capacity" is the correct answer.

INCORRECT: "Reduction in inbound data transfer charges" is incorrect $

INCORRECT: "Discounts for using a wider variety of services" is incorrect $

INCORRECT: "Removal of termination fees for customers who spend more" is incorrect $

References:

https://aws.amazon.com/pricing/

Save time with our exam-specific cheat sheets:

https://digitalcloud.training/certification-training/aws-certified-cloud-practitioner/aws-billing-and-pricing/

QUESTION 16

Which type of Amazon RDS automated backup allows you to restore the database with a granularity of as little as 5 minutes?

1. Snapshot backup
2. Full backup
3. Incremental backup
4. Point-in-time recovery

Answer: 4

Explanation:

You can restore an Amazon RDS database instance to a specific point in time with a granularity of 5 minutes. Amazon RDS uses transaction logs which it uploads to Amazon S3 to do this.

CORRECT: "Point-in-time recovery" is the correct answer.

INCORRECT: "Snapshot backup" is incorrect. This is not a point-in-time backup with 5 minute granularity.

INCORRECT: "Full backup" is incorrect. This just describes taking a fully backup of the database, typically with backup software.

INCORRECT: "Incremental backup" is incorrect. This describes taking a backup of items that have changed since the last backup.

References:

https://docs.aws.amazon.com/AmazonRDS/latest/UserGuide/USER_PIT.html

Save time with our exam-specific cheat sheets:

https://digitalcloud.training/certification-training/aws-certified-cloud-practitioner/aws-databases/

QUESTION 17

Which DynamoDB feature provides in-memory acceleration to tables that result in significant performance improvements?

1. Amazon ElastiCache
2. Amazon DynamoDB Accelerator (DAX)
3. Amazon EFS
4. Amazon CloudFront

Answer: 2

Explanation:

Amazon DynamoDB Accelerator (DAX) is a fully managed, highly available, in-memory cache for DynamoDB that delivers up to a 10x performance improvement – from milliseconds to microseconds – even at millions of requests per second.

DAX does all the heavy lifting required to add in-memory acceleration to your DynamoDB tables, without requiring developers to manage cache invalidation, data population, or cluster management.

CORRECT: "Amazon DynamoDB Accelerator (DAX)" is the correct answer.

INCORRECT: "Amazon ElastiCache" is incorrect. This service is also an in-memory cache but it is not a feature of DynamoDB.

INCORRECT: "Amazon EFS" is incorrect. This is an elastic filesystem based on the NFS protocol.

INCORRECT: "Amazon CloudFront" is incorrect. This is a content delivery network for caching content.

References:

https://aws.amazon.com/dynamodb/dax/

Save time with our exam-specific cheat sheets:

https://digitalcloud.training/certification-training/aws-certified-cloud-practitioner/aws-databases/

QUESTION 18

Which AWS service lets connected devices easily and securely interact with cloud applications and other devices?

1. Amazon Workspaces
2. AWS Directory Service
3. AWS IoT Core
4. AWS Server Migration Service (SMS)

Answer: 3

Explanation:

AWS IoT Core is a managed cloud service that lets connected devices easily and securely interact with cloud applications and other devices. AWS IoT Core can support billions of devices and trillions of messages, and can process and route those messages to AWS endpoints and to other devices reliably and securely.

Devices publish & subscribe

Billions of devices can publish and subscribe to messages

AWS IoT Core

Messages are transmitted and received using the MQTT protocol which minimizes the code footprint on the device and reduces network bandwidth requirements

Devices communicate

AWS IoT Core enables devices to communicate with AWS services and each other

CORRECT: "AWS IoT Core" is the correct answer.

INCORRECT: "AWS Directory Service" is incorrect. AWS Directory Service for Microsoft Active Directory, also known as AWS Managed Microsoft AD, enables your directory-aware workloads and AWS resources to use managed Active Directory in the

AWS Cloud

INCORRECT: "Amazon Workspaces" is incorrect. Amazon WorkSpaces is a managed, secure cloud desktop service

INCORRECT: "AWS Server Migration Service (SMS)" is incorrect. AWS Server Migration Service (SMS) is an agentless service which makes it easier and faster for you to migrate thousands of on-premises workloads to AWS.

References:

https://aws.amazon.com/iot-core/

Save time with our exam-specific cheat sheets:

https://digitalcloud.training/certification-training/aws-certified-cloud-practitioner/additional-aws-services-tools/

QUESTION 19

Which AWS service enables developers and data scientists to build, train, and deploy machine learning models?

1. Amazon Rekognition
2. Amazon Comprehend
3. Amazon SageMaker
4. Amazon MQ

Answer: 3

Explanation:

Amazon SageMaker is a fully-managed platform that enables developers and data scientists to quickly and easily build, train, and deploy machine learning models at any scale. Amazon SageMaker removes all the barriers that typically slow down developers who want to use machine learning.

CORRECT: "Amazon SageMaker" is the correct answer.

INCORRECT: "Amazon Rekognition" is incorrect. Amazon Rekognition makes it easy to add image and video analysis to your applications.

INCORRECT: "Amazon Comprehend" is incorrect. Amazon Comprehend is a natural language processing (NLP) service that uses machine learning to find insights and relationships in text

INCORRECT: "Amazon MQ" is incorrect. Amazon MQ is a managed message broker service for Apache ActiveMQ that makes it easy to set up and operate message brokers in the cloud.

References:

https://aws.amazon.com/sagemaker/

Save time with our exam-specific cheat sheets:

https://digitalcloud.training/certification-training/aws-certified-cloud-practitioner/additional-aws-services-tools/

QUESTION 20

Which service provides alerts and remediation guidance when AWS is experiencing events that may impact you?

1. AWS Trusted Advisor
2. AWS Inspector
3. AWS Personal Health Dashboard
4. AWS Shield

Answer: 3

Explanation:

AWS Personal Health Dashboard provides alerts and remediation guidance when AWS is experiencing events that may impact you.

CORRECT: "AWS Personal Health Dashboard" is the correct answer.

INCORRECT: "AWS Trusted Advisor" is incorrect. Trusted Advisor is an online resource that helps to reduce cost, increase performance and improve security by optimizing your AWS environment.

INCORRECT: "AWS Inspector" is incorrect. Inspector is an automated security assessment service that helps improve the security and compliance of applications deployed on AWS.

INCORRECT: "AWS Shield" is incorrect. AWS Shield is a managed Distributed Denial of Service (DDoS) protection service.

References:

https://docs.aws.amazon.com/health/latest/ug/getting-started-phd.html

Save time with our exam-specific cheat sheets:

https://digitalcloud.training/certification-training/aws-certified-cloud-practitioner/cloud-security/

QUESTION 21

What are the primary benefits of using AWS Elastic Load Balancing? (Select TWO.)

1. High availability
2. Elasticity
3. Automation
4. Caching
5. Regional resilience

Answer: 1, 2

Explanation:

High availability – ELB automatically distributes traffic across multiple EC2 instances in different AZs within a region.

Elasticity – ELB is capable of handling rapid changes in network traffic patterns.

CORRECT: "High availability" is a correct answer.

CORRECT: "Elasticity" is also a correct answer.

INCORRECT: "Automation" is incorrect. Automation is not a primary benefit of ELB.

INCORRECT: "Caching" is incorrect. Caching is not a benefit of ELB

INCORRECT: "Regional resilience" is incorrect. An ELB can distribute incoming traffic across your Amazon EC2 instances in a single Availability Zone or multiple Availability Zones, but not across regions (for regional resilience).

References:

https://aws.amazon.com/elasticloadbalancing/

Save time with our exam-specific cheat sheets:

https://digitalcloud.training/2018/10/19/cloud-computing-basics-compute/

QUESTION 22

What is an Edge location?

1. A public endpoint for Amazon S3
2. A content delivery network (CDN) endpoint for CloudFront
3. A virtual private gateway for VPN
4. A VPC peering connection endpoint

Answer: 2

Explanation:

Edge locations are Content Delivery Network (CDN) endpoints for CloudFront. There are many more edge locations than regions.

CORRECT: "A content delivery network (CDN) endpoint for CloudFront" is the correct answer.

INCORRECT: "A public endpoint for Amazon S3" is incorrect as it is not related to S3.

INCORRECT: "A virtual private gateway for VPN" is incorrect as it is not related to VPN.

INCORRECT: "A VPC peering connection endpoint" is incorrect as it is not related to VPC.

References:

Save time with our exam-specific cheat sheets:

QUESTION 23

What is the relationship between subnets and availability zones?

1. You can create one or more subnets within each availability zone
2. Subnets span across multiple availability zones
3. You can create one subnet per availability zone
4. Subnets contain one or more availability zones

Answer: 1

Explanation:

You can create one or more subnets within each availability zone but subnets cannot span across availability zones.

CORRECT: "You can create one or more subnets within each availability zone" is the correct answer.

INCORRECT: "Subnets span across multiple availability zones" is incorrect as they are contained within a single AZ.

INCORRECT: "You can create one subnet per availability zone" is incorrect as you can create many subnets per AZ.

INCORRECT: "Subnets contain one or more availability zones" is incorrect as they are created within a single AZ.

References:

https://docs.aws.amazon.com/AmazonRDS/latest/UserGuide/Concepts.RegionsAndAvailabilityZones.html

Save time with our exam-specific cheat sheets:

https://digitalcloud.training/certification-training/aws-certified-cloud-practitioner/aws-networking/

QUESTION 24

How can you configure Amazon Route 53 to monitor the health and performance of your application?

1. Using DNS lookups
2. Using Route 53 health checks
3. Using the Route 53 API
4. Using CloudWatch

Answer: 2

Explanation:

Amazon Route 53 health checks monitor the health and performance of your web applications, web servers, and other resources.

None of the other options provide a solution that can check the health and performance of an application.

CORRECT: "Using Route 53 health checks" is the correct answer.

INCORRECT: "Using DNS lookups" is incorrect as explained above.

INCORRECT: "Using the Route 53 API" is incorrect as explained above.

INCORRECT: "Using CloudWatch" is incorrect as explained above.

References:

https://docs.aws.amazon.com/Route53/latest/DeveloperGuide/dns-failover.html

Save time with our exam-specific cheat sheets:

https://digitalcloud.training/certification-training/aws-certified-cloud-practitioner/content-delivery-and-dns-services/

QUESTION 25

A developer needs a way to automatically provision a collection of AWS resources. Which AWS service is primarily used for deploying infrastructure as code?

1. AWS Elastic Beanstalk
2. AWS CloudFormation

3. AWS CodeDeploy
4. Jenkins

Answer: 2

Explanation:

AWS CloudFormation is a service that gives developers and businesses an easy way to create a collection of related AWS resources and provision them in an orderly and predictable fashion. AWS CloudFormation provides a common language for you to describe and provision all the infrastructure resources in your cloud environment. Think of CloudFormation as deploying infrastructure as code.

CORRECT: "AWS CloudFormation" is the correct answer.

INCORRECT: "AWS Elastic Beanstalk" is incorrect. Elastic Beanstalk is more focused on deploying applications on EC2 (PaaS).

INCORRECT: "AWS CodeDeploy" is incorrect. AWS CodeDeploy is a fully managed deployment service that automates software deployments to a variety of compute services such as Amazon EC2, AWS Lambda, and your on-premises servers.

INCORRECT: "Jenkins" is incorrect. Jenkins deploys infrastructure as code but is not an AWS service.

References:

https://aws.amazon.com/cloudformation/

Save time with our exam-specific cheat sheets:

https://digitalcloud.training/certification-training/aws-certified-cloud-practitioner/additional-aws-services-tools/

QUESTION 26

How can a company connect from their on-premises network to VPCs in multiple regions using private connections?

1. AWS Managed VPN
2. AWS Direct Connect Gateway
3. Amazon CloudFront
4. Inter-Region VPC Peering

Answer: 2

Explanation:

You can use an AWS Direct Connect gateway to connect your AWS Direct Connect connection over a private virtual interface to one or more VPCs in your account that are located in the same or different Regions

CORRECT: "AWS Direct Connect Gateway" is the correct answer.

INCORRECT: "AWS Managed VPN" is incorrect. AWS Managed VPN uses the public Internet and is therefore not a private connection.

INCORRECT: "Amazon CloudFront" is incorrect. Amazon CloudFront is a content delivery network used for caching data.

INCORRECT: "Inter-Region VPC Peering" is incorrect. Inter-Region VPC peering does not help you to connect from an on-premise network.

References:

https://docs.aws.amazon.com/directconnect/latest/UserGuide/direct-connect-gateways.html

Save time with our exam-specific cheat sheets:

https://digitalcloud.training/certification-training/aws-certified-cloud-practitioner/aws-networking/

QUESTION 27

Which of the following descriptions is incorrect in relation to the design of Availability Zones?

1. AZ's have direct, low-latency, high throughput and redundant network connections between each other
2. Each AZ is designed as an independent failure zone
3. AZs are physically separated within a typical metropolitan region and are located in lower risk flood plains
4. Each subnet in a VPC is mapped to all AZs in the region

Answer: 4

Explanation:

Subnets are created within a single AZ and do not get mapped to multiple AZs.

CORRECT: "Each subnet in a VPC is mapped to all AZs in the region" is the correct answer.

INCORRECT: "AZ's have direct, low-latency, high throughput and redundant network connections between each other" is incorrect as this is true.

INCORRECT: "Each AZ is designed as an independent failure zone" is incorrect as this is true.

INCORRECT: "AZs are physically separated within a typical metropolitan region and are located in lower risk flood plains" is incorrect as this is true.

References:

https://docs.aws.amazon.com/AWSEC2/latest/UserGuide/using-regions-availability-zones.html

Save time with our exam-specific cheat sheets:

https://digitalcloud.training/certification-training/aws-certified-cloud-practitioner/aws-global-infrastructure/

https://digitalcloud.training/certification-training/aws-certified-cloud-practitioner/aws-networking/

QUESTION 28

When designing a VPC, what is the purpose of an Internet Gateway?

1. Provides Internet access for EC2 instances in private subnets
2. Enables Internet communications for instances in public subnets
3. It's a bastion host for inbound management connections
4. It's used for making VPN connections to a VPC

Answer: 2

Explanation:

An internet gateway is a horizontally scaled, redundant, and highly available VPC component that allows communication between instances in your VPC and the internet. It therefore imposes no availability risks or bandwidth constraints on your network traffic.

An internet gateway serves two purposes: to provide a target in your VPC route tables for internet-routable traffic, and to perform network address translation (NAT) for instances that have been assigned public IPv4 addresses.

CORRECT: "Enables Internet communications for instances in public subnets" is the correct answer.

INCORRECT: "Provides Internet access for EC2 instances in private subnets" is incorrect. You cannot connect instances in a private subnet to the Internet using an Internet Gateway, you need a NAT Gateway or NAT Instance for this purpose.

INCORRECT: "It's a bastion host for inbound management connections" is incorrect. You cannot use an Internet Gateway as a bastion host, deploy an EC2 instance in a public subnet for this purpose.

INCORRECT: "It's used for making VPN connections to a VPC" is incorrect. You cannot use the Internet Gateway for making VPN connections to a VPC, you need a Virtual Private Gateway for this purpose.

References:

https://docs.aws.amazon.com/vpc/latest/userguide/VPC_Internet_Gateway.html

Save time with our exam-specific cheat sheets:

https://digitalcloud.training/certification-training/aws-certified-cloud-practitioner/aws-networking/

QUESTION 29

What is the name of the online, self-service portal that AWS provides to enable customers to view reports and, such as PCI reports, and accept agreements?

1. AWS Compliance Portal
2. AWS Documentation Portal
3. AWS Artifact
4. AWS DocuFact

Answer: 3

Explanation:

AWS Artifact is your go-to, central resource for compliance-related information that matters to you. It provides on-demand access to AWS' security and compliance reports and select online agreements.

Reports available in AWS Artifact include our Service Organization Control (SOC) reports, Payment Card Industry (PCI) reports, and certifications from accreditation bodies across geographies and compliance verticals that validate the implementation and operating effectiveness of AWS security controls.

Agreements available in AWS Artifact include the Business Associate Addendum (BAA) and the Nondisclosure Agreement (NDA).

CORRECT: "AWS Artifact" is the correct answer.

INCORRECT: "AWS Compliance Portal" is incorrect as this is not a real service.

INCORRECT: "AWS Documentation Portal" is incorrect as this is not a real service.

INCORRECT: "AWS DocuFact" is incorrect as this is not a real service.

References:

https://aws.amazon.com/artifact/

Save time with our exam-specific cheat sheets:

https://digitalcloud.training/certification-training/aws-certified-cloud-practitioner/additional-aws-services-tools/

QUESTION 30

What are two correct statements about AWS Organizations with consolidated billing? (Select TWO.)

1. Multiple bills are provided per organization
2. One bill provided for multiple accounts
3. Linked accounts lose their management independence
4. Volume pricing discounts applied across multiple accounts
5. CloudTrail can be configured per organization

Answer: 2, 4

Explanation:

With AWS organizations you create a paying account and linked accounts. One bill is provided for multiple accounts within an organization. Volume pricing discounts can be applied across resources in multiple accounts.

CORRECT: "One bill provided for multiple accounts" is a correct answer.

CORRECT: "Volume pricing discounts applied across multiple accounts" is also a correct answer.

INCORRECT: "Multiple bills are provided per organization" is incorrect as one bill is provided for multiple accounts within an organization.

INCORRECT: "Linked accounts lose their management independence" is incorrect. Linked accounts can still be managed independently.

INCORRECT: "CloudTrail can be configured per organization" is incorrect. CloudTrail is on a per account basis and per region basis but can be aggregated into a single bucket in the paying account.

References:

https://aws.amazon.com/organizations/

Save time with our exam-specific cheat sheets:

https://digitalcloud.training/certification-training/aws-certified-cloud-practitioner/aws-billing-and-pricing/

QUESTION 31

Which AWS IAM best practice recommends applying the minimum permissions necessary to perform a task when creating IAM policies?

1. Create individual IAM users

2. Use roles to delegate permissions
3. Grant least privilege
4. Enable MFA for privileged users

Answer: 3

Explanation:

When you create IAM policies, follow the standard security advice of granting least privilege that is, granting only the permissions required to perform a task. Determine what users need to do and then craft policies for them that let the users perform only those tasks.

The other answer are all valid best practices but are not related to applying minimum permissions to IAM policies.

CORRECT: "Grant least privilege" is the correct answer.

INCORRECT: "Create individual IAM users" is incorrect as explained above.

INCORRECT: "Use roles to delegate permissions" is incorrect as explained above.

INCORRECT: "Enable MFA for privileged users" is incorrect as explained above.

References:

https://docs.aws.amazon.com/IAM/latest/UserGuide/best-practices.html#grant-least-privilege

Save time with our exam-specific cheat sheets:

https://digitalcloud.training/certification-training/aws-certified-cloud-practitioner/identity-and-access-management/

QUESTION 32

What are the benefits of using IAM roles for applications that run on EC2 instances? (Select TWO.)
1. Easier to configure than using storing access keys within the EC2 instance
2. More secure than storing access keys within applications
3. Can apply multiple roles to a single instance
4. It is easier to manage IAM roles
5. Role credentials are permanent

Answer: 2, 4

Explanation:

Using IAM roles instead of storing credentials within EC2 instances is more secure It is also easier to manage roles.

CORRECT: "More secure than storing access keys within applications" is the correct answer.

CORRECT: "It is easier to manage IAM roles" is the correct answer.

INCORRECT: "Easier to configure than using storing access keys within the EC2 instance" is incorrect. It is not easier to configure as there are extra steps that need to be completed.

INCORRECT: "Can apply multiple roles to a single instance" is incorrect. You cannot apply multiple roles to a single instance.

INCORRECT: "Role credentials are permanent" is incorrect. Role credentials are temporary, not permanent, and are rotated automatically.

References:

https://docs.aws.amazon.com/IAM/latest/UserGuide/id_roles_use_switch-role-ec2.html

Save time with our exam-specific cheat sheets:

https://digitalcloud.training/certification-training/aws-certified-cloud-practitioner/identity-and-access-management/

QUESTION 33

Under the AWS Shared Responsibility Model, which of the following is the customer NOT responsible for?
1. Adding firewall rules to security groups and network ACLs
2. Applying encryption to data stored on an EBS volume
3. Applying bucket policies to share Amazon S3 data
4. Installing firmware updates on host servers

Answer: 4

Explanation:

AWS customers are not responsible for installing firmware updates on the underlying infrastructure. AWS customers must protect their AWS services through policies, encryption, and firewall rules.

CORRECT: "Installing firmware updates on host servers" is the correct answer.

INCORRECT: "Adding firewall rules to security groups and network ACLs" is incorrect as this is a customer responsibility.

INCORRECT: "Applying encryption to data stored on an EBS volume" is incorrect as this is a customer responsibility.

INCORRECT: "Applying bucket policies to share Amazon S3 data" is incorrect as this is a customer responsibility.

References:

https://aws.amazon.com/compliance/shared-responsibility-model/

Save time with our exam-specific cheat sheets:

https://digitalcloud.training/certification-training/aws-certified-cloud-practitioner/aws-shared-responsibility-model/

QUESTION 34

Which type of storage stores objects comprised of key, value pairs?

1. Amazon DynamoDB
2. Amazon EBS
3. Amazon EFS
4. Amazon S3

Answer: 4

Explanation:

Amazon Simple Storage Service is storage for the Internet. It is designed to make web-scale computing easier for developers. Amazon S3 is an object-based storage system that stores objects that are comprised of key, value pairs.

CORRECT: "Amazon S3" is the correct answer.

INCORRECT: "Amazon DynamoDB" is incorrect. Amazon DynamoDB stores items, not objects, based on key, value pairs.

INCORRECT: "Amazon EBS" is incorrect. Amazon EBS is a block-based storage system.

INCORRECT: "Amazon EFS" is incorrect. Amazon EFS is a file-based storage system.

References:

https://docs.aws.amazon.com/AmazonS3/latest/dev/Welcome.html

Save time with our exam-specific cheat sheets:

https://digitalcloud.training/certification-training/aws-certified-cloud-practitioner/aws-storage/

QUESTION 35

Which type of EBS volumes can be encrypted?

1. Non-root volumes only
2. Both non-root and root volumes
3. Only non-root volumes created from snapshots
4. Only root volumes can have encryption applied at launch time

Answer: 2

Explanation:

Amazon EBS encryption offers a straight-forward encryption solution for your EBS resources that doesn't require you to build, maintain, and secure your own key management infrastructure. It uses AWS Key Management Service (AWS KMS) customer master keys (CMK) when creating encrypted volumes and snapshots.

Encryption operations occur on the servers that host EC2 instances, ensuring the security of both data-at-rest and data-in-transit between an instance and its attached EBS storage.

All volumes can now be encrypted at launch time and it's possible to set this as the default setting.

CORRECT: "Both non-root and root volumes" is the correct answer.

INCORRECT: "Non-root volumes only" is incorrect as this is not true.

INCORRECT: "Only non-root volumes created from snapshots" is incorrect as you can encrypt all EBS volumes whether created from snapshots or not.

INCORRECT: "Only root volumes can have encryption applied at launch time" is incorrect as all volumes can have encryption applied at launch time.

References:

https://docs.aws.amazon.com/AWSEC2/latest/UserGuide/EBSEncryption.html

Save time with our exam-specific cheat sheets:

https://digitalcloud.training/certification-training/aws-certified-cloud-practitioner/aws-storage/

QUESTION 36

What feature of Amazon S3 enables you to set rules to automatically transfer objects between different storage classes at defined time intervals?

1. Elastic Data Management
2. Object Lifecycle Management
3. Auto Lifecycle Scaling
4. S3 Archiving

Answer: 2

Explanation:

Object lifecycle management can be used with objects so that they are stored cost effectively throughout their lifecycle. Objects can be transitioned to another storage class or expired.

All other options are incorrect as they are not services that can automatically transfer objects between S3 storage classes.

CORRECT: "Object Lifecycle Management" is the correct answer.

INCORRECT: "Elastic Data Management" is incorrect as explained above.

INCORRECT: "Auto Lifecycle Scaling" is incorrect as explained above.

INCORRECT: "S3 Archiving" is incorrect as explained above.

References:

https://docs.aws.amazon.com/AmazonS3/latest/dev/object-lifecycle-mgmt.html

Save time with our exam-specific cheat sheets:

https://digitalcloud.training/certification-training/aws-certified-cloud-practitioner/aws-storage/

QUESTION 37

What charges are applicable to Amazon S3 Standard storage class? (Select TWO.)

1. Per GB/month storage fee
2. Retrieval fee
3. Minimum capacity charge per object
4. Data ingress
5. Data egress

Answer: 1,5

Explanation:

With the standard storage class you pay a per GB/month storage fee, and data transfer out of S3. Standard-IA and One Zone-IA have a minimum capacity charge per object. Standard-IA, One Zone-IA, and Glacier also have a retrieval fee. You don't pay for data into S3 under any storage class.

CORRECT: "Per GB/month storage fee" is the correct answer.

CORRECT: "Data egress" is the correct answer.

INCORRECT: "Retrieval fee" is incorrect as explained above.

INCORRECT: "Minimum capacity charge per object" is incorrect as explained above.

INCORRECT: "Data ingress" is incorrect as explained above.

References:

https://aws.amazon.com/s3/pricing/

Save time with our exam-specific cheat sheets:

https://digitalcloud.training/certification-training/aws-certified-cloud-practitioner/aws-storage/

QUESTION 38

How can a company protect their Amazon S3 data from a regional disaster?

1. Archive to Amazon Glacier
2. Use Cross-Region Replication (CRR) to copy to another region
3. Use lifecycle actions to move to another S3 storage class
4. Enable Multi-Factor Authentication (MFA) delete

Answer: 2

Explanation:

Cross-Region replication (CRR) is used to copy objects across Amazon S3 buckets in different AWS Regions. The only option here that will help is to use CRR to copy the data to another region. This will provide disaster recovery.

CORRECT: "Use Cross-Region Replication (CRR) to copy to another region" is the correct answer.

INCORRECT: "Archive to Amazon Glacier" is incorrect. Moving to Glacier does not copy the data out of the region.

INCORRECT: "Use lifecycle actions to move to another S3 storage class" is incorrect as this will not move the data to another region.

INCORRECT: "Enable Multi-Factor Authentication (MFA) delete" is incorrect. Enabling MFA delete will not protect the data from a regional disaster.

References:

https://docs.aws.amazon.com/AmazonS3/latest/dev/replication.html

Save time with our exam-specific cheat sheets:

https://digitalcloud.training/certification-training/aws-certified-cloud-practitioner/aws-storage/

QUESTION 39

Which AWS support plan provides email only support by Cloud Support Associates?

1. Basic
2. Developer
3. Business
4. Enterprise

Answer: 2

Explanation:

Developer provides email support by the Cloud Support Associates team whereas Business and Enterprise provide email, 24×7 phone and chat access to Cloud Support Engineers. Basic does not provide email support at all.

	Developer	Business	Enterprise
	Recommended if you are experimenting or testing in AWS.	*Recommended if you have production workloads in AWS.*	*Recommended if you have business and/or mission critical workloads in AWS.*
AWS Trusted Advisor Best Practice Checks	7 Core checks	Full set of checks	Full set of checks
Enhanced Technical Support	Business hours** email access to Cloud Support Associates Unlimited cases / 1 primary contact	24x7 phone, email, and chat access to Cloud Support Engineers Unlimited cases / unlimited contacts (IAM supported)	24x7 phone, email, and chat access to Cloud Support Engineers Unlimited cases / unlimited contacts (IAM supported)

CORRECT: "Developer" is the correct answer.

INCORRECT: "Basic" is incorrect as explained above.

INCORRECT: "Business" is incorrect as explained above.

INCORRECT: "Enterprise" is incorrect as explained above.

References:

https://aws.amazon.com/premiumsupport/plans/

Save time with our exam-specific cheat sheets:

https://digitalcloud.training/certification-training/aws-certified-cloud-practitioner/aws-billing-and-pricing/

QUESTION 40

Which support plan is the lowest cost option that allows unlimited cases to be open?

1. Basic
2. Developer
3. Business
4. Enterprise

Answer: 2

Explanation:

With the Developer plan you can open unlimited cases. You can also open unlimited cases with the Business and Enterprise plans but these are more expensive. You cannot open any support cases with the basic support plan.

	Developer	Business	Enterprise
	Recommended if you are experimenting or testing in AWS.	*Recommended if you have production workloads in AWS.*	*Recommended if you have business and/or mission critical workloads in AWS.*
AWS Trusted Advisor Best Practice Checks	7 Core checks	Full set of checks	Full set of checks
Enhanced Technical Support	Business hours** email access to Cloud Support Associates Unlimited cases / 1 primary contact	24x7 phone, email, and chat access to Cloud Support Engineers Unlimited cases / unlimited contacts (IAM supported)	24x7 phone, email, and chat access to Cloud Support Engineers Unlimited cases / unlimited contacts (IAM supported)

CORRECT: "Developer" is the correct answer.

INCORRECT: "Basic" is incorrect as explained above.

INCORRECT: "Business" is incorrect as explained above.

INCORRECT: "Enterprise" is incorrect as explained above.

References:

https://aws.amazon.com/premiumsupport/plans/

Save time with our exam-specific cheat sheets:

https://digitalcloud.training/certification-training/aws-certified-cloud-practitioner/aws-billing-and-pricing/

QUESTION 41

Which service allows an organization to bring their own licensing on host hardware that is physically isolated from other AWS accounts?

1. EC2 Dedicated Instances
2. EC2 Spot Instances
3. EC2 Dedicated Hosts
4. EC2 Reserved Instances

Answer: 3

Explanation:

An Amazon EC2 Dedicated Host is a physical server with EC2 instance capacity fully dedicated to your use. Dedicated Hosts allow you to use your existing per-socket, per-core, or per-VM software licenses, including Windows Server, Microsoft SQL Server, SUSE, Linux Enterprise Server, and so on.

CORRECT: "EC2 Dedicated Hosts" is the correct answer.

INCORRECT: "EC2 Dedicated Instances" is incorrect. Dedicated Instances are Amazon EC2 instances that run in a VPC on hardware that's dedicated to a single customer. Bring your own licensing (BYOL) is not supported for dedicated instances.

INCORRECT: "EC2 Spot Instances" is incorrect. Spot instances allow you to bid in the marketplace for EC2 instances to reduce cost, they do not allow BYOL.

INCORRECT: "EC2 Reserved Instances" is incorrect. Reserved instances allow you to reduce on-demand price by up to 70% by committing to a 1- or 3-year term.

References:

https://docs.aws.amazon.com/AWSEC2/latest/UserGuide/dedicated-hosts-overview.html

Save time with our exam-specific cheat sheets:

https://digitalcloud.training/certification-training/aws-certified-cloud-practitioner/aws-compute/

QUESTION 42

Which of the below is an example of optimizing for cost?

1. Choosing the fastest EC2 instance to ensure performance
2. Provision extra capacity to allow for growth
3. Replace an EC2 compute instance with AWS Lambda
4. Deploy resources with AWS CloudFormation

Answer: 3

Explanation:

Where possible, you should replace EC2 workloads with AWS managed services that don't require you to take any capacity decisions. AWS Lambda is a serverless services and you only pay for actual processing time. Other examples of services that you don't need to make capacity decisions with include: ELB, CloudFront, SQS, Kinesis Firehose, SES, and CloudSearch.

CORRECT: "Replace an EC2 compute instance with AWS Lambda" is the correct answer.

INCORRECT: "Choosing the fastest EC2 instance to ensure performance" is incorrect. You should not choose the fastest EC2 instance if you're trying to optimize for cost as this will be expensive, you should right-size your EC2 instances, so you use the cheapest EC2 instance to suit your workload's requirements.

INCORRECT: "Provision extra capacity to allow for growth" is incorrect. Provisioning extra capacity for growth is not an example of cost optimization. With cloud computing you no longer need to do this as you can configure applications, databases and storage systems to grow on demand.

INCORRECT: "Deploy resources with AWS CloudFormation" is incorrect. Deploying resources with CloudFormation is great for consistently deploying application configurations from a template. However, this is not an example of cost optimization, it is more an example of operational optimization.

References:

https://aws.amazon.com/aws-cost-management/

QUESTION 43

Which service is used for caching data?

1. Amazon Simple Queue Service (SQS)
2. Amazon DynamoDB DAX
3. AWS Key Management Service (KMS)
4. Amazon Elastic File System (EFS)

Answer: 2

Explanation:

Amazon DynamoDB Accelerator (DAX) is a fully managed, highly available, in-memory cache for DynamoDB that delivers up to a 10x performance improvement – from milliseconds to microseconds – even at millions of requests per second.

CORRECT: "Amazon DynamoDB DAX" is the correct answer.

INCORRECT: "Amazon Simple Queue Service (SQS)" is incorrect. Amazon Simple Queue Service (SQS) is a fully managed message queuing service that enables you to decouple and scale microservices, distributed systems, and serverless applications.

INCORRECT: "Amazon Key Management Service (KMS)" is incorrect. AWS Key Management Service (KMS) makes it easy for you to create and manage keys and control the use of encryption across a wide range of AWS services and in your applications.

INCORRECT: "Amazon Elastic File System (EFS)" is incorrect. Amazon Elastic File System (Amazon EFS) provides a simple, scalable, elastic file system for Linux-based workloads for use with AWS Cloud services and on-premises resources.

References:

https://aws.amazon.com/dynamodb/dax/

QUESTION 44

Which service is used introduce fault tolerance into an application architecture?

1. Amazon CloudFront
2. Amazon ElastiCache
3. Amazon Elastic Load Balancing
4. Amazon DynamoDB

Answer: 3

Explanation:

Amazon Elastic Load Balancing is used to spread load and introduce fault tolerance by distributing connections across multiple identically configured back-end EC2 instances.

CORRECT: "Amazon Elastic Load Balancing" is the correct answer.

INCORRECT: "Amazon CloudFront" is incorrect. Amazon CloudFront is a content delivery network that is used for caching content and serving it to web-based users quickly.

INCORRECT: "Amazon ElastiCache" is incorrect. Amazon ElastiCache is an in-memory database cache and is used to introduce improved performance rather than fault tolerance.

INCORRECT: "Amazon DynamoDB" is incorrect. Amazon DynamoDB is fault tolerant; however, it is not something you add to an architecture to introduce fault tolerance to the application stack.

References:

https://aws.amazon.com/elasticloadbalancing/

https://digitalcloud.training/certification-training/aws-certified-cloud-practitioner/aws-databases/

QUESTION 45

Which tools can you use to manage identities in IAM? (choose 2)

1. Amazon CloudWatch API
2. AWS Management Console
3. AWS Command Line Tools
4. EC2 Management Console
5. EC2 Management Console
6. Amazon Workspaces

Answer: 2,3

Explanation:

You can manage AWS Identity and Access Management identities through the AWS Management Console, AWS Command Line Tools, AWS SDKs, and IAM HTTPS API.

CORRECT: "AWS Management Console" is a correct answer.

CORRECT: "AWS Command Line Tools" is also a correct answer.

INCORRECT: "Amazon CloudWatch API" is incorrect. CloudWatch is not used for managing identities in IAM. It is a service used for monitoring the state of your AWS resources.

INCORRECT: "EC2 Management Console" is incorrect. The EC2 management console cannot be used for managing identities in IAM.

INCORRECT: "Amazon Workspaces" is incorrect. Amazon WorkSpaces is a managed desktop computing service running on the AWS cloud.

References:

https://aws.amazon.com/iam/

Save time with our exam-specific cheat sheets:

https://digitalcloud.training/certification-training/aws-certified-cloud-practitioner/identity-and-access-management/

QUESTION 46

Which of the following would be good reasons to move from on-premises to the AWS Cloud? (Select TWO.)

1. Gain access to free technical support services
2. Reduce costs through easier right-sizing of workloads
3. Improve agility and elasticity
4. Gain end-to-end operational management of the entire infrastructure stack
5. Outsource all security responsibility

Answer: 2,3

Explanation:

There are many benefits to moving to the AWS Cloud and these include reducing costs through right-sizing workloads. This is easier with elastic computing and the ability to easily adjust workloads, monitor utilization and programmatically make changes. You can improve agility and elasticity through services such as Auto Scaling, Elastic Load Balancing and highly scalable services such as S3 and Lambda.

CORRECT: "Reduce costs through easier right-sizing of workloads" is a correct answer.

CORRECT: "Improve agility and elasticity" is also a correct answer.

INCORRECT: "Gain access to free technical support services" is incorrect. You do not get free technical support services with AWS.

INCORRECT: "Gain end-to-end operational management of the entire infrastructure stack" is incorrect. You do not gain end-to-end operational management of your entire infrastructure stack. AWS manage the infrastructure and, for some services, the application too.

INCORRECT: "Outsource all security responsibility" is incorrect. You do not outsource all security responsibility with AWS – you are still responsible for ensuring the security of your applications, users, and data.

References:

https://docs.aws.amazon.com/whitepapers/latest/aws-overview/six-advantages-of-cloud-computing.html

Save time with our exam-specific cheat sheets:

https://digitalcloud.training/certification-training/aws-certified-cloud-practitioner/cloud-computing-concepts/

QUESTION 47

Which service runs your application code only when needed without needing to run servers?

1. Amazon EC2
2. Amazon ECS
3. AWS Lambda
4. AWS LightSail

Answer: 3

Explanation:

AWS Lambda is a serverless service that runs code as "functions". That means that your code is run when needed but there are no servers running (at least not servers that you see or manage). This reduces cost and operational overhead.

CORRECT: "AWS Lambda" is the correct answer.

INCORRECT: "Amazon EC2" is incorrect. Amazon EC2 is used for running server instances so this is an incorrect answer.

INCORRECT: "Amazon ECS" is incorrect. Amazon ECS is used for running Docker containers which do need to run waiting for requests.

INCORRECT: "AWS LightSail" is incorrect. AWS LightSail is a service that is used for running virtual instances and databases using a simplified user interface for users who are less experienced with AWS (also at a much lower cost than EC2).

References:

https://aws.amazon.com/lambda/

Save time with our exam-specific cheat sheets:

https://digitalcloud.training/certification-training/aws-certified-cloud-practitioner/aws-compute/

QUESTION 48

Which AWS feature of Amazon EC2 allows an administrator to create a standardized image that can be used for launching new instances?

1. Amazon Golden Image
2. Amazon Block Template
3. Amazon Machine Image
4. Amazon EBS Mount Point

Answer: 3

Explanation:

An Amazon Machine Image (AMI) provides the information required to launch an instance. You can use an AMI to launch identical instances from a standard template. This is also known as a Golden Image (though no such feature exists in AWS with this name). An AMI is created from an EBS snapshot and also includes launch permissions and a block device mapping.

CORRECT: "Amazon Machine Image" is the correct answer.

INCORRECT: "Amazon Golden Image" is incorrect as this is not an AWS feature.

INCORRECT: "Amazon Block Template" is incorrect. Amazon Block Templates do not exist.

INCORRECT: "Amazon EBS Mount Point" is incorrect. An Amazon EBS Mount Point is not an AWS feature. You do mount EBS volumes however this is within the operating system. Block device mappings are used in AMIs to specify how to mount the EBS volume.

References:

https://docs.aws.amazon.com/AWSEC2/latest/UserGuide/AMIs.html

Save time with our exam-specific cheat sheets:

https://docs.aws.amazon.com/AWSEC2/latest/UserGuide/AMIs.html

QUESTION 49

What information must be entered into the AWS TCO Calculator?

1. The number of end users in your company
2. The number of applications in your company
3. The number of storage systems in your company
4. The number of servers in your company

Answer: 4

Explanation:

The TCO calculator asks for the number of servers (Physical or VMs) you are running on-premises. You also need to supply the resource information (CPU, RAM) and specify whether the server is a DB or non-DB.

Use this new calculator to compare the cost of your applications in an on-premises or traditional hosting environment to AWS. Describe your on-premises or hosting environment configuration to produce a detailed cost comparison with AWS.

1. Describe your existing or planned on-premises or hosting infrastructure in four steps, or enter detailed configurations.

2. Get an instant summary report which shows you the three year TCO comparison by cost categories.

3. Download a full report including detailed cost breakdowns, Methodology, Assumptions, and FAQ or store the report in Amazon S3 for sharing with others.

CORRECT: "The number of servers in your company" is the correct answer.

INCORRECT: "The number of end users in your company" is incorrect. You do not need to supply the number of end users.

INCORRECT: "The number of applications in your company" is incorrect. You do not need to supply the number of applications.

INCORRECT: "The number of storage systems in your company" is incorrect. You don't need to specify the number of storage systems, you just need to specify the raw capacity.

References:

https://aws.amazon.com/tco-calculator/

https://awstcocalculator.com/

Save time with our exam-specific cheat sheets:

https://digitalcloud.training/certification-training/aws-certified-cloud-practitioner/aws-billing-and-pricing/

QUESTION 50

An Elastic IP Address can be remapped between EC2 instances across which boundaries?

1. Regions
2. Edge Locations
3. Availability Zones
4. DB Subnets

Answer: 3

Explanation:

Elastic IP addresses are for use in a specific region only and can therefore only be remapped between instances within that region. You can use Elastic IP addresses to mask the failure of an instance in one Availability Zone by rapidly remapping the address to an instance in another Availability Zone.

CORRECT: "Availability Zones" is the correct answer.

INCORRECT: "Regions" is incorrect as you cannot remap across regions.

INCORRECT: "Edge Locations" is incorrect. Edge Locations are used by CloudFront and are not places where you can run EC2 instances.

INCORRECT: "DB Subnets" is incorrect. DB subnets (groups) are used by the RDS relational database service and are not used for running EC2 instances.

References:

https://docs.aws.amazon.com/AWSEC2/latest/UserGuide/elastic-ip-addresses-eip.html

Save time with our exam-specific cheat sheets:

https://digitalcloud.training/certification-training/aws-certified-cloud-practitioner/aws-global-infrastructure/

QUESTION 51

Which AWS service can assist with providing recommended actions on cost optimization?

1. AWS Inspector
2. AWS Trusted Advisor
3. AWS Artifact
4. Amazon CloudWatch Events

Answer: 2

Explanation:

Trusted Advisor is an online resource that helps to reduce cost, increase performance and improve security by optimizing your AWS environment.

CORRECT: "AWS Trusted Advisor" is the correct answer.

INCORRECT: "AWS Inspector" is incorrect. Inspector is an automated security assessment service that helps improve the security and compliance of applications deployed on AWS.

INCORRECT: "AWS Artifact" is incorrect. AWS Artifact is a resource for obtaining compliance-related information.

INCORRECT: "Amazon CloudWatch Events" is incorrect. Amazon CloudWatch Events delivers a near real-time stream of system events that describe changes in Amazon Web Services (AWS) resources.

References:

https://aws.amazon.com/premiumsupport/technology/trusted-advisor/

Save time with our exam-specific cheat sheets:

https://digitalcloud.training/certification-training/aws-certified-cloud-practitioner/cloud-security/

QUESTION 52

How can an online education company ensure their video courses play with minimal latency for their users around the world?

1. Use Amazon S3 Transfer Acceleration to speed up downloads
2. Use Amazon EBS Cross Region Replication to get the content close to the users
3. Use Amazon Aurora Global Database
4. Use Amazon CloudFront to get the content closer to users

Answer: 4

Explanation:

Amazon CloudFront is a content delivery network (CDN) that enables you to cache content in Edge Locations that are located around the world. This brings your media closer to your end users which reduces latency and improves the user experience.

CORRECT: "Use Amazon CloudFront to get the content closer to users" is the correct answer.

INCORRECT: "Use Amazon S3 Transfer Acceleration to speed up downloads" is incorrect. Amazon S3 Transfer Acceleration is a feature that is used for accelerating uploads to Amazon S3, not for downloads.

INCORRECT: "Use Amazon EBS Cross Region Replication to get the content close to the users" is incorrect. Amazon EBS Cross Region Replication does not exist (S3 Cross Region Replication does). You can copy EBS volumes across regions manually (or programmatically), however EBS is not a good way to get your content closer to your users as you would need to mount the volume to an EC2 instance (additional cost) and would also need to find a way to keep your files in sync.

INCORRECT: "Use Amazon Aurora Global Database" is incorrect. Amazon Aurora Global Database is designed for globally distributed applications, allowing a single Amazon Aurora database to span multiple AWS regions. This is a way to have an SQL database across regions, which is not a good use case for hosting media files.

References:

https://aws.amazon.com/cloudfront/

Save time with our exam-specific cheat sheets:

https://digitalcloud.training/certification-training/aws-certified-cloud-practitioner/content-delivery-and-dns-services/

QUESTION 53

Which AWS security service provides a firewall at the subnet level within a VPC?

1. Security Group
2. IAM Policy
3. Bucket Policy
4. Network Access Control List

Answer: 4

Explanation:

A Network ACL is a firewall that is associated with a subnet within your VPC. It is used to filter the network traffic that enters and exits the subnet.

CORRECT: "Network Access Control List" is the correct answer.

INCORRECT: "Security Group" is incorrect. A Security Group is a firewall that is associated with an EC2 instances (not the subnet). Security Groups control the traffic the inbound and outbound network traffic from/to the instance.

INCORRECT: "IAM Policy" is incorrect. An IAM Policy is used to assign permissions to users and roles.

INCORRECT: "Bucket Policy" is incorrect. A Bucket Policy is used with Amazon S3 buckets to control access.

References:

https://docs.aws.amazon.com/vpc/latest/userguide/vpc-network-acls.html

Save time with our exam-specific cheat sheets:

https://digitalcloud.training/certification-training/aws-certified-cloud-practitioner/aws-networking/

QUESTION 54

Which services allow you to store files on AWS? (Select TWO.)

1. AWS Lambda
2. Amazon LightSail
3. Amazon EBS
4. Amazon EFS
5. Amazon SQS

Answer: 3,4

Explanation:

You can store files on the Elastic Block Store (EBS), and Elastic File System (EFS). EBS volumes are mounted as block devices to EC2 instances and EFS volumes are mounted to the instance using the NFS protocol.

CORRECT: "Amazon EBS" is a correct answer.

CORRECT: "Amazon EFS" is also a correct answer.

INCORRECT: "AWS Lambda" is incorrect. AWS Lambda is a compute service for running code as functions.

INCORRECT: "Amazon LightSail" is incorrect. Amazon LightSail is a compute service for running instances.

INCORRECT: "Amazon SQS" is incorrect. Amazon Simple Queue Service (SQS) is a message bus for temporarily storing data that is being passed between application components.

References:

https://aws.amazon.com/ebs/

https://aws.amazon.com/efs/

Save time with our exam-specific cheat sheets:

https://digitalcloud.training/certification-training/aws-certified-cloud-practitioner/aws-storage/

QUESTION 55

Which AWS program can help an organization to design, build, and manage their workloads on AWS?

1. APN Consulting Partners
2. APN Technology Consultants
3. AWS Business Development Manager
4. AWS Technical Account Manager

Answer: 1

Explanation:

APN Consulting Partners are professional services firms that help customers of all sizes design, architect, build, migrate, and manage their workloads and applications on AWS. Consulting Partners include System Integrators (SIs), Strategic Consultancies, Agencies, Managed Service Providers (MSPs), and Value-Added Resellers (VARs).

None of the other options are AWS Programs that can assist a customer with the design, build and management of their workloads.

CORRECT: "APN Consulting Partners" is the correct answer.

INCORRECT: "APN Technology Consultants" is incorrect as explained above.

INCORRECT: "AWS Business Development Manager" is incorrect as explained above.

INCORRECT: "AWS Technical Account Manager" is incorrect as explained above.

References:

https://aws.amazon.com/partners/consulting/

Save time with our exam-specific cheat sheets:

QUESTION 56

Which of the following statements is correct about Amazon S3 cross-region replication?

1. Both source and destination S3 buckets must have versioning disabled
2. The source and destination S3 buckets cannot be in different AWS Regions
3. S3 buckets configured for cross-region replication can be owned by a single AWS account or by different accounts
4. The source S3 bucket owner must have the source and destination AWS Regions disabled for their account

Answer: 3

Explanation:

Replication enables automatic, asynchronous copying of objects across Amazon S3 buckets. Buckets that are configured for object replication can be owned by the same AWS account or by different accounts. You can copy objects between different AWS Regions or within the same Region.

Both source and destination buckets must have versioning enabled. The source bucket owner must have the source and destination AWS Regions enabled for their account. The destination bucket owner must have the destination Region-enabled for their account.

CORRECT: "S3 buckets configured for cross-region replication can be owned by a single AWS account or by different accounts" is the correct answer.

INCORRECT: "Both source and destination S3 buckets must have versioning disabled" is incorrect as explained above.

INCORRECT: "The source and destination S3 buckets cannot be in different AWS Regions" is incorrect as explained above.

INCORRECT: "The source S3 bucket owner must have the source and destination AWS Regions disabled for their account" is incorrect as explained above.

References:

https://docs.aws.amazon.com/AmazonS3/latest/dev/replication.html

Save time with our exam-specific cheat sheets:

https://digitalcloud.training/certification-training/aws-certified-cloud-practitioner/aws-storage/

QUESTION 57

Which of the following Amazon EC2 pricing models allows customers to use existing server-bound software licenses?

1. Spot Instances
2. Reserved Instances
3. Dedicated Hosts
4. On-Demand Instances

Answer: 3

Explanation:

Amazon EC2 Dedicated Hosts allow you to use your eligible software licenses from vendors such as Microsoft and Oracle on Amazon EC2, so that you get the flexibility and cost effectiveness of using your own licenses, but with the resiliency, simplicity and elasticity of AWS. An Amazon EC2 Dedicated Host is a physical server fully dedicated for your use, so you can help address corporate compliance requirements.

CORRECT: "Dedicated Hosts" is the correct answer.

INCORRECT: "On-Demand Instances" is incorrect. This is a standard pricing model and does not offer the advantages requested.

INCORRECT: "Spot Instances" is incorrect. This is used to obtain discounted pricing for short-term requirements that can be interrupted.

INCORRECT: "Reserved Instances" is incorrect. This is used to lower cost by reserving usage of an instance for a term of 1 or 3 years.

References:

https://aws.amazon.com/ec2/dedicated-hosts/

Save time with our exam-specific cheat sheets:

https://digitalcloud.training/certification-training/aws-certified-cloud-practitioner/aws-billing-and-pricing/

QUESTION 58

A company has deployed several relational databases on Amazon RDS. Every month, the database software vendor releases new security patches that need to be applied to the database.

What is the MOST efficient way to apply the security patches?

1. Connect to each database instance on a monthly basis, and download and apply the necessary security patches from the vendor
2. Enable automatic patching for the instances using the Amazon RDS console
3. In AWS Config, configure a rule for the instances and the required patch level
4. Use AWS Systems Manager to automate database patching according to a schedule

Answer: 2

Explanation:

Periodically, Amazon RDS performs maintenance on Amazon RDS resources. Maintenance most often involves updates to the DB instance's underlying hardware, underlying operating system (OS), or database engine version. Updates to the operating system most often occur for security issues and should be done as soon as possible.

Required patching is automatically scheduled only for patches that are related to security and instance reliability. Such patching occurs infrequently (typically once every few months) and seldom requires more than a fraction of your maintenance window.

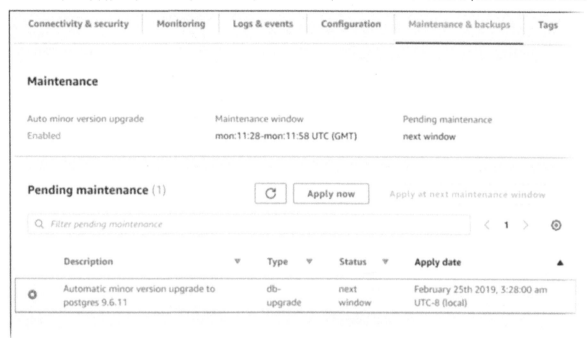

All you need to do to get enable patching is specify the maintenance window in which the patching will take place. This can be done at instance creation time or at any time afterwards.

CORRECT: "Enable automatic patching for the instances using the Amazon RDS console" is the correct answer.

INCORRECT: "Connect to each database instance on a monthly basis, and download and apply the necessary security patches from the vendor" is incorrect. Amazon RDS is a managed service and you do not need to do this manually.

INCORRECT: "In AWS Config, configure a rule for the instances and the required patch level" is incorrect. This service is used for auditing and evaluating resource configurations.

INCORRECT: "Use AWS Systems Manager to automate database patching according to a schedule" is incorrect. Systems Manager can be used to manage EC2 instances but it cannot be used to patch RDS instances.

References:

https://docs.aws.amazon.com/AmazonRDS/latest/UserGuide/USER_UpgradeDBInstance.Maintenance.html

Save time with our exam-specific cheat sheets:

https://digitalcloud.training/certification-training/aws-certified-cloud-practitioner/aws-databases/

QUESTION 59

A Cloud Practitioner needs to rapidly deploy a popular IT solution and start using it immediately.

What should the Cloud Practitioner use?

1. AWS Well-Architected Framework documentation
2. Amazon CloudFront
3. AWS Elastic Beanstalk
4. AWS Quick Start reference deployments

Answer: 4

Explanation:

Quick Starts are built by AWS solutions architects and partners to help you deploy popular technologies on AWS, based on AWS best practices for security and high availability. These accelerators reduce hundreds of manual procedures into just a few steps, so you can build your production environment quickly and start using it immediately.

Each Quick Start includes AWS CloudFormation templates that automate the deployment and a guide that discusses the architecture and provides step-by-step deployment instructions.

CORRECT: "AWS Quick Start reference deployments" is the correct answer.

INCORRECT: "AWS Well-Architected Framework documentation" is incorrect. The well architected framework is documentation that provides guidance on design best practices. It is not used to actually deploy anything.

INCORRECT: "Amazon CloudFront" is incorrect. CloudFront is a content delivery network (CDN) that caches content for better performance.

INCORRECT: "AWS Elastic Beanstalk" is incorrect. Elastic Beanstalk can be used to easily deploy certain web applications. However, you still need to supply the code and it is limited to EC2 instances.

References:

https://aws.amazon.com/quickstart/

Save time with our exam-specific cheat sheets:

QUESTION 60

A cloud practitioner needs to decrease application latency and increase performance for globally distributed users.

Which services can assist? (Select TWO.)

1. Amazon ECS
2. Amazon S3
3. Amazon AppStream 2.0
4. Amazon ElastiCache
5. Amazon CloudFront

Answer: 2,5

Explanation:

Amazon S3 is an object-based storage system. It can be used to store data such as files and images that need to be served. Optionally, an S3 bucket can be configured as a static website. Amazon CloudFront is a content delivery network (CDN) that caches content at Edge Locations around the world.

These two services can work together with an S3 bucket configured as an origin for the CloudFront distribution. Users around the world will then be able to pull the content from the local Edge Location with lower latency and better performance.

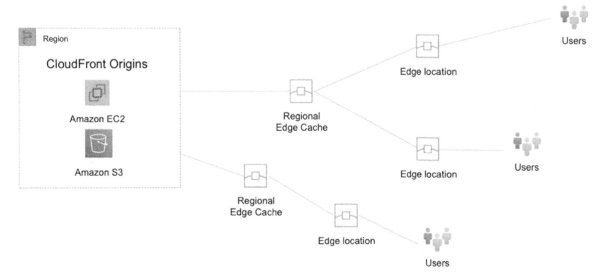

CORRECT: "Amazon S3" is a correct answer.

CORRECT: "Amazon CloudFront" is also a correct answer.

INCORRECT: "Amazon ECS" is incorrect. The Elastic Container Service (ECS) is used for running Docker containers on AWS. This is not going to help with reducing latency or increasing performance for global users.

INCORRECT: "Amazon AppStream 2.0" is incorrect. This is an application streaming service for streaming applications to computers. It is unsuitable for these requirements.

INCORRECT: "Amazon ElastiCache" is incorrect. ElastiCache caches data from a database in-memory. It is unsuitable for these requirements.

References:

https://aws.amazon.com/cloudfront/

https://aws.amazon.com/s3/

Save time with our exam-specific cheat sheets:

https://digitalcloud.training/certification-training/aws-certified-cloud-practitioner/content-delivery-and-dns-services/

https://digitalcloud.training/certification-training/aws-certified-cloud-practitioner/aws-storage/

QUESTION 61

A company needs protection from distributed denial of service (DDoS) attacks on its website and assistance from AWS experts during such events.

Which AWS managed service will meet these requirements?

5. AWS Shield Advanced
1. AWS Firewall Manager
2. AWS Web Application Firewall
3. Amazon GuardDuty

Answer: 1

Explanation:

AWS Shield Advanced provides enhanced detection and includes a specialized support team for customers on Enterprise or Business support plans. The AWS DDoS Response Team (DRT) are available 24/7 and can be engaged before, during, or after a DDoS attack.

CORRECT: "AWS Shield Advanced" is the correct answer.

INCORRECT: "AWS Firewall Manager" is incorrect. This service is used to simplify management of AWS WAF, AWS Shield Advanced, and Amazon VPC security groups.

INCORRECT: "AWS Web Application Firewall" is incorrect. AWS WAF is used for protecting web applications and APIs against malicious attacks. This is not a DDoS prevention service.

INCORRECT: "Amazon GuardDuty" is incorrect. This service is used for continuously monitoring AWS resources for threats. It is not a DDoS prevention service, it uses machine learning and anomaly detection to identify security vulnerabilities in resources.

References:

https://aws.amazon.com/shield/getting-started/

Save time with our exam-specific cheat sheets:

https://digitalcloud.training/certification-training/aws-certified-cloud-practitioner/cloud-security/

QUESTION 62

Which of the following must be used together to gain programmatic access to an AWS account? (Select TWO.)

1. An access key ID
2. A primary key
3. A secret access key
4. A user ID
5. A secondary key

Answer: 1,3

Explanation:

Access keys are long-term credentials for an IAM user or the AWS account root user. You can use access keys to sign programmatic requests to the AWS CLI or AWS API (directly or using the AWS SDK).

Access keys consist of two parts: an access key ID (for example, AKIAIOSFODNN7EXAMPLE) and a secret access key (for example, wJalrXUtnFEMI/K7MDENG/bPxRfiCYEXAMPLEKEY).

Like a user name and password, you must use both the access key ID and secret access key together to authenticate your requests. Manage your access keys as securely as you do your user name and password.

CORRECT: "An access key ID" is the correct answer.

CORRECT: "A secret access key" is the correct answer.

INCORRECT: "A primary key" is incorrect. Primary keys are not associated with authentication.

INCORRECT: "A user ID" is incorrect. A user ID is used to logon using the AWS Management Console, not programmatically.

INCORRECT: "A secondary key" is incorrect. Secondary keys are not associated with authentication.

References:

https://docs.aws.amazon.com/IAM/latest/UserGuide/id_credentials_access-keys.html

Save time with our exam-specific cheat sheets:

https://digitalcloud.training/certification-training/aws-certified-cloud-practitioner/identity-and-access-management/

QUESTION 63

An application that is deployed across multiple Availability Zones could be described as:

1. Being highly available
2. Having global reach
3. Being secure
4. Having elasticity

Answer: 1

Explanation:

When you deploy an application across multiple Availability Zones the application can be considered to be highly available. You must also have a way of directing traffic to the application in each AZ such as an Elastic Load Balancer.

The diagram below depicts an example of a highly available application deployed on EC2 instances in multiple AZs and using an ELB to direct traffic:

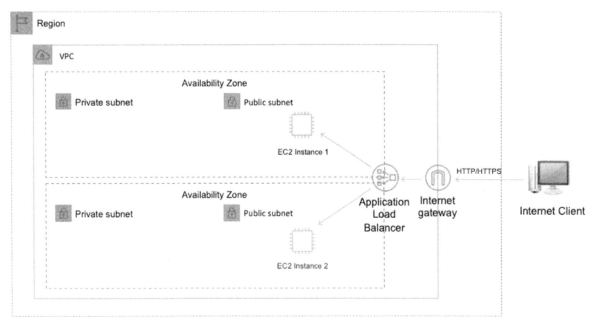

CORRECT: "Being highly available" is the correct answer.

INCORRECT: "Having global reach" is incorrect as this refers to deploying applications that can be connected to from around the world and also deploying applications into different regions.

INCORRECT: "Being secure" is incorrect as this is not an example of the implementation of security.

INCORRECT: "Having elasticity" is incorrect. Auto Scaling is an example of elasticity and it is not mentioned in this question.

References:

https://aws.amazon.com/about-aws/global-infrastructure/regions_az/

Save time with our exam-specific cheat sheets:

https://digitalcloud.training/certification-training/aws-certified-cloud-practitioner/architecting-for-the-cloud/

QUESTION 64

A Cloud Practitioner is developing a disaster recovery plan and intends to replicate data between multiple geographic areas.

Which of the following meets these requirements?

1. AWS Accounts
2. AWS Regions
3. Availability Zones
4. Edge locations

Answer: 2

Explanation:

AWS has the concept of a Region, which is a physical location around the world where we cluster data centers. We call each group of logical data centers an Availability Zone. Each AWS Region consists of multiple, isolated, and physically separate AZ's within a geographic area.

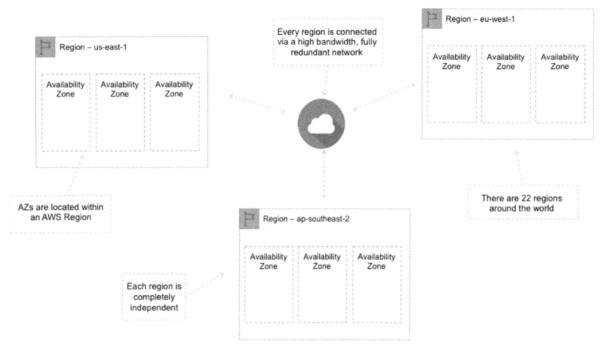

Therefore, the Cloud Practitioner should replicate data between multiple Regions as these are separate geographical areas.

CORRECT: "AWS Regions" is the correct answer.

INCORRECT: "AWS Accounts" is incorrect. An account is not a geographic area.

INCORRECT: "Availability Zones" is incorrect. AZs are within a Region, not across geographical areas.

INCORRECT: "Edge locations" is incorrect. These are not locations to which you can replicate your data. They are used primarily by Amazon CloudFront for caching content, not for disaster recovery.

References:

https://aws.amazon.com/about-aws/global-infrastructure/regions_az/

Save time with our exam-specific cheat sheets:

https://digitalcloud.training/certification-training/aws-certified-cloud-practitioner/aws-global-infrastructure/

QUESTION 65

A user deploys an Amazon Aurora database instance in multiple Availability Zones.

This strategy involves which pillar of the AWS Well-Architected Framework?

1. Performance efficiency
2. Reliability
3. Cost optimization
4. Security

Answer: 2

Explanation:

The reliability pillar includes the ability of a system to recover from infrastructure or service disruptions, dynamically acquire computing resources to meet demand, and mitigate disruptions such as misconfigurations or transient network issues.

There are five design principles for reliability in the cloud:

- Test recovery procedures
- Automatically recover from failure
- Scale horizontally to increase aggregate system availability
- Stop guessing capacity

- Manage change in automation

The example given in the question is related to "Automatically recover from failure".

CORRECT: "Reliability" is the correct answer.

INCORRECT: "Performance efficiency" is incorrect as this is an example of reliability.

INCORRECT: "Cost optimization" is incorrect as this is an example of reliability.

INCORRECT: "Security" is incorrect as this is an example of reliability.

References:

https://aws.amazon.com/blogs/apn/the-5-pillars-of-the-aws-well-architected-framework/

Save time with our exam-specific cheat sheets:

https://digitalcloud.training/certification-training/aws-certified-cloud-practitioner/architecting-for-the-cloud/

SET 6: PRACTICE QUESTIONS ONLY

For training purposes, go directly to Set 6: Practice Questions, Answers & Explanations

QUESTION 1

The AWS Cost Management tools give users the ability to do which of the following? (Select TWO.)

1. Terminate all AWS resources automatically if budget thresholds are exceeded
2. Break down AWS costs by day, service, and linked AWS account
3. Create budgets and receive notifications if current or forecasted usage exceeds the budgets
4. Switch automatically to Reserved Instances or Spot Instances, whichever is most cost-effective
5. Move data stored in Amazon S3 to a more cost-effective storage class

QUESTION 2

Which AWS service or feature helps restrict the AWS service, resources, and individual API actions the users and roles in each member account can access?

1. Amazon Cognito
2. AWS Organizations
3. AWS Shield
4. AWS Firewall Manager

QUESTION 3

Under the shared responsibility model, which of the following tasks are the responsibility of the AWS customer? (Select TWO.)

1. Ensuring that application data is encrypted at rest
2. Ensuring that AWS NTP servers are set to the correct time
3. Ensuring that users have received security training in the use of AWS services
4. Ensuring that access to data centers is restricted
5. Ensuring that hardware is disposed of properly

QUESTION 4

Under the AWS shared responsibility model, which of the following are customer responsibilities? (Select TWO.)

1. Setting up server-side encryption on an Amazon S3 bucket
2. Amazon RDS instance patching
3. Network and firewall configurations
4. Physical security of data center facilities
5. Compute capacity availability

QUESTION 5

A web application running on AWS has been received malicious requests from the same set of IP addresses.

Which AWS service can help secure the application and block the malicious traffic?

1. AWS IAM
2. Amazon GuardDuty
3. Amazon SNS
4. AWS WAF

QUESTION 6

Which AWS service provides the ability to detect inadvertent data leaks of personally identifiable information (PII) and user credential data?

1. Amazon GuardDuty
2. Amazon Inspector
3. Amazon Macie
4. AWS Shield

QUESTION 7

According to the AWS Well-Architected Framework, what change management steps should be taken to achieve reliability in the AWS Cloud? (Select TWO.)

1. Use AWS Config to generate an inventory of AWS resources
2. Use service limits to prevent users from creating or making changes to AWS resources
3. Use AWS CloudTrail to record AWS API calls into an auditable log file
4. Use AWS Certificate Manager to create a catalog of approved services
5. Use Amazon GuardDuty to record API activity to an S3 bucket

QUESTION 8

Which of the following acts as a virtual firewall at the Amazon EC2 instance level to control traffic for one or more instances?

1. Route table
2. Virtual private gateways (VPG)
3. Security groups
4. Network Access Control Lists (ACL)

QUESTION 9

Which AWS Cloud design principles can help increase reliability? (Select TWO.)

1. Using monolithic architecture
2. Measuring overall efficiency
3. Testing recovery procedures
4. Adopting a consumption model
5. Automatically recovering from failure

QUESTION 10

Which pricing model will interrupt a running Amazon EC2 instance if capacity becomes temporarily unavailable?

1. On-Demand Instances
2. Standard Reserved Instances
3. Spot Instances
4. Convertible Reserved Instances

QUESTION 11

Which of the following statements about AWS's pay-as-you-go pricing model is correct?

1. It results in reduced capital expenditures
2. It requires payment up front for AWS services
3. It is relevant only for Amazon EC2, Amazon S3, and Amazon DynamoDB
4. It reduces operational expenditures

QUESTION 12

Which AWS service can serve a static website?

1. Amazon S3
2. Amazon Route 53
3. Amazon QuickSight

4.   AWS X-Ray

QUESTION 13

A startup eCommerce company needs to quickly deliver new website features in an iterative manner, minimizing the time to market.

Which AWS Cloud feature allows this?

1.   Elasticity
2.   High availability
3.   Agility
4.   Reliability

QUESTION 14

What is the most efficient way to establish network connectivity from on-premises to multiple VPCs in different AWS Regions?

1.   Use AWS Direct Connect
2.   Use AWS VPN
3.   Use AWS Client VPN
4.   Use an AWS Transit Gateway

QUESTION 15

A company is using the AWS CLI and programmatic access of AWS resources from its on-premises network.

What is a mandatory requirement in this scenario?

1.   Using an AWS Direct Connect connection
2.   Using an AWS access key and a secret key
3.   Using Amazon API Gateway
4.   Using an Amazon EC2 key pair

QUESTION 16

Which AWS service is suitable for an event-driven workload?

1.   Amazon EC2
2.   AWS Elastic Beanstalk
3.   AWS Lambda
4.   Amazon Lumberyard

QUESTION 17

Based on the shared responsibility model, which of the following security and compliance tasks is AWS responsible for?

1.   Granting access to individuals and services
2.   Encrypting data in transit
3.   Updating Amazon EC2 host firmware
4.   Updating operating systems

QUESTION 18

Which AWS service can be used to run Docker containers?

5.   AWS Lambda
6.   Amazon ECR
7.   AWS Fargate
8.   Amazon AMI

QUESTION 19

Which type of Elastic Load Balancer operates at the TCP connection level?

1. Application Load Balancer (ALB)
2. Network Load Balancer (NLB)
3. Classic Load Balancer (CLB)
4. Amazon Route 53 Load Balancer

QUESTION 20

Which AWS technology can be referred to as a "virtual hard disk in the cloud"?

1. Amazon EFS Filesystem
2. Amazon S3 Bucket
3. Amazon EBS volume
4. Amazon ENI

QUESTION 21

In which ways does AWS' pricing model benefit organizations?

1. Eliminates licensing costs
2. Focus spend on capital expenditure, rather than operational expenditure
3. Reduce the cost of maintaining idle resources
4. Reduces the people cost of application development

QUESTION 22

Which service allows you to monitor and troubleshoot systems using system and application log files generated by those systems?

1. CloudTrail Logs
2. CloudWatch Metrics
3. CloudWatch Logs
4. CloudTrail Metrics

QUESTION 23

According to the AWS Shared Responsibility Model, which of the following is a shared control?

1. Operating system patching
2. Awareness and training
3. Protection of infrastructure
4. Client-side data encryption

QUESTION 24

Where do Amazon Identity and Access Management (IAM) accounts need to be created for a global organization?

1. In each region where the users are located
2. Just create them once, as IAM is a global service
3. Create them globally, and then replicate them regionally
4. In each geographical area where the users are located

QUESTION 25

What is the name for the top-level container used to hold objects within Amazon S3?

1. Folder

2. Directory
3. Instance Store
4. Bucket

QUESTION 26

Which of the following are examples of horizontal scaling? (Select TWO.)

1. Add more CPU/RAM to existing instances as demand increases
2. Add more instances as demand increases
3. Requires a restart to scale up or down
4. Automatic scaling using services such as AWS Auto Scaling
5. Scalability is limited by maximum instance size

QUESTION 27

Which resource should you use to access AWS security and compliance reports?

1. AWS Artifact
2. AWS Business Associate Addendum (BAA)
3. AWS IAM
4. AWS Organizations

QUESTION 28

What methods are available for scaling an Amazon RDS database? (Select TWO.)

1. You can scale up by moving to a larger instance size
2. You can scale out automatically with EC2 Auto Scaling
3. You can scale up by increasing storage capacity
4. You can scale out by implementing Elastic Load Balancing
5. You can scale up automatically using AWS Auto Scaling

QUESTION 29

Which type of scaling does Amazon EC2 Auto Scaling provide?

1. Vertical
2. Linear
3. Horizontal
4. Incremental

QUESTION 30

Which feature of Amazon S3 enables you to create rules to control the transfer of objects between different storage classes?

1. Object sharing
2. Versioning
3. Lifecycle management
4. Bucket policies

QUESTION 31

How can a database administrator reduce operational overhead for a MySQL database?

1. Migrate the database onto an EC2 instance
2. Migrate the database onto AWS Lambda
3. Use AWS CloudFormation to manage operations
4. Migrate the database onto an Amazon RDS instance

QUESTION 32

Which AWS database service is schema-less and can be scaled dynamically without incurring downtime?

1. Amazon RDS
2. Amazon Aurora
3. Amazon RedShift
4. Amazon DynamoDB

QUESTION 33

Which type of AWS database is ideally suited to analytics using SQL queries?

1. Amazon DynamoDB
2. Amazon RedShift
3. Amazon RDS
4. Amazon S3

QUESTION 34

Which AWS service is designed to be used for operational analytics?

1. Amazon EMR
2. Amazon Athena
3. Amazon QuickSight
4. Amazon Elasticsearch Service

QUESTION 35

You need to connect your company's on-premise network into AWS and would like to establish an AWS managed VPN service. Which of the following configuration items needs to be setup on the Amazon VPC side of the connection?

1. A Virtual Private Gateway
2. A Customer Gateway
3. A Network Address Translation device
4. A Firewall

QUESTION 36

Where are Amazon EBS snapshots stored?

1. On an Amazon EBS instance store
2. On an Amazon EFS filesystem
3. Within the EBS block store
4. On Amazon S3

QUESTION 37

Which AWS service makes it easy to coordinate the components of distributed applications as a series of steps in a visual workflow?

1. Amazon SWF
2. AWS Step Functions
3. Amazon SNS
4. Amazon SES

QUESTION 38

A Cloud Practitioner is creating the business process workflows associated with an order fulfilment system. Which AWS service can assist with coordinating tasks across distributed application components?

1. AWS STS
2. Amazon SQS
3. Amazon SWF
4. Amazon SNS

QUESTION 39

Your manager has asked you to explain some of the security features available in the AWS cloud. How can you describe the function of Amazon CloudHSM?

1. It provides server-side encryption for S3 objects
2. It is a Public Key Infrastructure (PKI)
3. It can be used to generate, use and manage encryption keys in the cloud
4. It is a firewall for use with web applications

QUESTION 40

Which AWS Glacier data access option retrieves data from an archive in 1-5 minutes?

1. Standard
2. Express
3. Accelerated
4. Expedited

QUESTION 41

How can a systems administrator specify a script to be run on an EC2 instance during launch?

1. Metadata
2. User Data
3. Run Command
4. AWS Config

QUESTION 42

What advantages does the AWS cloud provide in relation to cost? (Select TWO.)

1. Fine-grained billing
2. One-off payments for on-demand resources
3. Ability to turn off resources and not pay for them
4. Enterprise licensing discounts
5. Itemized power costs

QUESTION 43

Which of the authentication options below can be used to authenticate using AWS APIs? (Select TWO.)

1. Key pairs
2. Access keys
3. Server passwords
4. Security groups
5. Server certificates

QUESTION 44

Under the AWS Shared Responsibility Model, who is responsible for what? (Select TWO.)

1. Customers are responsible for compute infrastructure
2. AWS are responsible for network and firewall configuration
3. Customers are responsible for networking traffic protection

4. AWS are responsible for networking infrastructure
5. Customers are responsible for edge locations

QUESTION 45

Which HTTP code indicates a successful upload of an object to Amazon S3?

1. 200
2. 300
3. 400
4. 500

QUESTION 46

Which AWS support plans provide 24×7 access to customer service?

1. Basic
2. Business
3. Developer
4. All plans

QUESTION 47

Which of the following are NOT features of AWS IAM? (Select TWO.)

1. Shared access to your AWS account
2. Logon using local user accounts
3. Identity federation
4. PCI DSS compliance
5. Charged for what you use

QUESTION 48

How can a company facilitate the sharing of data over private connections between two accounts they own within a region?

1. Create an internal ELB
2. Create a subnet peering connection
3. Create a VPC peering connection
4. Configure matching CIDR address ranges

QUESTION 49

How can you deploy your EC2 instances so that if a single data center fails you still have instances available?

1. Across regions
2. Across subnets
3. Across Availability Zones
4. Across VPCs

QUESTION 50

Your manager has asked you to explain the benefits of using IAM groups. Which of the below statements are valid benefits? (Select TWO.)

1. You can restrict access to the subnets in your VPC
2. Groups let you specify permissions for multiple users, which can make it easier to manage the permissions for those users
3. Provide the ability to create custom permission policies
4. Enables you to attach IAM permission policies to more than one user at a time
5. Provide the ability to nest groups to create an organizational hierarchy

QUESTION 51

Which of the following are pillars from the five pillars of the AWS Well-Architected Framework? (Select TWO.)

1. Resilience
2. Operational excellence
3. Confidentiality
4. Economics
5. Performance efficiency

QUESTION 52

What do you need to log into the AWS console?

1. User name and password
2. Key pair
3. Access key and secret ID
4. Certificate

QUESTION 53

What are the advantages of running a database service such as Amazon RDS in the cloud versus deploying on-premise? (Select TWO.)

1. You have full control of the operating system and can install your own operational tools
2. Scalability is improved as it is quicker to implement and there is an abundance of capacity
3. You can use any database software you like, allowing greater flexibility
4. High availability is easier to implement due to built-in functionality for deploying read replicas and multi-AZ
5. There are no costs for replicating data between DBs in different data centers or regions

QUESTION 54

Which of the statements below does NOT characterize cloud computing?

1. Cloud computing is the on-demand delivery of compute power
2. With cloud computing you get to benefit from massive economies of scale
3. Cloud computing allows you to swap variable expense for capital expense
4. With cloud computing you can increase your speed and agility

QUESTION 55

Which AWS technology enables you to group resources that share one or more tags?

1. Tag groups
2. Organization groups
3. Resource groups
4. Consolidation groups

QUESTION 56

What is the easiest way to store a backup of an EBS volume on Amazon S3?

1. Write a custom script to copy the data into a bucket
2. Use S3 lifecycle actions to backup the volume
3. Create a snapshot of the volume
4. Use Amazon Kinesis to process the data and store the results in S3

QUESTION 57

Which AWS security tool uses an agent installed in EC2 instances and assesses applications for vulnerabilities and deviations from best practices?

1. AWS Trusted Advisor
2. AWS Personal Health Dashboard
3. AWS TCO Calculator
4. AWS Inspector

QUESTION 58

Which of the following is NOT a best practice for protecting the root user of an AWS account?

1. Don't share the root user credentials
2. Enable MFA
3. Remove administrative permissions
4. Lock away the AWS root user access keys

QUESTION 59

You are evaluating AWS services that can assist with creating scalable application environments. Which of the statements below best describes the Elastic Load Balancer service?

1. Helps you ensure that you have the correct number of Amazon EC2 instances available to handle the load for your application
2. A highly available and scalable Domain Name System (DNS) service
3. Automatically distributes incoming application traffic across multiple targets, such as Amazon EC2 instances, containers, and IP addresses
4. A network service that provides an alternative to using the Internet to connect customers' on-premise sites to AWS

QUESTION 60

What is an example of scaling vertically?

1. AWS Auto Scaling adding more EC2 instances
2. AWS Lambda adding concurrently executing functions
3. Increasing the instance size with Amazon RDS
4. Adding read replicas to an Amazon RDS database

QUESTION 61

To reduce cost, which of the following services support reservations? (Select TWO.)

1. Amazon ElastiCache
2. Amazon CloudFormation
3. Amazon RedShift
4. AWS Elastic Beanstalk
5. Amazon S3

QUESTION 62

What type of cloud computing service type do AWS Elastic Beanstalk and Amazon RDS correspond to?

1. IaaS
2. PaaS
3. SaaS
4. Hybrid

QUESTION 63

How can a company configure automatic, asynchronous copying of objects in Amazon S3 buckets across regions?

1. This is done by default by AWS
2. By configuring multi-master replication
3. Using cross-region replication
4. Using lifecycle actions

QUESTION 64

Your company has recently migrated to AWS. How can your CTO monitor the organization's costs?

1. AWS Cost Explorer
2. AWS CloudTrail
3. AWS Consolidated Billing
4. AWS Simple Monthly calculator

QUESTION 65

Your organization has offices around the world and some employees travel between offices. How should their accounts be setup?

1. IAM is a global service, just create the users in one place
2. Create a separate account in IAM within each region in which they will travel
3. Set the user account as a "global" account when created
4. Enable MFA for the accounts

SET 6: PRACTICE QUESTIONS AND ANSWERS

QUESTION 1

The AWS Cost Management tools give users the ability to do which of the following? (Select TWO.)

1. Terminate all AWS resources automatically if budget thresholds are exceeded
2. Break down AWS costs by day, service, and linked AWS account
3. Create budgets and receive notifications if current or forecasted usage exceeds the budgets
4. Switch automatically to Reserved Instances or Spot Instances, whichever is most cost-effective
5. Move data stored in Amazon S3 to a more cost-effective storage class

Answer: 2, 3

Explanation:

AWS has a set of solutions to help you with cost management and optimization. This includes services, tools, and resources to organize and track cost and usage data, enhance control through consolidated billing and access permission, enable better planning through budgeting and forecasts, and further lower cost with resources and pricing optimizations.

However, these tools do not terminate resources, manipulate resources, or make changes to pricing models.

CORRECT: "Break down AWS costs by day, service, and linked AWS account" is the correct answer.

CORRECT: "Create budgets and receive notifications if current or forecasted usage exceeds the budgets" is the correct answer.

INCORRECT: "Terminate all AWS resources automatically if budget thresholds are exceeded" is incorrect as explained above.

INCORRECT: "Switch automatically to Reserved Instances or Spot Instances, whichever is most cost-effective" is incorrect as explained above.

INCORRECT: "Move data stored in Amazon S3 to a more cost-effective storage class" is incorrect as explained above.

References:

https://aws.amazon.com/aws-cost-management/

Save time with our exam-specific cheat sheets:

https://digitalcloud.training/certification-training/aws-certified-cloud-practitioner/aws-billing-and-pricing/

QUESTION 2

Which AWS service or feature helps restrict the AWS service, resources, and individual API actions the users and roles in each member account can access?

1. Amazon Cognito
2. AWS Organizations
3. AWS Shield
4. AWS Firewall Manager

Answer: 2

Explanation:

AWS Organizations offers the following policy types:

- Service control policies (SCPs) offer central control over the maximum available permissions for all of the accounts in your organization.
- Tag policies help you standardize tags across resources in your organization's accounts.

SCPs are used to restrict access within member accounts. For instance you can create an SCP that restricts a specific API action such as deploying a particular Amazon EC2 instance type. The policy would then prevent anyone, including administrators, from being able to launch EC2 instances using that instance type.

CORRECT: "AWS Organizations" is the correct answer.

INCORRECT: "Amazon Cognito" is incorrect as this service is used for providing sign-in and sign-up services for mobile applications.

INCORRECT: "AWS Shield" is incorrect as this is a security service for protecting against DDoS attacks.

INCORRECT: "AWS Firewall Manager" is incorrect as this service is used for managing various security services within AWS.

References:

https://docs.aws.amazon.com/organizations/latest/userguide/orgs_manage_policies_scp.html

QUESTION 3

Under the shared responsibility model, which of the following tasks are the responsibility of the AWS customer? (Select TWO.)

1. Ensuring that application data is encrypted at rest
2. Ensuring that AWS NTP servers are set to the correct time
3. Ensuring that users have received security training in the use of AWS services
4. Ensuring that access to data centers is restricted
5. Ensuring that hardware is disposed of properly

Answer: 1, 3

Explanation:

As a customer on AWS you take responsibility for encrypting data. This includes encrypting data at rest and data in transit. It's also a customer's responsibility to properly train their staff in security best practices and procedures for the AWS services they use.

CORRECT: "Ensuring that application data is encrypted at rest" is a correct answer.

CORRECT: "Ensuring that users have received security training in the use of AWS services" is also a correct answer.

INCORRECT: "Ensuring that AWS NTP servers are set to the correct time" is incorrect. Network Time Protocol (NTP) servers are an AWS responsibility.

INCORRECT: "Ensuring that access to data centers is restricted" is incorrect as this is security of the cloud and is an AWS responsibility.

INCORRECT: "Ensuring that hardware is disposed of properly" is incorrect as this is an AWS responsibility.

References:

https://aws.amazon.com/compliance/shared-responsibility-model/

Save time with our exam-specific cheat sheets:

https://digitalcloud.training/certification-training/aws-certified-cloud-practitioner/aws-shared-responsibility-model/

QUESTION 4

Under the AWS shared responsibility model, which of the following are customer responsibilities? (Select TWO.)

1. Setting up server-side encryption on an Amazon S3 bucket
2. Amazon RDS instance patching
3. Network and firewall configurations
4. Physical security of data center facilities
5. Compute capacity availability

Answer: 1, 3

Explanation:

As a customer on AWS you take responsibility for encrypting data. This includes encrypting data at rest and data in transit. Another security responsibility the customer owns is setting network and firewall configurations. For instance, you must configure Network ACLs and Security Groups, and any operating system-level firewalls on your EC2 instances.

CORRECT: "Setting up server-side encryption on an Amazon S3 bucket" is a correct answer.

CORRECT: "Network and firewall configurations" is also a correct answer.

INCORRECT: "Amazon RDS instance patching" is incorrect. With RDS you can define the maintenance window but AWS actually perform the patching for you.

INCORRECT: "Physical security of data center facilities" is incorrect as this is security of the cloud and is an AWS responsibility.

INCORRECT: "Compute capacity availability" is incorrect as this is an AWS responsibility.

References:

https://aws.amazon.com/compliance/shared-responsibility-model/

Save time with our exam-specific cheat sheets:

https://digitalcloud.training/certification-training/aws-certified-cloud-practitioner/aws-shared-responsibility-model/

QUESTION 5

A web application running on AWS has been received malicious requests from the same set of IP addresses.

Which AWS service can help secure the application and block the malicious traffic?

1. AWS IAM
2. Amazon GuardDuty
3. Amazon SNS
4. AWS WAF

Answer: 4

Explanation:

The AWS Web Application Firewall (WAF) is used to protect web applications or APIs against common web exploits. Rules can be created that block traffic based on source IP address.

CORRECT: "AWS WAF" is the correct answer.

INCORRECT: "AWS IAM" is incorrect. The Identity and Access Management service is used for creating users, groups, roles and policies. It is not used for controlling network access.

INCORRECT: "Amazon GuardDuty" is incorrect. This is a service that analyzes your resources using anomaly detection and machine learning. It can alert and trigger other tools to take action but it is not a network firewall service.

INCORRECT: "Amazon SNS" is incorrect as this is service is used for sending notifications using a publisher/subscriber model.

References:

https://aws.amazon.com/waf/

Save time with our exam-specific cheat sheets:

https://digitalcloud.training/certification-training/aws-certified-cloud-practitioner/cloud-security/

QUESTION 6

Which AWS service provides the ability to detect inadvertent data leaks of personally identifiable information (PII) and user credential data?

1. Amazon GuardDuty
2. Amazon Inspector
3. Amazon Macie
4. AWS Shield

Answer: 3

Explanation:

Amazon Macie is a fully managed data security and data privacy service that uses machine learning and pattern matching to discover and protect your sensitive data in Amazon S3.

Macie applies machine learning and pattern matching techniques to the Amazon S3 buckets you select to identify and alert you to sensitive data, such as personally identifiable information (PII).

© 2022 Digital Cloud Training

Amazon Macie
Enable Amazon Macie with one-click in the AWS Management Console or a single API call

Continually evaluate your S3 environment
Automatically generates an inventory of S3 buckets and details on the bucket-level security and access controls

Discover sensitive data
Analyzes buckets using machine learning and pattern matching to discover sensitive data, such as personally identifiable information (PII)

Take action
Generates findings and sends to Amazon CloudWatch Events for integration into workflows and remediation actions

CORRECT: "Amazon Macie" is the correct answer.

INCORRECT: "Amazon GuardDuty" is incorrect. This is a service that analyzes your resources using anomaly detection and machine learning. It does not detect personally identifiable information.

INCORRECT: "Amazon Inspector" is incorrect. Amazon Inspector automatically assesses applications for exposure, vulnerabilities, and deviations from best practices. It does not detect personally identifiable information.

INCORRECT: "AWS Shield" is incorrect. This service is involved with protecting your resources of distributed denial of service (DDoS) attacks.

References:

https://aws.amazon.com/macie/

Save time with our exam-specific cheat sheets:

https://digitalcloud.training/certification-training/aws-certified-cloud-practitioner/cloud-security/

QUESTION 7

According to the AWS Well-Architected Framework, what change management steps should be taken to achieve reliability in the AWS Cloud? (Select TWO.)

1. Use AWS Config to generate an inventory of AWS resources
2. Use service limits to prevent users from creating or making changes to AWS resources
3. Use AWS CloudTrail to record AWS API calls into an auditable log file
4. Use AWS Certificate Manager to create a catalog of approved services
5. Use Amazon GuardDuty to record API activity to an S3 bucket

Answer: 1, 3

Explanation:

AWS Config can be used to track the configuration state of your resources and how the state has changed over time. With CloudTrail you can audit who made what API calls on what resources at what time. This can help with identifying changes that cause reliability issues.

CORRECT: "Use AWS Config to generate an inventory of AWS resources" is the correct answer.

CORRECT: "Use AWS CloudTrail to record AWS API calls into an auditable log file" is the correct answer.

INCORRECT: "Use service limits to prevent users from creating or making changes to AWS resources" is incorrect. Service limits result in a maximum limit for launching resources, but you can still make changes to existing resources (so long as you don't exceed the limit).

INCORRECT: "Use AWS Certificate Manager to create a catalog of approved services" is incorrect. Certificate manager is used for issuing and managing SSL/TLS certificates, it does not maintain a catalog of approved services.

INCORRECT: "Use Amazon GuardDuty to record API activity to an S3 bucket" is incorrect. GuardDuty does not record API activity to an S3 bucket.

References:

Save time with our exam-specific cheat sheets:

https://digitalcloud.training/certification-training/aws-certified-cloud-practitioner/architecting-for-the-cloud/

QUESTION 8

Which of the following acts as a virtual firewall at the Amazon EC2 instance level to control traffic for one or more instances?

1. Route table
2. Virtual private gateways (VPG)
3. Security groups
4. Network Access Control Lists (ACL)

Answer: 3

Explanation:

A security group is an instance-level firewall that can be used to control traffic the that reaches (ingress/inbound) and is sent out from (egress/outbound) your EC2 instances. Rules are created for inbound or outbound traffic. A security group can be attached to multiple EC2 instances.

CORRECT: "Security groups" is the correct answer.

INCORRECT: "Network Access Control Lists (ACL)" is incorrect as this is subnet-level firewall. You do not attach a Network ACL to an instance, you attach it to a subnet.

INCORRECT: "Virtual private gateways (VPG)" is incorrect. A VPG is the Amazon side of an AWS Managed VPN.

INCORRECT: "Route table" is incorrect as this is not a firewall but a table of routes for directing traffic between subnets within a VPC.

References:

https://docs.aws.amazon.com/vpc/latest/userguide/VPC_SecurityGroups.html

Save time with our exam-specific cheat sheets:

https://digitalcloud.training/certification-training/aws-certified-cloud-practitioner/aws-networking/

QUESTION 9

Which AWS Cloud design principles can help increase reliability? (Select TWO.)

1. Using monolithic architecture
2. Measuring overall efficiency
3. Testing recovery procedures
4. Adopting a consumption model
5. Automatically recovering from failure

Answer: 3, 5

Explanation:

Recovery procedures should always be tested ahead of any outage of disaster recovery situation. This is the only way to be sure your recovery procedures are effective.

When designing systems it is also a good practice to implement automatic recovery when possible. This reduces or eliminates the operational burden and potential downtime associated with a failure of a system or application component.

CORRECT: "Testing recovery procedures" is the correct answer.

CORRECT: "Automatically recovering from failure" is the correct answer.

INCORRECT: "Using monolithic architecture" is incorrect. A monolithic architecture means you have multiple components of an application running on a single system. This results in a bigger issue if that system fails. A distributed architecture is preferred.

INCORRECT: "Measuring overall efficiency" is incorrect. Efficiency has more of a bearing on cost management than reliability.

INCORRECT: "Adopting a consumption model" is incorrect. A consumption model has benefits more aligned with cost and agility than reliability.

References:

https://aws.amazon.com/blogs/apn/the-5-pillars-of-the-aws-well-architected-framework/

Save time with our exam-specific cheat sheets:

https://digitalcloud.training/certification-training/aws-certified-cloud-practitioner/architecting-for-the-cloud/

QUESTION 10

Which pricing model will interrupt a running Amazon EC2 instance if capacity becomes temporarily unavailable?

1. On-Demand Instances
2. Standard Reserved Instances
3. Spot Instances
4. Convertible Reserved Instances

Answer: 3

Explanation:

Amazon EC2 Spot Instances let you take advantage of unused EC2 capacity in the AWS cloud. Spot Instances are available at up to a 90% discount compared to On-Demand prices. When AWS need to reclaim the capacity you get a 2 minute warning and then your instances are terminated.

With all other pricing models your instances will not be terminated by AWS once they are running.

CORRECT: "Spot Instances" is the correct answer.

INCORRECT: "On-Demand Instances" is incorrect as explained above.

INCORRECT: "Standard Reserved Instances" is incorrect as explained above.

INCORRECT: "Convertible Reserved Instances" is incorrect as explained above.

References:

https://aws.amazon.com/ec2/spot/

Save time with our exam-specific cheat sheets:

https://digitalcloud.training/certification-training/aws-certified-cloud-practitioner/aws-billing-and-pricing/

QUESTION 11

Which of the following statements about AWS's pay-as-you-go pricing model is correct?

1. It results in reduced capital expenditures
2. It requires payment up front for AWS services
3. It is relevant only for Amazon EC2, Amazon S3, and Amazon DynamoDB
4. It reduces operational expenditures

Answer: 1

Explanation:

The pay-as-you-go pricing model means you only pay for the services and consumption you actually use. You are charged for compute, storage and outbound data transfer. This model reduces capital expenditure as you pay a monthly bill (operational expenditure).

CORRECT: "It results in reduced capital expenditures" is the correct answer.

INCORRECT: "It requires payment up front for AWS services" is incorrect. You can pay upfront for some services such as EC2 reserved instances to get better pricing but most services are offered on a consumption basis.

INCORRECT: "It is relevant only for Amazon EC2, Amazon S3, and Amazon DynamoDB" is incorrect. This is not true most AWS services are offered on a pay-as-you-go pricing model.

INCORRECT: "It reduces operational expenditures" is incorrect. This is not true, it reduces capital expenditures.

References:

https://aws.amazon.com/pricing/

Save time with our exam-specific cheat sheets:

https://digitalcloud.training/certification-training/aws-certified-cloud-practitioner/aws-billing-and-pricing/

QUESTION 12

Which AWS service can serve a static website?

1. Amazon S3
2. Amazon Route 53
3. Amazon QuickSight
4. AWS X-Ray

Answer: 1

Explanation:

You can use Amazon S3 to host a static website. On a *static* website, individual webpages include static content. They might also contain client-side scripts.

To host a static website on Amazon S3, you configure an Amazon S3 bucket for website hosting and then upload your website content to the bucket. When you configure a bucket as a static website, you must enable website hosting, set permissions, and create and add an index document. Depending on your website requirements, you can also configure redirects, web traffic logging, and a custom error document.

CORRECT: "Amazon S3" is the correct answer.

INCORRECT: "Amazon Route 53" is incorrect. This is an intelligent DNS service.

INCORRECT: "Amazon QuickSight" is incorrect. Amazon QuickSight is a fast, cloud-powered business intelligence service that makes it easy to deliver insights to everyone in your organization.

INCORRECT: "AWS X-Ray" is incorrect. This is used for tracing and debugging applications.

References:

https://docs.aws.amazon.com/AmazonS3/latest/dev/WebsiteHosting.html

Save time with our exam-specific cheat sheets:

https://digitalcloud.training/certification-training/aws-certified-cloud-practitioner/aws-storage/

QUESTION 13

A startup eCommerce company needs to quickly deliver new website features in an iterative manner, minimizing the time to market.

Which AWS Cloud feature allows this?

1. Elasticity
2. High availability
3. Agility
4. Reliability

Answer: 3

Explanation:

In a cloud computing environment, new IT resources are only a click away, which means that you reduce the time to make those resources available to your developers from weeks to just minutes.

This results in a dramatic increase in agility for the organization, since the cost and time it takes to experiment and develop is significantly lower.

CORRECT: "Agility" is the correct answer.

INCORRECT: "High availability" is incorrect as this is associated with increased resilience, not agility.

INCORRECT: "Elasticity" is incorrect as this associated with the ability to adjust to demand and reduce the need to guess capacity requirements.

INCORRECT: "Reliability" is incorrect as this does not assist with bringing features to market faster.

References:

https://docs.aws.amazon.com/whitepapers/latest/aws-overview/six-advantages-of-cloud-computing.html

Save time with our exam-specific cheat sheets:

https://digitalcloud.training/certification-training/aws-certified-cloud-practitioner/cloud-computing-concepts/

QUESTION 14

What is the most efficient way to establish network connectivity from on-premises to multiple VPCs in different AWS Regions?

1. Use AWS Direct Connect
2. Use AWS VPN
3. Use AWS Client VPN
4. Use an AWS Transit Gateway

Answer: 4

Explanation:

AWS Transit Gateway is a service that enables customers to connect their Amazon Virtual Private Clouds (VPCs) and their on-premises networks to a single gateway.

Without AWS Transit Gateway

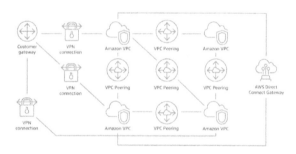

With AWS Transit Gateway

With AWS Transit Gateway, you only have to create and manage a single connection from the central gateway in to each Amazon VPC, on-premises data center, or remote office across your network. Transit Gateway acts as a hub that controls how traffic is routed among all the connected networks which act like spokes.

CORRECT: "Use an AWS Transit Gateway" is the correct answer.

INCORRECT: "Use AWS Direct Connect" is incorrect as this only connects you to a single Amazon VPC, not multiple VPCs in different Regions.

INCORRECT: "Use AWS VPN" is incorrect as this is a point-to-point connection between an on-premises location and a single Amazon VPC.

INCORRECT: "Use AWS Client VPN" is incorrect as this service allows end users to connect to AWS using a VPN client.

References:

https://aws.amazon.com/transit-gateway/

Save time with our exam-specific cheat sheets:

https://digitalcloud.training/certification-training/aws-certified-cloud-practitioner/aws-networking/

QUESTION 15

A company is using the AWS CLI and programmatic access of AWS resources from its on-premises network.

What is a mandatory requirement in this scenario?

1. Using an AWS Direct Connect connection
2. Using an AWS access key and a secret key
3. Using Amazon API Gateway
4. Using an Amazon EC2 key pair

Answer: 2

Explanation:

Access keys are long-term credentials for an IAM user or the AWS account root user. You can use access keys to sign programmatic requests to the AWS CLI or AWS API (directly or using the AWS SDK).

Access keys consist of two parts: an access key ID (for example, AKIAIOSFODNN7EXAMPLE) and a secret access key (for example, wJalrXUtnFEMI/K7MDENG/bPxRfiCYEXAMPLEKEY). Like a user name and password, you must use both the access key ID and secret access key together to authenticate your requests.

CORRECT: "Using an AWS access key and a secret key" is the correct answer.

INCORRECT: "Using an AWS Direct Connect connection" is incorrect. It is not a requirement that you use a Direct Connect connection. You can access public services via the API using the internet. For private services you can use Direct Connect, a VPN, or a bastion host.

INCORRECT: "Using Amazon API Gateway" is incorrect. You do not need API Gateway for programmatic access to the AWS API.

INCORRECT: "Using an Amazon EC2 key pair" is incorrect. A key pair is used to securely access EC2 resources and should not be confused with access keys.

References:

https://docs.aws.amazon.com/IAM/latest/UserGuide/id_credentials_access-keys.html

Save time with our exam-specific cheat sheets:

https://digitalcloud.training/certification-training/aws-certified-cloud-practitioner/identity-and-access-management/

QUESTION 16

Which AWS service is suitable for an event-driven workload?

1. Amazon EC2
2. AWS Elastic Beanstalk
3. AWS Lambda
4. Amazon Lumberyard

Answer: 3

Explanation:

AWS Lambda is an event-driven service. For example you can configure an Amazon S3 bucket with event notifications that trigger an AWS Lambda function when data is uploaded to an S3 bucket.

CORRECT: "AWS Lambda" is the correct answer.

INCORRECT: "Amazon EC2" is incorrect as this is not an event-driven service.

INCORRECT: "AWS Elastic Beanstalk" is incorrect as this is not an event-driven service.

INCORRECT: "Amazon Lumberyard" is incorrect as this is a game engine service.

References:

https://docs.aws.amazon.com/lambda/latest/dg/with-s3.html

Save time with our exam-specific cheat sheets:

https://digitalcloud.training/certification-training/aws-certified-cloud-practitioner/aws-compute/

QUESTION 17

Based on the shared responsibility model, which of the following security and compliance tasks is AWS responsible for?

1. Granting access to individuals and services
2. Encrypting data in transit
3. Updating Amazon EC2 host firmware
4. Updating operating systems

Answer: 3

Explanation:

AWS are responsible for updating Amazon EC2 host firmware. This is considered "security of the cloud". All other tasks are the responsibility of the customer.

CORRECT: "Updating Amazon EC2 host firmware" is the correct answer.

INCORRECT: "Granting access to individuals and services" is incorrect. This is something a customer must perform to control access to the resources they use on AWS.

INCORRECT: "Encrypting data in transit" is incorrect. Encryption at rest and in-transit is a customer responsibility.

INCORRECT: "Updating operating systems" is incorrect. Customers are responsible for patching operating systems on Amazon EC2. AWS are only responsible for the host servers.

References:

https://digitalcloud.training/certification-training/aws-certified-cloud-practitioner/aws-shared-responsibility-model/

Save time with our exam-specific cheat sheets:

https://aws.amazon.com/compliance/shared-responsibility-model/

QUESTION 18

Which AWS service can be used to run Docker containers?

1. AWS Lambda
2. Amazon ECR
3. AWS Fargate
4. Amazon AMI

Answer: 3

Explanation:

AWS Fargate is a serverless compute engine for containers that works with both Amazon Elastic Container Service (ECS) and Amazon Elastic Kubernetes Service (EKS).

Fargate makes it easy for you to focus on building your applications. Fargate removes the need to provision and manage servers, lets you specify and pay for resources per application, and improves security through application isolation by design.

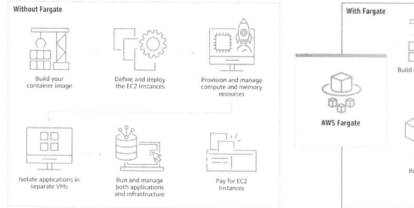
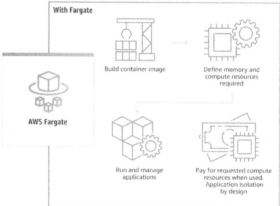

CORRECT: "Amazon ECS" is the correct answer.

INCORRECT: "AWS Lambda" is incorrect. AWS Lambda is a serverless technology that lets you run code in response to events as functions

INCORRECT: "Amazon ECR" is incorrect. Amazon Elastic Container Registry (ECR) is a fully-managed Docker container registry that makes it easy for developers to store, manage, and deploy Docker container images

INCORRECT: "Amazon AMI" is incorrect. Amazon Machine Images (AMI) store configuration information for Amazon EC2 instances.

References:

https://aws.amazon.com/fargate/

Save time with our exam-specific cheat sheets:

https://digitalcloud.training/certification-training/aws-certified-cloud-practitioner/aws-compute/

QUESTION 19

Which type of Elastic Load Balancer operates at the TCP connection level?

1. Application Load Balancer (ALB)
2. Network Load Balancer (NLB)
3. Classic Load Balancer (CLB)
4. Amazon Route 53 Load Balancer

Answer: 2

Explanation:

A Network Load Balancer functions at the fourth layer of the Open Systems Interconnection (OSI) model. NLBs direct connections based on information at the TCP connection level.

CORRECT: "Network Load Balancer (NLB)" is the correct answer.

INCORRECT: "Application Load Balancer (ALB)" is incorrect. ALBs process traffic at the application level (layer 7) based on information in the HTTP/HTTPS headers.

INCORRECT: "Classic Load Balancer (CLB)" is incorrect. CLBs process traffic at the TCP, SSL, HTTP and HTTPS levels (layer 4 & 7).

INCORRECT: "Amazon Route 53 Load Balancer" is incorrect. There is no feature called a load balancer that is associated with Route 53. You can perform a type of load balancing using multivalue answer routing.

References:

https://docs.aws.amazon.com/elasticloadbalancing/latest/network/introduction.html

Save time with our exam-specific cheat sheets:

https://digitalcloud.training/certification-training/aws-certified-cloud-practitioner/elastic-load-balancing-and-auto-scaling/

QUESTION 20

Which AWS technology can be referred to as a "virtual hard disk in the cloud"?

1. Amazon EFS Filesystem
2. Amazon S3 Bucket
3. Amazon EBS volume
4. Amazon ENI

Answer: 3

Explanation:

An Amazon Elastic Block Store (EBS) volume is often described as a "virtual hard disk in the cloud". EBS volumes are block-level storage volumes that are attached to EC2 instances much as you would attach a virtual hard disk to a virtual machine in a virtual infrastructure.

CORRECT: "Amazon EBS volume" is the correct answer.

INCORRECT: "Amazon EFS Filesystem" is incorrect. An Amazon EFS filesystem is a file-level storage system that is accessed using the NFS protocol. Filesystems are mounted at the file, rather than the block level and are therefore not similar to a virtual hard disk.

INCORRECT: "Amazon S3 Bucket" is incorrect. Amazon S3 is an object-level storage service and is not mounted or attached. You use a REST API over HTTPS to access objects in an object store.

INCORRECT: "Amazon ENI" is incorrect. An Amazon Elastic Network Interface is a networking construct, not a storage construct.

References:

https://docs.aws.amazon.com/AWSEC2/latest/UserGuide/ebs-volumes.html

Save time with our exam-specific cheat sheets:

QUESTION 21

In which ways does AWS' pricing model benefit organizations?

1. Eliminates licensing costs
2. Focus spend on capital expenditure, rather than operational expenditure
3. Reduce the cost of maintaining idle resources
4. Reduces the people cost of application development

Answer: 3

Explanation:

Using AWS you can provision only what you need and adjust resources automatically and elastically. This reduces the amount of resources that are sitting idle which reduces cost.

CORRECT: "Reduce the cost of maintaining idle resources" is the correct answer.

INCORRECT: "Eliminates licensing costs" is incorrect. AWS does not eliminate licensing costs or application development costs as you still need to licence and develop your application.

INCORRECT: "Focus spend on capital expenditure, rather than operational expenditure" is incorrect. AWS allows you to focus your spend on operational costs, not capital costs.

INCORRECT: "Reduces the people cost of application development" is incorrect as you still need people to develop applications.

References:

https://aws.amazon.com/pricing/

Save time with our exam-specific cheat sheets:

https://digitalcloud.training/certification-training/aws-certified-cloud-practitioner/cloud-computing-concepts/

QUESTION 22

Which service allows you to monitor and troubleshoot systems using system and application log files generated by those systems?

1. CloudTrail Logs
2. CloudWatch Metrics
3. CloudWatch Logs
4. CloudTrail Metrics

Answer: 3

Explanation:

Amazon CloudWatch Logs lets you monitor and troubleshoot your systems and applications using your existing system, application and custom log files. CloudWatch Logs can be used for real time application and system monitoring as well as long term log retention.

CORRECT: "CloudWatch Logs" is the correct answer.

INCORRECT: "CloudTrail Logs" is incorrect. CloudTrail is used for logging who does what in AWS by recording API calls. It is used for auditing, not performance or system operational monitoring.

INCORRECT: "CloudWatch Metrics" is incorrect. CloudWatch metrics are the standard method by which CloudWatch collects data

INCORRECT: "CloudTrail Metrics" is incorrect. CloudTrail does not record metrics, it records logs.

References:

https://aws.amazon.com/cloudtrail/

Save time with our exam-specific cheat sheets:

https://digitalcloud.training/certification-training/aws-certified-cloud-practitioner/monitoring-and-logging-services/

QUESTION 23

According to the AWS Shared Responsibility Model, which of the following is a shared control?

1. Operating system patching
2. Awareness and training
3. Protection of infrastructure
4. Client-side data encryption

Answer: 2

Explanation:

Shared Controls are controls which apply to both the infrastructure layer and customer layers, but in completely separate contexts or perspectives. In a shared control, AWS provides the requirements for the infrastructure and the customer must provide their own control implementation within their use of AWS services. Examples include patch management, configuration management, and awareness and training.

CORRECT: "Awareness and training" is the correct answer.

INCORRECT: "Operating system patching" is incorrect. Though patch management is a shared control, operating system patching specifically is a customer responsibility.

INCORRECT: "Protection of infrastructure" is incorrect. Protection of infrastructure is solely an AWS responsibility.

INCORRECT: "Client-side data encryption" is incorrect. Client and server-side data encryption are both customer responsibilities.

References:

https://aws.amazon.com/compliance/shared-responsibility-model/

Save time with our exam-specific cheat sheets:

https://digitalcloud.training/certification-training/aws-certified-cloud-practitioner/aws-shared-responsibility-model/

QUESTION 24

Where do Amazon Identity and Access Management (IAM) accounts need to be created for a global organization?

1. In each region where the users are located
2. Just create them once, as IAM is a global service
3. Create them globally, and then replicate them regionally
4. In each geographical area where the users are located

Answer: 2

Explanation:

IAM is a global service so you only need to create your users once and can then use those user accounts anywhere globally. The other options are all incorrect. as you do not create IAM accounts regionally, replicate them regionally, or create them within geographical areas.

CORRECT: "Just create them once, as IAM is a global service" is the correct answer.

INCORRECT: "In each region where the users are located" is incorrect as explained above.

INCORRECT: "Create them globally, and then replicate them regionally" is incorrect as explained above.

INCORRECT: "In each geographical area where the users are located" is incorrect as explained above.

References:

https://aws.amazon.com/iam/

Save time with our exam-specific cheat sheets:

https://digitalcloud.training/certification-training/aws-certified-cloud-practitioner/identity-and-access-management/

QUESTION 25

What is the name for the top-level container used to hold objects within Amazon S3?

1. Folder
2. Directory
3. Instance Store
4. Bucket

Answer: 4

Explanation:

Amazon S3 is an object-based storage system. You upload your objects into buckets.

CORRECT: "Bucket" is the correct answer.

INCORRECT: "Folder" is incorrect. Though S3 is a flat structure (not hierarchical), folders can be used for grouping objects. However, this is not the top-level container.

INCORRECT: "Directory" is incorrect. Directories are usually associated with filesystems rather than object-based storage systems.

INCORRECT: "Instance Store" is incorrect. An Instance Store is a type of ephemeral block-based storage service available to EC2 instances.

References:

https://docs.aws.amazon.com/AmazonS3/latest/dev/UsingBucket.html#create-bucket-intro

https://docs.aws.amazon.com/AmazonS3/latest/user-guide/using-folders.html

Save time with our exam-specific cheat sheets:

https://digitalcloud.training/certification-training/aws-certified-cloud-practitioner/aws-storage/

QUESTION 26

Which of the following are examples of horizontal scaling? (Select TWO.)
1. Add more CPU/RAM to existing instances as demand increases
2. Add more instances as demand increases
3. Requires a restart to scale up or down
4. Automatic scaling using services such as AWS Auto Scaling
5. Scalability is limited by maximum instance size

Answer: 2,4

Explanation:

With horizontal scaling you add more instances to a fleet of instances to service demand as it increases. This can be achieved automatically by using AWS Auto Scaling to add instances in response to CloudWatch performance metrics.

With vertical scaling you are adding CPU, RAM or storage to an existing instance. This may involve modifying the instance type which typically requires a restart. With vertical scaling on AWS scalability is limited by the maximum instance size.

CORRECT: "Add more instances as demand increases" is a correct answer.

CORRECT: "Automatic scaling using services such as AWS Auto Scaling" is also a correct answer.

INCORRECT: "Add more CPU/RAM to existing instances as demand increases" is incorrect as this is an example of vertical scaling.

INCORRECT: "Requires a restart to scale up or down" is incorrect as horizontal scaling does not require a restart of existing instances/applications.

INCORRECT: "Scalability is limited by maximum instance size" is incorrect as with horizontal scaling you add more instances.

References:

https://aws.amazon.com/architecture/

Save time with our exam-specific cheat sheets:

https://digitalcloud.training/certification-training/aws-certified-cloud-practitioner/architecting-for-the-cloud/

QUESTION 27

Which resource should you use to access AWS security and compliance reports?

1. AWS Artifact
2. AWS Business Associate Addendum (BAA)
3. AWS IAM
4. AWS Organizations

Answer: 1

Explanation:

AWS Artifact, available in the console, is a self-service audit artifact retrieval portal that provides our customers with on-demand access to AWS' compliance documentation and AWS agreements.

CORRECT: "AWS Artifact" is the correct answer.

INCORRECT: "AWS Business Associate Addendum (BAA)" is incorrect. The Business Associate Addendum (BAA) is an agreement you can choose to accept within AWS Artifact Agreements.

INCORRECT: "AWS IAM" is incorrect. AWS Identity and Access Management (IAM) is the service used for creating and managing users, groups, roles and policies.

INCORRECT: "AWS Organizations" is incorrect. AWS Organizations helps you centrally govern your environment as you grow and scale your workloads on AWS. Using AWS Organizations, you can automate account creation, create groups of accounts to reflect your business needs, and apply policies for these groups for governance.

References:

https://aws.amazon.com/artifact/

Save time with our exam-specific cheat sheets:

https://digitalcloud.training/certification-training/aws-certified-cloud-practitioner/cloud-security/

QUESTION 28

What methods are available for scaling an Amazon RDS database? (Select TWO.)

1. You can scale up by moving to a larger instance size
2. You can scale out automatically with EC2 Auto Scaling
3. You can scale up by increasing storage capacity
4. You can scale out by implementing Elastic Load Balancing
5. You can scale up automatically using AWS Auto Scaling

Answer: 1,3

Explanation:

To handle a higher load in your database, you can vertically scale up your master database with a simple push of a button. There are currently over 18 instance sizes that you can choose from when resizing your RDS MySQL, PostgreSQL, MariaDB, Oracle, or Microsoft SQL Server instance.

For Amazon Aurora, you have 5 memory-optimized instance sizes to choose from. The wide selection of instance types allows you to choose the best resource and cost for your database server.

In addition to scaling your master database vertically, you can also improve the performance of a read-heavy database by using read replicas to horizontally scale your database. RDS MySQL, PostgreSQL, and MariaDB can have up to 5 read replicas, and Amazon Aurora can have up to 15 read replicas.

CORRECT: "You can scale up by moving to a larger instance size" is a correct answer.

CORRECT: "You can scale up by increasing storage capacity" is also a correct answer.

INCORRECT: "You can scale out automatically with EC2 Auto Scaling" is incorrect. You cannot use EC2 Auto Scaling with Amazon RDS.

INCORRECT: "You can scale out by implementing Elastic Load Balancing" is incorrect. You cannot use Elastic Load Balancing with

RDS.

INCORRECT: "You can scale up automatically using AWS Auto Scaling" is incorrect. You cannot use EC2 Auto Scaling or AWS (Application) Auto Scaling to automatically scale your RDS database. EC2 Auto Scaling is involved with launching additional instances (scale out) and this is not a method of scaling an RDS database. Application auto scaling is involved with automatically adjusting the assignment of resources to the database which is not supported with RDS (you can do it with DynamoDB).

References:

https://aws.amazon.com/blogs/database/scaling-your-amazon-rds-instance-vertically-and-horizontally/

Save time with our exam-specific cheat sheets:

https://digitalcloud.training/certification-training/aws-certified-cloud-practitioner/aws-databases/

QUESTION 29

Which type of scaling does Amazon EC2 Auto Scaling provide?

1. Vertical
2. Linear
3. Horizontal
4. Incremental

Answer: 3

Explanation:

Amazon EC2 Auto Scaling scales horizontally by adding launching and terminating EC2 instances based on actual demand for your application.

CORRECT: "Horizontal" is the correct answer.

INCORRECT: "Vertical" is incorrect as EC2 auto scaling scales horizontally.

INCORRECT: "Linear" is incorrect as this is not the way Auto Scaling works.

INCORRECT: "Incremental" is incorrect as this is not the way Auto Scaling works.

References:

https://aws.amazon.com/ec2/autoscaling/

Save time with our exam-specific cheat sheets:

https://digitalcloud.training/certification-training/aws-certified-cloud-practitioner/architecting-for-the-cloud/

QUESTION 30

Which feature of Amazon S3 enables you to create rules to control the transfer of objects between different storage classes?

1. Object sharing
2. Versioning
3. Lifecycle management
4. Bucket policies

Answer: 3

Explanation:

To manage your objects so that they are stored cost effectively throughout their lifecycle, configure their *Amazon S3 Lifecycle*. An *S3 Lifecycle configuration* is a set of rules that define actions that Amazon S3 applies to a group of objects. There are two types of actions:

- **Transition actions**—Define when objects transition to another storage class. For example, you might choose to transition objects to the S3 Standard-IA storage class 30 days after you created them, or archive objects to the S3 Glacier storage class one year after creating them.

- **Expiration actions**—Define when objects expire. Amazon S3 deletes expired objects on your behalf. The lifecycle expiration costs depend on when you choose to expire objects.

CORRECT: "Lifecycle management" is the correct answer.

INCORRECT: "Object sharing" is incorrect. Object sharing refers to the ability to make any object publicly available via a URL.

INCORRECT: "Versioning" is incorrect. Versioning enabled you to automatically keep multiple versions of an object (when enabled).

INCORRECT: "Bucket policies" is incorrect. Bucket policies are used for controlling access to buckets, they can't be used to move data between storage classes.

References:

https://docs.aws.amazon.com/AmazonS3/latest/dev/object-lifecycle-mgmt.html

Save time with our exam-specific cheat sheets:

https://digitalcloud.training/certification-training/aws-certified-cloud-practitioner/aws-storage/

QUESTION 31

How can a database administrator reduce operational overhead for a MySQL database?

1. Migrate the database onto an EC2 instance
2. Migrate the database onto AWS Lambda
3. Use AWS CloudFormation to manage operations
4. Migrate the database onto an Amazon RDS instance

Answer: 4

Explanation:

Amazon RDS is a managed database service that supports MySQL. The DBA can reduce operational overhead by moving to RDS and having less work to do to manage the database.

CORRECT: "Migrate the database onto an Amazon RDS instance" is the correct answer.

INCORRECT: "Migrate the database onto an EC2 instance" is incorrect. Migrating onto an EC2 instance will not reduce operational overhead as the DBA will still need to manage both the operating system and the database.

INCORRECT: "Migrate the database onto AWS Lambda" is incorrect. AWS Lambda provides functions as a service. It therefore a compute service, not a database service and cannot be used to run a MySQL database.

INCORRECT: "Use AWS CloudFormation to manage operations" is incorrect. AWS CloudFormation is used for automating the deployment of infrastructure on AWS, not for automating operations.

References:

https://aws.amazon.com/rds/

Save time with our exam-specific cheat sheets:

https://digitalcloud.training/certification-training/aws-certified-cloud-practitioner/aws-databases/

QUESTION 32

Which AWS database service is schema-less and can be scaled dynamically without incurring downtime?

1. Amazon RDS
2. Amazon Aurora
3. Amazon RedShift
4. Amazon DynamoDB

Answer: 4

Explanation:

Amazon DynamoDB is a fully managed NoSQL database service that provides fast and predictable performance with seamless scalability. Push button scaling means that you can scale the DB at any time without incurring downtime. DynamoDB is schema-less.

All other options are SQL type of databases and therefore have a schema. They also rely on EC2 instances so cannot be scaled dynamically without incurring downtime (you have to change instance types).

CORRECT: "Amazon DynamoDB" is the correct answer.

INCORRECT: "Amazon RDS" is incorrect as explained above.

INCORRECT: "Amazon Aurora" is incorrect as explained above.

INCORRECT: "Amazon RedShift" is incorrect as explained above.

References:

https://aws.amazon.com/dynamodb/

Save time with our exam-specific cheat sheets:

https://digitalcloud.training/certification-training/aws-certified-cloud-practitioner/aws-databases/

QUESTION 33

Which type of AWS database is ideally suited to analytics using SQL queries?

1. Amazon DynamoDB
2. Amazon RedShift
3. Amazon RDS
4. Amazon S3

Answer: 2

Explanation:

Amazon Redshift is a fast, fully managed data warehouse that makes it simple and cost-effective to analyze all your data using standard SQL and existing Business Intelligence (BI) tools. RedShift is a SQL based data warehouse used for **analytics** applications.

CORRECT: "Amazon RedShift" is the correct answer.

INCORRECT: "Amazon DynamoDB" is incorrect. Amazon DynamoDB is a NoSQL type of database and is not suited to analytics using SQL queries.

INCORRECT: "Amazon RDS" is incorrect. Amazon RDS is a transactional DB, not an analytics DB.

INCORRECT: "Amazon S3" is incorrect. Amazon S3 is an object storage solution not a database.

References:

https://aws.amazon.com/redshift/

Save time with our exam-specific cheat sheets:

https://digitalcloud.training/certification-training/aws-certified-cloud-practitioner/aws-databases/

QUESTION 34

Which AWS service is designed to be used for operational analytics?

1. Amazon EMR
2. Amazon Athena
3. Amazon QuickSight
4. Amazon Elasticsearch Service

Answer: 4

Explanation:

Amazon Elasticsearch Service is involved with operational analytics such as application monitoring, log analytics and clickstream analytics. Amazon Elasticsearch Service allows you to search, explore, filter, aggregate, and visualize your data in near real-time.

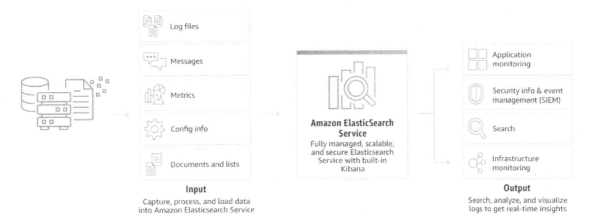

Input
Capture, process, and load data
into Amazon Elasticsearch Service

Output
Search, analyze, and visualize
logs to get real-time insights

CORRECT: "Amazon Elasticsearch Service" is the correct answer.

INCORRECT: "Amazon EMR" is incorrect. For big data processing using the Spark and Hadoop frameworks, Amazon EMR provides a managed service for processing vast amounts data.

INCORRECT: "Amazon Athena" is incorrect. Amazon Athena is used to analyze data directly in S3 and Glacier using standard SQL queries.

INCORRECT: "Amazon QuickSight" is incorrect. Amazon QuickSight provides a fast, cloud-powered business analytics service, that that makes it easy to build stunning visualizations and rich dashboards that can be accessed from any browser or mobile device.

References:

https://aws.amazon.com/elasticsearch-service/

https://aws.amazon.com/big-data/datalakes-and-analytics/

Save time with our exam-specific cheat sheets:

https://digitalcloud.training/certification-training/aws-certified-cloud-practitioner/additional-aws-services-tools/

QUESTION 35

You need to connect your company's on-premise network into AWS and would like to establish an AWS managed VPN service. Which of the following configuration items needs to be setup on the Amazon VPC side of the connection?

1. A Virtual Private Gateway
2. A Customer Gateway
3. A Network Address Translation device
4. A Firewall

Answer: 1

Explanation:

A *virtual private gateway* is the VPN concentrator on the Amazon side of the VPN connection. You create a virtual private gateway and attach it to the VPC from which you want to create the VPN connection.

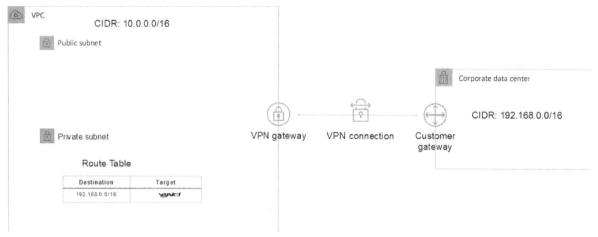

CORRECT: "A Virtual Private Gateway" is the correct answer.

INCORRECT: "A Customer Gateway" is incorrect. A *customer gateway* is a physical device or software application on your side of the VPN connection.

INCORRECT: "A Network Address Translation device" is incorrect. NAT devices and firewalls are not required for an AWS managed VPN.

INCORRECT: "A Firewall" is incorrect. A firewall is not required for a VPN connection.

References:

https://docs.aws.amazon.com/vpc/latest/userguide/VPC_VPN.html#VPN

Save time with our exam-specific cheat sheets:

https://digitalcloud.training/certification-training/aws-certified-cloud-practitioner/aws-networking/

QUESTION 36

Where are Amazon EBS snapshots stored?

1.   On an Amazon EBS instance store
2.   On an Amazon EFS filesystem
3.   Within the EBS block store
4.   On Amazon S3

Answer: 4

Explanation:

You can back up the data on your Amazon EBS volumes to Amazon S3 by taking point-in-time snapshots. Snapshots are *incremental* backups, which means that only the blocks on the device that have changed after your most recent snapshot are saved.

CORRECT: "On Amazon S3" is the correct answer.

INCORRECT: "On an Amazon EBS instance store" is incorrect as explained above.

INCORRECT: "On an Amazon EFS filesystem" is incorrect as explained above.

INCORRECT: "Within the EBS block store" is incorrect as explained above.

References:

https://docs.aws.amazon.com/AWSEC2/latest/UserGuide/EBSSnapshots.html

Save time with our exam-specific cheat sheets:

https://digitalcloud.training/certification-training/aws-certified-cloud-practitioner/aws-storage/

QUESTION 37

Which AWS service makes it easy to coordinate the components of distributed applications as a series of steps in a visual workflow?

1. Amazon SWF
2. AWS Step Functions
3. Amazon SNS
4. Amazon SES

Answer: 2

Explanation:

AWS Step Functions lets you coordinate multiple AWS services into serverless workflows so you can build and update apps quickly. AWS Step Functions lets you build visual workflows that enable fast translation of business requirements into technical requirements.

CORRECT: "AWS Step Functions" is the correct answer.

INCORRECT: "Amazon SWF" is incorrect. Amazon SWF helps developers build, run, and scale background jobs that have parallel or sequential steps. SWF is not a visual workflow tool.

INCORRECT: "Amazon SNS" is incorrect. Amazon Simple Notification Service (SNS) is a highly available, durable, secure, fully managed pub/sub messaging service.

INCORRECT: "Amazon SES" is incorrect. Amazon Simple Email Service (Amazon SES) is a cloud-based email sending service designed to help digital marketers and application developers send marketing, notification, and transactional emails.

References:

https://aws.amazon.com/step-functions/

Save time with our exam-specific cheat sheets:

https://digitalcloud.training/certification-training/aws-certified-cloud-practitioner/additional-aws-services-tools/

QUESTION 38

A Cloud Practitioner is creating the business process workflows associated with an order fulfilment system. Which AWS service can assist with coordinating tasks across distributed application components?

1. AWS STS
2. Amazon SQS
3. Amazon SWF
4. Amazon SNS

Answer: 3

Explanation:

Amazon Simple Workflow Service (SWF) is a web service that makes it easy to coordinate work across distributed application components. SWF enables applications for a range of use cases, including media processing, web application back-ends, business process workflows, and analytics pipelines, to be designed as a coordination of tasks.

CORRECT: "Amazon SWF" is the correct answer.

INCORRECT: "AWS STS" is incorrect. AWS Security Token Service (STS) is used for requesting temporary credentials..

INCORRECT: "Amazon SQS" is incorrect. Amazon Simple Queue Service (SQS) is a message queue used for decoupling application components.

INCORRECT: "Amazon SNS" is incorrect. Amazon Simple Notification Service (SNS) is a web service that makes it easy to set up, operate, and send notifications from the cloud. SNS supports notifications over multiple transports including HTTP/HTTPS, Email/Email-JSON, SQS and SMS.

References:

https://aws.amazon.com/swf/

Save time with our exam-specific cheat sheets:

https://digitalcloud.training/certification-training/aws-certified-cloud-practitioner/additional-aws-services-tools/

QUESTION 39

Your manager has asked you to explain some of the security features available in the AWS cloud. How can you describe the function of Amazon CloudHSM?

1. It provides server-side encryption for S3 objects
2. It is a Public Key Infrastructure (PKI)
3. It can be used to generate, use and manage encryption keys in the cloud
4. It is a firewall for use with web applications

Answer: 3

Explanation:

AWS CloudHSM is a cloud-based hardware security module (HSM) that allows you to easily add secure key storage and high-performance crypto operations to your AWS applications.

CloudHSM has no upfront costs and provides the ability to start and stop HSMs on-demand, allowing you to provision capacity when and where it is needed quickly and cost-effectively.

CloudHSM is a managed service that automates time-consuming administrative tasks, such as hardware provisioning, software patching, high availability, and backups.

CORRECT: "It can be used to generate, use and manage encryption keys in the cloud" is the correct answer.

INCORRECT: "It provides server-side encryption for S3 objects" is incorrect. CloudHSM performs key management but it does not perform encryption of S3 objects.

INCORRECT: "It is a Public Key Infrastructure (PKI)" is incorrect. It can be used to generate asymmetric keys, however it is not a PKI.

INCORRECT: "It is a firewall for use with web applications" is incorrect as it does not provide any firewall functionality.

References:

https://aws.amazon.com/cloudhsm/details/

Save time with our exam-specific cheat sheets:

https://digitalcloud.training/certification-training/aws-certified-cloud-practitioner/cloud-security/

QUESTION 40

Which AWS Glacier data access option retrieves data from an archive in 1-5 minutes?

1. Standard
2. Express
3. Accelerated
4. Expedited

Answer: 4

Explanation:

Expedited retrievals allow you to quickly access your data when occasional urgent requests for a subset of archives are required. For all but the largest archives (250 MB+), data accessed using Expedited retrievals are typically made available within 1–5 minutes.

CORRECT: "Expedited" is the correct answer.

INCORRECT: "Standard" is incorrect. Standard takes 3-5 hours.

INCORRECT: "Express" is incorrect as this is not a retrieval option.

INCORRECT: "Accelerated" is incorrect as this is not a retrieval option.

References:

https://docs.aws.amazon.com/amazonglacier/latest/dev/downloading-an-archive-two-steps.html

Save time with our exam-specific cheat sheets:

https://digitalcloud.training/certification-training/aws-certified-cloud-practitioner/aws-billing-and-pricing/

QUESTION 41

How can a systems administrator specify a script to be run on an EC2 instance during launch?

1. Metadata
2. User Data
3. Run Command
4. AWS Config

Answer: 2

Explanation:

When you launch an instance in Amazon EC2, you have the option of passing user data to the instance that can be used to perform common automated configuration tasks and even run scripts after the instance starts.

You can pass two types of user data to Amazon EC2: shell scripts and cloud-init directives. User data is data that is supplied by the user at instance launch in the form of a script. User data is limited to 16KB. User data and meta data are not encrypted.

CORRECT: "User Data" is the correct answer.

INCORRECT: "Metadata" is incorrect as metadata retrieves information about the instance.

INCORRECT: "Run Command" is incorrect as this operates separately to the launch process.

INCORRECT: "AWS Config" is incorrect as this service stores configuration information relating to AWS services.

References:

https://docs.aws.amazon.com/AWSEC2/latest/UserGuide/user-data.html

Save time with our exam-specific cheat sheets:

https://digitalcloud.training/certification-training/aws-certified-cloud-practitioner/aws-compute/

QUESTION 42

What advantages does the AWS cloud provide in relation to cost? (Select TWO.)

1. Fine-grained billing
2. One-off payments for on-demand resources
3. Ability to turn off resources and not pay for them
4. Enterprise licensing discounts
5. Itemized power costs

Answer: 1,3

Explanation:

With the AWS cloud you get fine-grained billing and can turn off resources you are not using easily and not have to pay for them (pay for what you use model).

CORRECT: "Fine-grained billing" is a correct answer.

CORRECT: "Ability to turn off resources and not pay for them" is also a correct answer.

INCORRECT: "One-off payments for on-demand resources" is incorrect. You do not get the option for one-off payments for on-demand resources. You can for reserved instances which can be paid all upfront.

INCORRECT: "Enterprise licensing discounts" is incorrect. You do not get enterprise licensing discounts from AWS and you do not pay anything for power as the cost is built in.

INCORRECT: "Itemized power costs" is incorrect. You do not get any power costs on your bill

References:

https://aws.amazon.com/ec2/pricing/

Save time with our exam-specific cheat sheets:

https://digitalcloud.training/certification-training/aws-certified-cloud-practitioner/architecting-for-the-cloud/

QUESTION 43

Which of the authentication options below can be used to authenticate using AWS APIs? (Select TWO.)

1. Key pairs
2. Access keys
3. Server passwords
4. Security groups
5. Server certificates

Answer: 2,5

Explanation:

Access keys are long-term credentials for an IAM user or the AWS account root user. You can use access keys to sign programmatic requests to the AWS CLI or AWS API (directly or using the AWS SDK).

Server certificates are SSL/TLS certificates that you can use to authenticate with some AWS services.

CORRECT: "Access keys" is a correct answer.

CORRECT: "Server certificates" is also a correct answer.

INCORRECT: "Key pairs" is incorrect. Key pairs are used for encrypting logon information when accessing EC2 instances.

INCORRECT: "Server passwords" is incorrect. A server password cannot be used to authenticate with an API.

INCORRECT: "Security groups" is incorrect. Security groups are an instance-level firewall used for controlling access to AWS resources.

References:

https://docs.aws.amazon.com/IAM/latest/UserGuide/id_credentials_access-keys.html

https://docs.aws.amazon.com/IAM/latest/UserGuide/id_credentials_server-certs.html

Save time with our exam-specific cheat sheets:

https://digitalcloud.training/certification-training/aws-certified-cloud-practitioner/identity-and-access-management/

QUESTION 44

Under the AWS Shared Responsibility Model, who is responsible for what? (Select TWO.)

1. Customers are responsible for compute infrastructure
2. AWS are responsible for network and firewall configuration
3. Customers are responsible for networking traffic protection
4. AWS are responsible for networking infrastructure
5. Customers are responsible for edge locations

Answer: 3,4

Explanation:

AWS is responsible for protecting the infrastructure that runs all of the services offered in the AWS Cloud. Customers are responsible for security in the cloud and responsibilities vary by service.

Customers are responsible for networking traffic protection. This includes applying encryption and using security groups and Network ACLs.

AWS are responsible for networking infrastructure. The underlying networking equipment is maintained by AWS.

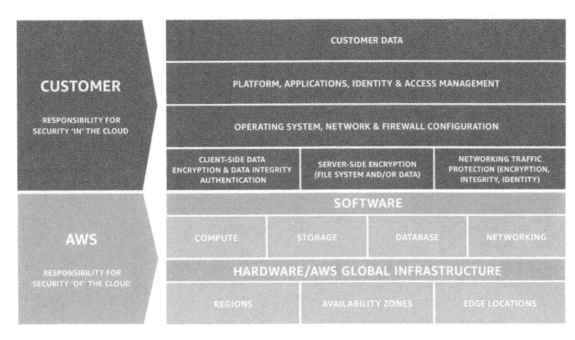

CORRECT: "Customers are responsible for networking traffic protection" is a correct answer.

CORRECT: "AWS are responsible for networking infrastructure" is also a correct answer.

INCORRECT: "Customers are responsible for compute infrastructure" is incorrect. AWS are responsible for compute infrastructure

INCORRECT: "AWS are responsible for network and firewall configuration" is incorrect. Customers are responsible for network and firewall configuration.

INCORRECT: "Customers are responsible for edge locations" is incorrect. AWS are responsible for edge locations.

References:

https://aws.amazon.com/compliance/shared-responsibility-model/

Save time with our exam-specific cheat sheets:

https://digitalcloud.training/certification-training/aws-certified-cloud-practitioner/aws-shared-responsibility-model/

QUESTION 45

Which HTTP code indicates a successful upload of an object to Amazon S3?

1. 200
2. 300
3. 400
4. 500

Answer: 1

Explanation:

HTTP response status codes indicate whether a specific HTTP request has been successfully completed.

- A HTTP 200 codes indicates a successful upload.
- A HTTP 300 code indicates a redirection.
- A HTTP 400 code indicates a client error.
- A HTTP 500 code indicates a server error.

CORRECT: "200" is the correct answer.

INCORRECT: "300" is incorrect as explained above.

INCORRECT: "400" is incorrect as explained above.

INCORRECT: "500" is incorrect as explained above.

References:

https://en.wikipedia.org/wiki/List_of_HTTP_status_codes

Save time with our exam-specific cheat sheets:

https://digitalcloud.training/certification-training/aws-certified-cloud-practitioner/aws-storage/

QUESTION 46

Which AWS support plans provide 24×7 access to customer service?

1. Basic
2. Business
3. Developer
4. All plans

Answer: 4

Explanation:

All support plans provide 24×7 access to customer service, documentation, whitepapers, and support forums.

CORRECT: "All plans" is the correct answer.

INCORRECT: "Basic" is incorrect as explained above.

INCORRECT: "Business" is incorrect as explained above.

INCORRECT: "Developer" is incorrect as explained above.

References:

https://aws.amazon.com/premiumsupport/plans/

Save time with our exam-specific cheat sheets:

https://digitalcloud.training/certification-training/aws-certified-cloud-practitioner/aws-billing-and-pricing/

QUESTION 47

Which of the following are NOT features of AWS IAM? (Select TWO.)

1. Shared access to your AWS account
2. Logon using local user accounts
3. Identity federation
4. PCI DSS compliance
5. Charged for what you use

Answer: 2,5

Explanation:

You cannot use IAM to create local user accounts on any system. You are also not charged for what you use, IAM is free to use The other options are all features of AWS IAM.

CORRECT: "Logon using local user accounts" is the correct answer.

CORRECT: "Charged for what you use" is the correct answer.

INCORRECT: "Shared access to your AWS account" is incorrect as explained above.

INCORRECT: "Identity federation" is incorrect as explained above.

INCORRECT: "PCI DSS compliance" is incorrect as explained above.

References:

https://docs.aws.amazon.com/IAM/latest/UserGuide/introduction.html

Save time with our exam-specific cheat sheets:

https://digitalcloud.training/certification-training/aws-certified-cloud-practitioner/identity-and-access-management/

QUESTION 48

How can a company facilitate the sharing of data over private connections between two accounts they own within a region?

1. Create an internal ELB
2. Create a subnet peering connection
3. Create a VPC peering connection
4. Configure matching CIDR address ranges

Answer: 3

Explanation:

A VPC peering connection helps you to facilitate the transfer of data. For example, if you have more than one AWS account, you can peer the VPCs across those accounts to create a file sharing network. You can also use a VPC peering connection to allow other VPCs to access resources you have in one of your VPCs.

CORRECT: "Create a VPC peering connection" is the correct answer.

INCORRECT: "Create an internal ELB" is incorrect. An internal ELB will not help you to transfer data between accounts.

INCORRECT: "Create a subnet peering connection" is incorrect. You cannot peer subnets.

INCORRECT: "Configure matching CIDR address ranges" is incorrect. Configuring matching CIDR address ranges will not mean you can route between accounts. Also, you cannot peer with an account with a matching (or overlapping) address range.

References:

https://docs.aws.amazon.com/vpc/latest/peering/what-is-vpc-peering.html

Save time with our exam-specific cheat sheets:

https://digitalcloud.training/certification-training/aws-certified-cloud-practitioner/aws-networking/

QUESTION 49

How can you deploy your EC2 instances so that if a single data center fails you still have instances available?

1. Across regions
2. Across subnets
3. Across Availability Zones
4. Across VPCs

Answer: 3

Explanation:

An AZ spans one or more data centers and each AZ is physically isolated from other AZs and connected by high speed networking. If you want to deploy a highly available application you should spread your instances across AZs and they will be resilient to the failure of a single DC

CORRECT: "Across Availability Zones" is the correct answer.

INCORRECT: "Across regions" is incorrect. You could deploy your instances across separate regions but this is not necessary to create a highly available application and introduces complexity and cost. For example you may need multiple ELBs (one per region), complex name resolution and potential data transfer charges.

INCORRECT: "Across subnets" is incorrect. Subnets are created within AZs. Therefore, if you deploy resources into multiple subnets within an AZ and a data center fails, you may lose all of your instances.

INCORRECT: "Across VPCs" is incorrect. You should deploy across AZs within a VPC.

References:

https://docs.aws.amazon.com/AWSEC2/latest/UserGuide/using-regions-availability-zones.html

Save time with our exam-specific cheat sheets:

https://digitalcloud.training/certification-training/aws-certified-cloud-practitioner/aws-global-infrastructure/

QUESTION 50

Your manager has asked you to explain the benefits of using IAM groups. Which of the below statements are valid benefits?

(Select TWO.)

1. You can restrict access to the subnets in your VPC
2. Groups let you specify permissions for multiple users, which can make it easier to manage the permissions for those users
3. Provide the ability to create custom permission policies
4. Enables you to attach IAM permission policies to more than one user at a time
5. Provide the ability to nest groups to create an organizational hierarchy

Answer: 2,4

Explanation:

Groups are collections of users and have policies attached to them. This enables you to organize groups of users by job function or role and apply relevant policies to the group.

You can use groups to assign permissions to users and should follow the principal of least privilege when assigning permissions.

CORRECT: "Groups let you specify permissions for multiple users, which can make it easier to manage the permissions for those users" is a correct answer.

CORRECT: "Enables you to attach IAM permission policies to more than one user at a time" is also a correct answer.

INCORRECT: "You can restrict access to the subnets in your VPC" is incorrect as this describes Network ACLs.

INCORRECT: "Provide the ability to create custom permission policies" is incorrect as this describes IAM policies.

INCORRECT: "Provide the ability to nest groups to create an organizational hierarchy" is incorrect. You cannot nest groups (groups within groups).

References:

https://docs.aws.amazon.com/IAM/latest/UserGuide/id.html

Save time with our exam-specific cheat sheets:

https://digitalcloud.training/certification-training/aws-certified-cloud-practitioner/identity-and-access-management/

QUESTION 51

Which of the following are pillars from the five pillars of the AWS Well-Architected Framework? (Select TWO.)

1. Resilience
2. Operational excellence
3. Confidentiality
4. Economics
5. Performance efficiency

Answer: 2,5

Explanation:

The five pillars of the AWS Well-Architected Framework are operation excellence, security, reliability, performance efficiency, and cost optimization

CORRECT: "Operational excellence" is a correct answer.

CORRECT: "Performance efficiency" is also a correct answer.

INCORRECT: "Resilience" is incorrect as this is not one of the five pillars.

INCORRECT: "Confidentiality" is incorrect as this is not one of the five pillars.

INCORRECT: "Economics" is incorrect as this is not one of the five pillars.

References:

https://aws.amazon.com/blogs/apn/the-5-pillars-of-the-aws-well-architected-framework/

Save time with our exam-specific cheat sheets:

https://digitalcloud.training/certification-training/aws-certified-cloud-practitioner/architecting-for-the-cloud/

QUESTION 52

What do you need to log into the AWS console?

1. User name and password
2. Key pair
3. Access key and secret ID
4. Certificate

Answer: 1

Explanation:

You can log into the AWS console using a user name and password. You cannot log in to the AWS console using a key pair, access key & secret ID or certificate.

CORRECT: "User name and password" is the correct answer.

INCORRECT: "Key pair" is incorrect as explained above.

INCORRECT: "Access key and secret ID" is incorrect as explained above.

INCORRECT: "Certificate" is incorrect as explained above.

References:

https://aws.amazon.com/console/

Save time with our exam-specific cheat sheets:

https://digitalcloud.training/certification-training/aws-certified-cloud-practitioner/identity-and-access-management/

QUESTION 53

What are the advantages of running a database service such as Amazon RDS in the cloud versus deploying on-premise? (Select TWO.)

1. You have full control of the operating system and can install your own operational tools
2. Scalability is improved as it is quicker to implement and there is an abundance of capacity
3. You can use any database software you like, allowing greater flexibility
4. High availability is easier to implement due to built-in functionality for deploying read replicas and multi-AZ
5. There are no costs for replicating data between DBs in different data centers or regions

Answer: 2,4

Explanation:

The advantages of using Amazon RDS include being able to easily scale by increasing your instance type without having to go through a long procurement cycle for getting new hardware or worrying about whether capacity exists on your existing private cloud infrastructure. You can also implement fault tolerance and scalability features through multi-AZ and read replicas easily

With Amazon RDS you do not have control of the operating system and you cannot use any database software you like as you are restricted to a list of several engines. There are costs for replicating data between AZs and regions so this must be taken into account in any cost analysis.

CORRECT: "Scalability is improved as it is quicker to implement and there is an abundance of capacity" is a correct answer.

CORRECT: "High availability is easier to implement due to built-in functionality for deploying read replicas and multi-AZ" is also a correct answer.

INCORRECT: "You have full control of the operating system and can install your own operational tools" is incorrect as explained above.

INCORRECT: "You can use any database software you like, allowing greater flexibility" is incorrect as explained above.

INCORRECT: "There are no costs for replicating data between DBs in different data centers or regions" is incorrect as explained above.

References:

https://aws.amazon.com/rds/

Save time with our exam-specific cheat sheets:

https://digitalcloud.training/certification-training/aws-certified-cloud-practitioner/architecting-for-the-cloud/

QUESTION 54

Which of the statements below does NOT characterize cloud computing?

1. Cloud computing is the on-demand delivery of compute power
2. With cloud computing you get to benefit from massive economies of scale
3. Cloud computing allows you to swap variable expense for capital expense
4. With cloud computing you can increase your speed and agility

Answer: 3

Explanation:

Cloud computing is not a one-off capital expense, it is an ongoing operating expense. The caveat to this is that if you purchase reserved capacity you have an option to partially or fully pay upfront. However, it is still an operating cost as you do not own and depreciate the assets.

CORRECT: "Cloud computing allows you to swap variable expense for capital expense" is the correct answer.

INCORRECT: "Cloud computing is the on-demand delivery of compute power" is incorrect as this is a valid statement.

INCORRECT: "With cloud computing you get to benefit from massive economies of scale" is incorrect as this is a valid statement.

INCORRECT: "With cloud computing you can increase your speed and agility" is incorrect as this is a valid statement.

References:

https://docs.aws.amazon.com/whitepapers/latest/aws-overview/six-advantages-of-cloud-computing.html

Save time with our exam-specific cheat sheets:

https://digitalcloud.training/certification-training/aws-certified-cloud-practitioner/cloud-computing-concepts/

QUESTION 55

Which AWS technology enables you to group resources that share one or more tags?

1. Tag groups
2. Organization groups
3. Resource groups
4. Consolidation groups

Answer: 3

Explanation:

You can use *resource groups* to organize your AWS resources. Resource groups make it easier to manage and automate tasks on large numbers of resources at one time.

Resource groups make it easy to group resources using the tags that are assigned to them. You can group resources that share one or more tags.

CORRECT: "Resource groups" is the correct answer.

INCORRECT: "Tag groups" is incorrect as this is not a feature.

INCORRECT: "Organization groups" is incorrect as this is not a feature.

INCORRECT: "Consolidation groups" is incorrect as this is not a feature.

References:

https://docs.aws.amazon.com/ARG/latest/userguide/welcome.html

Save time with our exam-specific cheat sheets:

https://digitalcloud.training/certification-training/aws-certified-cloud-practitioner/aws-billing-and-pricing/

QUESTION 56

What is the easiest way to store a backup of an EBS volume on Amazon S3?

1. Write a custom script to copy the data into a bucket
2. Use S3 lifecycle actions to backup the volume
3. Create a snapshot of the volume
4. Use Amazon Kinesis to process the data and store the results in S3

Answer: 3

Explanation:

You can back up the data on your Amazon EBS volumes to Amazon S3 by taking point-in-time snapshots. Snapshots are *incremental* backups, which means that only the blocks on the device that have changed after your most recent snapshot are saved.

CORRECT: "Create a snapshot of the volume" is the correct answer.

INCORRECT: "Write a custom script to copy the data into a bucket" is incorrect. Writing a custom script could work but would not be the easiest method.

INCORRECT: "Use S3 lifecycle actions to backup the volume" is incorrect. You cannot apply S3 lifecycle actions to EBS volumes.

INCORRECT: "Use Amazon Kinesis to process the data and store the results in S3" is incorrect. Amazon Kinesis is used for processing streaming data, not data in EBS volumes.

References:

https://docs.aws.amazon.com/AWSEC2/latest/UserGuide/EBSSnapshots.html

Save time with our exam-specific cheat sheets:

https://digitalcloud.training/certification-training/aws-certified-cloud-practitioner/aws-storage/

QUESTION 57

Which AWS security tool uses an agent installed in EC2 instances and assesses applications for vulnerabilities and deviations from best practices?

1. AWS Trusted Advisor
2. AWS Personal Health Dashboard
3. AWS TCO Calculator
4. AWS Inspector

Answer: 4

Explanation:

Inspector is an automated security assessment service that helps improve the security and compliance of applications deployed on AWS. Inspector automatically assesses applications for vulnerabilities or deviations from best practices. Inspector uses an agent installed on EC2 instances.

CORRECT: "AWS Inspector" is the correct answer.

INCORRECT: "AWS Trusted Advisor" is incorrect. Trusted Advisor is an online resource that helps to reduce cost, increase performance and improve security by optimizing your AWS environment.

INCORRECT: "AWS Personal Health Dashboard" is incorrect. AWS Personal Health Dashboard provides alerts and remediation guidance when AWS is experiencing events that may impact you.

INCORRECT: "AWS TCO Calculator" is incorrect. The AWS TCO calculator can be used to compare the cost of running your applications in an on-premises or colocation environment to AWS.

References:

https://aws.amazon.com/inspector/

Save time with our exam-specific cheat sheets:

https://digitalcloud.training/certification-training/aws-certified-cloud-practitioner/cloud-security/

QUESTION 58

Which of the following is NOT a best practice for protecting the root user of an AWS account?

1. Don't share the root user credentials
2. Enable MFA
3. Remove administrative permissions
4. Lock away the AWS root user access keys

Answer: 3

Explanation:

You cannot remove administrative permissions from the root user of an AWS account. Therefore, you must protect the account through creating a complex password, enabling MFA, locking away access keys (assuming they're even required), and not sharing the account details.

CORRECT: "Remove administrative permissions" is the correct answer.

INCORRECT: "Don't share the root user credentials" is incorrect as this is a best practice.

INCORRECT: "Enable MFA" is incorrect as this is a best practice.

INCORRECT: "Lock away the AWS root user access keys" is incorrect as this is a best practice.

References:

https://docs.aws.amazon.com/IAM/latest/UserGuide/best-practices.html

Save time with our exam-specific cheat sheets:

https://digitalcloud.training/certification-training/aws-certified-cloud-practitioner/identity-and-access-management/

QUESTION 59

You are evaluating AWS services that can assist with creating scalable application environments. Which of the statements below best describes the Elastic Load Balancer service?

1. Helps you ensure that you have the correct number of Amazon EC2 instances available to handle the load for your application
2. A highly available and scalable Domain Name System (DNS) service
3. Automatically distributes incoming application traffic across multiple targets, such as Amazon EC2 instances, containers, and IP addresses
4. A network service that provides an alternative to using the Internet to connect customers' on-premise sites to AWS

Answer: 3

Explanation:

Elastic Load Balancing automatically distributes incoming application traffic across multiple targets, such as Amazon EC2 instances, containers, and IP addresses.

Elastic Load Balancing provides fault tolerance for applications by automatically balancing traffic across targets – Amazon EC2 instances, containers and IP addresses – and Availability Zones while ensuring only healthy targets receive traffic.

CORRECT: "Automatically distributes incoming application traffic across multiple targets, such as Amazon EC2 instances, containers, and IP addresses" is the correct answer.

INCORRECT: "Helps you ensure that you have the correct number of Amazon EC2 instances available to handle the load for your application" is incorrect as this describes EC2 Auto Scaling.

INCORRECT: "A highly available and scalable Domain Name System (DNS) service" is incorrect as this describes Amazon Route 53.

INCORRECT: "A network service that provides an alternative to using the Internet to connect customers' on-premise sites to AWS" is incorrect as this describes AWS Direct Connect.

References:

https://aws.amazon.com/elasticloadbalancing/

Save time with our exam-specific cheat sheets:

QUESTION 60

What is an example of scaling vertically?

1. AWS Auto Scaling adding more EC2 instances
2. AWS Lambda adding concurrently executing functions
3. Increasing the instance size with Amazon RDS
4. Adding read replicas to an Amazon RDS database

Answer: 3

Explanation:

A good example of vertical scaling is changing the instance size of an EC2 instance or RDS database to one with more CPU and RAM.

All of the other options are examples of scaling horizontally.

CORRECT: "Increasing the instance size with Amazon RDS" is the correct answer.

INCORRECT: "AWS Auto Scaling adding more EC2 instances" is incorrect as explained above.

INCORRECT: "AWS Lambda adding concurrently executing functions" is incorrect as explained above.

INCORRECT: "Adding read replicas to an Amazon RDS database" is incorrect as explained above.

References:

https://aws.amazon.com/blogs/database/scaling-your-amazon-rds-instance-vertically-and-horizontally/

Save time with our exam-specific cheat sheets:

https://digitalcloud.training/certification-training/aws-certified-cloud-practitioner/architecting-for-the-cloud/

QUESTION 61

To reduce cost, which of the following services support reservations? (Select TWO.)

1. Amazon ElastiCache
2. Amazon CloudFormation
3. Amazon RedShift
4. AWS Elastic Beanstalk
5. Amazon S3

Answer: 1,3

Explanation:

Amazon ElastiCache and Amazon Redshift both support reserved nodes. Reservations can be used to gain a large discount from the on-demand rate in exchange for the commitment to a contract for 1 or 3 years.

CORRECT: "Amazon ElastiCache" is a correct answer.

CORRECT: "Amazon RedShift" is also a correct answer.

INCORRECT: "Amazon CloudFormation" is incorrect as you do not pay for CloudFormation.

INCORRECT: "AWS Elastic Beanstalk" is incorrect as you do not pay for Elastic Beanstalk.

INCORRECT: "Amazon S3" is incorrect as you pay for usage and cannot reserve capacity.

References:

https://d1.awsstatic.com/whitepapers/aws_pricing_overview.pdf

Save time with our exam-specific cheat sheets:

https://digitalcloud.training/certification-training/aws-certified-cloud-practitioner/aws-billing-and-pricing/

QUESTION 62

What type of cloud computing service type do AWS Elastic Beanstalk and Amazon RDS correspond to?

1. IaaS
2. PaaS
3. SaaS
4. Hybrid

Answer: 2

Explanation:

Both Elastic Beanstalk and RDS are services that are managed at the platform level meaning you don't need to manage the infrastructure level yourself. Therefore, tasks like OS management and patching are performed for you.

CORRECT: "PaaS" is the correct answer.

INCORRECT: "IaaS" is incorrect. IaaS is a model where the underlying hardware platform and hypervisor are managed for you and you are delivered tools and interfaces for working with operating system instances.

INCORRECT: "SaaS" is incorrect. SaaS is a model where the whole stack is managed for you right up to the application and you are delivered working software that you can customize and populate with data.

INCORRECT: "Hybrid" is incorrect. Hybrid is a type of cloud delivery model in which you consume both public and private cloud and connect the two together.

References:

https://aws.amazon.com/types-of-cloud-computing/

Save time with our exam-specific cheat sheets:

https://digitalcloud.training/certification-training/aws-certified-cloud-practitioner/cloud-computing-concepts/

QUESTION 63

How can a company configure automatic, asynchronous copying of objects in Amazon S3 buckets across regions?

1. This is done by default by AWS
2. By configuring multi-master replication
3. Using cross-region replication
4. Using lifecycle actions

Answer: 3

Explanation:

Cross-region replication (CRR) enables automatic, asynchronous copying of objects across buckets in different AWS Regions. Buckets configured for cross-region replication can be owned by the same AWS account or by different account

CORRECT: "Using cross-region replication" is the correct answer.

INCORRECT: "This is done by default by AWS" is incorrect as this is not true.

INCORRECT: "By configuring multi-master replication" is incorrect. Multi-master replication is not something you can do with Amazon S3 (Amazon Aurora has this feature).

INCORRECT: "Using lifecycle actions" is incorrect. Lifecycle actions cannot be configured to move to another storage class in a different region.

References:

https://docs.aws.amazon.com/AmazonS3/latest/dev/crr.html

Save time with our exam-specific cheat sheets:

https://digitalcloud.training/certification-training/aws-certified-cloud-practitioner/aws-storage/

QUESTION 64

Your company has recently migrated to AWS. How can your CTO monitor the organization's costs?

1. AWS Cost Explorer
2. AWS CloudTrail
3. AWS Consolidated Billing
4. AWS Simple Monthly calculator

Answer: 1

Explanation:

AWS Cost Explorer – enables you to visualize your usage patterns over time and to identify your underlying cost drivers.

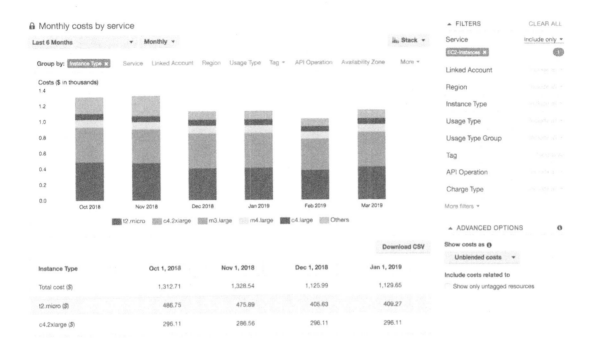

CORRECT: "AWS Cost Explorer" is the correct answer.

INCORRECT: "AWS CloudTrail" is incorrect. AWS CloudTrail provides a record of API activity in your account. I.e. who did what to which resource..

INCORRECT: "AWS Consolidated Billing" is incorrect. AWS Consolidated Billing is a feature of AWS Organizations that allows you to consolidate billing across multiple linked accounts and benefit from volume pricing discounts.

INCORRECT: "AWS Simple Monthly calculator" is incorrect. AWS Simple Monthly calculator – shows you how much you would pay in AWS if you move your resources.

References:

https://aws.amazon.com/aws-cost-management/aws-cost-explorer/

Save time with our exam-specific cheat sheets:

https://digitalcloud.training/certification-training/aws-certified-cloud-practitioner/aws-billing-and-pricing/

QUESTION 65

Your organization has offices around the world and some employees travel between offices. How should their accounts be setup?

1. IAM is a global service, just create the users in one place
2. Create a separate account in IAM within each region in which they will travel
3. Set the user account as a "global" account when created
4. Enable MFA for the accounts

Answer: 1

Explanation:

IAM is a global service and all users that are created are able to login to the AWS Management Console from any location.

CORRECT: "IAM is a global service, just create the users in one place" is the correct answer.

INCORRECT: "Create a separate account in IAM within each region in which they will travel" is incorrect. You do not create separate IAM accounts in different regions as IAM is a global service.

INCORRECT: "Set the user account as a "global" account when created" is incorrect. There is no such thing as setting the account as "global".

INCORRECT: "Enable MFA for the accounts" is incorrect. Enabling multi-factor authentication is a good security practice but not necessary to enable users to travel to different locations.

References:

https://docs.aws.amazon.com/IAM/latest/UserGuide/introduction_identity-management.html

Save time with our exam-specific cheat sheets:

https://digitalcloud.training/certification-training/aws-certified-cloud-practitioner/identity-and-access-management/

CONCLUSION

Congratulations on completing these exam-difficulty practice tests! We truly hope that these high-quality questions along with the supporting explanations helped to fully prepare you for the AWS Certified Cloud Practitioner exam.

The **CLF-C01** exam covers a broad set of technologies and it's vital to ensure you are armed with the knowledge to answer whatever questions come up in your certification exam. So, it's best to review these practice questions until you're confident in all areas. We recommend re-taking these practice tests until you consistently score 80% or higher - that's when you're ready to sit the exam and achieve a great score!

REACH OUT AND CONNECT

We want you to have a 5-star learning experience. If anything is not 100% to your liking, please email us at support@digitalcloud.training. We promise to address all questions and concerns. We really want you to get great value from these training resources.

The AWS platform is evolving quickly, and the exam tracks these changes with a typical lag of around 6 months. We are therefore reliant on student feedback to keep track of what is appearing in the exam. If there are any topics in your exam that weren't covered in our training resources, please provide us with feedback using this form https://digitalcloud.training/student-feedback/. We appreciate any feedback that will help us further improve our AWS training resources.

To discuss any exam-specific questions you may have, please join the discussion on Slack. Visit http://digitalcloud.training/slack for instructions.

Also, remember to join our private Facebook group to ask questions and share knowledge and exam tips with the AWS community: https://www.facebook.com/groups/awscertificationqa

LIMITED TIME BONUS OFFER

As a special bonus, we are now offering **FREE Access to the Exam** Simulator on the Digital Cloud Training website. The exam simulator randomly selects 65 questions from our pool of 500 questions - mimicking the real AWS exam environment. The practice exam has the same format, style, time limit and passing score as the real AWS exam.

To gain FREE access to all 500 Practice Questions, simply send us a **screenshot of your review on Amazon** to info@digitalcloud.training with "**CCP500**" in the subject line. You will then get FREE access to our Online Exam Simulator within 48 hours. Should you encounter ANY problems with your review, please reach out. We're here to support you on your cloud journey.

Your reviews help us improve our courses and help your fellow AWS students make the right choices. We celebrate every honest review and truly appreciate it. You can leave a review at any time by visiting amazon.com/ryp or your local amazon store (e.g. amazon.co.uk/ryp).

HOW TO ACCESS YOUR FREE EXTENDED PDF VERSION

To ensure a positive learning experience, we're offering our Amazon customers a downloadable PDF version of this book at no additional charge. This extended version includes additional diagrams, images and reference links. To download your free version, simply scan the QR code below or visit: https://digitalcloud.training/amazon-customers-ccp-practice-tests/

Best wishes for your AWS certification journey!

OTHER BOOKS, COURSES & CHALLENGE LABS FROM DIGITAL CLOUD TRAINING

At Digital Cloud Training, we offer a wide range of training courses that help students successfully prepare for their AWS Certification exams and beyond.

All of our on-demand courses are available on digitalcloud.training/aws-training-courses

Apply coupon code **AMZ20** for a 20% discount at checkout.

AWS Certification	Available Training Courses
AWS Certified Cloud Practitioner	• Video Course (Instructor-led) • Practical Exam Reviewer (Guided Video Walkthrough) • Practice Exam Course (incl. Online Exam Simulator) • Training Notes (ebook) for Offline Study • Practice Tests (ebook) for Offline Study
AWS Certified Solutions Architect Associate	• Video Course (Instructor-led) • Practice Exam Course (incl. Online Exam Simulator) • Training Notes (ebook) for Offline Study • Practice Tests (ebook) for Offline Study
AWS Certified Developer Associate	• Video Course (Instructor-led) • Practice Exam Course (incl. Online Exam Simulator) • Training Notes (ebook) for Offline Study • Practice Tests (ebook) for Offline Study
AWS Certified SysOps Administrator Associate	• Video Course (Instructor-led) • Practice Exam Course (incl. Online Exam Simulator) • Training Notes (ebook) for Offline Study • Practice Tests (ebook) for Offline Study
AWS Certified Solutions Architect Professional	• Video Course (Instructor-led) • Practice Exam Course (incl. Online Exam Simulator)
AWS Certified Advanced Networking Specialty	• Video Course (Instructor-led) – coming soon • Practice Exam Course (incl. Online Exam Simulator)
AWS Certified Machine Learning Specialty	• Video Course (Instructor-led) – coming soon • Practice Exam Course (incl. Online Exam Simulator)
AWS Certified Security Specialty	• Video Course (Instructor-led) – coming soon • Practice Exam Course (incl. Online Exam Simulator)

CHALLENGE LABS

Keen to gain practical, real-world cloud skills? Then Challenge Labs are for you. Hone your skills across the most in-demand technologies, practice role-based cloud skills, and get the hands-on experience you need for certification exams.

Hands-on Challenge Labs are scenario-based exercises that run in a secure sandbox environment. These online scored labs offer extensive hands-on opportunities for all skill levels without the risk of cloud bills!

Ranging from fully guided to advanced hands-on exercises, Challenge Labs cater for all skill levels. At Digital Cloud Training we offer Challenge Labs for different levels of learners:

- **Guided** – Simply follow the step-by-step instructions in the guided labs with detailed hints to learn the fundamentals.
- **Advanced** – Create solutions according to requirements with supporting documentation – each step is checked / validated.
- **Expert** – Create solutions according to requirements with basic instructions and no supporting information – receive a final score.

Our Challenge Labs catalog includes over 850 on-demand challenges across multiple cloud platforms and technologies including AWS, Azure, Docker, Linux, Microsoft, VMware and Cybersecurity.

To learn more, visit https://digitalcloud.training/hands-on-challenge-labs/

ABOUT THE AUTHOR

Neal Davis is the founder of Digital Cloud Training, AWS Cloud Solutions Architect and successful IT instructor. With more than 20 years of experience in the tech industry, Neal is a true expert in virtualization and cloud computing. His passion is to help others achieve career success by offering in-depth AWS certification training resources.

Neal started **Digital Cloud Training** to provide a variety of training resources for Amazon Web Services (AWS) certifications that represent a higher standard of quality than is otherwise available in the market.

Digital Cloud Training provides AWS Certification exam preparation resources including instructor-led Video Courses, guided Hands-on Labs, in-depth Training Notes, Exam-Cram lessons for quick revision, Hands-on Challenge Labs and exam-difficulty Practice Exams to assess your exam readiness.

With Digital Cloud Training, you get access to highly experienced staff who support you on your AWS Certification journey and help you elevate your career through achieving highly valuable certifications. Join the AWS Community of over 500,000 happy students that are currently enrolled in Digital Cloud Training courses.

CONNECT WITH NEAL ON SOCIAL MEDIA

All Links available on https://digitalcloud.training/neal-davis

  digitalcloud.training/neal-davis

  youtube.com/c/digitalcloudtraining

  facebook.com/digitalcloudtraining

  Twitter @nealkdavis

  linkedin.com/in/nealkdavis

  Instagram @digitalcloudtraining

Printed in Great Britain
by Amazon